Critical magnetic fields

Thermodynamic (two-fluid model)

$$H_c(T) = H_c(0)\left[1 - \left(\frac{T}{T_c}\right)^2\right]$$

[272]

Lower critical fields (type II)

$$H_{c1} = H_c(\ln\kappa)(\sqrt{2}\,\kappa)^{-1}$$

[313]

Upper critical field (type II)

$$H_{c2} = \sqrt{2}\,\kappa H_c$$

[318]

Surface-sheath field

$$H_{c3} = 1.7 H_{c2}$$

[319]

Circuit parameters

Inductance of parallel-plate transmission line (width w; spaced d; thick plates; $w \gg d$)

$$L = \frac{\mu_0 d}{w}\left(1 + \frac{\lambda_1}{d} + \frac{\lambda_2}{d}\right)$$

[114]

Phase velocity in transmission line with identical thick plates ($w \gg d$)

$$v_{ph} = \left[\mu_0\varepsilon\left(1 + \frac{2\lambda}{d}\right)\right]^{-1/2}$$

[134]

Josephson junctions

Current-phase relation

$$J = J_c \sin\phi$$

[141]

Voltage-phase relation

$$\frac{\partial\phi}{\partial t} = \frac{2eV}{\hbar}$$

[142]

Tunneling current density

$$J_c = \frac{G_n}{A}\left(\frac{\pi\Delta(T)}{2e}\right)\tanh\frac{\Delta(T)}{2k_B T}$$

[142]

Josephson penetration depth

$$\lambda_J^2 = \hbar\left[2eJ_c\mu_0(2\lambda + d)\right]^{-1}$$

[150]

Junction phase velocity

$$v_{ph} = \left[\mu_0\varepsilon\left(\frac{2\lambda}{d} + 1\right)\right]^{-1/2}$$

[149]

Josephson plasma frequency (zero-loss approximation)

$$\omega_p^2 = (v_{ph}/\lambda_J)^2\cos\phi_0$$

[151]

$$\omega_p^2 = \frac{2eI_c}{\hbar C}\cos\phi_0$$

[175]

McCumber admittance parameter

$$\beta_c \overset{\Delta}{=} \frac{2e}{\hbar}I_c C G^{-2}$$

[171]

Small-signal inductance of Josephson junction

$$L_J = \hbar(2eI_c\cos\phi_0)^{-1}$$

[185]

Principles of
Superconductive
Devices and Circuits

Principles of Superconductive Devices and Circuits

T. Van Duzer
University of California, Berkeley

C. W. Turner
King's College, London University

Elsevier
New York • Amsterdam • London

Elsevier North Holland, Inc.
52 Vanderbilt Avenue, New York, New York 10017

Distributors outside the United States and Canada:

Edward Arnold (Publishers,), Ltd.
41 Bedford Square, London WC1B 3DQ, England

Library of Congress Cataloging in Publication Data

Van Duzer, Theodore.
    Principles of superconductive devices and circuits.

    Bibliography: p.
    Includes index.
    1. Superconductivity. 2. Superconductors.
    I. Turner, Charles William, joint author.
QC612.S8 V36   537.6′23   80-17471
ISBN 0-444-00411-4

Current printing (last digit)
10 9 8 7 6 5 4 3 2

Manufactured in the United States of America

To

Janice   Shan
  Jeff   Deanna
    Margie   Charles
      Eric
        Leslie

with loving appreciation

Contents

Preface

The purpose of this book is to present the principles of superconductivity underlying its use in devices and circuits of both low- and high-power types. It is principally intended for first-year graduate electrical engineering and experimental physics students, but some of the material can also be used at the undergraduate level. It is expected that the problems found at the ends of most of the sections will aid in its use, not only within the university setting, but also for self-study of practicing engineers and physicists. We have attempted to present each subject in the simplest, most readily applicable way possible. The basic relations are given for each subject, and the reader is led to more detailed treatments through carefully selected references. The key formulas, constants, and data on the most useful materials are given inside the covers for quick reference. We expect that this structuring of the book will lead to its use as a reference volume for those working in the field.

We have chosen to introduce some principal phenomena of superconductivity in Chapter 1 through the properties of normal metals at low temperatures. This choice is made partly because electrical engineers usually have some knowledge of semiconductor physics but little acquaintance with metals and, therefore, need to review certain key properties. Having seen the behavior of a normal metal at low temperatures, it is easier to appreciate the remarkable change that takes place when the material becomes superconductive. The Bardeen–Cooper–Schrieffer microscopic theory of superconductivity is the main subject of the second chapter; it is presented in a way that can be understood at the level required for applications by a reader who has had a senior-level course in quantum mechanics. Quantum-mechanical electron tunneling through an insulating barrier is used to illustrate one of the key features of the superconducting state. Some aspects of superconductivity and its applications can be explained in the context of a macroscopic theory of superconductivity by London, which predates the microscopic theory. The London theory and applications to circuits are given in Chapter 3; for these, undergraduate quantum mechanics and electromagnetic field theory are adequate. Chapter 4 introduces the Josephson effects in the context of the oxide-barrier junction, and Chapter 5 gives an extensive review of the properties and applications of more general types of Josephson junction based on a simple circuit model. The remainder of the book is directed toward understanding and application of the thermodynamically based Ginzburg–Landau theory, which permits analysis of situations where the strength of the superconducting property is spatially dependent. It is assumed that the reader has had an introduction to thermodynamics at the sophomore or junior level but, as is usually the case, is not conversant with the free energies in the presence of magnetic fields. Chapter 6 gives a review of some important concepts in thermodynamics and electromagnetic fields. The Ginzburg–Landau theory is introduced in Chapter 7 and some key results are derived. Normal-metal–superconductor contacts and metal- and semiconductor-coupled Josephson junctions are analyzed. Chapter 8 develops the properties of type II superconductors and their applications in situations involving high magnetic fields and currents. The special properties of superconducting thin films, which can exhibit type II behavior even if made of type I material, are discussed in some detail.

Since our principal aim has been to bring the subject of superconductive devices and circuits to electrical engineers, we have chosen to express all equations in MKS units. The question of whether to use $\exp(-i\omega t)$ as done in the physics literature or $\exp(j\omega t)$ as in electrical engineering proved more difficult. Recasting quantum-mechanical expressions, especially those in the Bardeen–Cooper–Schrieffer theory, in $\exp(j\omega t)$ seemed as unwise as having inductive reactance be a negative quantity. We have chosen the middle ground of using $\exp(-i\omega t)$ for the quantum mechanics and $\exp(j\omega t)$ for circuits. The reader will understand that the use of i implies the minus sign for time dependence.

The book has developed over a number of years of teaching in the Department of Electrical Engineering and Computer Sciences at the University of California at Berkeley and has benefitted greatly from the many comments, corrections, and suggestions of present and former students. We should especially note the generous help of K.E. Chen, G.A. Cooper, S.H. Dhong, C.L. Huang, D.P. Hornbuckle, J.A. Stubstad, and J.P. Uyemura. A number of colleagues in the field have kindly reviewed portions of the text or discussed some of the subjects. We should like especially to express appreciation for the help of M.R. Beasley, R. Chiao, J. Clarke, M.L. Cohen, L.M. Falicov, T.F. Finnegan, H. Kanter, J.E. Lukens, P.L. Richards, M. Sugahara, J.R. Tucker, and B.T. Ulrich. The suggestions of the anonymous reviewers, although not all heeded, partly because of time pressures, are greatly appreciated. The typing of the manuscript was done by several secretaries, with the major part by Bettye Fuller, Mary Yoshikawa, and Rosemary Ainsworth. Their patience and expertise were essential to the completion of this work and we extend our thanks to them. Finally, to our wives and offspring for whom the publication of this work brings to an end a cause of missed companionship, we offer our deep appreciation.

T. Van Duzer
Berkeley

C.W. Turner
London

**Principles of
Superconductive
Devices and Circuits**

Chapter 1

Normal Metals and the Transition
to the Superconducting State

1.01. Introduction

Many metallic elements, compounds, and alloys undergo phase transitions
when temperature is reduced to near the absolute zero. At the transition
temperature, there are drastic changes in the properties of the conduction
electrons. Materials in this *superconductive* state possess perfect dc conductivity, the tendency to exclude magnetic fields, a gap for energy absorption
somewhat like that in a semiconductor, long-range order of the electronic
wave function, and remarkable behavior of weakly coupled junctions.
These features are now largely explained theoretically and two families of
applications have been spawned. The low-power electronics applications
are principally in magnetometry, millimeter-wave electromagnetic detection, and digital circuits; these excel with regard to low operating power,
response time, and noise. The other family of applications is for high-
energy and includes magnets, electric motors and generators, and power
transmission. In this text we lay the theoretical foundations of superconductivity and introduce elements of a number of applications.

The logical starting point for the discussion of superconducting materials
is a look at the physical processes governing electrical conductivity at
cryogenic temperatures. The central theme of this chapter is, therefore, the
behavior of the electrons and phonons in metals. Electron states in crystals
and the free-electron theory of metals are reviewed with emphasis on the
Fermi surface. The concept of excitations from the ground state is introduced and used to calculate the electronic specific heat of normal metals.
This, in turn, is used to introduce one of the basic features of the
superconducting state—the existence of a gap in the excitation-energy
spectrum. The Debye idealization of the phonon spectrum is presented and
compared with that of a real metal. Scattering of electrons by phonons and
its effect on the conduction process is studied as the temperature approaches the absolute zero. This leads to a discussion of the discovery of
the perfect-conductor property of superconductors. We then consider the

behavior that would be expected of a perfect conductor in a magnetic field and see that the additional characteristic of perfect diamagnetism is an essential feature of superconductivity.

1.02. Independent Electrons in a Periodic Lattice

In solids, the conduction or valence electrons are shared among all the assembled atoms. If two atoms are put in close proximity, their valence electrons follow orbitals around both. As many atoms are brought together, the orbitals extend over all of them. We find the electron orbitals (states) for a crystal containing typically 10^{22}–10^{23} atoms cm^{-3} by considering each electron to be moving independently through the periodic potential produced by the positive ions. The states that the electron can occupy are the solutions of the Schrödinger equation:

$$-(\hbar^2/2m)\nabla^2\Psi(\vec{r}) + V(\vec{r})\Psi(\vec{r}) = \mathcal{E}\Psi(\vec{r}) \tag{1}$$

where $V(\vec{r})$ is the electric potential of the lattice of ions. The solutions are well known to be expressible in the form of Bloch functions:

$$\Psi_{\vec{k}} = U(\vec{r})e^{i\vec{k}\cdot\vec{r}} \tag{2}$$

where $U(\vec{r})$ has the same periodicity as $V(\vec{r})$. The real part of a typical Bloch function is shown in Fig. 1.02a. The Bloch function varies in the region of the ion core in such a way as to be orthogonal to the other electron states in the ion and has a slow variation between ions somewhat in the form of a wave of wave number k.

For a perfectly free electron, $U(\vec{r})$ is a constant and $\vec{k}$ is related to the momentum through the de Broglie relation $\vec{p} = \hbar\vec{k}$. In the same way, we refer to the *crystal momentum* k of the electrons in a periodic lattice. It is

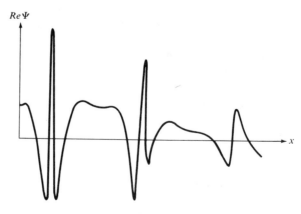

Figure 1.02a. Real part of a typical Bloch function.

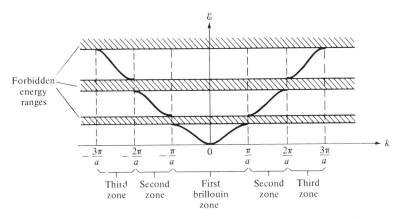

Figure 1.02b. The relation between energy and wave number in a one-dimensional periodic lattice: the extended-zone representation.

important to find k in terms of energy $\mathcal{E}$ of a state; this relation can be found in a variety of ways. Perhaps the simplest way to determine the $\mathcal{E}-k$ relation is through use of the one-dimensional Kronig–Penney model.[1] This simplification takes the potential to have the form of a regularly spaced series of rectangular wells. The solution of (1) with the Kronig–Penney potential yields the relation between $\mathcal{E}$ and k shown in Fig. 1.02b, where it is seen that there are ranges of energy that are forbidden for real values of k. Although it is possible to excite states in the "forbidden" range, these are in the form of decaying waves since they have complex values of k; we shall be concerned only with states with real k.

The range of k from $-\pi/a$ to π/a, where a is the lattice spacing, is called the *first Brillouin zone*; the second and higher-numbered zones are as indicated in Fig. 1.02b. It is clear from (2) that k could be replaced by $k + 2\pi n/a$ without changing the validity of the solution since $\exp(i2\pi n/a)x$ has the same periodicity as $U(x)$ and can be combined with it to give a $U(x)$ that is different but has the same periodicity. As a result, the entire $\mathcal{E}-k$ diagram can be mapped into the first (or any other) Brillouin zone, making Figs. 1.02c and 1.02d as valid as Fig. 1.02b. The forms of the diagrams shown in Figs. 1.02c and 1.02d are called the *reduced-zone* and *repeated-zone* representations, respectively, and are each useful under different circumstances.

By assuming a crystal of some given size and applying suitable boundary

[1] The development of the Kronig–Penney model is found in most introductory solid-state physics books: J. P. McKelvey, *Solid-State and Semiconductor Physics*. New York: Harper and Row, 1966. C. Kittel, *Introduction to Solid-State Physics*, 5th Ed. New York: John Wiley and Sons, 1976.

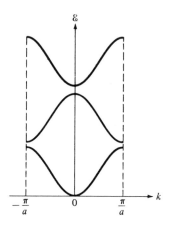

Figure 1.02c. The relation between energy and wave number in a one-dimensional periodic lattice: the reduced-zone representation (equivalent to Fig. 1.02b).

conditions at its edges, one finds the set of discrete allowed values of $\vec{k}$, which are the same for all bands. These can be shown to have a density in $\vec{k}$ space given by $1/8\pi^3$ per unit real volume of crystal. The density of states is twice this value or $1/4\pi^3$ since each $\vec{k}$ state can contain two electrons of opposite spin. The density of states for typical crystal sizes is so large that the states can be considered to form a continuum, for most purposes. Each value of $\vec{k}$ in a given energy band is associated with a certain value of energy. For very small values of $\vec{k}$, the locus of points of equal energy may form spheres in $\vec{k}$-space. For larger values of $\vec{k}$, the shapes of the equal-energy surfaces change in a way dependent on the crystal structure to which the array of points in $\vec{k}$-space corresponds. This is illustrated in Fig. 1.02e for the simple cubic crystal using the first Brillouin

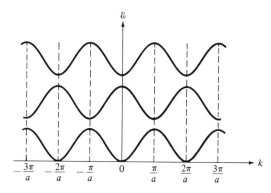

Figure 1.02d. The relation between energy and wave number in a one-dimensional periodic lattice: the repeated-zone representation (equivalent to Fig. 1.02b).

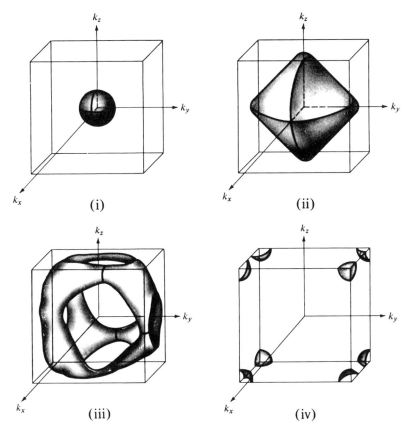

Figure 1.02e. Surfaces of successively higher energies in the first Brillouin zone for the simple cubic crystal.(From J. P. McKelvey, *Solid-State and Semiconductor Physics*. New York: Harper and Row, 1966, p. 239.)

zone. There are several methods for calculating the relation between $\mathcal{E}$ and $\vec{k}$ for three-dimensional Bloch functions.[2]

Problem

1.02. Assuming spherical energy surfaces at $|k| \cong \pi/2a$ for a simple cubic crystal, calculate the number of allowed values of $\vec{k}$ lying in a range of energy $k_B T$ about $|k| = \pi/2a$, where k_B is Boltzmann's constant and $T = 4.2$ K. Take

---

[2] J. M. Ziman, *Principles of the Theory of Solids*, 2nd Ed. Cambridge: University Press, 1972. N. W. Ashcroft and N. D. Mermin, *Solid-State Physics*. New York: Holt, Rinehart, and Winston, 1976.

the crystal dimensions to be $1 \times 1 \times 1$ mm^3 and the lattice spacing to be 4 Å and assume the free-electron mass.

1.03. Energy Distribution and the Fermi Surface

Electrons obey the Pauli exclusion principle and are indistinguishable; it follows that they are distributed with respect to energy by the Fermi–Dirac function[3] which gives the probability of occupancy of

$$f(\mathcal{E}) = \frac{1}{1 + \exp\left[(\mathcal{E} - \mu)/k_B T\right]} \tag{1}$$

for the state having energy $\mathcal{E}$. Here k_B is the Boltzmann constant, T is absolute temperature, and μ is a weak function of temperature called the *chemical potential* (or *Fermi level* or *Fermi potential*). The chemical potential is defined such that the sum of the number of electrons n occupying the available states equals the total number of electrons:

$$n = \sum_i f(\mathcal{E}_i)$$

The Fermi–Dirac function (1) falls to the value $1/2$ where the energy equals μ at all temperatures, as shown in Fig. 1.03a. It falls abruptly to zero for $T = 0$ K. At the absolute zero, the chemical potential is equal to the *Fermi energy*, which is defined as the uppermost level of energy occupied at absolute-zero temperature. Since our primary concern is with superconduc-

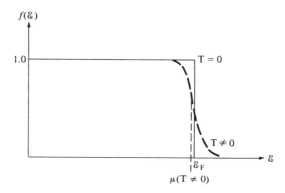

Figure 1.03a. Fermi–Dirac distribution function at zero and nonzero temperatures.

[3]See, for example, R. B. Leighton, *Principles of Modern Physics*. New York: McGraw-Hill, 1959, pp. 327–339, where the Fermi–Dirac, Bose–Einstein, and Maxwell–Boltzmann distributions are given in a unified presentation.

tivity, and therefore with temperatures near the absolute zero, there is very little difference between the Fermi energy and the Fermi (chemical) potential at any temperature of interest.

In k-space, one of the energy surfaces, of the kind shown in Fig. 1.02e, is at the Fermi energy and is known as the Fermi surface.[4] The surface in the reduced-zone representation could be approximately that of Fig. 1.02e(i) for a material with a simple cubic structure and one valence electron per atom. The corresponding picture in the repeated-zone representation is shown in Fig. 1.03b, given for convenience in two dimensions. For materials with more valence electrons, the Fermi surface will be connected from zone to zone and will appear in more than one energy band, The Brillouin zone of a face-centered-cubic (fcc) material such as lead is a truncated octahedron. A portion of the Fermi surface for lead is shown in Fig. 1.03c. The important point is that, like lead, many materials have Fermi surfaces that intersect the zone boundary.[5] We shall see later that this has an important effect on all physical processes involving electronic transitions near the Fermi surface, such as the conduction of electric current. States below the Fermi surface by more than $k_B T$ are inaccessible, since they are occupied with unity probability and the Pauli exclusion principle precludes additional occupancy. Thus only the states near the Fermi surface play a

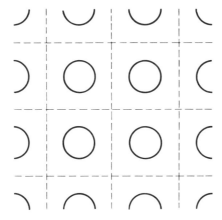

Figure 1.03b. Repeated-zone representation of a Fermi surface in two dimensions for a low-valence material with a simple cubic crystal structure.

---

[4] See works by C. Kittel, J. M. Ziman, and N. W. Ashcroft and N. Mermin in footnotes 1 and 2.

[5] A. P. Cracknell and K. C. Wong, *The Fermi Surface*. Oxford: Clarendon Press, 1973. A. V. Gold, "An experimental determination of the Fermi surface in lead," *Phil. Trans. Royal Soc.*, London, Vol. A251, pp. 85–112, 6 November 1958.

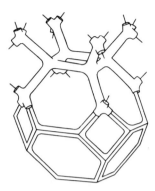

Figure 1.03c. A portion of the Fermi surface of lead. The top half is in the repeated-zone representation and the lower half in the reduced-zone representation. (From A. V. Gold, *Phil. Trans. Royal Soc.*, London, Vol. A251, p. 96, 6 November 1958.)

role in transport processes and in thermal properties like the specific heat. As we shall see, it is only these states that are important to superconductivity.

Problems

1.03a.   Calculate the group velocity

$$v_{gr}(k) = (1/\hbar)[\partial \mathscr{E}(k)/\partial k]$$

at the Fermi surface for the conditions stated in Problem 1.02, assuming the Fermi surface to lie at $|k| = \pi/2a$. Compare this velocity with the mean thermal velocity for $T = 4.2$ K.

1.03b.   It can be shown[6] that the temperature dependence of the chemical potential is

$$\mu \cong \mathscr{E}_F\left[1 - \tfrac{1}{12}\pi^2(k_B T/\mathscr{E}_F)^2\right]$$

Compare $\mu - \mathscr{E}_F$ in aluminum at the temperature of its transition to the superconducting state (1.196 K) with $k_B T$ and with the Fermi energy ($\mathscr{E}_F = 11.6$ eV).

1.04.   Free-Electron Gas

We saw in Section 1.02 that the stationary states for electrons in a periodic potential have the form of Bloch functions. The coefficient $U(\vec{r})$ represents the effect of the periodic potential. If $U(\vec{r})$ were just a constant, the function would be a plane wave, which is the wave representation of a free

---

[6] F. Seitz, *Modern Theory of Solids.* New York: McGraw-Hill, 1940, pp. 146–149.

particle with a definite momentum. It is found that the conduction electrons in a metal have a relation between energy and momentum much like that of a free particle. The free-electron theory of metals[7] assumes such a relation and gives accurate results. The electrons are assumed to move about the crystal freely, virtually without interaction with the strong potentials of the ion cores. In Chapter 2 the free-electron model is used as the basis for the theory of superconductivity. Some preliminary explanation is in order here to account for the relatively good results obtained from such an obviously simplified approach. First let us see how we can construct wave functions suitable for the conduction electrons and then proceed to argue the validity of the free-electron model.

The wave functions of the conduction electrons must be orthogonal to the core states; otherwise occupation of one of the former would imply partial additional population of an already fully occupied core state, and thus violate the Pauli principle. The *orthogonalized-plane-wave* (OPW) method assumes a plane-wave solution in the nearly constant-potential regions outside the cores and combines with it a set of functions in the core region such that the result is orthogonal to every core state. Making the function orthogonal to the core states gives it more nodes than the core states, as is appropriate to the electron states for the next higher shell. The result is a function that is nearly a plane wave outside the core region and is a rapidly varying function inside.

The rapid oscillation required for orthogonality represents the high kinetic energy that the electron must have to enter the core region. This kinetic energy can be replaced by an equivalent repulsive pseudopotential in the core region which, when added to the attractive potential of the ion, leaves only a small net equivalent potential. One can then consider that the electrons encounter only small potential-energy perturbations at the ion sites. The energies found for the electrons with this equivalent potential function are quite accurate and are not far different from those of the free electron. Although the plane-wave solutions give approximately the right energies, the actual wave functions, of course, have the rapid variations in the core region illustrated in Fig. 1.02a.

Hereafter, we shall not be interested in the detailed form of the wave functions but shall be concerned principally with the $\mathscr{E}-k$ relation. For this purpose we shall neglect the small net potential and consider the potential energy $V(\vec{r})$ in the Hamiltonian in Eq. 1.02(1) to be essentially zero. The solutions are then plane-wave states

$$\Psi_{\vec{k}} = ae^{i\vec{k}\cdot\vec{r}} \tag{1}$$

As was true for the Bloch functions for a periodic potential, the imposition

[7]The free-electron theory appears in a number of texts including those by J. P. McKelvey, C. Kittel, and N. W. Ashcroft and N. D. Mermin in footnotes 1 and 2.

of boundary conditions appropriate to a crystal of finite size leads to a set of allowed values for $\vec{k}$. In this case, however, the energy eigenvalues [found by substitution of the plane-wave functions (1) into Eq. 1.02(1) with $V(\vec{r})$ set to zero] take the form

$$\mathcal{E} = (\hbar^2/2m)k^2 \tag{2}$$

Therefore, all energy surfaces in $\vec{k}$-space are spheres. In particular, the Fermi surface is a sphere with energy

$$\mathcal{E}_F = (\hbar^2/2m)k_F^2 \tag{3}$$

Equating (3) with $mv^2/2$ appropriate to free particles, we find the velocity of electrons at the Fermi surface.

$$v_F = (\hbar/m)k_F \tag{4}$$

The velocity v_F is typically orders of magnitude greater than thermal velocities, i.e., around 10^6-10^7 m/s.

For calculations of various properties of conductors such as thermal and electric transport, it is necessary to have an expression for the density of states as a function of energy, i.e., the number of states per unit energy interval (for a unit volume of material). Though this is not easily obtained in systems with complex Fermi surfaces, it can be found quite simply in the free-electron-gas model. An energy interval $d\mathcal{E}$ corresponds to a spherical shell of thickness dk in $\vec{k}$-space. The number of states in the energy interval $d\mathcal{E}$ must equal that for the corresponding interval dk. As pointed out in Section 1.02, the density of states in $\vec{k}$-space is $1/8\pi^3$. If we account for the fact that the number of states is doubled by the allowance of occupations by opposite-spin particles, we can consider the density in $\vec{k}$-space to be $1/4\pi^3$. Then the number of states in the volume d^3k is

$$N(k)\,d^3k = (1/4\pi^3)4\pi k^2\,dk \tag{5}$$

Using $N(\mathcal{E})d\mathcal{E} = N(k)d^3k$ and substituting (2) in (5) gives

$$N(\mathcal{E}) = \frac{1}{2\pi^2}\left(\frac{2m}{\hbar^2}\right)^{3/2}\mathcal{E}^{1/2} \tag{6}$$

as the density of states. The form of this expression is shown in Fig. 1.04.

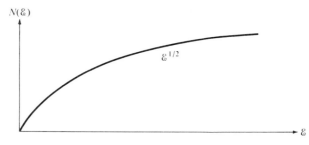

Figure 1.04. Density of states for the three-dimensional free-electron gas.

If we multiply the density of states (6) by the probability of occupation [the Fermi–Dirac function, Eq. 1.03(1)] with $T = 0$ and integrate up to the Fermi energy $\mathscr{E}_F$, the result gives the number of electrons n in the conduction band per unit volume. In this way we can express the Fermi energy as

$$\mathscr{E}_F = (\hbar^2/2m)(3\pi^2 n)^{2/3} \tag{7}$$

For a typical metal the number of electrons n in the conduction band is on the order of 10^{23}, and we find that a typical Fermi energy is several electron volts. Since an energy of no more than a few millivolts about the Fermi energy is involved in superconducting phenomena, the density-of-states function can generally be considered to be constant.

It is useful for future reference to express the Fermi velocity in terms of the number of valence electrons. Using (3), (4), and (7) one obtains

$$v_F = (\hbar/m)(3\pi^2 n)^{1/3} \tag{8}$$

Problems

1.04a. Aluminum has a face-centered-cubic (fcc) structure with a lattice constant of 4.05 Å, a Fermi energy of 11.6 eV, and a valence of 3. Calculate the ratio (effective mass/free-electron rest mass) for the electrons, using the free-electron-gas model.

1.04b. Verify the assertion that the total kinetic energy of the electrons in the conduction band is proportional to $n^{5/3}$. Give an explanation of the result in physical terms.

1.05. Excitations: The Energy Gap in a Superconductor

In Section 1.03 we discussed the Fermi gas at both zero and nonzero temperatures and saw that there is a smearing of the edge for the latter case, as in Fig. 1.03a. Another way to view the physical situation is to consider a ground state, that existing at $T = 0$, and deviations from it, called *excitations*. For electrons, the allowed states form a continuous spectrum in energy (neglecting the discreteness of states imposed by the finite dimensions of the crystal) so that any arbitrarily small amount of energy added to a system in its ground state can cause an excitation (that is, raise an electron out of the ground-state Fermi gas to place it in a higher-energy state). It will be seen that an important determinant of the properties of the superconducting state is a gap that exists between the lowest excitation state and the energy level of the ground state of the system.

As groundwork for the study of superconductors in Chapter 2, it is useful

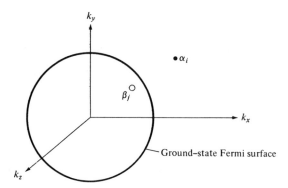

Figure 1.05a. The excited state $|\alpha_i; \beta_j\rangle$.

to consider a symbolic way of describing the excited states of an electron system. States above the Fermi energy $\mathscr{E}_F$ are designated α and states below $\mathscr{E}_F$ are called β. The ground state is written as $|F\rangle$. If we take one electron from the β_j state inside the Fermi surface and put it in the α_i state, as shown in Fig. 1.05a, we can describe the new excited state as $|\alpha_i; \beta_j\rangle$.

The operators that perform the function of *annihilating* the electron in the β_j state and *creating* the electron in the α_i state may be represented by c_{β_j} and $c_{\alpha_i}^*$, respectively.[8] Thus

$$|\alpha_i; \beta_j\rangle = c_{\alpha_i}^* c_{\beta_j} |F\rangle \qquad (1)$$

The energy of this state exceeds that of the ground state $|F\rangle$ by $\mathscr{E}_{\alpha_i} - \mathscr{E}_{\beta_j}$. It is useful to express this in terms of energies measured from the Fermi energy at absolute zero. The energy of the state (1) above the ground state can thus be written as

$$E = (\mathscr{E}_{\alpha_i} - \mathscr{E}_F) - (\mathscr{E}_{\beta_j} - \mathscr{E}_F) = (\mathscr{E}_{\alpha_i} - \mathscr{E}_F) + (\mathscr{E}_F - \mathscr{E}_{\beta_j}) \qquad (2)$$

Then the energy required to populate the state $|\alpha_i; \beta_j\rangle$ is the sum of the energy required to move the electron from the state β_j to the Fermi energy $(\mathscr{E}_F - \mathscr{E}_{\beta_j})$ plus that required to move it from the Fermi energy to the state α_i, $(\mathscr{E}_{\alpha_i} - \mathscr{E}_F)$. These excitation energies are illustrated in Fig. 1.05b. Since excitation energy is always positive, it is convenient to replot it as in Fig. 1.05c where the relation $E = |\mathscr{E} - \mathscr{E}_F|$ is manifested. The energy required for the annihilation of an electron in the ground state decreases as $k_\beta \to k_F$, and the energy required for the creation of an electron above the Fermi surface increases as k_α increases.

States with more than one excitation above the ground state can be

---

[8] These operators must satisfy anticommutation relations since they apply to fermions. We do not wish to emphasize the operator algebra here and the interested reader is referred to texts on quantum mechanics.

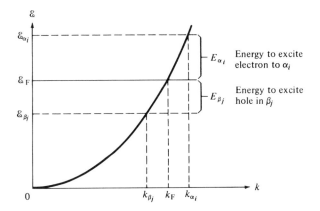

Figure 1.05b. Definitions of excitation energies in terms of Bloch-state energies.

described using the same formalism. A state with $2n$ excitations

$$c^*_{\alpha_1}c^*_{\alpha_2}c^*_{\alpha_3} \cdots c^*_{\alpha_n}c_{\beta_1}c_{\beta_2}c_{\beta_3} \cdots c_{\beta_n}|F\rangle \tag{3}$$

in which electrons in states $\beta_1, \beta_2, \beta_3, \ldots, \beta_n$ have been annihilated and electrons in states $\alpha_1, \alpha_2, \alpha_3, \ldots, \alpha_n$ have been created, has an energy relative to the ground-state energy of

$$E = \left(\mathcal{E}_{\alpha_1} - \mathcal{E}_F\right) + \left(\mathcal{E}_{\alpha_2} - \mathcal{E}_F\right) + \left(\mathcal{E}_{\alpha_3} - \mathcal{E}_F\right) + \cdots + \left(\mathcal{E}_{\alpha_n} - \mathcal{E}_F\right)$$
$$+ \left(\mathcal{E}_F - \mathcal{E}_{\beta_1}\right) + \left(\mathcal{E}_F - \mathcal{E}_{\beta_2}\right) + \left(\mathcal{E}_F - \mathcal{E}_{\beta_3}\right) + \cdots + \left(\mathcal{E}_F - \mathcal{E}_{\beta_n}\right) \tag{4}$$

If a continuum of states is considered and the free-electron-gas model used, one can write the excitation energy at temperature T as

$$E(T) = \int_{\mathcal{E}_F}^{\infty} d\mathcal{E}(\mathcal{E} - \mathcal{E}_F)f(\mathcal{E},T)N(\mathcal{E})$$
$$+ \int_0^{\mathcal{E}_F} d\mathcal{E}(\mathcal{E}_F - \mathcal{E})\left[1 - f(\mathcal{E},T)\right]N(\mathcal{E}) \tag{5}$$

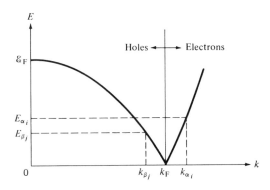

Figure 1.05c. Excitation energies for holes below the Fermi energy (at $k = k_F$) and electrons for $k > k_F$.

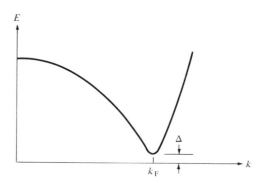

Figure 1.05d. Excitation-energy spectrum of a superconductor showing a gap Δ, which is typically on the order of 1 meV.

where $f(\mathcal{E})$ is the Fermi function [Eq. 1.03(1)] and $N(\mathcal{E})$ is the density of states [Eq. 1.04(6)]. In the next section, we shall make use of (5) to determine the specific heat of an electron gas.

Since arbitrarily small energies can produce excitations in normal metals, one expects, and finds, that absorption takes place for photons of any frequency ν and energy $h\nu$. On the other hand, experiments with superconductors have revealed the result that there is little absorption for photons of energy less than about 1 meV, which corresponds to photon frequencies in the millimeter-wave range. Thus it can be deduced that there must be a gap in the excitation energy spectrum as shown in Fig. 1.05d. This has been corroborated theoretically and is of great importance in determining the properties of superconductors.

1.06. Electronic Heat Capacity

There are two reasons for studying the electronic heat capacity (or electronic specific heat) of normal metals. First, measurements of the heat capacity can be used to determine the density of states at the Fermi surface, a parameter of great importance in the theory of superconductivity. Second, the heat-capacity expression is derived using the excitations from the ground-state Fermi gas. With it we can argue qualitatively the effect of a gap in the excitation spectrum of a superconductor.

The electronic heat capacity for a unit volume of material is defined by

$$c_V^e \triangleq \left(\frac{\partial E}{\partial T} \right)_V \tag{1}$$

Henceforth, we neglect the subscript V since we deal only with constant-volume processes. The energy per degree of freedom for a classical particle is $k_B T/2$, or $3k_B T/2$ for its three degrees of freedom. Using (1), the heat capacity of a collection of particles of density n per unit volume is $(3n/2)k_B$, a result that, for electrons, is orders of magnitude too high. The reason is that all states in the Fermi gas are essentially full except within a range of energy $k_B T$ at the Fermi surface.

Electrons in lower-lying states cannot move to unoccupied states above $\mathcal{E}_F$ since the available energy is only about $k_B T$. Thus, only electrons near the Fermi surface can move to higher energy states, and the change of energy of the whole system is much less than that obtained where all electrons are able to absorb heat.

Let us now derive the electronic specific heat. Substituting the expression for excitation energy [Eq. 1.05(5)] into (1) and using

$$\frac{\partial[1 - f(\mathcal{E})]}{\partial T} = -\frac{\partial f(\mathcal{E})}{\partial T} \tag{2}$$

we find

$$c^e = \int_0^\infty d\mathcal{E}(\mathcal{E} - \mathcal{E}_F) \frac{\partial f(\mathcal{E})}{\partial T} N(\mathcal{E}) \tag{3}$$

At low temperatures $\partial f/\partial T$ is sharply peaked at $\mathcal{E}_F$, and $N(\mathcal{E})$ is nearly constant there (Fig. 1.04), so (3) can be written approximately as

$$c^e = N(\mathcal{E}_F) \int_0^\infty d\mathcal{E}(\mathcal{E} - \mathcal{E}_F) \frac{\partial f(\mathcal{E})}{\partial T} \tag{4}$$

At low temperatures, $\mu \cong \mathcal{E}_F$ (see Section 1.03) so

$$\frac{\partial f(\mathcal{E})}{\partial T} = \frac{\mathcal{E} - \mathcal{E}_F}{k_B T^2} \frac{\exp[(\mathcal{E} - \mathcal{E}_F)/k_B T]}{\{\exp[(\mathcal{E} - \mathcal{E}_F)/k_B T] + 1\}^2} \tag{5}$$

Using the change of variables $x \equiv (\mathcal{E} - \mathcal{E}_F)/k_B T$, (4) becomes

$$c^e = N(\mathcal{E}_F) k_B^2 T \int_{-\mathcal{E}_F/k_B T}^\infty dx \frac{x^2 e^x}{(e^x + 1)^2} \tag{6}$$

The integrand of (6) is entirely negligible at the lower limit, so the latter can be replaced by $-\infty$. The integration yields

$$c^e = \pi^2 N(\mathcal{E}_F) k_B^2 T/3 = \gamma T \tag{7}$$

where γ is the *electronic heat constant*; values for superconductive elements are given on the inside back cover. This is the form that is useful for determination of $N(\mathcal{E}_F)$ from measurements of the heat capacity. One could observe roughly that about $k_B T N(\mathcal{E}_F)$ electrons receive an energy of about $k_B T$ each, so $E \approx k_B^2 T^2 N(\mathcal{E}_F)$ and c^e is on the order of $k_B^2 T N(\mathcal{E}_F)$, in rough agreement with (7).

To make the comparison with the heat capacity of classical particles we make use of

$$N(\mathcal{E}_F) = 3n/2\mathcal{E}_F \tag{8}$$

which is found from Eqs. 1.04(6) and 1.04(7). Substitution of (8) into (7)

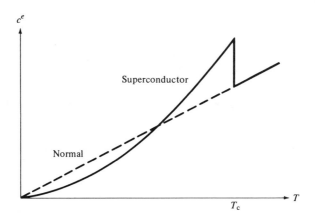

Figure 1.06. Comparison of the specific heat of a metal in the superconducting state with the form it would have if the material were not superconducting below T_c.

and division by the specific heat of classical particles gives

$$c^e/c_{cl} = \tfrac{1}{3}\pi^2 k_B T/\mathscr{E}_F \tag{9}$$

Noting that Fermi energies are typically a few electron volts and $k_B T$ is a fraction of a millielectron volt at cryogenic temperatures, we see that there is a difference of four orders of magnitude between the classical and electronic specific heats.

In the case of the superconductor, there is the additional difference that an energy gap exists between the ground state and the excitation spectrum, as discussed in the preceding section. At the lowest temperatures, almost no excitations can be produced; the heat capacity rises much more slowly than the linear rise for normal metals. As the transition temperature is approached, the number of excitations increases rapidly and the superconductor heat capacity exceeds that for the normal metal. A qualitative comparison is shown in Fig. 1.06. The effect of a gap is also seen in Prob. 1.06b. At the temperature T_c, the superconductor reverts to the normal state and there is an abrupt change of the heat capacity back to the normal-metal value.

Problems

1.06a. Argue the validity of the assumptions that $N(\mathscr{E}) \simeq N(\mathscr{E}_F)$ over the range of significant values of $\partial f/\partial T$, that $\mathscr{E}_F \simeq \mu$, and that $\exp(-\mathscr{E}_F/k_B T) \simeq 0$. Verify the integration leading to (7). Note that

$$\int_{-\infty}^{\infty} \frac{x^2 e^x}{(e^x + 1)^2}\, dx = \frac{\pi^2}{3}$$

1.06b. It is of interest at this point to see the effect of a gap in the energy-excitation spectrum. Assume that there are no occupiable states in a region from

$\mathcal{E}_F - \delta$ to $\mathcal{E}_F + \delta$ in a normal Fermi gas. Further, take $\delta = 1$ meV and consider temperatures only in the range of 0–3 K so that $\delta \gg k_B T$ and the Fermi function can be approximated by the Boltzmann function. Show that in this temperature range the electronic heat capacity has approximately the form

$$c^e = 2N(\mathcal{E}_F)(\delta^2/T)\exp(-\delta/k_B T)$$

This is essentially the same form as for a superconductor with a gap in its excitation-energy spectrum and at temperatures far below T_c.

1.07. The Phonon Spectrum

The interaction between the conduction electrons and lattice vibrations leads to the phenomenon of electrical resistance and also, strangely enough, to the zero-resistance superconducting state. In this section we review briefly the vibrational modes in crystal lattices and the excitations (phonons) that populate these modes. The interaction with electrons is treated in the next section.

The most easily tractable model for lattice vibrations is one-dimensional; it gives a useful picture of the main features of the mechanical behavior of a periodic array of atoms. Calculation of the relation between frequency and wave number q will be left to Problem 1.07a. Here we review only the results. Analysis of one-dimensional compressional waves on a lattice represented schematically by the structure in Fig. 1.07a yields the dispersion relation shown by the solid line in Fig. 1.07b. For long wavelengths (small q), the discreteness of the structure is unimportant and the dispersion relation reduces to that of a continuum, shown by the broken line. Complete Bragg reflection takes place at $q = \pi/a$ where the wavelength equals twice the atomic spacing, and no propagating modes exist at higher frequencies. Relations similar to the one shown for compressional waves can be derived for waves of shear motion in the lattice. Since the restoring forces are different for shear motion from those involved in longitudinal motion, the dispersion relation is also different.

A simple model of a diatomic lattice is shown in Fig. 1.07c. The dispersion diagram for this structure is shown in Fig. 1.07d. The lower curves are called the *acoustic branches* and the upper, *optical branches*. As in the monatomic case, the dispersion relations for transverse motion differ from those of longitudinal motion. At $q = \pi/2a$ one-half wavelength equals

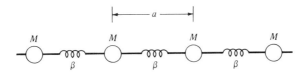

Figure 1.07a. One-dimensional mass–spring model for lattice vibrations in a monatomic crystal.

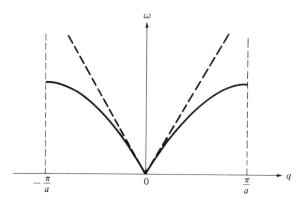

Figure 1.07b. Dispersion diagram for longitudinal oscillations on the system in Fig. 1.07a and for a continuum (dashed line). The slope v_s of the dashed line is the low-frequency velocity of sound.

the basic periodicity of the lattice $2a$. Complete Bragg reflection occurs over a range of frequencies, the size of which increases with the difference between the masses M and m. Here q should be understood to be the wave number of a wave describing the motion of the centers of mass of the cells shown by vertical broken lines in Fig. 1.07c. Thus, at the $q = 0$ point on the optical branch the cells are stationary but the atoms within the cell are oscillating $180°$ out of phase, as shown in Fig. 1.07e.

The situation in three dimensions becomes more complicated and, in general, there are different dispersion relations for waves propagating in different directions in a crystal as a result of anisotropy of the force constants. Furthermore, it is not always possible to separate longitudinal and transverse waves since the characteristic modes may have both kinds of motion. The reader is referred to the texts on solid-state physics mentioned earlier[9] for further details.

As in the case of the electrons in a finite crystal, which was described in Section 1.03, only certain values of wave number will permit satisfaction of

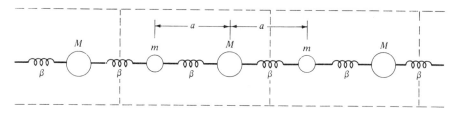

Figure 1.07c. One-dimensional mass–spring model for lattice vibrations in a diatomic crystal.

---

[9] See footnotes 1 and 2.

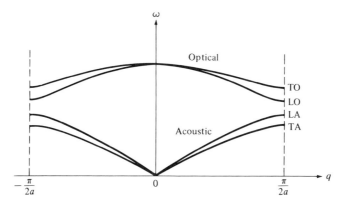

Figure 1.07d. Dispersion diagram for longitudinal (L) and transverse (T) vibrations in the model of Fig. 1.07c.

the boundary conditions at the edges of the crystal. By the same methods, one finds that the density of points in $\vec{q}$-space (the acoustical wave number) is $1/8\pi^3$ per unit volume of crystal. Each of these allowed modes will be populated by vibrational quanta, phonons having an energy $\hbar\omega_q$, where ω_q is the classical frequency of that mode, according to Bose–Einstein statistics.[10] The energy (and therefore amplitude of vibration) of a mode depends on its phonon population. The average population in the mode of wave number q is

$$n_q = \left[\exp(\hbar\omega_q/k_BT) - 1 \right]^{-1} \tag{1}$$

Counting the zero-point energy,[11] these contribute to the system an energy

$$E_q = \left(n_q + \tfrac{1}{2} \right)\hbar\omega_q \tag{2}$$

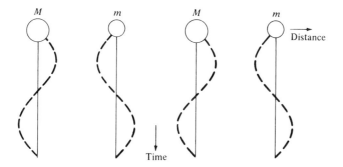

Figure 1.07e. Lattice vibrations in the model of Fig. 1.07c at $q = 0$ in the optical branch.

[10] See Leighton (footnote 3).
[11] See McKelvey (footnote 1), p. 99.

Since we are only interested in the change of energy of the system as population is changed, we may drop the zero-point energy. We then have as the total excitation energy in the system at temperature T:

$$E = \sum_q \frac{\hbar\omega_q}{\exp(\hbar\omega_q/k_B T) - 1} \tag{3}$$

Lattice Specific Heat

The Debye spectrum of phonon energies is used in the superconducting pairing theory so it is of value to examine it here. Its origin lies in the theoretical treatment used by Debye to calculate the specific heat of the lattice. In the Debye model one assumes that the energies available are insufficient to excite the optical modes (Fig. 1.07d). The Brillouin zone, which bounds the allowed values of $\vec{q}$, is replaced by a sphere of the same volume in $\vec{q}$-space and therefore contains the same number of modes. The maximum q of the sphere is called the *Debye wave number* q_D. The Debye model does not distinguish between the various acoustic branches, nor does it take into account the gaps at the zone boundaries, even though a sphere large enough to contain all values of q in the zone necessarily includes q values outside the zone. Since we are considering here only the acoustic branches of the dispersion relation, there is one mode per lattice point per branch. (The modes in the optical branch result from motion of the atoms within the unit cells.) Then the number of lattice points N per unit volume of material equals the product of the density of modes in $\vec{q}$-space and the volume of the Debye sphere,

$$N = (1/8\pi^3)(\tfrac{4}{3}\pi q_D^3) \tag{4}$$

and the number in a spherical shell in $\vec{q}$-space is

$$D(q)\,d^3q = q^2\,dq/2\pi^2 \tag{5}$$

The Debye model further assumes a linear relation between ω and q, as in the continuum model (the dashed line in Fig. 1.07b). Thus $\omega = v_s q$ and $\omega_D = v_s q_D$, where ω_D is the phonon frequency at the edge of the Debye sphere (v_s is sound velocity). Combining these relations with (4) and (5), one can show that the density of modes as a function of frequency is .

$$D(\omega) = 3N\omega^2/\omega_D^3 \tag{6}$$

which is plotted as the solid line in Fig. 1.07f.

The Debye theory of specific heat gives good agreement with experiment. However, it should be kept in mind that the actual phonon spectrum does not have the sharp cutoff at ω_D; there are usually several peaks corresponding to different wave polarizations and normally a strong one at a high frequency arising from the strong dispersion at the zone boundary. The Debye spectrum is compared with a more precise calculation in Fig. 1.07f.

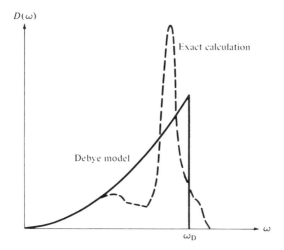

Figure 1.07f. Vibrational spectrum in the Debye model compared with a more exact calculation.

The constant-volume specific heat of the lattice is defined as the change of the excitation energy with temperature, keeping volume unchanged:

$$c_V^L = (\partial E / \partial T)_V \tag{7}$$

Since our interest in this text is in solids, for which the volume can be assumed constant, the subscript V will henceforth be omitted. Substituting the excitation energy (3) in (7), converting the summation to an integral by using the density of states per branch (6), and accounting for the three acoustic branches, we obtain

$$c^L = \frac{9N\hbar^2}{k_B T^2 \omega_D^3} \int_0^{\omega_D} \frac{\omega^4 \exp(\hbar\omega/k_B T)}{\left[\exp(\hbar\omega/k_B T) - 1\right]^2} \, d\omega \tag{8}$$

which, incidentally, is not integrable in closed form. Introducing the Debye temperature θ_D, which is defined by

$$k_B \theta_D \overset{\Delta}{=} \hbar \omega_D \tag{9}$$

so $k_B \theta_D$ is the energy of the highest-energy phonon in the Debye sphere, we can plot the lattice specific heat (8) as shown in Fig. 1.07g. At high temperatures, the specific heat reaches a constant value of $3Nk_B$. Debye temperatures for metals are typically greater than 100 K, so for metals in the superconducting temperature range (less than ≈ 23 K), $T \ll \theta_D$. In this case the lattice contribution to the specific heat has the approximate form

$$c^L \cong \tfrac{12}{5} \pi^4 N k_B (T/\theta_D)^3 \tag{10}$$

Notice that the normal-state electronic specific heat, discussed in Section 1.06 and shown for reference by the broken line in Fig. 1.07g, dominates at very low temperatures (typically for $T < \theta_D/10$).

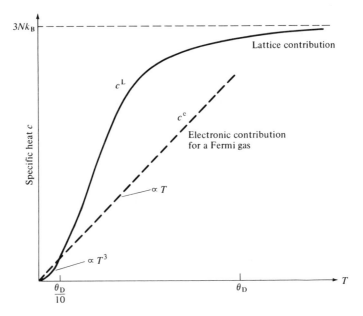

Figure 1.07g. Specific heats of the electrons and phonons in a metal. At low temperatures, $T < \theta_D/10$, the electronic contribution dominates since the lattice heat capacity falls as T^3.

The lattice is not affected by the transition to the superconducting state. If the lattice and electronic specific heats are summed for the normal and superconducting states, a result qualitatively the same as that shown in Fig. 1.06 for the electronic specific heat is obtained.

Problems

1.07a. Consider the one-dimensional diatomic-lattice model shown in Fig. 1.07c and designate the masses as $\ldots, 2n-2, 2n-1, 2n, 2n+1, 2n+2, \ldots$ with the even numbers for the smaller masses. Set up a force equation for the longitudinal motion of the $2n$th mass and one for the $(2n+1)$th mass, taking account of the interaction with adjacent masses through the spring constants β. Assume solutions for the mass displacements in the form $\exp[-i(\omega t - 2nqa)]$ for the $2n$th mass and corresponding forms for the others. Show that this leads to

$$\omega_{\pm}^2 = \frac{\beta(m+M)}{mM}\left[1 \pm \left(1 - \frac{4mM}{(m+M)^2}\sin^2 qa\right)^{1/2}\right]$$

Plot the result as in Fig. 1.07d. Show how the plotted result would be affected if the ends of the system were held fixed. Show that the group velocity is zero at the zone boundary for all values of M except $M \equiv m$.

1.07b. Find the ratio of the lattice (Debye) specific heat to the electronic specific heat for aluminum as a function of temperature in the range 0–20 K. At what temperature are the two specific heats equal? In what range of temperatures should specific-heat measurements be made if one wishes to deduce reasonably accurate values of $N(\mathscr{E}_F)$ from the results? The lattice constant a is 4.05 Å for the face-centered-cubic aluminum crystal. Assume valence is 3 and the effective mass of the conduction electrons can be taken as 1.5 m_0, where m_0 is the electron rest mass. The Debye temperature is 420 K.

1.08. Scattering of Electrons by Phonons

In the preceding sections we have discussed the free-electron gas and the phonon spectrum. Now we shall consider the scattering of electrons by phonons as groundwork for the discussion of electrical resistance in Section 1.09 and for the treatment of phonon-mediated electron-pair formation presented in Chapter 2. There are several different kinds of scattering that take place, but the most important for our present purposes is the scattering of electrons by phonons. Consider a single electron scattered by a single phonon. A typical situation is illustrated in Fig. 1.08a, in which an electron initially in state $\vec{k}$ is scattered into a final state $\vec{k}'$ by the absorption of a phonon of wave vector $\vec{q}$. Since we are describing a real event, in which well-defined particles or entities participate, it is meaningful to apply the conservation laws of momentum and energy. We have then

$$\hbar\vec{k} \pm \hbar\vec{q} = \hbar\vec{k}' \tag{1}$$

and

$$(\hbar^2 k^2 / 2m) \pm \hbar\omega_q = \hbar^2 k'^2 / 2m \tag{2}$$

These equations include the process in which an electron emits a phonon on being scattered to a new state $\vec{k}'$ as well as the absorption event. Although these two processes are quite distinct from a physical point of view and involve separate numerical factors, it turns out, when the full calculation is completed, that they make identical contributions to the electrical and thermal resistivities.[12]

It is convenient to consider scattering in two different temperature ranges; there is an important difference between the very low- and high-temperature regimes. First note that, for practical temperatures, no unoccupied electron states exist deep inside the Fermi gas. That is, the energy range of partially occupied states is of the order of $k_B T$ at the Fermi surface. Even at 1000 K (727 °C) the value of $k_B T$ is only 0.087 eV, and this is to be compared with typical Fermi energies in metals of several electron volts. This means that we are always dealing with electron momenta comparable with the value at the Fermi surface. On the other hand, the phonon momenta depend on temperature in an important way, as can

---

[12] F. J. Blatt, *Physics of Electronic Conduction in Solids*. New York: McGraw-Hill, 1968.

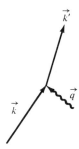

Figure 1.08a. Electron scattering by absorption of a phonon.

be seen from the Bose–Einstein population factor given in Eq. 1.07(1). For low temperatures there is very little occupation of phonon states of appreciable ω_q and q. For example, at $T = 4.2$ K, the occupation of phonon states for $q = \pi/10a$ is typically 5×10^4 greater than for $q = \pi/a$. The small phonon momenta are only sufficient to make small angular changes in the electron momenta as shown in Fig. 1.08b. At high temperatures there is appreciable population of the phonon states of highest allowed energy. The momenta in this regime are comparable with the electron momenta since the zone boundaries are the same and, therefore, large-angle scattering can take place, as shown in Fig. 1.08b. The importance of the difference between small- and large-angle scattering will be brought out in the next section in connection with temperature dependence of electrical resistivity.

The scattering processes described above are referred to as *normal* scattering. There is another type of electron–phonon interaction called an *umklapp*, or *reversing*, process which involves a transfer of momentum to the lattice as a whole through Bragg reflection. In this case, instead of the

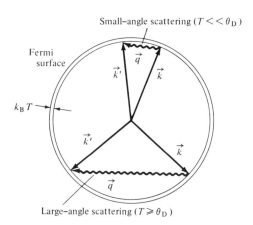

Figure 1.08b. Phonon scattering of electrons in the small range of unoccupied and energetically accessible electron states.

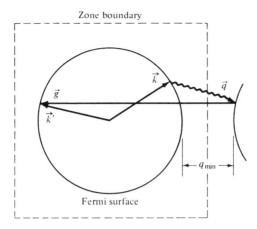

Figure 1.08c. The umklapp scattering process in which there occurs a momentum transfer to the lattice equal to the reciprocal lattice vector $\vec{q}$. The minimum phonon momentum for this process is that necessary to reach the Fermi surface in the next zone in the repeated-zone representation.

electron's momentum satisfying (1), it is described by

$$\hbar\vec{k} \pm \hbar\vec{q} + \hbar\vec{g} = \hbar\vec{k}' \tag{3}$$

where $\vec{g}$ is a reciprocal lattice vector (π/a in the simple monatomic lattice of Figs. 1.07a, b). In the repeated-zone representation, the free-electron Fermi surface is repeated as shown in Fig. 1.03b. If an electron is scattered by a phonon of sufficient momentum, it can have its momentum changed as shown in Fig. 1.08c by scattering into an adjacent zone. In scattering across the zone boundary, a momentum $\hbar\vec{g}$ is transferred to the lattice as a whole and the final $\vec{k}'$ is as shown. It may be noted that the umklapp processes are of considerable importance at high temperatures, contributing as much as half of the resistivity at room temperature for some metals.

Since a minimum phonon wave vector is required, the probability of the process diminishes rapidly as the temperature is reduced below the Debye temperature. Of course, actual metals do not conform to the ideal model and in many cases the Fermi surface is grossly distorted and even touches the edge of the Brillouin zone, as shown in Fig. 1.03c, with the result that no simple conclusions can be drawn about the role of umklapp processes at low temperatures.

1.09. Electrical Conductivity and Resistivity: The Superconducting State

In this section we discuss the factors that affect the conductivity of normal metals. The temperature dependences of conductivity and resistivity expected at low temperatures are analyzed and compared with the actual

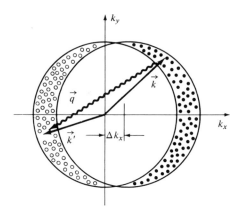

Figure 1.09a. Fermi sphere displaced by application of an electric field E_x with steady state maintained by scattering back to empty equilibrium states.

behavior of a superconductor, as exhibited in the original experiment of Kamerlingh Onnes[13] in 1911.

In an electron gas with an applied electric field $\vec{E}$, there are two opposing influences on the momenta of the electrons. The differential equation for the average x-directed electron velocity can be written as

$$m \frac{d\langle v_x \rangle}{dt} + \frac{m \langle v_x \rangle}{\tau} = -eE_x \tag{1}$$

where τ is the momentum relaxation time and e is the magnitude of the electronic charge. That is, if a field were applied for some time and then removed, the established average velocity would decay in a characteristic time τ. This requires electrons to scatter back from the leading edge of the displaced Fermi surface to the trailing edge as shown in Fig. 1.09a. If the scattering is over large angles as indicated for high temperatures in Fig. 1.08b, the relaxation time and collision time are approximately equal. If, however, each collision only causes a small angular change of the electron momentum as shown for low temperatures in Fig. 1.08b, the relaxation time can be many times larger than the collision time. Where field changes are slow compared with τ (typically 10^{-13} s), the first term in (1) vanishes and we have

$$\langle v_x \rangle = -(e\tau/m)E_x \tag{2}$$

To find the expression for conductivity σ, we note that the current density is

$$J_x = \sigma E_x = -ne \langle v_x \rangle \tag{3}$$

[13] H. Kamerlingh Onnes, *Akad. van Wetenschappen (Amsterdam)*, Vol. 14, pp. 113, 818, 1911. See also selected reprints of *Superconductivity*. New York: American Institute of Physics, 1964.

From (2) and (3), we have

$$\sigma = (ne^2\tau/m) \qquad (4)$$

Whereas this *kinetic* formulation of conductivity is accurate for a semiconductor where the electrons in the conduction band are far from Brillouin-zone boundaries, a more general approach should be used to get correct results for a metal. Starting with the Boltzmann transport equation, introducing the relaxation time approximation, and defining the current density by

$$\vec{J} = \int e\vec{v}_{\vec{k}} f_{\vec{k}} \, dk$$

where $f_{\vec{k}}$ is the distribution function, one can derive a general expression for conductivity.[14] In the case of crystals of cubic symmetry where conductivity is a scalar, this result is

$$\sigma = \frac{e^2}{12\pi^3\hbar} \int l_0 \, dS_F \qquad (5)$$

where the intrinsic relaxation mean free path $l_0 = \tau v_F$, v_F is the total velocity magnitude at the Fermi surface, and the integration is over the Fermi surface. It is easily shown (Prob. 1.09a) that this reduces to the kinetic formula (4) for a free-electron gas. More generally, (5) should be used since the Fermi surfaces are normally complex.

There are two equivalent ways of considering the conduction process. In the kinetic view, all conduction electrons take part and move with a small velocity v_x. Another view is that the electrons in the center of the Fermi gas are unaffected and only those in a thin layer at the Fermi surface are moved from the back to the front of the Fermi gas (Fig. 1.09a). That this is an equivalent view is seen by the following argument. In the kinetic picture, the average energy is related to the shift of the Fermi gas; thus $v_x = \hbar\Delta k/m$, so the current is $J_x = ne\hbar\Delta k/m$. If only the electrons at the surface are involved, there is one group of electrons at the front with a velocity $v_F \cos\theta$ and a group of holes at the rear with a velocity $-v_F \cos\theta$ and these comprise current components of the same sign. Their average x-directed velocities can be shown to be $2v_F/3$. The number of electrons in the sector shaded in Fig. 1.09a is $3n\Delta k/4k_F$ with an equal number of holes on the other side. These together give a current of $J_x = nev_F\Delta k/k_F = ne\hbar\Delta k/m$, which is the same as in the kinetic formulation. In this view, the inner electrons play the role of raising the velocity of those at the surface which carry the current. This provides some understanding of why the conductivity is expressible as an integral over the Fermi surface as in (5).

----

[14]See Ziman (footnote 2), p. 216.

Temperature Dependence of Conductivity and Resistivity

At high temperatures, $T \gtrsim \theta_D$, the density of phonons increases linearly with temperature (Prob. 1.09b) and the collision time decreases as T^{-1}, as shown in Fig. 1.09b. Large-angle scattering dominates so the relaxation time approximately equals the collision time. Thus, the conductivity has a T^{-1} dependence and the resistivity $\rho = (1/\sigma) \propto T$, as shown in Fig. 1.09c.

At low temperatures, $T \ll \theta_D$, phonons scatter the electrons only through small angles, as shown in Fig. 1.08b, since the mean phonon wave number $\langle q \rangle$ is on the order of $(T/\theta_D)q_D$. The mean angle of scattering $\langle \phi \rangle \approx \langle q \rangle / k_F$, and k_F and q_D are of the same order, so it is easily seen that $\langle \phi \rangle \approx T/\theta_D$. Each collision event, therefore, is much less effective in restoring the equilibrium momentum distribution than at high temperatures where a single collision can carry $\vec{k}$ into $\vec{k}'$ on the other side of the Fermi gas. The fractional reduction of forward momentum per collision is $\Delta p/p = 1 - \cos\phi$. The relaxation time in the preceding equations is related to the collision time τ_c by

$$(1/\tau) = \langle (1 - \cos\phi)/\tau_c(\phi) \rangle$$
$$\cong (1/\tau_c)\langle 1 - \cos\phi \rangle \tag{6}$$

where the second form assumes that τ_c is approximately independent of the scattering angle. Making the further approximation that $\langle 1 - \cos\phi \rangle \cong 1 - \cos\langle\phi\rangle \cong \langle\phi\rangle^2/2$. We see that

$$\tau \approx 2(\theta_D/T)^2\tau_c \tag{7}$$

It can be shown (Prob. 1.09b) that the density of phonons at low

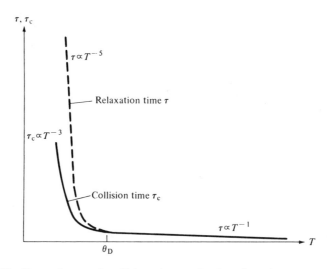

Figure 1.09b. Dependence of collision time and relaxation time on temperature. Effective collision time takes account of the temperature dependence of the mean scattering angle.

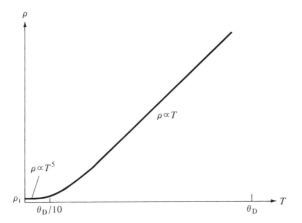

Figure 1.09c. Typical dependence of electrical resistivity on temperature with a residual resistivity at the lowest temperatures resulting from imperfection scattering.

temperatures increases as T^3. The collision time must vary as T^{-3}. Thus, the relaxation time is proportional to T^{-5} as shown in Fig. 1.09b and the conductivity dependence is T^{-5}. The resistivity is, therefore,

$$\rho_{ph}(T) \propto T^5, \qquad \text{where} \quad T \ll \theta_D \tag{8}$$

The processes at low temperatures are actually more complicated than suggested above. For example, it is known that umklapp processes increase the resistivity where the normal process is becoming less efficient because of small-angle scattering.

The phonon contribution to resistance is summarized in the semi-empirical Bloch–Grüneisen formula which has been shown to give good agreement with experiment,[15] though it should be used with some care. In particular, it does not account for the very structure-dependent umklapp processes that modify the T^5 dependence at low temperatures.

The resistance contribution of the phonon scattering is not the whole story. If there were no other effects, the resistance would vanish at $T = 0$; but the electrons are also scattered by structural imperfections of the lattice and by impurities, causing a residual resistivity ρ_i. The Matthiessen rule states that these independent resistivity components can be added:

$$\rho = \rho_i + \rho_{ph}(T) \tag{9}$$

Thus in normal metals one finds an overall temperature dependence as shown in Fig. 1.09c.

Experimental observations of electrical conductivity provide a means for comparing the strengths of the electron–phonon interaction in different

---

[15] See Ziman (footnote 2), p. 225.

metals. For those obtainable in sufficiently pure single-crystal form, the electron–phonon scattering is the dominant agent except at the lowest temperatures. The residual resistivity is a sensitive test of the purity, and the resistance ratio $R_{273 \text{ K}}/R_{4.2 \text{ K}}$ is a common measure. For example, 99.999% ("five-nines") purity copper has a resistance ratio of about 1000. Some materials, such as magnesium, can be made so pure that the mean free path exceeds usual crystal dimensions and they appear to be perfect conductors in all but the most precise measurements.

The Superconducting Transition

Resistivity measurements of the type described above were made on mercury by Kamerlingh Onnes in 1911.[16] He had developed a method of liquifying helium and thereby could reach temperatures in the neighborhood of 4.2 K. He found that, at a temperature slightly below the boiling point of helium, the resistance of a mercury filament dropped abruptly to a value thousands of times lower than the value just above 4.2 K, as shown in the reproduction of his original published graph, Fig. 1.09d. He realized

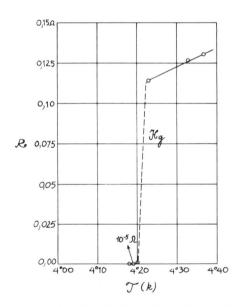

Figure 1.09d. Experimental data by H. Kamerlingh Onnes (footnote 13) in 1911 which first showed the transition from the resistive state to the superconductive state. A mercury filament was used and its resistance at 273 K, extrapolated from the melting point, was about 60 Ω. Ordinate is resistance in ohms and abscissa is temperature in Kelvins.

---

[16] See footnote 13.

that the material had passed into a new state, and called it the "superconductive state." This was the first observed manifestation of superconductivity.

In Section 1.05, we discussed the superconductor energy gap and its effect on the optical absorption spectrum which was observed many years after Kamerlingh Onnes' resistance measurements. In the next section we shall introduce another remarkable aspect of superconductivity—the diamagnetic behavior of superconductors.

Problems

1.09a. Show that the formula (5) for the conductivity of crystals with cubic symmetry reduces to (4) in the case of the free-electron gas.

1.09b. Show that the density of phonons varies as T at high temperatures and as T^3 at low temperatures.

1.09c. The Bloch–Grüneisen formula for resistance is

$$\rho = C\left(\frac{T}{\theta_{\mathrm{D}}}\right)^5 \int_0^{\theta_{\mathrm{D}}/T} \frac{s^5\,ds}{(e^s - 1)(1 - e^{-s})}$$

where C is a constant and s is a variable of integration. This is not integrable in closed form. Show that this gives $\rho = 120C(T/\theta_{\mathrm{D}})^5$ and $\rho = CT/4\theta_{\mathrm{D}}$ for temperatures much less than and greater than the Debye temperature, respectively. (The constant C is the same in both relations.)

1.09d. The resistance of the mercury filament in Kamerlingh Onnes' experiment was about 60 Ω at $T = 0$ °C. Calculate the temperature dependence of resistance at low temperatures that would have occurred in the absence of the superconducting transition using the relations in Prob. 1.09c. Take $\theta_{\mathrm{D}} = 71.9$ K. Compare with Onnes' data at 4.3 K and suggest possible reasons for the difference.

1.10. Perfect Conductor vs Superconductor: The Meissner Experiment

In this section we examine the behavior of a perfectly pure crystal of a normal metal in which resistance vanishes at $T = 0$ because of the elimination of phonon scattering. The behavior of this fictitious perfect conductor is compared with that of a superconductor in one of the milestone experiments in the history of superconductivity, that done by Meissner and Ochsenfeld.[17] We shall see that whereas a perfect conductor would trap the

---

[17] W. Meissner and R. Ochsenfeld "Ein Neuer Effekt bei Eintritt der Supraleitfähigkeit," *Naturwissenschaften*, Vol. 21, pp. 787–788, 1933.

flux it contained upon becoming perfect, the superconductor expels flux in making the transition to the superconductive state.

Let us first examine the behavior of a conductor subjected to an ac field and see the result of letting relaxation time τ become infinite. If we let $d\langle v_x \rangle / dt \cong \partial \langle v_x \rangle / \partial t$ in Eq. 1.09(1)[18] and assume that all quantities vary with time as $e^{j\omega t}$, we obtain[19]

$$\langle v_x \rangle = \frac{-(e\tau/m)E_x}{1+j\omega\tau} \qquad (1)$$

Using Eq. 1.09(3) we find an expression for the ac current density:

$$J_x = \frac{ne^2\tau/m}{1+\omega^2\tau^2}(1-j\omega\tau)E_x \qquad (2)$$

If we let $\tau \to \infty$, we obtain the result for the perfect conductor with zero surface scattering also assumed:

$$J_x = -j(ne^2/\omega m)E_x \qquad (3)$$

Thus we see that the current density, like momentum, is at phase quadrature to the electric field for the perfect conductor. The Fermi gas oscillates in $\vec{k}$-space with a 90° phase shift from the electric field as shown in Fig. 1.10a. Here we see that the real part of the ac conductivity vanishes as it must to avoid having losses resulting from a current component in phase with the electric field. If we consider a perfect conductor of length l_1 and cross-sectional area A, and assume uniform current-density distribution, we can write from (3) a relation between current I and voltage. If this is compared with $I = (j\omega L)^{-1}V$, we can identify an inductance L associated with the inertia of the electrons:

$$L = ml_1/ne^2A \qquad (4)$$

Clearly, there can be an electric field in a perfect conductor if the frequency is not zero. We shall see in Chapter 3 that there can also be a nonvanishing electric field in a superconductor with ac fields. The same inductance effect arises there. However, though a superconductor at *finite* temperature has zero dc resistance, as does the fictitious perfect conductor at $T = 0$, there are ac losses because some of the electrons are not in the superconductive state (excitations) and these can be scattered by the phonons.

Now let us examine a magnetic property of a perfect conductor. With

---

[18] The neglect of the other components of $d\langle v \rangle / dt$ is commonly made because the spatial variations of velocity are small.

[19] Throughout the text, for topics with physics emphasis we shall use $-i$, which results from the use of $\exp(-i\omega t)$ time dependence common in physics. For subjects most often associated with electrical engineering, j will be used in accordance with the time dependence $\exp(j\omega t)$ used there. Conversions can be made easily where desired.

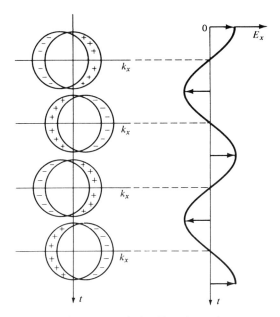

Figure 1.10a. Periodic displacement of the Fermi gas in a very pure conductor ($\omega\tau \gg 1$) subjected to an ac electric field. Note that there is a 90° phase shift between the field and the momentum.

$\tau = \infty$, Eq. 1.09(1) describes the dynamics of the electrons, and using Eq. 1.09(3) we can obtain (in the vector form)

$$\vec{E} = \frac{m}{ne^2}\frac{d\vec{J}}{dt} \cong \frac{m}{ne^2}\frac{\partial \vec{J}}{\partial t} \tag{5}$$

Taking the time derivative of Maxwell's equation $\nabla \times \vec{H} = \vec{J}$, neglecting displacement current, and substituting (5), one obtains

$$\nabla \times \dot{\vec{H}} = (ne^2/m)\vec{E} \tag{6}$$

where $\dot{\vec{H}} = \partial\vec{H}/\partial t$. Taking the curl of the above relation and substituting Maxwell's other curl equation gives

$$\nabla \times \nabla \times \dot{\vec{H}} = -(ne^2/m)\dot{\vec{B}} \tag{7}$$

The left side of (7) can be replaced using a common vector identity and making use of the facts[20] that $\nabla \cdot \vec{B} = 0$ and $\vec{B} = \mu_0\vec{H}$, obtaining finally for the time derivative of magnetic induction

$$\nabla^2\dot{\vec{B}} = (\mu_0 ne^2/m)\dot{\vec{B}} \tag{8}$$

---

[20] For many metals it is a very good approximation to take $\mu = \mu_0$.

To examine the conditions at the boundary of a perfect conductor, we specialize (8) to one dimension (assuming a perfectly conducting half-space from $y = 0$ to $y = \infty$):

$$\frac{\partial^2 \vec{B}}{\partial y^2} = \frac{\mu_0 n e^2}{m} \vec{B} \qquad (9)$$

The general solution of (9) can be written in the form:

$$\vec{B} = A_1 e^{\alpha y} + A_2 e^{-\alpha y} \qquad (10)$$

where $\alpha = (\mu_0 n e^2 / m)^{1/2}$. The solution that meets the boundary condition at infinity is the one in which $\vec{B}$ decays exponentially with distance from the boundary. The $1/e$ distance of decay is typically less than 100 nm so $\vec{B}$ is very effectively excluded from the interior of a perfect conductor.

The Meissner Experiment

In 1933 Meissner and Ochsenfeld[21] performed an experiment of fundamental importance to the development of the science of superconductivity. They subjected a lead sample to a weak magnetic field with $T > T_c$ and then reduced the temperature to make the lead superconducting. They

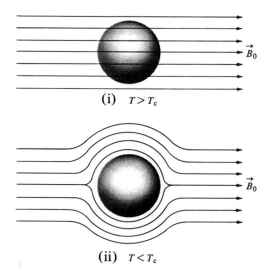

(i) $T > T_c$

(ii) $T < T_c$

Figure 1.10b. Superconductor sample subjected to an applied magnetic field with temperature (i) above and (ii) below T_c. The flux expulsion below T_c is called the *Meissner effect.*

---

[21] See footnote 17.

believed at the time that a superconductor was merely a perfect conductor. According to the above theory for a perfect conductor, flux should have been trapped and subsequent removal of the field should have left flux in the lead. What was actually observed is shown in Fig. 1.10b. In the first part (i) the temperature is above T_c and a magnetic field is applied; then the temperature is reduced below T_c and the result is as shown in (ii). The magnetic flux is expelled, giving a zero *effective* relative permeability; it was concluded that the superconductor in a weak field is therefore perfectly diamagnetic except for a thin layer at the suface of the body. It was later deduced that, in the superconductor, the magnetic induction $\vec{B}$ itself varies in the same way as is predicted for $\vec{B}$ in the perfect conductor. The induction therefore decays substantially in a distance of about 100 nm from the surface. This *Meissner effect* led to the formulation of the London theory which is discussed in Chapter 3.

Problems

1.10a. Consider a straight copper wire of 100 μm in diameter and long enough to treat as though infinite. Calculate the inductance per unit length arising from the inertia of the electrons, assuming very high purity and neglecting scattering at the wire surface ($\tau \to \infty$). Compare this with the internal inductance per unit length $L_{int} = \mu/8\pi$. Assume that the frequency is low enough to have uniform distribution of current in the wire. Take $n = 8.45 \times 10^{22}$ cm^{-3} and $m = m_0$, the electron rest mass.

1.10b. For the wire of the preceding problem, calculate the distance in which $\vec{B}$ falls to $1/e$ of its surface value. Assume that an ac field is applied parallel to the axis of the wire. Discuss the fields and currents in the sample.

Chapter 2

Microscopic Theory
of the Equilibrium Superconducting State
and Single-Particle Tunneling

2.01. Introduction

In Chapter 1 we studied the behavior of normal metals at low temperatures and saw that at a certain critical temperature, whose value depends on the material, there is an abrupt change of the thermal and electrodynamic characteristics. It is the purpose of the present chapter to examine the microscopic phenomena responsible for that change.

We shall see that the Bardeen–Cooper–Schrieffer (BCS) theory[1] of the superconducting state employs a very simple model of the electron dynamics in the metal, the spherical Fermi gas discussed in Chapter 1. Experimental evidence suggests that this model leads even to quantitatively correct results. For example, the crystal structure, which directly affects the shape of the Fermi surface, does not seem to play a determining role in the existence of the superconducting state.

The basic hypothesis of the BCS theory of the superconducting state is that the electrons occupy $\vec{k}$ states in pairs, as shown in Fig. 2.01. If a scattering event causes the electron in state $\vec{k}_1$ to take on a different value, say $\vec{k}_2$, its mate initially in the $-\vec{k}_1$ state must move almost simultaneously to the state $-\vec{k}_2$.

Under certain conditions, there is a net attractive interaction between members of the pairs. This attraction arises because, in making a state transition, one electron perturbs the lattice, yielding a distorted, positively charged lattice that attracts the other electron and overcomes the Coulomb repulsion force. In a common, though incomplete, analogy, a ball rolling across an elastic sheet distorts the sheet and attracts another ball rolling nearby.

In the superconducting ground state ($T = 0$), all electrons are paired and a certain minimum amount of energy is required to break a pair; this

---

[1] J. Bardeen, L. N. Cooper, and J. R. Schrieffer, "Theory of superconductivity," *Phys. Rev.*, Vol. 108, pp. 1175–1204, 1 December 1957. "Bardeen, Cooper, and Schrieffer share Nobel Physics Prize," *Phys. Today*, Vol. 25, p. 73, December 1972.

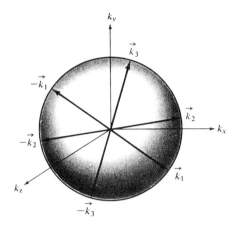

Figure 2.01. Paired-electron occupancy of $\vec{k}$ states in the superconducting ground state.

amount of energy is called the *energy gap*. At nonzero temperatures some pairs are broken and the resulting single electrons are distributed in energy according to the Fermi–Dirac law.

The chapter starts with a discussion of electron pairing and we show that in the absence of current flow the most probable way for the electrons to pair is by occupying opposite $\vec{k}$ states, as in Fig. 2.01.

We then present the model used by L. N. Cooper[2] to show that under certain conditions the normal Fermi gas is unstable and there is a tendency toward pairing. Cooper considered two electrons added to a completely filled, zero-temperature Fermi gas and showed that, if they are paired and there is an attractive interaction between them, the energy of the Fermi gas plus the two electrons is less than that of the Fermi gas alone. Therefore, to lower the system energy the other electrons should form pairs. This work suggested the direction that the microscopic theory of the superconducting state should take and led to the elegant BCS theory.

We then give an analysis of the origin of the attractive interaction requiring only a modest level of quantum mechanics. This approach reveals how the charge perturbation resulting when an electron changes state excites oscillations of other electrons and ions in such a way that there is an attractive force between electrons. The analysis is couched in terms of a dielectric function, which is the familiar dielectric constant, but with functional dependence on frequency and wave number.

With this background, the BCS theory for the superconducting ground state is presented. This theory eluded the efforts of theoreticians for many

---

[2]L. N. Cooper, "Bound electron pairs in a degenerate Fermi gas," *Phys. Rev.*, Vol. 104, pp. 1189–1190, 15 November 1956.

years. It employs creation and annihilation operators which were briefly introduced in Chapter 1. We have chosen to describe the theory in a way that, though complete, can be appreciated without requiring familiarity with operator algebra.

A key result is the probability of pair occupation of $\vec{k}$ states at $T = 0$, which has a form reminiscent of the Fermi distribution for $T \neq 0$, even though all electrons are in the ground state.

We then study the superconductor with $T \neq 0$ and analyze the excitations (broken pairs). The concept of minimum excitation energy, or energy gap, that was alluded to briefly in Section 1.05 and plays an important role in applications, is presented and its effect on the density of states available for occupation by excitations is analyzed. We then show that the excitations are distributed in energy according to the Fermi distribution.

The electron gas in the superconductor thus consists of two interpenetrating systems or fluids: one in the paired state and one in the excited, or single-particle, state. The next chapter exploits this *two-fluid* picture which, historically, preceded the BCS microscopic theory, in the study of electrodynamics for practical applications.

The last sections of the chapter deal with single-particle tunneling. It is brought in at this point as a practical illustration of the use of the theory of excitations. The last section presents a discussion of recent applications of single-particle tunneling for detection and mixing at millimeter-wave frequencies.

2.02. Electron Pairing

Basic to the microscopic theory of superconductivity is the concept of occupancy of $\vec{k}$ states in pairs. If one studies the case where occupancy of a certain state $\vec{k}_1$ implies occupancy of another state $\vec{k}_2$, and vice versa, it is found that there is a type of interaction that lowers the energy of the system. The system has its lowest energy if the spins of the electrons occupying the two states are oppositely directed. We shall assume opposite spins throughout this text. In the present section, we discuss pair occupancy and scattering between pair states.

We shall be considering pairs of plane-wave states with one electron with position coordinate $\vec{r}_1$ occupying the state $\exp(i\vec{k}_1 \cdot \vec{r}_1)$ and the other occupying $\exp(i\vec{k}_2 \cdot \vec{r}_2)$, as suggested in Fig. 2.02a. It will become evident in the next section that a pair of electrons requires for its representation a whole spectrum of such pairs of states. Also, for small values of the relative position vector $\vec{r} = \vec{r}_1 - \vec{r}_2$, there is an enhanced probability density for the pair when there is an attractive interaction.

We shall start with consideration of two noninteracting electrons. The eigenfunction for the noninteracting pair can be written as the product of

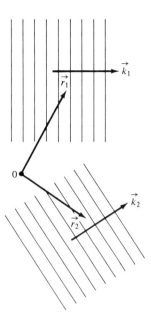

Figure 2.02a. Elemental pair of plane-wave states from which the wave function for a Cooper pair is formed.

their state functions:

$$\Phi(\vec{k}_1, \vec{k}_2; \vec{r}_1, \vec{r}_2) = \exp(i\vec{k}_1 \cdot \vec{r}_1)\exp(i\vec{k}_2 \cdot \vec{r}_2) \tag{1}$$

where $\vec{k}_1$ is assumed to have spin up and $\vec{k}_2$, spin down. This can be written in center-of-mass and relative-motion coordinates using the definitions $\vec{R} = \frac{1}{2}(\vec{r}_1 + \vec{r}_2)$, $\vec{r} = \vec{r}_1 - \vec{r}_2$, $\vec{K} = \vec{k}_1 + \vec{k}_2$, and $\vec{k} = \frac{1}{2}(\vec{k}_1 - \vec{k}_2)$, where $\vec{R}$ is the location of the center of mass and $\vec{K}$ is its momentum, $\vec{r}$ is the relative electron-position coordinate, and $2\vec{k}$ is the difference of the momenta. The result is

$$\Phi(\vec{K}, \vec{k}; \vec{R}, \vec{r}) = \exp\left[i(\vec{K} \cdot \vec{R} + \vec{k} \cdot \vec{r})\right] \tag{2}$$

We shall consider scattering between states such as (2) resulting from interactions between the electrons. The basic scattering process is shown in Fig. 2.02b. The electron occupying state $\vec{k}_1$ emits a phonon (i.e., vibrates the lattice) which is absorbed by the electron occupying state $\vec{k}_2$. The total momentum $\vec{K}$ in the final state is the same as in the initial state. The scattering takes place in a very short time so the uncertainty in time Δt is also very small. This means, by the Heisenberg uncertainty principle $\Delta t \Delta \mathcal{E} \geq \hbar$, that the uncertainty in energy $\Delta \mathcal{E}$ is very large and the final state energy can differ from that of the initial state (within $\Delta \mathcal{E}$). Therefore,

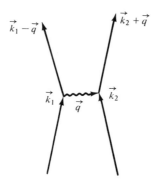

Figure 2.02b. Exchange of a virtual phonon between electrons occupying states $\vec{k}_1$ and $\vec{k}_2$.

though we assume that momentum is conserved in this scattering event, it is not necessary to require conservation of energy. The phonon is therefore called a "virtual" phonon.

Consider a pair of states as shown relative to the Fermi sea in Fig. 2.02c. The shell at the Fermi surface denotes the range of states into which $\vec{k}_1$ and $\vec{k}_2$ may scatter as a result of the exchange of a virtual phonon. As we saw in Section 1.07, the maximum energy of the phonons is about $k_B\theta_D$, where the Debye temperature θ_D is typically 150 K. Therefore, the shell of accessible

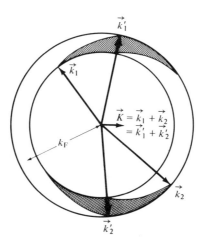

Figure 2.02c. Electron pairs occupying pairs of states (e.g., $\vec{k}_1, \vec{k}_2$ and $\vec{k}'_1, \vec{k}'_2$) lying in a range of energies within about $\hbar\omega_D$ around the Fermi energy. The total momentum $\vec{K}$ is conserved so pairs can only scatter into other k-state pairs within the darkly shaded region. The Fermi gas is spherical, so the shaded region is actually a ring on the surface of the sphere. The volume of the ring, as a function of the net pair momentum $\vec{K}$, is sharply peaked at $\vec{K} = 0$.

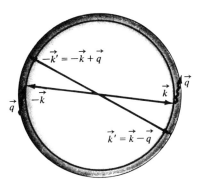

Figure 2.02d. Scattering of the state $\vec{k}, -\vec{k}$ into $\vec{k} - \vec{q}, -\vec{k} + \vec{q}$ upon emission of a virtual phonon by the electron in state $\vec{k}$ and its absorption by the electron in state $-\vec{k}$.

states has a thickness on the order of 13 meV which is to be compared with the typical Fermi energies of a few electron volts. Since $\vec{K}$ is conserved in the scattering, all pairs of $\vec{k}_1$ and $\vec{k}_2$ must be within the dark shaded ring in the shell at the Fermi surface. It is easy to see that the size of that region of accessible states increases sharply as $\vec{K}$ is reduced to zero since the whole spherical shell shown in Fig. 2.02c then becomes accessible. We shall see later that the amount by which the energy of the state with a Cooper pair present is reduced below the energy of the Fermi ground state increases as the number of states accessible for scattering increases. Therefore, the most probable equilibrium state is the one with $\vec{K} = 0$, i.e., zero center-of-mass motion. Thus, we are concerned with state pairs where $\vec{k}_2 = -\vec{k}_1$; in this case $\vec{k}$ in (2) equals $\vec{k}_1$. In Fig. 2.02d a typical scattering event is shown. The illustration shows the same phonon twice, once being emitted by the electron in the $\vec{k}$ state and simultaneously being absorbed by the electron in the $-\vec{k}$ state. The resulting new states are $\vec{k}' = \vec{k} - \vec{q}$ and $-\vec{k}' = -\vec{k} + \vec{q}$. It might be noted parenthetically here that consideration of scattering only with phonon wave vectors $\vec{q}$ limits consideration to normal scattering processes (see Section 1.08). Though umklapp processes also play a role, we shall consider only normal processes, for simplicity.

Problem

2.02. Show with vector diagrams the meanings of $\vec{R}$, $\vec{r}$, $\vec{K}$, and $\vec{k}$ in (2). Suppose all the electrons in a superconducting metal were in pairs with the same center-of-mass momentum $\vec{K}$ and there were 10^{22} pairs per cm³. Assume that each electron has the free-electron mass and the Fermi energy is 5 eV. Estimate the ratio of K to k_F, the momentum of the individual electron at the Fermi surface, if the momentum $\vec{K}$ produces a current density of 10^8 A/cm². Discuss the significance of the calculation.

2.03.   The Cooper Pair Model

In this section we consider an artificial but instructive model which shows in a relatively simple way some of the basic ideas of the general microscopic theory by Bardeen, Cooper, and Schrieffer, which is to be treated in Section 2.05. The Cooper model[3] assumes a filled Fermi sea so that all states for which $k \leqslant k_F$ are completely filled. Two electrons are added and must occupy states with $k > k_F$. It is assumed that there is an interaction between the electrons that can be expressed by a potential energy $V(\vec{r}_1 - \vec{r}_2)$ as shown in Fig. 2.03a, so the total Hamiltonian for the added pair is

$$H = H_0 + V(\vec{r}_1 - \vec{r}_2) \tag{1}$$

where H_0 is the Hamiltonian of the noninteracting pair using energies measured relative to the Fermi energy. Schrödinger's equation for the added pair is

$$H\Psi = W\Psi \tag{2}$$

and Ψ is a stationary state with energy W. Equations (1) and (2) can be rearranged to give

$$(W - H_0)\Psi = V(\vec{r}_1 - \vec{r}_2)\Psi \tag{3}$$

Assuming no interaction between electrons and taking all occupancy to be in pairs with zero center-of-mass momentum as in Fig. 2.02d, the functions given by Eq. 2.02(2),

$$\Phi = \exp\left[i\vec{k} \cdot (\vec{r}_1 - \vec{r}_2)\right] \tag{4}$$

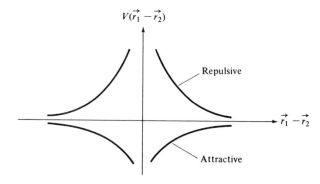

Figure 2.03a. Interaction potential energies for a pair of electrons.

---

[3] See footnote 2.

form a complete set. We shall write $\vec{r}_1 - \vec{r}_2$ in this form to emphasize the use of relative coordinates. Therefore, according to perturbation theory,[4] when there is a perturbing interaction between electrons, the stationary states can be expressed as

$$\Psi = \sum_k a_k \exp\left[i\vec{k} \cdot (\vec{r}_1 - \vec{r}_2) \right] \qquad (5)$$

We shall see that if the interaction potential $V(\vec{r}_1 - \vec{r}_2)$ is negative, a bound state exists which is to be interpreted as the wave function describing a bound-electron pair ("Cooper pair"). Since there is a finite range of magnitudes of k, those lying in the thin shell at the Fermi surface (Fig. 2.02c), the sum (5) then represents a wave function with dependence on relative coordinates $\vec{r}_1 - \vec{r}_2$, which is like a de Broglie wave packet for a single localized electron. The range of magnitudes of k is $\Delta k = (\partial k / \partial \mathcal{E})\Delta \mathcal{E}$, where $\mathcal{E} = \hbar^2 k^2 / 2m$ is the Bloch state energy. With Δk obtained this way and the Heisenberg relation $\Delta r \Delta k = 1$, we find $\Delta r = \hbar v_F / \Delta \mathcal{E}$. Using typical values of the Fermi velocity and taking the range of significant Bloch state energies to be $k_B T_c$ with a typical transition temperature, we find the "size" of a Cooper pair to be $\approx 1 \ \mu$m. (See Fig. 2.03b.) We shall see in Section 3.11 that the pair size in the BCS superconducting ground state is actually 0.18 of the value given by the present considerations of this artificial Cooper model.

Figure 2.03c shows a schematic illustration of a pair. The Fourier sum of plane-wave states in (5) represents a packet having an average wave number of k_F. Typically, the "diameter" of a pair will equal hundreds of wavelengths (schematically shown by just a few in Fig. 2.03c). The phase of the wave function evolves at a frequency $f = 2\mathcal{E}_F / h$, where the factor of 2

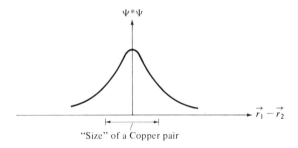

"Size" of a Copper pair

Figure 2.03b. A schematic representation of the probability distribution of a Cooper pair in relative coordinates. There is an enhanced probability of finding the electrons close to each other when an attractive potential exists.

---

[4]See, for example, L. I. Schiff, *Quantum Mechanics*, 3rd. Ed. New York: McGraw-Hill Book Co., 1968.

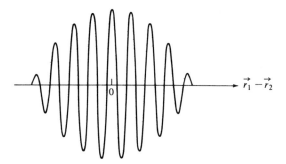

Figure 2.03c. Schematic illustration of the Cooper pair wave function. Typically, the diameter of a pair is about $1\mu m$, the wavelength is about 1nm, and the frequency of oscillation is on the order of 10^{15} Hz.

is easily seen to derive from the fact that two electrons are involved [the unwritten temporal part of (4)].

We shall analyze the scattering to obtain the eigenvalue W for the pair with interaction. It will be convenient to define the Bloch state energy relative to the Fermi energy: $\epsilon_k = \mathcal{E} - \mathcal{E}_F$. In these terms, the eigenvalue of H_0 for the pair without interaction is $2\epsilon_k$. Let us first substitute (5), with $\vec{k}$ replaced by $\vec{k}'$ into (3):

$$(W - H_0)\sum_{k'} a_{k'}\exp\left[i\vec{k}'\cdot(\vec{r}_1 - \vec{r}_2)\right] = V(\vec{r}_1 - \vec{r}_2)\sum_{k'} a_{k'}\exp\left[i\vec{k}'\cdot(\vec{r}_1 - \vec{r}_2)\right]$$

(6)

Then, to obtain a relation for the coefficients $a_{k'}$, we multiply by $\exp[-i\vec{k}\cdot(\vec{r}_1 - \vec{r}_2)]$ and integrate over the volume Ω of the system. Consider the left side first:

$$\frac{1}{\Omega}\int_{\Omega}\exp\left[-i\vec{k}\cdot(\vec{r}_1 - \vec{r}_2)\right](W - H_0)\sum_{k'} a_{k'}\exp\left[i\vec{k}'\cdot(\vec{r}_1 - \vec{r}_2)\right]d(\vec{r}_1 - \vec{r}_2)$$

$$= W\sum_{k'} a_{k'}\frac{1}{\Omega}\int_{\Omega}\exp\left[i(\vec{k}' - \vec{k})\cdot(\vec{r}_1 - \vec{r}_2)\right]d(\vec{r}_1 - \vec{r}_2)$$

$$- \sum_{k'} a_{k'}\frac{1}{\Omega}\int_{\Omega}\exp\left[-i\vec{k}\cdot(\vec{r}_1 - \vec{r}_2)\right]$$

$$\times H_0\exp\left[i\vec{k}'\cdot(\vec{r}_1 - \vec{r}_2)\right]d(\vec{r}_1 - \vec{r}_2)$$

$$= (W - 2\epsilon_k)a_k$$

Here we have made use of the fact that the unperturbed states are eigenfunctions and so are required to be orthogonal over the volume of the system. Thus, the first integral on the right side has the value unity if $k = k'$ and zero otherwise; the second integral gives the eigenvalues if

$\vec{k} = \vec{k}'$ and zero otherwise. The right side of (6) becomes

$$\frac{1}{\Omega} \int_{\Omega} \exp\left[-i\vec{k} \cdot (\vec{r}_1 - \vec{r}_2)\right] V(\vec{r}_1 - \vec{r}_2) \sum_{k'} a_{k'} \exp\left[i\vec{k}' \cdot (\vec{r}_1 - \vec{r}_2)\right] d(\vec{r}_1 - \vec{r}_2)$$

$$= \sum_{k'} a_{k'} \frac{1}{\Omega} \int_{\Omega} \exp\left[-i\vec{k} \cdot (\vec{r}_1 - \vec{r}_2)\right]$$

$$\times V(\vec{r}_1 - \vec{r}_2) \exp\left[i\vec{k}' \cdot (\vec{r}_1 - \vec{r}_2)\right] d(\vec{r}_1 - \vec{r}_2) \tag{7}$$

The integral in the last form is the scattering matrix element

$$V_{\vec{k}\vec{k}'} = \langle \vec{k}, -\vec{k} | V(\vec{r}_1 - \vec{r}_2) | \vec{k}', -\vec{k}' \rangle \tag{7a}$$

which represents the scattering by $V(\vec{r}_1 - \vec{r}_2)$ of the pair occupying $|\vec{k}', -\vec{k}'\rangle$ into the other pair states $|\vec{k}, -\vec{k}\rangle$. The potential $V_{\vec{k}\vec{k}'}$ represents the exchange of virtual phonons described in Section 2.02. Now we can rewrite (3) as

$$(W - 2\epsilon_{\vec{k}})a_{\vec{k}} = \sum_{k'} a_{k'} V_{\vec{k}\vec{k}'} \tag{8}$$

An important simplification is made by assuming $V_{\vec{k}\vec{k}'}$ to be a constant $-V$ ($V > 0$), where both $\hbar^2 k^2 / 2m$ and $\hbar^2 k'^2 / 2m$ are within the shell at the Fermi surface bounded by $\mathscr{E}_F$ and $\mathscr{E}_F + \hbar\omega_D$, and zero otherwise. That is, the amplitude for scattering between any two pair states in the shell is $-V$, but is zero if either lies outside. With this simplification, we have

$$(W - 2\epsilon_{\vec{k}})a_{\vec{k}} = -V \sum_{k'} a_{k'} \tag{9}$$

The right side is now independent of $\vec{k}$. Rearranging, we get

$$a_{\vec{k}} = \left(-V \sum_{k'} a_{k'}\right) / (W - 2\epsilon_{\vec{k}}) \tag{10}$$

Since this is true for any $a_{\vec{k}}$, where $\vec{k}$ is in the shell, we can substitute the form (10) into (9) giving

$$-V \sum_{k'} a_{k'} = -V \sum_{k'} \left(-V \sum_{k'} a_{k'}\right) / (W - 2\epsilon_{\vec{k}'}) \tag{11}$$

or

$$1 = -V \sum_{k'} \frac{1}{W - 2\epsilon_{\vec{k}'}} \tag{12}$$

The summation over $\vec{k}'$ can be converted to an integral over energy with the range bounded by $\epsilon = 0$ and $\hbar\omega_D$ (where V is nonzero):

$$1 = -V \int_0^{\hbar\omega_D} \frac{N(\epsilon)}{W - 2\epsilon} d\epsilon \tag{13}$$

Over the range of integration, the density of the states $N(\epsilon)$ is nearly constant and equal to its value at the Fermi surface $N(0)$, so (13) becomes

$$1 = - N(0)V \int_0^{\hbar\omega_D} \frac{1}{W - 2\epsilon} \, d\epsilon \qquad (14)$$

This can easily be integrated to give

$$W = 2\hbar\omega_D/(1 - e^{2/VN(0)}) \qquad (15)$$

If the interaction between the electrons is weak so that $VN(0) \ll 1$, then (15) is approximately

$$W = - 2\hbar\omega_D e^{-2/VN(0)} \qquad (16)$$

Thus we have shown that there is a *single negative eigenvalue*[5]; this signifies the existence of a bound state for the two added electrons. Cooper showed with the analysis that, where the interaction is attractive, the system energy is reduced by pairing; therefore, the Fermi sea of single electrons is unstable since any perturbation that moves two electrons above $\mathcal{E}_F$, where scattering is possible, will lower the system energy. It remains for the BCS theory (Section 2.07) to define the stable ground state in the presence of pairing.

The BCS theory yields a result that has an appearance similar to (16) with some different factors. It must be kept in mind that the Cooper model is not a model for the superconducting ground state and that (16) is an eigenvalue for a very artificial situation.

Problems

2.03a.   Use the argument based on the Heisenberg uncertainty relation to estimate the sizes of the Cooper pairs in aluminum, tin, and lead. Use Fermi velocities of $1.11 \times 10^6 \text{m/s}$, $6.37 \times 10^5 \text{m/s}$, and $4.07 \times 10^5 \text{m/s}$, respectively. How many atoms are contained within the volumes of the Cooper pairs? (See table on inside of the back cover.)

2.03b.   Show that the integration in (14) leads to (15) and determine the value of $VN(0)$ for which (16) approximates (15) with 5% accuracy.

●**2.03c.**[6]   Defining mean-square radius of a Cooper pair by

$$\rho^2 = \frac{\int |\Psi(\vec{r}_1 - \vec{r}_2)|^2 (\vec{r}_1 - \vec{r}_2)^2 d(\vec{r}_1 - \vec{r}_2)}{\int |\Psi(\vec{r}_1 - \vec{r}_2)|^2 d(\vec{r}_1 - \vec{r}_2)}$$

---

[5] Note that W increases with increasing $N(0)$, that is, with the increasing numbers of states for scattering. This lends justification to the choice of k, $-k$ pairs to maximize the number of states for scattering as discussed in Section 2.02.
[6] The most tedious or difficult problems are marked with a bullet (●).

show that

$$\rho^2 = \frac{\sum_{k}|\nabla_{\vec{k}} a_{\vec{k}}|^2}{\sum_{k}|a_{\vec{k}}|^2}$$

Show further that with $\epsilon = (\hbar^2 k^2/2m) - \mathscr{E}_F$ and the density of states

$$N(\epsilon) = \left[4\pi k^2/(2\pi)^3\right] dk/d\epsilon$$

one obtains

$$\rho^2 = \frac{\hbar^2 v_F^2 \int_0^\infty (da/d\epsilon)^2 d\epsilon}{\int_0^\infty a^2 \, d\epsilon}$$

Note that the Cooper model employs only states above k_F in forming a pair. Using the state amplitudes given by (10), show that

$$\rho = \left(2/\sqrt{3}\right)\hbar v_F/|W|$$

2.04. Dielectric Functions and Scattering Amplitudes

Our next task is to show the origin of the phonon-mediated attractive interaction. We shall do this in the simplest possible way in the next section. The approach to be used, however, requires familiarity with the concept of a dielectric function, so we devote the present section to showing how the dielectric function represents the response of a medium to a disturbing charge and indicating its relation to the scattering amplitude $V_{\vec{k}\vec{k}'}$. Let us consider first the Coulomb interaction between two electrons in a metal and the scattering it causes. The Coulomb interaction potential energy between electrons at $\vec{r}_1$ and $\vec{r}_2$ is as follows (potential energy is charge $\times$ electric potential Φ):

$$V(\vec{r}_1 - \vec{r}_2) = \frac{e^2}{4\pi\epsilon|\vec{r}_1 - \vec{r}_2|} \tag{1}$$

If there were no response by the Fermi gas of electrons, the dielectric constant ϵ would represent the effect of the ion cores in the lattice of the metal[7] and is only slightly different from the free-space constant ϵ_0. Using (1) in the scattering integral in Eq. 2.03(7), it is found that the transition amplitude between states $\vec{k}'$ and $\vec{k}$ is given by

$$V_{\vec{k}\vec{k}} = \langle \vec{k}', -\vec{k}'|V(\vec{r}_1 - \vec{r}_2)|\vec{k}, -\vec{k}\rangle = \frac{e^2}{\epsilon q^2} \tag{2}$$

---

[7] Though ϵ is not completely independent of frequency, it can be so assumed over the frequency range involved in the processes discussed in this section and in Section 2.05.

where $\vec{q}$ is the wave-vector difference between $\vec{k}'$ and $\vec{k}$. Notice that (2) is the qth component in a Fourier transform of (1).

If there is a Fermi gas of electrons present, the electric potential is modified because the electrons of the gas move in response to the potential and tend to shield it. Considering a static potential and assuming long wavelength ($q \ll k_F$), the shielding can be found in the simple Thomas–Fermi[8] model. The local electron density increases at points where the potential is more positive, being given by the relation

$$n + \delta n = (1/3\pi^2)(2m/\hbar^2)^{3/2}(\mathcal{E}_F + e\Phi)^{3/2} \tag{3}$$

where n is the equilibrium electron density

$$(1/3\pi^2)(2m/\hbar^2)^{3/2}\mathcal{E}_F^{3/2}$$

from Eq. 1.04(7). Equation (3) can be expanded in a power series to give

$$\delta n = 3ne\Phi/2\mathcal{E}_F \tag{4}$$

The charge density is given by $\rho = -e\delta n = -3ne^2\Phi/2\mathcal{E}_F$, so Poisson's equation is

$$\nabla^2\Phi = k_s^2\Phi \tag{5}$$

with $k_s^2 = 3e^2n/2\varepsilon\mathcal{E}_F$. This can be shown to have a spherically symmetric solution

$$\Phi(\vec{r}_1 - \vec{r}_2) = -\frac{e\left[\exp(-k_s|\vec{r}_1 - \vec{r}_2|)\right]}{4\pi\varepsilon|\vec{r}_1 - \vec{r}_2|} \tag{6}$$

which is, therefore, the shielded potential at $\vec{r}_2$ of an electron at $\vec{r}_1$ (or vice versa). This has a corresponding scattering amplitude

$$V_{\vec{k}\vec{k}'} = \frac{e^2}{\varepsilon(k_s^2 + q^2)} \tag{7}$$

which is the shielded equivalent of (2). By comparison with (2) we see that the response of the Fermi gas can be represented by an effective static dielectric function for low q of the form

$$\varepsilon(q,\omega)|_{\omega=0} = \varepsilon\left(1 + \frac{k_s^2}{q^2}\right) \tag{8}$$

It is conventional to write the dielectric function with ω dependence. Here, however, we have only considered the zero-frequency limit.

Now let us look at another way to find the dielectric function. One may

[8] J. M. Ziman, *Principles of the Theory of Solids*, 2nd Ed. Cambridge: Cambridge University Press, 1972, p. 150. C. Kittel, *Introduction to Solid-State Physics*, 5th Ed. New York: John Wiley and Sons, 1976, p. 296.

do this most simply in one dimension, where Poisson's equation has the form

$$\frac{d^2\Phi}{dx^2} = -\frac{\rho_T}{\varepsilon} \tag{9}$$

where it is assumed that the charge density ρ_T is the sum of any perturbing charge density $\delta\rho$ plus the screening response of the electronic and ionic fluids ρ_s. The perturbing charge, the response charge, and the potential all have the same wavelength and frequency, so we can substitute

$$\rho_T = (\delta\rho + \rho_s)e^{i(qx - \omega t)} \tag{10}$$

and

$$\Phi = \Phi_q e^{i(qx - \omega t)} \tag{11}$$

into (9) and get

$$\Phi_q = (\delta\rho + \rho_s)/q^2\varepsilon \tag{12}$$

If the response of the medium is characterized by a dielectric function $\varepsilon(q, \omega)$, so $\Phi_q = \delta\rho/q^2\varepsilon(q, \omega)$, then we can see that

$$\varepsilon(q, \omega) = \varepsilon\, \delta\rho/(\rho_s + \delta\rho) \tag{13}$$

We shall use this relation in Section 2.05 to determine the dielectric function and the corresponding scattering amplitude for screening by both electrons and ions.

Problems

2.04a. Verify that the scattering amplitude for the shielded Coulomb potential is given by (7).

2.04b. Find the electron separation $|\vec{r}_1 - \vec{r}_2|$ for which electronic shielding reduces the potential by 0.1 of its value without shielding, for indium. The atomic density of indium is $3.83 \times 10^{28}\,\mathrm{m}^{-3}$. Take its valence to be 3. Assume a spherical Fermi surface and that the electron mass is its free value, and $\varepsilon \cong \varepsilon_0$.

2.05. Attractive Electron–Electron Interaction

It was made clear in Section 2.03 that the occurrence of an attractive potential between electrons is central to the superconducting state. It is the purpose of this section to give a simple, approximate model that will convey how such a remarkable circumstance can exist. In this model the conduction electrons are considered to constitute a fluid or "jellium" that interpenetrates a positive fluid consisting of the ions of the lattice. The particles of the ion fluid are taken to have appropriately larger masses than those of the electron fluid. Single wave components of the perturbations of these fluids are analyzed to study the electron interaction. In a fluid model only longitudinal oscillations can be considered, so transverse modes of the lattice are neglected here. Furthermore, the ion fluid has no periodicity, so it is just the continuum model for the lattice.

Scattering theory tells us that, in the presence of a potential with a component of wave vector $\vec{q}$ [Eq. 2.04(11)], the state $\vec{k}$ is mixed with the state $\vec{k} + \vec{q}$, so the wave function becomes

$$\Psi_{\vec{k}}(\vec{r}, t) = \exp\left[i(\vec{k} \cdot \vec{r} - \mathcal{E}_{\vec{k}} t / \hbar)\right] + b_{\vec{k}+\vec{q}} \exp\left\{i\left[(\vec{k} + \vec{q}) \cdot \vec{r} - \mathcal{E}_{\vec{k}+\vec{q}} t / \hbar\right]\right\}$$

(1)

The value of the coefficient $b_{\vec{k}+\vec{q}}$ can be derived[9] but is incidental to the present purposes. The total charge-density perturbation resulting from scattering is

$$\delta\rho = e \sum_{k} \left[\Psi_{\vec{k}}^{*}\Psi_{\vec{k}} - 1\right]$$

(2)

where the sum is over states like (1) and the -1 appears because we are interested only in perturbations. We shall examine the response of the system to one component of the charge perturbation, that resulting from the scattering from state $\vec{k}$ into $\vec{k} + \vec{q}$. This component can be written as

$$\delta\rho_{\vec{q}}(\vec{r}, t) = \text{Re}\left[\delta\rho e^{i(\vec{q} \cdot \vec{r} - \omega t)}\right]$$

(3)

where ω is the beat frequency between the initial and final states; i.e.,

$$\omega = \mathcal{E}_{\vec{k}+\vec{q}} / \hbar - \mathcal{E}_{\vec{k}} / \hbar$$

Since the scattering takes place only between states in a thin shell in $\vec{k}$-space, the changes of energy are small, so ω is a low frequency. For convenience in the analysis we shall leave the perturbation in phasor notation and assume $\vec{q} = \hat{x}q$:

$$\delta\rho_{q} = \delta\rho e^{i(qx - \omega t)}$$

(4)

The response ρ_s to $\delta\rho$ is a wave of charge having the same spatial variation and the same frequency:

$$\rho_{sq} = \rho_s e^{i(qx - \omega t)}$$

(5)

There are two components of the response: that of the ion fluid ρ_i and that of the electron fluid ρ_e:

$$\rho_s = \rho_i + \rho_e$$

(6)

The response must be consistent, not only with $\delta\rho$, but also with itself. The initial perturbation is the wave (4) resulting from an electron scattering

---

[9] See Ziman (footnote 8), Section 5.1.

from state $\vec{k}$ to state $\vec{k} + \vec{q}$. To this are added waves of the ion and electron fluids which respond to the *total* potential perturbation. By analyzing this situation, we can find the dielectric function Eq. 2.04(13) and thence the Fourier components of the electron–electron interaction using the equivalent of Eq. 2.04(2).

Let us consider first the response of the electron fluid. It was pointed out above that the frequency of $\delta \rho$ is small. The electrons are very mobile and can respond essentially instantaneously; thus we can use the Thomas–Fermi static screening model discussed in Section 2.04. From Eq. 2.04(4) we find the potential concomitant to an electronic charge perturbation $\rho_e = -e\,\delta n$ to be

$$\Phi = (\delta n / \tfrac{3}{2} ne)\mathscr{E}_F = -\rho_e \mathscr{E}_F / \tfrac{3}{2} ne^2 \tag{7}$$

Assuming $e^{i(qx - \omega t)}$ variations, we can substitute (7) in the one-dimensional form of Poisson's equation to obtain

$$\frac{2q^2\rho_e\mathscr{E}_F}{3ne^2} = -\frac{\rho_T}{\varepsilon} = -\frac{\delta\rho + \rho_i + \rho_e}{\varepsilon} \tag{8}$$

in which all variables are phasors. We can solve this for the electronic portion of the response using $\rho_s = \rho_i + \rho_e$:

$$\rho_e = -\left(k_s^2 / q^2\right)(\rho_s + \delta\rho) \tag{9}$$

where $k_s^2 = 3e^2n/2\varepsilon\mathscr{E}_F$. The perturbation $\delta\rho$ results from the $\vec{k}$ to $\vec{k} + \vec{q}$ transition and this electronic response is the other half of the interaction shown in Fig. 2.02b. That is, if $\delta\rho$ results from $\vec{k}_2 \to \vec{k}_2 + \vec{q}$, then ρ_e results from $\vec{k}_1 \to \vec{k}_1 - \vec{q}$.

The ions respond more sluggishly and must be treated differently. The equation of motion for an ion is

$$M\frac{dv_i}{dt} = ZeE \tag{10}$$

where M is the ion mass, Z is the ion charge number, and E is the electric field. The current density J_i is related to the velocity v_i by

$$J_i = (n/Z)(Ze)v_i \tag{11}$$

where n is the free-electron density. Combining (10) and (11) and using $E = -\partial\Phi/\partial x$, we can write

$$M\frac{dJ_i}{dt} = -Ze^2n\frac{\partial\Phi}{\partial x} \tag{12}$$

The total derivative in (12) can be replaced by $\partial J_i/\partial t$ using the assumption that the ion velocities are small compared with the phase velocity ω/q (see Prob. 2.05a). This can then be substituted in the continuity equation

$$\frac{\partial\rho_i}{\partial t} + \frac{\partial J_i}{\partial x} = 0 \tag{13}$$

to obtain

$$\frac{\partial^2 \rho_i}{\partial t^2} = \frac{Ze^2 n}{M} \frac{\partial^2 \Phi}{\partial x^2} \tag{14}$$

Substituting the assumed wave form and using Poisson's equation, one finds

$$\rho_i = \left(\omega_{pi}^2 / \omega^2\right)(\rho_s + \delta\rho) \tag{15}$$

where $\omega_{pi} = (Ze^2 n / M\varepsilon)^{1/2}$ is the ion plasma frequency.

Taking the sum of (9) and (15) to form ρ_s and substituting that into the expression for the dielectric function [Eq. 2.04(13)], we find

$$\varepsilon(q, \omega) = \frac{\omega^2 \left(k_s^2 + q^2\right) - \omega_{pi}^2 q^2}{\omega^2 q^2} \varepsilon \tag{16}$$

It is useful to recast (16) in terms of the natural frequency of the ion (lattice) mode of the same wavelength (i.e., in the absence of electron perturbation but including electronic shielding). This can be found easily by noting that $\delta\rho$ is zero in this case, so $\varepsilon(q, \omega) = 0$ according to Eq. 2.04(13). From (16),

$$\omega_q^2 \overset{\Delta}{=} \omega^2|_{\delta\rho = 0} = \frac{\omega_{pi}^2 q^2}{k_s^2 + q^2} \tag{17}$$

Inserting (17) into (16) and substituting the result in the transition amplitude Eq. 2.04(2) in place of ε, we obtain

$$V_{kk'} = \frac{e^2}{\varepsilon\left(k_s^2 + q^2\right)} + \frac{e^2 \omega_q^2}{\varepsilon\left(k_s^2 + q^2\right)\left(\omega^2 - \omega_q^2\right)} \tag{18}$$

Note that the first term in (18) is just the electron-screened Coulomb scattering amplitude. The second term arises as a result of the ion screening and is the important one for superconductivity. Figure 2.05 shows $V_{kk'}$ as a function of frequency ω; we see that for $\omega < \omega_q$, the scattering amplitude is negative. In this frequency range, the ion-mediated interaction is negative and stronger than the screened repulsive Coulomb interaction. Recall that $\omega = (\mathcal{E}_{k+q} - \mathcal{E}_k)/\hbar$. The interpretation is that if the difference of energies of the final and initial states is small enough, ω is less than the natural frequency of the phonon of wave number q (i.e., the phonon absorbed in the electron transition from $\vec{k}$ to $\vec{k} + \vec{q}$); then $V_{kk'}$ is negative and, as we saw in Section 2.03, this transition makes a contribution to the reduction of the potential energy of the system. The entire process is represented by the electron–phonon–electron scattering shown in Fig. 2.02b.

The model used above is only approximate but contains the essential features of the attractive interaction. A more accurate expression for $V_{kk'}$

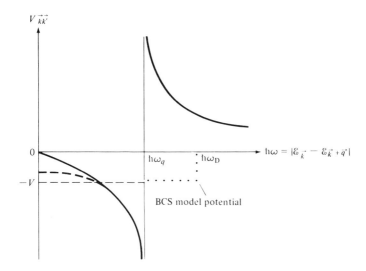

Figure 2.05. The interaction potential as a function of the difference of energies between final and initial states of an electron scattered by a phonon emitted by another electron making a similar transition. Solid lines show the results of the fluid model [Eq. 2.05(18)] and the broken line shows a more accurate calculation. The dotted line is the simplified potential assumed in the BCS analysis (see Section 2.08).

can be found in various references[10] and the form is shown by the broken line in Fig. 2.05. Clearly, the larger the ω_q, the greater the number of transitions for which $V_{\vec{k}\vec{k}'}$ is negative. The Cooper model in Section 2.02 and the BCS model to be discussed in the next section take $V_{\vec{k}\vec{k}'}$ to be negative up to the Debye frequency ω_D, as shown by the dotted line in Fig. 2.05. *They further simplify $V_{\vec{k}\vec{k}'}$ by assuming it to be a negative constant – V over a range where both $|\mathcal{E}_{\vec{k}} - \mathcal{E}_F|$ and $|\mathcal{E}_{\vec{k}'} - \mathcal{E}_F|$ are less than $\hbar\omega_D$, and zero otherwise.* We shall see in Section 2.07 that the actual range over which scattering takes place is on the order of $k_B T_c$, where T_c is the temperature of transition to the superconducting state. Thus $|\mathcal{E}_{\vec{k}} - \mathcal{E}_F|$ is no more that about 0.5 meV. Comparing this with typical values of $\hbar\omega_D$ of about 30 meV, we see that the exact choice of energy region for use of $V_{\vec{k}\vec{k}'} = -V$ is not too important.

Problems

2.05a. Show that $\partial J_i/\partial t \cong dJ/dt$ when the ion velocity is small compared with the phase velocity, as stated below (12).

---

[10] See Ziman (footnote 8), Section 11.1.

2.05b. Use (17) to estimate the long-wavelength value for the phase velocity of longitudinal lattice vibrations in bulk tin and compare with the handbook value of 3320 m/s.

2.06. Hamiltonian for the Superconducting Ground State

In this section and the next we shall introduce the theory of the superconducting ground state, which is a part of the microscopic theory of superconductivity published by Bardeen, Cooper, and Schrieffer in 1957.[11] The method of finding the ground state involves

   a. devising a Hamiltonian operator, which we do in this section,
   b. using an assumed ground-state wave function to find an expression for the energy, and finally
   c. minimizing the energy to find the coefficients in the ground-state wave function.

The latter two parts are done in the following section.

The BCS theory is presented in the formalism of second quantization involving creation and annihilation operators. The reader who is unfamiliar with operator algebra can appreciate the BCS theory by interpreting the equations pictorially—they lend themselves well to that. Those desiring a systematic introduction to operator algebra should consult a quantum mechanics text.[12]

The equations are written in terms of the creation and annihilation operators introduced in Section 1.05 for single electrons and an extension of that concept to electron pairs. The creation operator $c_{\vec{k}\uparrow}^{*}$ places an electron in state $\vec{k}$ with spin up, so if it operates on the "vacuum" state, in which all $\vec{k}$ states are empty, it produces a new state with one spin-up electron in state $\vec{k}$:

$$c_{\vec{k}\uparrow}^{*}|0\rangle = |1_{\vec{k}\uparrow}\rangle$$

Likewise, the annihilation operator $c_{\vec{k}\uparrow}$ causes the elimination of an electron:

$$c_{\vec{k}\uparrow}|1_{\vec{k}\uparrow}\rangle = |0\rangle$$

These operators are used to formulate the energy Hamiltonian. It is only necessary to consider the differences from the normal ground state, which are referred to as *reduced* energies.

Each electron–phonon–electron interaction of the type shown in Fig. 2.02b and discussed in the previous section contributes to the potential energy of the superconducting state relative to the ground state. As in the Cooper model, we restrict consideration to paired states $\vec{k}\uparrow, -\vec{k}\downarrow$. The pair

---

[11] See footnote 1.
[12] For example, Schiff (footnote 4).

transition can be represented by the product of creation and annihilation operators,

$$c_{\vec{k}+\vec{q}\uparrow}^{*} c_{-\vec{k}-\vec{q}\downarrow}^{*} c_{-\vec{k}\downarrow} c_{\vec{k}\uparrow}$$

If this operator operates on the ground state, it first removes the electrons from $\vec{k}$ and $-\vec{k}$ states and then places them in $\vec{k}+\vec{q}$ and $-\vec{k}-\vec{q}$ with their spin unaffected. Taking the sum of all such scattering events, one obtains the potential energy relative to the normal state, the reduced potential energy:

$$V_{\text{red}} = \sum_{k,\vec{q}} V_{kk'} c_{\vec{k}+\vec{q}\uparrow}^{*} c_{-\vec{k}-\vec{q}\downarrow}^{*} c_{-\vec{k}\downarrow} c_{\vec{k}\uparrow} \tag{1}$$

where $\vec{k}' = \vec{k} + \vec{q}$. It can be shown[13] that this gives an energy lowering for the superconducting state which increases with the number of scattering events, thus adding justification for using $\vec{k}$, $-\vec{k}$ pairs.

Since the theory involves only pairs of a certain kind (i.e., $\vec{k}\uparrow$ and $-\vec{k}\downarrow$), single-electron operators are replaced by pair operators

$$b_{\vec{k}}^{*} = c_{\vec{k}\uparrow}^{*} c_{-\vec{k}\downarrow}^{*} \quad \text{and} \quad b_{\vec{k}} = c_{-\vec{k}\downarrow} c_{\vec{k}\uparrow} \tag{2}$$

Since these pairs have the individual spins canceled, it might be expected that they would behave like bosons. However, this is not the case because the Pauli principle applies: no $\vec{k}\uparrow$, $-\vec{k}\downarrow$ state may be occupied by more than one pair at a time. It does turn out that the pair behavior is close enough to that of a boson so that boson electrodynamics gives a very good representation of the actual behavior of superconductors. This is discussed in more detail in Chapter 3.

Using (2), the reduced potential energy (1) may be rewritten as

$$V_{\text{red}} = \sum_{k,k'} V_{kk'} b_{\vec{k}'}^{*} b_{\vec{k}} \tag{3}$$

The kinetic energy can be written as the sum of the pair energies in each of the occupied pair states. The corresponding Hamiltonian thus must contain the number operator $\hat{n}_k$ which has the property

$$\hat{n}_{\vec{k}} |n_{\vec{k}}\rangle = n |n_{\vec{k}}\rangle$$

That is, the eigenstate of $\hat{n}_{\vec{k}}$ is the state having the wave number $\vec{k}$ and occupancy n, and the eigenvalue is the occupancy. The number operator in the case of pairs in $b_{\vec{k}}^{*} b_{\vec{k}}$. Then the pair kinetic energy relative to the Fermi energy is

$$H_{\text{KE}} = \sum_{k} 2\epsilon_{\vec{k}} b_{\vec{k}}^{*} b_{\vec{k}} \tag{4}$$

where $\epsilon_{\vec{k}} = (\hbar^2 k^2 / 2m) - \mathscr{E}_{\text{F}}$, the kinetic energy of a Bloch state measured

---

[13] M. Tinkham, *Superconductivity*. New York: Gordon and Breach, 1965, p. 31.

relative to the Fermi level. To get this in the reduced form, i.e., the kinetic energy relative to the normal ground state, we subtract

$$2 \sum_{k < k_F} \epsilon_{\vec{k}}$$

from (4). This can be done by using the pair commutation relations (see Prob. 2.06). Performing this operation on (4) and adding to (3), we get the total reduced Hamiltonian:

$$H_{\text{red}} = 2 \sum_{k < k_F} |\epsilon_{\vec{k}}| b_{\vec{k}} b_{\vec{k}}^* + 2 \sum_{k > k_F} \epsilon_{\vec{k}} b_{\vec{k}}^* b_{\vec{k}} + \sum_{kk'} V_{\vec{k}\vec{k}'} b_{\vec{k}'}^* b_{\vec{k}} \qquad (5)$$

The factors of 2 appear in these expressions because we count pairs and there are two possible spins for each $\vec{k}$. The summation puts a spin-up electron in each $\vec{k}$ state and a spin-down electron in the corresponding $-\vec{k}$ state with the result that each state for $k < k_F$ contains both spin-up electron and spin-down electrons.

Problem

●**2.06.** Show that the conversion of (4) into the first two terms of (5) follows from the pair commutation relations:

$$[b_{\vec{k}}, b_{\vec{k}'}^*] = (1 - \hat{n}_{\vec{k}\uparrow} - \hat{n}_{-\vec{k}\downarrow})\delta_{\vec{k}\vec{k}'}$$
$$\{b_{\vec{k}}, b_{\vec{k}'}\} = 2b_{\vec{k}} b_{\vec{k}'}(1 - \delta_{\vec{k}\vec{k}'})$$

2.07. Superconducting Ground State

In this section we use the reduced Hamiltonian Eq. 2.06(5), to find the distribution of pair occupancy in the superconducting ground state. According to the BCS theory,[14] the ground state should be written as the product of the occupation operators for all pair states:

$$|\Psi\rangle = \prod_{k} [u_{\vec{k}} + v_{\vec{k}} b_{\vec{k}}^*] |0\rangle \qquad (1)$$

Here $|0\rangle$ is the vacuum state, $v_{\vec{k}}^2$ is the probability of pair occupancy, and $u_{\vec{k}}^2 = 1 - v_{\vec{k}}^2$ is the probability of pair vacancy. The first term is included since it is needed for normalization of $|\Psi\rangle$ (see Prob. 2.07a). The formation of the BCS ground state (1) is illustrated in Fig. 2.07a.

The energy of the superconducting ground state relative to the normal ground state is the expectation value of the reduced Hamiltonian:

$$W = \langle \Psi | H_{\text{red}} | \Psi \rangle \qquad (2)$$

---

[14]See footnote 1.

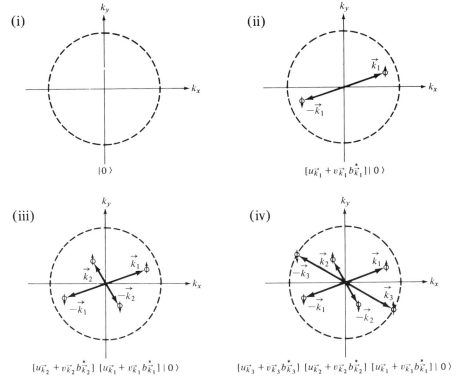

Figure 2.07a. Formation of the BCS ground state by successive addition of pairs. Not illustrated are the weighting $v_{\vec{k}}$ of the pairs. The oppositely directed spins are shown. (i) shows the vacuum state and (ii)–(iv) show successive additions of pairs.

Substituting (1) and Eq. 2.06(5) into (2), one obtains

$$W = 2 \sum_{k > k_{\mathrm{F}}} \epsilon_{\vec{k}} v_{\vec{k}}^2 + 2 \sum_{k < k_{\mathrm{F}}} |\epsilon_{\vec{k}}| u_{\vec{k}}^2 + \sum_{kk'} V_{\vec{k}\vec{k}'} u_{\vec{k}} v_{\vec{k}} u_{\vec{k}'} v_{\vec{k}'} \tag{3}$$

To find the equilibrium state this can be minimized with respect to $v_{\vec{k}}^2$ by setting $[\partial W / \partial(v_{\vec{k}}^2)] = 0$. The resulting probability of occupancy is

$$v_{\vec{k}}^2 = \tfrac{1}{2}\left[1 - \epsilon_{\vec{k}} / \left(\Delta_{\vec{k}}^2 + \epsilon_{\vec{k}}^2\right)^{1/2}\right] \tag{4}$$

The parameter $\Delta_{\vec{k}}$ will be seen in Section 2.08 to have special significance. It is called the *gap parameter* and is defined by

$$\Delta_{\vec{k}} \overset{\Delta}{=} -\sum_{k'} V_{\vec{k}\vec{k}'} v_{\vec{k}'} u_{\vec{k}'} \tag{5}$$

We can put (4) in a simpler form by defining another quantity

$$E_{\vec{k}} \overset{\Delta}{=} \left(\Delta_{\vec{k}}^2 + \epsilon_{\vec{k}}^2\right)^{1/2} \tag{6}$$

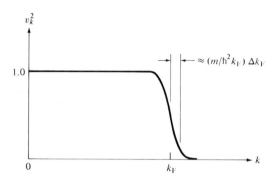

Figure 2.07b. Probability of pair occupancy in the superconducting ground state.

Using (6) the probability of occupancy (4) becomes

$$v_k^2 = \tfrac{1}{2}\left[1 - \epsilon_k / E_k\right] \tag{7}$$

which is shown in Fig. 2.07b. The probability of pair occupancy does not vanish above $\mathcal{E}_F$. We saw in the Cooper model that the normal ground state is unstable to pair formation when there is an attractive electron–electron interaction. Pairs move to $\vec{k}$ states of higher kinetic energy [first term in (3)] in order to maximize scattering possibilities since that reduces the potential energy [third term in (3)] by more than the increase of kinetic energy. The equilibrium distribution is reached when a further increase of kinetic energy is not offset by the decrease of potential energy. The distribution is reminiscent of the normal state with $T \neq 0$; but for the superconducting state, it obtains at $T = 0$. The region of $\epsilon_{\vec{k}}$ over which v_k^2 is significantly different from both unity and zero is of the order of a few $\Delta_{\vec{k}_F}$ (typically, a few millielectron volts).

Long-range Coherence

The electron occupation of the paired $\vec{k}$ states can be considered to be that of the Cooper pair [Eq. 2.03(5)]. Within a spatial region having a diameter on the order of 1 μm, there is phase coherence much like that in a de Broglie wave packet for a single electron. This distance is called the *coherence length* and is denoted by the symbol ξ. The center-of-mass coordinates of about a million interacting pairs lie within a sphere of diameter ξ. It is energetically favorable for overlapping pairs to lock phases. The whole superconducting fluid can be viewed as consisting of a large number of overlapping pairs. As was discussed in connection with Fig. 2.03c, the individual pairs are comprised of a large number of $\vec{k}$ states centered in magnitude about k_F. The resulting wave packet has a wavelength of about one-thousandth of the pair diameter. The waves oscillate at

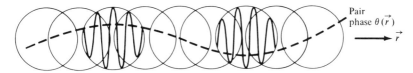

Figure 2.07c. The superconducting ground state is composed of a very large number of overlapping Cooper pairs. The phases are locked together since that minimizes the energy. If there is net momentum, there is a gradient of phase, as illustrated.

a frequency $f = 2\mathcal{E}_F/h$. In the absence of a net pair momentum, the phases of all pairs are locked together and they oscillate in unison.

If the pairs of k states have a nonzero net wave vector $\vec{K}$ [see Eq. 2.02(2)], the wave function representing the superconducting fluid is multiplied by $\exp(i\vec{K} \cdot \vec{r})$. We can represent the fluid by an ensemble-average function $\psi = |\psi(\vec{r})|$ when $K = 0$ and by

$$\psi = |\psi(\vec{r})|e^{i\vec{K} \cdot \vec{r}} \tag{8}$$

when $K \neq 0$. This is usually written in the more general form

$$\psi = |\psi(\vec{r})|e^{i\theta(\vec{r})} \tag{9}$$

where θ is the phase of the electron pairs. Figure 2.07c shows the situation where there is a phase variation, as in (9). The phases of just two pairs are shown to avoid confusion; the phases of these are seen to differ from one another by 180°. The phases of all the pairs evolve at the frequency $2\mathcal{E}_F/h$ while maintaining the $\theta(\vec{r})$ relative phase differences.

Problems

●2.07a. Since v_k^2 is the probability of pair occupancy and u_k^2 is the probability of vacancy, $v_k^2 + u_k^2 = 1$. Use this to show that the ground state (1) is normalized, i.e., $\langle \Psi | \Psi \rangle = 1$.

●2.07b. Show that minimization of the ground-state energy leads to the given expressions for pair occupation probability and gap parameter.

2.08. Gap Parameter and Condensation Energy at $T = 0$

Let us examine further the gap parameter Δ_k. Substitution of Eq. 2.07(7) into Eq. 2.07(5) gives

$$\Delta_k = -\sum_{k'} V_{kk'} \frac{\Delta_{k'}}{2E_{k'}} \tag{1}$$

At this point some simplifying assumptions are made to solve (1). As discussed at the end of Section 2.05, *one assumes that $V_{kk'} = -V$ if both $|\epsilon_k|$*

and $|\epsilon_{k'}|$ are less than $\hbar\omega_D$ and is zero otherwise. It is further assumed that $\Delta_{\vec{k}} = \Delta$, a constant, for $|\epsilon_{\vec{k}}| < \hbar\omega_D$ and is zero otherwise. Thus the quantity in Eq. 2.07(6) becomes

$$E = \left(\Delta^2 + \epsilon^2\right)^{1/2} \tag{1a}$$

with Δ taken as a constant and ϵ and E understood to be functions of $\vec{k}$. The summation over $\vec{k}'$ in (1) is replaced by an integral over the corresponding energy range. Further, we make use of the fact that the density of states is nearly constant close to $\mathscr{E}_F$, so $N(\epsilon) \cong N(0)$ over the range $|\epsilon_{\vec{k}}| < \hbar\omega_D$. With these simplifications, (1) becomes

$$\frac{2}{N(0)V} = \int_{-\hbar\omega_D}^{\hbar\omega_D} \frac{d\epsilon}{\left[\epsilon^2 + \Delta^2\right]^{1/2}} \tag{2}$$

Performing the integration and rearranging, one obtains

$$\Delta = \hbar\omega_D / \sinh\left[1/N(0)V\right] \tag{3}$$

If $N(0)V \ll 1$, the superconductor has *weak coupling* between electrons and phonons, as in most of the elemental materials, and (3) can be reduced to

$$\Delta = 2\hbar\omega_D e^{-1/N(0)V} \tag{4}$$

A typical value of Δ is about 1 meV.

Condensation Energy

We can calculate the difference of energies of the superconducting and normal states; this is the energy of *condensation* into the superconducting state. The difference of kinetic energies is [from Eq. 2.07(3)]

$$(\text{KE})_s - (\text{KE})_n = 2\sum_{\vec{k} < \vec{k}_F} |\epsilon_{\vec{k}}|\left(v_{\vec{k}}^2 - 1\right) + 2\sum_{\vec{k} > \vec{k}_F} \epsilon_{\vec{k}} v_{\vec{k}}^2 \tag{5}$$

Using (4) and Eqs. 2.07(6) and 2.07(7), (5) can be converted to

$$(\text{KE})_s - (\text{KE})_n = N(0)\Delta^2\left[(1/N(0)V) - \tfrac{1}{2}(1 - e^{-2/N(0)V})\right] \tag{6}$$

Similarly, the difference of potential energies from Eq. 2.07(3) is

$$V_s - V_n = -\Delta^2/V \tag{7}$$

since $V_n = 0$. The total difference of energies is the sum of (6) and (7). Noting that the change of potential energy is just canceled by the first term in (6), we have the following for the condensation energy:

$$W_s - W_n = -\tfrac{1}{2}N(0)\Delta^2\left[1 - e^{-2/N(0)V}\right]$$

$$\cong -\tfrac{1}{2}N(0)\Delta^2 \tag{8}$$

A useful physical understanding of (8) can be derived by taking the energy range of pairing interactions to be Δ and noting that the number of pairs there is about $N(0)\Delta$. Consider 2Δ to be the binding energy of each electron pair (as will be shown in the next section). Then the product of the number of pairs and the binding energy is approximately the condensation energy. Thus, it is clear that, although the BCS theory of the ground state has all electrons paired [Eq. 2.07(1)], only those in a narrow energy range of order Δ participate in the condensation. Those farther below the Fermi level are described mathematically as pairs with no loss of veracity but they are too far from the surface to be scattered by the electron–phonon interaction, and, hence, do not participate in the reduction of the system energy.

Problems

2.08a. Verify equations (2) and (3).

●**2.08b.** Verify equations (6) and (7).

2.08c. Find the value of current in a 2-mm-diam In wire at which the kinetic energy equals the condensation energy at $T = 2.1$ K. Assume the current flows only in a surface layer of 64-nm depth, assume three conduction electrons per atom, take the atomic density of In to be $3.83 \times 10^{28} \, \text{m}^{-3}$, and use the free-electron mass. Use inside back cover and Fig. 2.11.

2.09. Excitations from the Ground State

Electrons may be excited out of the ground state by thermal lattice vibrations or by incident photons. In this section we examine the peculiar properties of the excitations.

Let us recall first the nature of excitations from the ground state in a normal metal (Section 1.05). Figure 2.09a(i) shows the Fermi distribution at $T = 0$ with a hole excitation and an electron excitation, and Fig. 2.09a(ii) shows the corresponding excitation energies. At any nonzero temperature, the overall state of the electrons in a normal system is that of the $T = 0$ Fermi gas plus a set of excitations.

Now consider a superconductor. Since the excitations involve both positive and negative $\vec{k}$ states, it is convenient to show the occupation probability as in Fig. 2.09b(i). An excitation in state $\vec{k}$ is defined by:

$$\vec{k}\uparrow \qquad \text{surely occupied}$$
$$-\vec{k}\downarrow \qquad \text{surely empty}$$

which serves to increase the system momentum by $\vec{k}$. In Fig. 2.09b(i) we show four different excitations. At $\vec{k}_1$, the ground-state occupation proba-

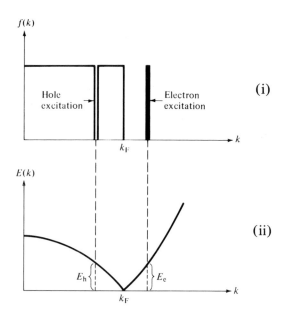

Figure 2.09a. Hole and electron excitations in a normal metal: (i) Fermi function; (ii) excitation energies.

bility is essentially unity, so placing an electron in $\vec{k}_1$ does not change its occupation; however, making $-\vec{k}_1$ surely empty creates a hole in a state that was full with nearly unity occupation probability. We say that the entire excitation is, therefore, strongly *hole-like* and is called a *quasihole*. For an excitation in states $\vec{k}_4\uparrow$ and $-\vec{k}_4\downarrow$, the opposite situation occurs. The vacancy in $-\vec{k}_4\downarrow$ makes almost no change there, whereas the occupation in $\vec{k}_4\uparrow$ fills an almost empty state. This excitation is strongly electron-like and is called a *quasielectron*. Near k_F the situation is more complex. Consider the excitation in $\vec{k}_2\uparrow$ and $-\vec{k}_2\downarrow$. The ground-state occupation probability is about 0.7, so when $\vec{k}_2\uparrow$ has sure occupancy in the excited state, its average occupation has increased by 0.3. Likewise, the vacancy at $-\vec{k}_2\downarrow$ causes a loss of 0.7 electron. The net result is that this excitation causes a loss of 0.4 electron. It is said to be *hole-like* (though not very strongly). The same line of reasoning leads to the $\vec{k}_3$ excitation adding 0.4 electron to the system and therefore being electron-like.

Of course, electrons do not come in fractions. We must keep in mind that the pair occupation probability v_k^2 is an ensemble average. What we mean by sure occupancy is that every member system of the ensemble has an electron in that state. If $v_{k_1}^2 = 0.7$, it means that 70% of the systems in the ensemble have an electron in state k_1. Sure occupancy for all systems thus requires the addition of 0.3 electron to each system, on the average.

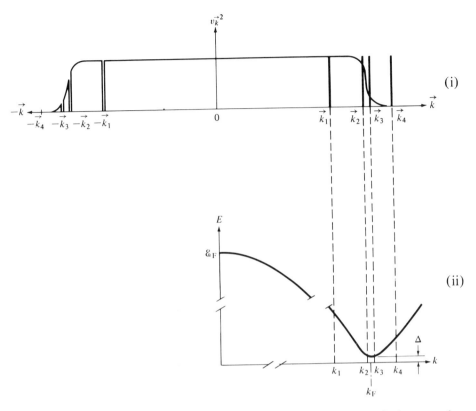

Figure 2.09b. Excitations from the superconducting ground state: (i) the ground state with four quasiparticle excitations; (ii) the excitation energy for each of these excitations.

The state of the system, with an excitation in state $\vec{k}_1$ and all other states occupied by pairs, is written as

$$|\Psi_{\vec{k}_1}\rangle = c^*_{\vec{k}_1\uparrow} \prod_{\vec{k}\neq\vec{k}_1} (u_{\vec{k}} + v_{\vec{k}}b^*_{\vec{k}})|0\rangle \tag{1}$$

The creation operator $c^*_{\vec{k}_1\uparrow}$ gives sure occupancy in state $\vec{k}_1\uparrow$. The operators in (1) do nothing to state $-\vec{k}_1\downarrow$, so it remains empty. The kinetic energy of state (1) relative to the ground state is reduced by the absence of the pairs occupying $\vec{k}_1\uparrow, -\vec{k}_1\downarrow$ with probability $v_{\vec{k}_1}^2$ and increased by the sure occupancy of $\vec{k}_1\uparrow$ by the excitation. Therefore,

$$\delta(\text{KE}) = \epsilon_{\vec{k}_1}\left(1 - 2v_{\vec{k}_1}^2\right) \tag{2}$$

The potential-energy term in Eq. 2.07(3) is modified by eliminating pair scattering from and into $(\vec{k}_1\uparrow, -\vec{k}_1\downarrow)$. This change can be expressed as

$$\delta(\text{PE}) = -2u_{\vec{k}_1}v_{\vec{k}_1}\sum_k V_{\vec{k}_1\vec{k}}u_{\vec{k}}v_{\vec{k}}$$

$$= 2u_{\vec{k}_1}v_{\vec{k}_1}\Delta_{\vec{k}_1} \cong 2u_{\vec{k}_1}v_{\vec{k}_1}\Delta \qquad (3)$$

The last line is obtained using Eq. 2.07(5) and the argument after Eq. 2.08(1). If we sum (2) and (3) and use the values of $E_{\vec{k}}$ and $v_{\vec{k}}^2$ from Eqs. 2.07(6) and 2.07(7) with $\Delta_{\vec{k}_1} = \Delta$, the total change of energy from the ground state to the excited state (1) is

$$\delta(\text{KE} + \text{PE}) = \epsilon_{\vec{k}_1}^2/E_{\vec{k}_1} + \Delta^2/E_{\vec{k}_1} = E_{\vec{k}_1} \qquad (4)$$

Thus we have identified $E_{\vec{k}_1}$ as the energy that must be added to the ground-state energy to produce an excitation in state $(\vec{k}_1\uparrow, -\vec{k}_1\downarrow)$. A plot of E_k as a function of k, as shown in Fig. 2.09b(ii), is the excitation-energy diagram corresponding to that for the normal metal, Fig. 2.09a(ii). Note that $E_k \cong |\epsilon_k|$ for k not close to k_F. When the excitation is strongly electron-like [as discussed above in connection with Fig. 2.09b(i)], the excitation energy is almost that of an electron in a normal metal, and similarly for holes. The most important feature is that the excitation energy has a minimum value Δ. Excitations cannot be created with an arbitrarily small energy as in the case of the normal metal. This explains the phenomenon that a superconductor absorbs little energy from an electromagnetic wave if its constituent photons have too little energy $\hbar\omega$. *To break a pair, one must create two excitations, and this requires at least 2Δ*. Thus, absorption of the electromagnetic energy by pair breaking takes place for frequencies $\omega \gtrsim 2\Delta/\hbar$.[15]

It might be pointed out that to conserve electrons, creation of excitations must be done in pairs in states symmetrically located relative to k_F. This is illustrated in Fig. 2.09c where a state of 0.3 average occupancy goes to

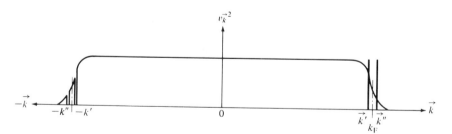

Figure 2.09c. A pair of excitations that conserves electrons. The increased average occupation in $\vec{k}''$ is 0.4 and decreased average occupation in $\vec{k}'$ is 0.4.

[15] A low level of absorption takes place at frequencies below $\omega \approx 2\Delta/\hbar$ if $T \neq 0$ by virtue of the presence of unpaired electrons which can absorb energy from the field and transfer it to the phonons.

unity for $\vec{k} = \vec{k}''$ and to zero for $\vec{k} = -\vec{k}''$, leading to a net increase of 0.4 electron. If, in addition, an excitation is caused in $\vec{k}'$, $-\vec{k}'$ which is symmetrically located about k_F with respect to $\vec{k}''$, $-\vec{k}''$, so $v_{k'}^2 = 1 - v_{k''}^2$, there is a net decrease of average occupancy of 0.4. Thus the combination leaves the total number of electrons unchanged.

It can be shown that if excitations occupy both states $\vec{k}_1\!\uparrow$ and $-\vec{k}_1\!\downarrow$ (which means sure occupancy of both), the energy required is $2E_{k_1}$, so this does not have to be considered as a special case.

Problem

2.09. Consider the excited state in Fig. 2.09b. Write the state expression corresponding to (1). From the values of $\vec{k}$ involved in the excitations, judge whether electrons have been conserved so this state could have come about by breaking two pairs in the ground state. A typical value of Δ is 1 meV; estimate the total energy required to create this excited state.

2.10. Occupation Statistics for Pairs and Excitations for $T \neq 0$

In this section we outline the method of calculating the equilibrium pair occupancy v_k^2 and the probability of occupation of excitation states f_k for $T \neq 0$. The actual calculation[16] requires concepts that are presented later in the text, so only a summary is given here. To find equilibrium conditions in physical problems, one finds a minimum energy situation. As we shall see in Chapter 6, the choice of energy to be minimized depends on the nature of the constraints on the system of interest. In the present analysis, it is assumed that the superconductor can exchange energy with a constant-temperature reservoir (e.g., a liquid-helium bath) with which it is in contact, and thereby seek its equilibrium state. In this situation, there is a minimization of the so-called Helmholtz free energy (see Section 6.04), which involves kinetic energy, potential energy, and entropy. To show the factors that come into play, let us examine the kinetic energy:

$$ \text{KE} = 2 \sum_k |\epsilon_k| f_k + 2 \sum_k |\epsilon_k| (1 - 2f_k) v_k^2 $$

The first term is the sum over all excitations and the second is the sum over all pair states. The outer factors of 2 represent the two allowed spin orientations in each $\vec{k}$ state. The quantity $(1-2f_k)$ measures the blocking of pair states by excitation occupancy of $\vec{k}\!\uparrow$, where the factor of 2 is present because occupancy of $\vec{k}\!\uparrow$ means both $\vec{k}\!\uparrow$ and $-\vec{k}\!\downarrow$ are unavailable for pair

---

[16] See Tinkham (footnote 13), p. 39.

occupancy. The important point to notice is that both the excitation occupancy factor $f_{\vec{k}}$ and that for pair occupancy $v_{\vec{k}}^2$ come into the expression. The same is true for potential energy, but the entropy involves only $f_{\vec{k}}$.

The probability of pair occupancy $v_{\vec{k}}^2$, the derivation of which was outlined in Section 2.07 for the ground state $(T = 0)$, is temperature dependent. The form of $v_{\vec{k}}^2$ with $T \neq 0$ is found by minimizing the Helmholtz free energy with respect to $v_{\vec{k}}^2$. The result has the same form as Eq. 2.07(7), with the same definition of the excitation energy $E_{\vec{k}}$ as given by Eq. 2.07(6). The difference lies in the expression for the gap parameter, which here becomes

$$\Delta_{\vec{k}} = -\sum_{\vec{k}'} V_{\vec{k}\vec{k}'} v_{\vec{k}'} u_{\vec{k}'} (1 - 2f_{\vec{k}'}) \tag{1}$$

Since the probability of excitation occupancy $f_{\vec{k}}$ increases with increasing temperature, the gap $\Delta_{\vec{k}}$ decreases; this idea will be developed further in Section 2.11. To obtain $v_{\vec{k}}^2$ as a function of $\epsilon_{\vec{k}}$ or $\vec{k}$, one must solve self-consistently Eqs. 2.07(6) and 2.07(7) with (1).

If the Helmholtz free energy is also minimized with respect to $f_{\vec{k}}$, we obtain

$$f_{\vec{k}} = \left[\exp(E_{\vec{k}}/k_{\mathrm{B}}T) + 1 \right]^{-1} \tag{2}$$

Thus it is seen that the Fermi function describes the excitation occupation probability. As the temperature is increased from zero, the gap parameter $\Delta_{\vec{k}}$ decreases (Fig. 2.10a), causing a decrease of the excitation energy $E_{\vec{k}}$ for each $\vec{k}$, and the probability of excitation occupancy (2) increases, as shown in Fig. 2.10b.

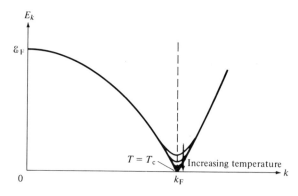

Figure 2.10a. Temperature variation of the gap in the excitation spectrum.

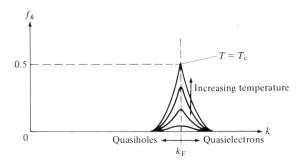

Figure 2.10b. Temperature variation of the occupation probability of excitations. The curve at $T = T_c$ is the normal-state Fermi function, and quasiholes and quasielectrons are just holes and electrons, in the sense used in Section 1.05.

2.11. Temperature Dependence of the Gap Parameter

In this section we continue analysis of the effect of temperature on the gap parameter $\Delta_{\vec{k}}$ and find a relation between the gap at $T = 0$ and the transition temperature.

Substituting Eq. 2.10(2) into Eq. 2.10(1), we obtain

$$\Delta_{\vec{k}} = - \sum_{\vec{k}} V_{\vec{k}\vec{k}'} \frac{\Delta_{\vec{k}'}}{2E_{\vec{k}'}} \left[1 - \frac{2}{\exp(E_{\vec{k}'}/k_B T) + 1} \right] \tag{1}$$

As was done in Section 2.08, where $\Delta_{\vec{k}}$ of the ground state was developed, we assume that $V_{\vec{k}\vec{k}'}$ is an average value $-V$ for all $\vec{k}$ and $\vec{k}'$ such that $|\epsilon_{\vec{k}}| < \hbar\omega_D$ and $|\epsilon_{\vec{k}'}| < \hbar\omega_D$, where ω_D is the Debye frequency, and is zero otherwise. It is also assumed that $\Delta_{\vec{k}} = \Delta$, a quantity independent of $\vec{k}$ for $|\epsilon_{\vec{k}}| < \hbar\omega_D$, and is zero otherwise. With these assumptions (1) becomes

$$\frac{1}{V} = \sum_{\vec{k}} \frac{1}{2E_{\vec{k}}} \tanh \frac{E_{\vec{k}}}{2k_B T} \tag{2}$$

with limits on the sum as defined above. Equation (2) can be expressed in integral form assuming a constant density of states $N(0)$ for the contributing states in (2):

$$\frac{1}{N(0)V} = \int_{-\hbar\omega_D}^{\hbar\omega_D} \frac{\tanh\left\{ \left[\epsilon^2 + \Delta^2(T) \right]^{1/2} / 2k_B T \right\}}{2\left[\epsilon^2 + \Delta^2(T) \right]^{1/2}} \, d\epsilon \tag{3}$$

Equation (3) is an implicit relation for the temperature-dependent gap parameter $\Delta(T)$. The temperature dependence of $\Delta(T)$ is shown in Fig. 2.11, where it is normalized to $\Delta(0)$, the value for the ground state given by Eq. 2.08(4). Experimental values agree well with the theoretical depen-

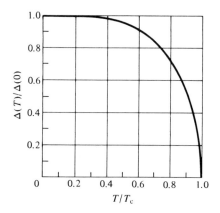

Figure 2.11. Temperature dependence of the superconductor energy gap.

dence. As the temperature approaches T_c, the gap vanishes and the metal reverts to the normal state; the effect on the excitation spectrum was shown in Fig. 2.10a. It is of interest to note that there is very little variation of $\Delta(T)$ up to $T_c/2$. In the neighborhood of T_c the gap function follows the approximate relation:

$$\Delta(T) \cong 3.2k_B T_c (1 - T/T_c)^{1/2} \tag{4}$$

Since the gap vanishes at the critical temperature, we may substitute $\Delta = 0$ and $T = T_c$ in (3) and obtain

$$\frac{1}{N(0)V} = \int_0^{\hbar\omega_D} \frac{\tanh(\epsilon/2k_B T_c)}{\epsilon} \, d\epsilon \tag{5}$$

Where $k_B T_c \ll \hbar\omega_D$, which corresponds to weak electron–phonon–electron coupling defined by $N(0)V \ll 1$, (5) reduces to

$$k_B T_c = 1.13\hbar\omega_D e^{-1/N(0)V} \tag{6}$$

By comparing (6) with

$$2\Delta(0) = 4\hbar\omega_D e^{-1/N(0)V} \tag{7}$$

which is derived from Eq. 2.08(4), we see that

$$\boxed{2\Delta(0) = 3.52k_B T_c} \tag{8}$$

The actual values of the constant (3.52) in (8) found from tunneling and electromagnetic-absorption experiments depend on the material and vary from experiment to experiment but generally lie within about 30% of 3.52.[17]

---

[17]Values of this coefficient for some important superconductors are found on the inside of the back cover.

Problem

●**2.11.** Integrate (5) by parts to obtain (6) for superconductors with $\hbar\omega_D/k_B T_c \gg 1$. In strong-coupling superconductors, the constant in (8) is appreciably larger than 3.52 (e.g., 4.3 for Pb). Make a simple correction in the analysis used to verify (6) for $\hbar\omega_D/k_B T_c = 12$ as in Pb to show that, even for a relatively strong-coupling superconductor, (6) is still accurate. Verify that Eq. 2.08(4) is also a good approximation even for Pb and thus that the explanation for the differences of the constant in (8) found experimentally cannot be found in the BCS theory.

2.12. Density of Excitation States

In order to know the actual occupation of the excitation states one must know not only the occupation probabilities given in Section 2.10 but also the density of excitation states. Furthermore, knowledge of the density of excitation states is essential in the theory of tunneling, as we shall see in later sections. For a normal metal, each of the Bloch states above the Fermi energy can be occupied by an electron and those below can be occupied by a hole. Thus the excitations can occupy the Bloch states and the density of excitation states is identical with the density of Bloch states. That the density of excitation states for a superconductor is remarkably different from that of the Bloch states is evident from the fact that there are no excitation states for energies lying within the half gap Δ about the Fermi energy.

It is clear from Fig. 2.09b(ii) that for every value of k there corresponds an excitation energy E. Likewise, there is a Bloch state energy for every k. Then the states in a differential range dk will fall in a corresponding range of excitation energies dE and also in a corresponding range of Bloch state energies $d\mathcal{E}$.[18] Thus, the number of states in dE equals that in $d\mathcal{E}$. We use this fact to define the density of excitation states according to

$$N(E)dE = N_n(\mathcal{E})d\mathcal{E} \qquad \text{or} \qquad N(E) = N_n(\mathcal{E})d\mathcal{E}/dE \qquad (1)$$

For the *normal metal*, the excitation energy E equals the absolute value of the difference between the Bloch state energy and the Fermi energy, $E = |\mathcal{E} - \mathcal{E}_F|$, as discussed in Section 1.05. It is clear that $d\mathcal{E}/dE = 1$ in that case, so $N_n(E) = N_n(\mathcal{E})$, as mentioned above. As an aid in understanding the reason for the remarkable density-of-states function that exists for a superconductor, consider the graphical construction shown in Fig. 2.12a. For a given range $\Delta\mathcal{E}$ of Bloch state energies, there is a corresponding number of states as shown by the cross-hatched region in the $\mathcal{E}$-vs-$N_n(\mathcal{E})$

---

[18] Following the usual convention, we designate the density of Bloch states by a subscript n ("normal metal"), though it is really only a property of the lattice.

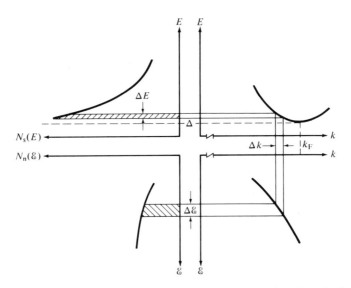

Figure 2.12a. Diagram showing by construction why the density of excitation states $N_s(E)$ has a singularity at $E = \Delta$. The two cross-hatched zones have the same area —for each Bloch state, there is an excitation state.

graph. Projecting the chosen range of Bloch state energies onto the $\mathscr{E}-k$ relation for Bloch states, the range of k is determined. Because of the shape of the relation of the excitation energy to k, the corresponding range of excitation energies ΔE in the $E - k$ diagram is smaller than the range of Bloch state energies. In order to have the same number of states as in the $\mathscr{E}$-vs-$N_n(\mathscr{E})$ diagram, it is necessary to have a larger density of states as a function of excitation energy. It is clear that for k values approaching k_F, the range of excitation energies approaches zero for a given range of Bloch state energies, so $N_s(E)$ must approach infinity.

To get an analytic expression for $N_s(E)$ we use Eq. 2.08(1a), in evaluating $d\mathscr{E}/dE$. Note that $\epsilon = \mathscr{E} - \mathscr{E}_F$, so $d\mathscr{E}/dE = d\epsilon/dE$. Making these substitutions in (1), we obtain the excitation density of states in the superconductor

$$N_s(E) = \frac{N_n(\mathscr{E})E}{\left(E^2 - \Delta^2\right)^{1/2}} \tag{2}$$

The excitation-state densities for quasiholes and quasielectrons are shown in relation to the excitation-energy diagram in Fig. 2.12b. As usual, it is necessary to distort the scales in order to reveal the important features. In particular, Δ is shown many times greater than its actual magnitude.

It is customary to approximate the result in (2) using the fact that $N_n(\mathscr{E})$ is essentially constant and equal to $N_n(0)$ over the energy range of interest, which is generally up to tens of millielectron volts (compare with the Fermi

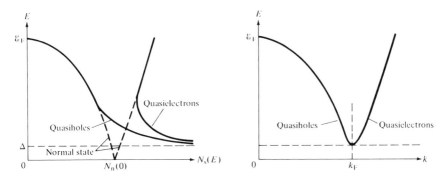

Figure 2.12b. Excitation energy and density-of-states diagrams for a superconductor. The left diagram shows the density of states on the abscissa for a given excitation energy and the right diagram shows the k values for the corresponding energies. The magnitude of Δ is greatly exaggerated in order to include the whole range of quasihole excitation energies.

energy of several volts). Then (2) becomes

$$N_s(E) = \frac{N_n(0)E}{(E^2 - \Delta^2)^{1/2}} \tag{3}$$

and this is shown in Fig. 2.12c. Note that the densities of quasiholes and quasielectrons are identical in this approximation. In either of the figures, we see that there are no excitation states in the range $0 \leqslant E < \Delta$; all the states in that range have been pushed beyond $E = \Delta$ within a range of a few times Δ. Beyond that the densities are essentially the same for a normal metal.

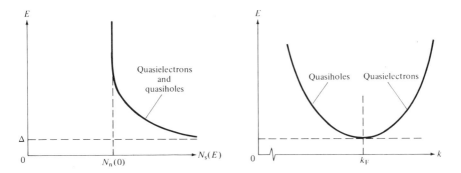

Figure 2.12c. These figures are similar to those of Fig. 2.12b except that an expanded scale is used for the region around k_F and the density of Bloch states is assumed to be constant over the very small range of excitation energies considered.

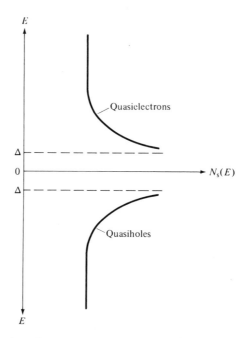

Figure 2.12d. Density of states vs excitation energy in the "semiconductor-like" representation using the approximation in Eq. 2.12(3). In this diagram, excitation energy is measured positive in both directions.

The density-of-states diagram is often drawn as in Fig. 2.12d. It is to be kept in mind that excitation energy is measured positive outward in both directions from the center. The lower half gives the density for quasiholes and the upper, the density for quasielectrons. This kind of diagram is used extensively in tunneling calculations.

Problem

2.12.   Sketch for a normal metal the diagrams corresponding to Figs. 2.12b–d.

2.13.   Tunneling Barriers

In this and the following several sections, we discuss tunneling both as an illustration of the use of excitation diagrams and to provide understanding of single-particle tunneling $I-V$ characteristics.

The term *tunneling* is applicable when an electron passes through a region in which the potential is such that a classical particle with the same kinetic energy could not pass. In quantum mechanics, one finds that an electron incident on such a barrier has a certain probability of passing

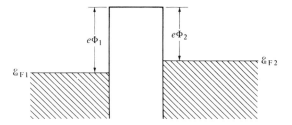

Figure 2.13a. Fermi levels in two isolated metals with different work functions.

through, depending on the height, width, and shape of the barrier. In this section we examine the origin of the tunneling barriers between metals.

The energy required to remove a Fermi level electron from a metal is the work function $e\Phi$, and the electrons removed from two different isolated metals can be considered to be at the same energy, as shown in Fig. 2.13a. As the metals are brought together or connected through a circuit, electrons are transferred from one to the other, thus creating a potential difference $\Phi_1 - \Phi_2$ sufficient to eliminate the energy difference between the two Fermi levels. The result is a barrier as shown by the solid line in Fig. 2.13b. The barrier is modified by image forces acting on an electron located between the metals. The effect of the image forces is to lower the barrier as shown by the broken line in Fig. 2.13b.[19]

Barriers are normally made of an insulating material since it is physically almost impossible to achieve the very small spacings required (≈ 5 nm or less) with a vacuum barrier. The energy required to remove an electron from an insulator is $e\chi$, the *electron affinity* for that material. Transfer of an electron from the metal into the insulator requires less energy than its removal to free space. The barrier is correspondingly reduced by $e\chi$.

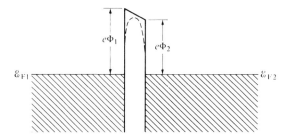

Figure 2.13b. Closely spaced metals where transfer of electrons between them leads to an equalization of the Fermi levels. The broken line shows the reduction of the barrier by image forces.

[19] J. G. Simmons, "Electric tunnel effect between dissimilar electrodes separated by a thin insulating film," *J. Appl. Phys.*, Vol. 34, pp. 2581–2590, September 1963.

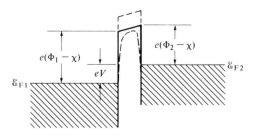

Figure 2.13c. Energy levels in a metal–insulator–metal junction with a bias V applied to the left side. The barrier height is reduced by the electron affinity of the insulator. The curved broken line shows the reduction of the barrier by image forces.

If a voltage V is applied between the metals, there is a displacement of the Fermi levels by an amount eV with the positive side lowered. This is shown for an insulating barrier in Fig. 2.13c. The modification of the barrier by image forces is shown by a broken line. To illustrate a practical situation, let us consider a niobium–insulator–lead sandwich. Typically one would begin by depositing a strip of niobium on an insultating substrate as shown in Fig. 2.13d. This would be oxidized to form an insulating layer of perhaps 3-nm thickness. Subsequently, a cross strip of lead would be deposited as shown to complete the junction.

The barriers described here for normal metals apply equally well to superconductors.

The barrier can be thought of as a center of elastic scattering which causes a transition from a state k_1 in region 1 into state k_2 in region 2. The energies of the initial and final states are identical since the scattering is elastic. The rate at which electrons are scattered from k_1 into k_2 is given by "Fermi's golden rule number 2" of time-dependent perturbation theory.[20] The rate, or probability per unit time, of transition from state 1 to state 2 is given by that rule as

$$w(t)_{1\to2} = (2\pi/\hbar)|\langle 2|H^{(1)}|1\rangle|^2 N_2(\mathscr{E})$$

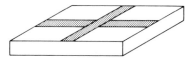

Figure 2.13d. A simple crossed-strip junction. One metal strip is deposited and then oxidized to make an insulating barrier. The second strip is then deposited. Junctions for applications would take other forms, depending on the purpose.

---

[20] See Schiff (footnote 4).

where $H^{(1)}$ is the perturbation Hamiltonian causing the scattering and $N_2(\mathcal{E})$ is the density of states at the energy of state 2. To adapt this to the tunneling problem, we denote the expectation value of the perturbation Hamiltonian by the tunneling matrix element T_{12} and use the fact that current is the rate of transfer times the electronic charge. Thus,

$$J_2 = -(2\pi e/\hbar)|T_{12}|^2 N_2(\mathcal{E}) \tag{1}$$

An example of tunneling is given in Appendix A, where the tunneling current and tunneling matrix element are evaluated for a rectangular barrier.

2.14. Tunneling Between Normal Metals

In this section we analyze tunneling through a barrier between two normal-metal bodies as a simple context in which to see the principles. Two kinds of tunneling diagram will be introduced. The first is used to show the physics of the process and the second is an aid to setting up the calculation of the tunneling current.

The tunneling process can be discussed in terms of excitations in the two metal regions. The use of this concept is not necessary in the case of normal metals, but it is easier to introduce it here than in the case of tunneling involving a superconductor, where it is very important. Figure 2.14a shows an excitation-energy diagram for each of the metals. The presence of a bias is represented by the displacement of the zero-excitation levels. As illustrated, the metal on the right side is positively biased with respect to that on the left and, as a result, there is a net transfer of electrons from left to right. We show the transfer of one electron; this is represented by the excitation of a hole in the k state from which the electron is removed on the left side and an excitation of an electron in the k state on the right side into which

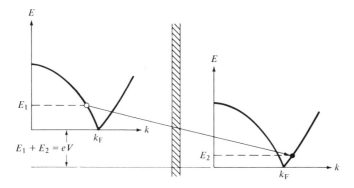

Figure 2.14a. Excitation tunneling diagram with bias shown applied to the right side of the junction.

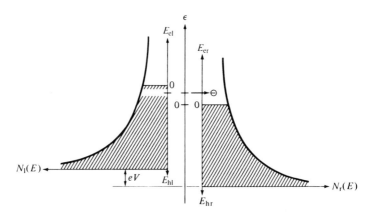

Figure 2.14b. "Semiconductor-type" of diagram for tunneling calculations between two normal metals ($T = 0$). The density of states shown is the one-dimensional form since a one-dimensional subset is involved in tunneling.

the electron is injected. The sum of the excitation energies $E_1 + E_2$ for the hole and the electron must equal the energy eV provided by the applied bias (neglecting possible phonon excitations). A tunneling current consists of a succession of many such pairs of excitations as the electrons cross the barrier. Of course, the holes created on the left side are continually refilled by electrons flowing through the circuit by which the bias is applied.[21]

To calculate the tunneling current between two normal metals, it is more useful to use the diagram shown in Fig. 2.14b. The density of states is shown for each metal on the two sides of the barrier. As discussed in the previous section, the states involved in the tunneling process are those with velocities normal to the barrier. This means that we can tunnel from and into only that subset of states; the appropriate density of states is therefore the one-dimensional form shown.[22] We have plotted the density of states as a function of the excitation energy, which is measured positively in both directions from the zero point. In the normal-metal case, the excitation energy is just equal to the absolute magnitude of the Bloch state energy measured relative to the Fermi level $\epsilon = \mathcal{E} - \mathcal{E}_F$, as discussed in Section 1.05. Figure 2.14b would be a little easier to understand if the reduced Bloch state energy ϵ were used exclusively instead of the excitation energy, but part of the point here is to lay the groundwork for the more difficult problem of tunneling between superconductors, where excitation energy must be used. Note that the zeros of the excitation energies are displaced

[21] For an introduction to this kind of tunneling diagram, see J. M. Rowell, "Tunneling and superconductivity," in *Superconductivity*, Vol. 2. (P. R. Wallace, Ed.). New York: Gordon and Breach, 1969.

[22] See works by Ziman and by Kittel cited in footnote 8.

by the energy of the applied bias eV. The shading is used to show states available for hole excitation, that is, states from which electrons can be extracted. The diagram is drawn for $T = 0$, so all states in the hole-excitation range are shown filled. The direct horizontal transition conserves energy; this feature is the principal virtue of the diagram. The tunneling of one electron is shown by the dotted line. To calculate the tunneling current, we must count all possible events of this kind. Tunneling can take place only from left to right at $T = 0$ with the given bias polarity because no empty states on the left side are in line with filled states on the right side.

In the preceding section we discussed the use of the tunneling matrix element for calculating tunneling current from a given state on one side into energy-conserving states on the other side. To get the tunneling between states in a differential range of excitation energy on the left side and the corresponding states on the right side, we multiply Eq. 2.13(1) by the density of states on the left and the differential energy range. Then the total current is the integral over the range where tunneling can take place. It is most convenient to set up the integrals in terms of Bloch state energies on one side of the junction rather than excitation energy. As mentioned above, $E = |\epsilon|$ for the normal metal. In the $T = 0$ case shown in Fig. 2.14b, tunneling can take place for values of the right-side excitation energy from zero to eV. Thus the total current from right to left is positive (V is positive, right to left) and has the value

$$I_{nn}(T = 0) = \frac{2\pi eA}{\hbar} \int_0^{eV} |T_{lr}|^2 N_l(\epsilon - eV) N_r(\epsilon) \, d\epsilon \qquad (1)$$

where A is the junction area, l and r (left and right) subscripts are employed in place of the 1 and 2 subscripts used in the preceding sections, and ϵ is the reduced Bloch state energy corresponding to the excitation energy in Fig. 2.14b.

If $T \neq 0$ the problem is somewhat more complicated. In this case partially occupied states on one side face partially occupied states on the other side, as shown in Fig. 2.14c, so tunneling can take place in either direction.

The net tunneling current is the difference of the rightward and leftward currents. In setting up the integral, we must take into account that an electron cannot tunnel into a occupied state or out of an unoccupied state; this is done by multiplying the densities of states by the appropriate Fermi functions. We make use of the fact that letting E_e and E_h range from zero to ∞ is equivalent to taking $-\infty \leqslant \epsilon \leqslant \infty$. Of course, the proper range of integration is finite, but a simplification is achieved by taking the infinite range and negligible error is made because of the rapid decay of the Fermi function. The electron flow from left to right is

$$(F_e)_{lr} = \frac{2\pi A}{\hbar} \int_{-\infty}^{\infty} |T_{lr}|^2 N_l(\epsilon - eV) N_r(\epsilon) f(\epsilon - eV) \left[1 - f(\epsilon) \right] d\epsilon \qquad (2)$$

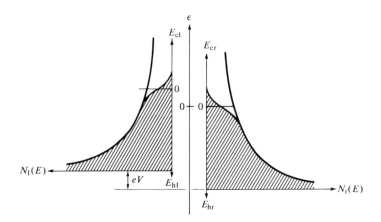

Figure 2.14c. Tunneling diagram for $T \neq 0$.

and that from right to left is

$$(F_e)_{rl} = \frac{2\pi A}{\hbar} \int_{-\infty}^{\infty} |T_{rl}|^2 N_l(\epsilon - eV)N_r(\epsilon)f(\epsilon)\left[1 - f(\epsilon - eV)\right]d\epsilon \quad (3)$$

where $f(\xi) = [1 + \exp(\xi/k_B T)]^{-1}$ and ϵ is the Bloch state energy on the right side. Combining (2) and (3) and making use of the symmetry of the tunneling matrix element so $|T_{lr}|^2 = |T_{rl}|^2 = |T|^2$, we obtain the following for the tunneling current (right to left):

$$I_{nn} = \frac{2\pi eA}{\hbar} \int_{-\infty}^{\infty} |T|^2 N_l(\epsilon - eV)N_r(\epsilon)\left[f(\epsilon - eV) - f(\epsilon)\right]d\epsilon \quad (4)$$

Over a small range of bias voltage, the tunneling matrix element and the densities of states can be considered as constants and removed from the integral. For low temperatures, the remaining integral can be shown to be approximately equal to eV, where V is the applied bias. Therefore

$$I_{nn} = G_n V \quad (5)$$

where

$$G_n = (2\pi e^2 A/\hbar)|T|^2 N_l(0)N_r(0) \quad (6)$$

Thus the I–V characteristic has the simple form shown in Fig. 2.14d and G_n is the normal–normal tunneling conductance of the junction.

Problems

2.14a. Show that (5) has the correct approximate form and evaluate the tunneling matrix element for the data given in Fig. 2.14d. Take the electron effective mass to equal the free-electron mass and assume a spherical Fermi sea. Assume a valence of 3 and atomic density of $6 \times 10^{28} \, \text{m}^{-3}$ for Al.

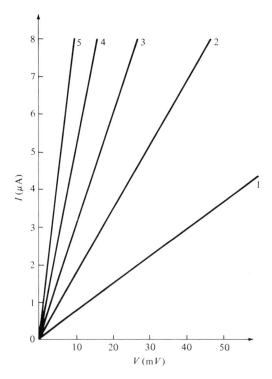

Figure 2.14d. Tunneling currents through five different $Al-Al_2O_3-Al$ junctions having area ratios as shown $(5:4:3:2:1)$ with the smallest having an area of 4.72×10^{-3} cm^2. Assuming a dielectric constant of 8, the oxide thicknesses were estimated from capacitance measurements to be 4.8, 4.5, 4.8, 4.7, and 4.8 nm, respectively.

After J. C. Fisher and I. Giaever, "Tunneling through thin insulating layers," *J. Appl. Phys.*, Vol. 32, p. 173, February 1961.

2.14b. Determine which factors in (4) lead to a deviation from the linear dependence on voltage given in (5). Estimate the voltage at which I_{nn} differs by 2% from the value given by (5). Assume $|T|^2 = $ constant.

2.15. Tunneling Between a Normal Metal and a Superconductor

In the previous section we introduced tunneling diagrams which relate excitation energy E to wave number k on both sides of a tunnel junction. These will be seen to be very helpful in understanding tunneling in situations involving superconductors. Figure 2.15a shows excitation-energy diagrams for normal-metal–insulator–superconductor (NIS) tunneling. An electron tunneling out of the normal metal from a state with excitation energy E_1 may tunnel into any unoccupied state whose excitation energy E_2 is such that energy is conserved; i.e., $E_1 + E_2 = eV$, where V is the bias

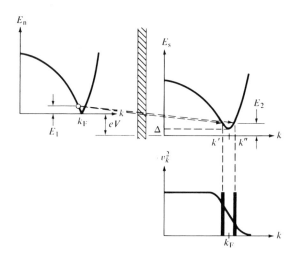

Figure 2.15a. Tunneling between a normal metal and a superconductor. An electron tunnels into either of the two states, conserving energy, with probabilities that depend on the pair occupancy. ($T = 0$, excitations neglected.)

voltage.[23] The probability that the state k' is empty is the probability that it is not occupied by pairs, $u_{k'}^2$. The state k'' has the same excitation energy and its probability of vacancy is $u_{k''}^2$. The states with the same excitation energies have occupation probabilities such that $u_{k''}^2 = v_{k'}^2$ (assuming $\Delta_k = \Delta$, a constant) so the probability of a vacant state is $u_{k'}^2 + v_{k'}^2 = 1$. It should be kept in mind that the occupation probabilities are calculated for an infinite ensemble of identical junctions. In any ensemble member junction, the electron is injected either into the k' or k'' states. Though the excitations in the superconductor are really in states both above and below k_F, we can calculate tunneling current by considering only states above k_F and taking the vacancy there to be unity, as shown in Fig. 2.15b.

As we saw in Section 2.14, one must know the one-dimensional density of states on both sides of the barrier in order to calculate the tunneling current. For the purpose of the NIS junction, we need the density of states in the superconductor. The modification of the normal-metal density of states described by Eq. 2.12(2) also applies to the one-dimensional case. Thus the appropriate density of states here is

$$N_s(E) = \begin{cases} N_n(\epsilon)E/(E^2 - \Delta^2)^{1/2} & |E| \geqslant \Delta \\ 0 & |E| < \Delta \end{cases} \tag{1}$$

---

[23] As in Section 2.14, we neglect possible excitation of phonons by the electron as it crosses the insulating barrier.

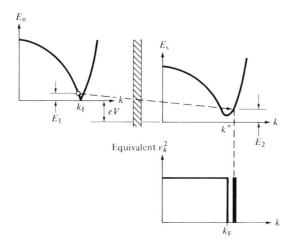

Figure 2.15b. Scheme for counting tunneling electrons equivalent to the correct representation in Fig. 2.15a.

which is shown in Fig. 2.15c. We shall make the very adequate assumption that the normal-metal density of states is essentially constant over the energy range of interest (typically less than 0.1 eV, compared with a Fermi energy of several electron volts). With this assumption for both sides of the junction, we can use the diagram in Fig. 2.15d to calculate the tunneling current for $T = 0$. The equivalent pair occupation shown in Fig. 2.15b is used. The shaded areas in the diagram indicate the states available for hole

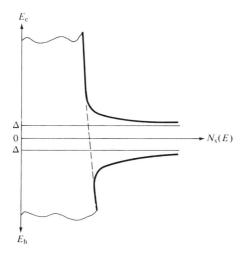

Figure 2.15c. One-dimensional density of states in a superconductor plotted as a function of excitation energy of electron-like and hole-like states.

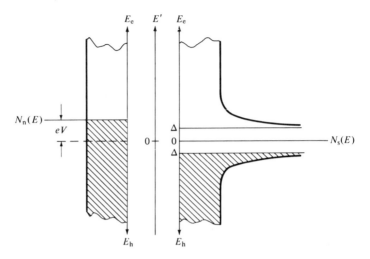

Figure 2.15d. Diagram for determining tunneling currents between a normal metal and a superconductor for $T = 0$. In this kind of diagram, all the states above the gap are assumed empty and those below, full, for $T = 0$.

occupancy and the unshaded regions are available for electron occupancy. Note that this diagram suggests that electrons tunnel into the superconductor only above k_F and holes only below k_F, whereas states both above and below k_F are involved for each kind of tunneling. This fact should be kept in mind to avoid inferring incorrect physics. For $T \neq 0$, the tunneling diagram is modified as shown in Fig. 2.15e. Now some of the states both

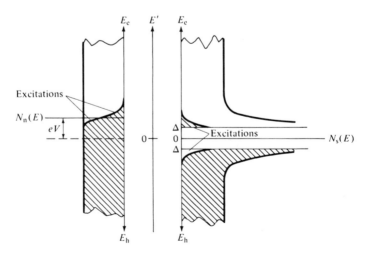

Figure 2.15e. Diagram for determining tunneling currents between a normal metal and a superconductor with $T \neq 0$. Unshaded areas are empty electron states and shaded areas are empty hole states.

above and below k_F are partially occupied by excitations distributed according to the Fermi function, as discussed in Section 2.09, so they are partially unavailable for tunneling.

Now let us see how to calculate the tunneling current. The integration necessary is simplified by introducing a dummy variable E', which is shown in the center of the diagram in Fig. 2.15d. For the superconductor, this variable is the same as E_e and the negative of E_h over their respective ranges. It has the role played by the Bloch state energy ϵ in the case of normal tunneling (see Figs. 2.14b and 2.14c). We cover the entire range of electron- and hole-excitation energies by taking E' over the range $-\infty \le E' \le \infty$.

Consider first the tunneling current at $T = 0$ for which we refer to Fig. 2.15d. The calculation parallels that of the previous case [Eq. 2.14(1)] with E' replacing the reduced Bloch state energy ϵ. Tunneling can only occur at those values of E' for which there is an occupied state on the left side and an unoccupied state on the right side. Here the range of E' in which tunneling can occur is $\Delta < E' \le eV$. Using the appropriate densities of state and noting that there are no states in the gap, we have

$$I_{sn}(T = 0) = \frac{2\pi e A}{\hbar} \int_{\Delta}^{eV} |T|^2 N_n(E' - eV) N_s(E') \, dE' \qquad (2)$$

Note that in this case ($T = 0$), current is only in one direction, and that the tunneling matrix element refers to transitions between Bloch states whether in the normal or superconducting states, so $|T|^2$ in (2) is the same as in Eqs. 2.14(1)–(4). With the usual assumption of nearly constant density of states and tunneling matrix element, (2) becomes

$$I_{sn}(T = 0) = \frac{G_n}{e} \int_{\Delta}^{eV} \frac{E' \, dE'}{(E'^2 - \Delta^2)^{1/2}}$$

$$= \begin{cases} (G_n/e)\left[(eV)^2 - \Delta^2\right]^{1/2} & \text{for} \quad eV \ge \Delta \\ 0 & \text{for} \quad eV < \Delta \end{cases} \qquad (3)$$

where G_n is the normal tunneling conductance given by Eq. 2.14(6). The result given by (3) is shown by the solid line in Fig. 2.15f.[24]

Now let us turn to the case where $T \ne 0$ for which we refer to Fig. 2.15e. We must now take into account the excitations which are distributed according to the Fermi function. By using the dummy variable E', which has both positive and negative values, the Fermi function gives directly the

[24] Measurement of this kind of tunneling was first reported in I. Giaever, "Energy gap in superconductors measured by electron tunneling," *Phys. Rev. Lett.*, Vol. 5, pp. 147–148, 15 August 1960.

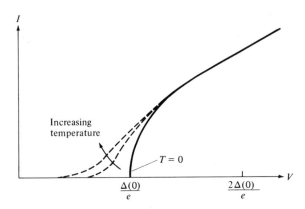

Figure 2.15f. Tunneling current between a normal metal and a superconductor for various temperatures. Note that as the temperature increases both the excitation occupancy and the gap change. Here, as elsewhere, $2\Delta(0)$ is the energy gap at $T = 0$.

probability of electron occupancy.[25] The tunneling integral becomes, by direct analogy with Eq. 2.14(4),

$$I_{sn} = \frac{G_n}{e} \int_{-\infty}^{\infty} \frac{E'}{(E'^2 - \Delta^2)^{1/2}} \left[f(E' - eV) - f(E') \right] dE' \qquad (4)$$

where the range of energy $|E'| < \Delta$ is excluded from the integration. Here, and in subsequent sections, it should be kept in mind that Δ is a function of temperature. The form of current variation given by (4) is shown for various temperatures in Fig. 2.15f.

It is of interest to note that at $T = 0$ the conductance is given by

$$\left(\frac{dI_{sn}}{dV} \right)_{T=0} = \begin{cases} G_n |V| / \left[V^2 - (\Delta/e)^2 \right] & |eV| \geqslant \Delta \\ 0 & |eV| < \Delta \end{cases} \qquad (5)$$

Thus measurements of conductance for $T \rightarrow 0$ yield the form of the density of states in the superconductor, as seen by comparing (1) and (5).

Problem

2.15. Derive (4) by first calculating the rightward and leftward tunneling. Write a paragraph discussing the tunneling process in terms of electron and hole excitations to reveal the processes hidden by using the variable E'.

---

[25] The reader should keep in mind that a rather complex system of excitations and ground-state electrons is being described (with mathematical accuracy) by the simple expedient of introducing E' as a dummy variable.

2.16. Quasiparticle Tunneling Between Superconductors

In Section 2.15, it was argued that whereas the actual excitations produced by tunneling of an electron into a superconductor involve states both below and above k_F, calculation of tunneling currents can conveniently be done by considering only states above k_F and taking these to have zero pair occupancy. The same treatment can be used for tunneling out of a superconductor. Thus, we assume that all pair states are fully occupied below k_F and empty above for both superconductors.

There are two types of process to consider. A pair may be broken, creating a hole excitation on the side where the pair was and injecting the electron into the other side. This is shown in Fig. 2.16a. The second type is the transfer of an excited electron from one side to the other. These can both be taken into account by Fig. 2.16b, which shows the density of states and occupations for $T \neq 0$, where two different superconductors are assumed. Here, as in Section 2.15, we use a dummy variable E' to facilitate the integration. The tunneling current (right to left) is

$$I_{ss} = \frac{G_n}{e} \int_{-\infty}^{\infty} \frac{|E' - eV|}{\left[(eV - E')^2 - \Delta_1^2 \right]^{1/2}} \frac{|E'|}{\left[E'^2 - \Delta_2^2 \right]^{1/2}}$$

$$\times \left[f(E' - eV) - f(E') \right] dE' \tag{1}$$

At $T = 0$, I_{ss} has the form shown by the heavy line in Fig. 2.16c; the discontinuity in the current at $V = (\Delta_1 + \Delta_2)/e$ is $\frac{1}{2}\pi(G_n/e)(\Delta_1\Delta_2)^{1/2}$. For $T \neq 0$ the tunneling current follows the heavy line in Fig. 2.16d. For low temperatures it is possible to observe negative resistance between $|\Delta_1 - \Delta_2|/e$ and $(\Delta_1 + \Delta_2)/e$. The excited electrons on the left side (Fig. 2.16b) first face a high density of states as the voltage is raised from zero, so the

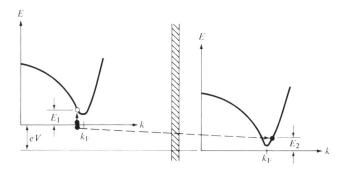

Figure 2.16a. Tunneling from a pair state in one superconductor creating a hole excitation there and an electron excitation in the other superconductor. In this representation we assume unity occupancy for $k < k_F$ and zero for $k > k_F$.

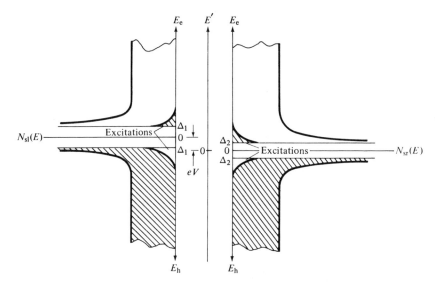

Figure 2.16b. Diagram for determination of tunneling currents between two different superconductors with $T \neq 0$ and an applied voltage V.

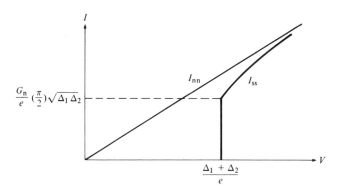

Figure 2.16c. Tunneling between superconductors at $T = 0$ compared with tunneling between the same materials in the normal state.

current increases. It subsequently decreases because the available density of states decreases; this is the negative-resistance region. Finally, at $(\Delta_1 + \Delta_2)/e$, pairs in the left side break and provide a large increase in tunneling current.

The actual values of the tunneling currents and the corresponding conductance in the gap region $V < (\Delta_1 + \Delta_2)/e$ can be of appreciable

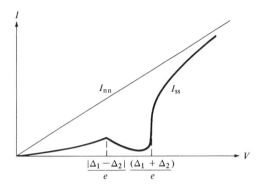

Figure 2.16d. Tunneling between superconductors for $T \neq 0$.

practical importance. For the general case with $T \neq 0$, (1) must be integrated numerically. There are some special cases for which useful analytic results have been obtained. The discontinuity of I_{ss} at $V = (\Delta_1 + \Delta_2)/e$ is of magnitude

$$\Delta I_{ss} = \frac{\pi G_n \sqrt{\Delta_1 \Delta_2}}{4e} \frac{\sinh[(\Delta_1 + \Delta_2)/2k_BT]}{(\cosh \Delta_1/2k_BT)(\cosh \Delta_2/2k_BT)} \tag{2}$$

When the superconductors are identical ($\Delta_1 = \Delta_2 = \Delta$) and for $T \ll \Delta/k_B$ and $eV < 2\Delta$, the current is well approximated by

$$I_{ss} = \frac{2G_n}{e} e^{-\Delta/k_BT} \left(\frac{2\Delta}{eV + 2\Delta} \right)^{1/2} (eV + \Delta) \left(\sinh \frac{eV}{2k_BT} \right) K_0 \left(\frac{eV}{2k_BT} \right) \tag{3}$$

where K_0 is the zeroth-order modified Bessel function.[26]

Problem

2.16. Figure 2.16e shows experimental data on an Al–Al$_2$O$_3$–Al junction. Calculate the dependence of I_{ss} on V for $T = 0.756$ K, using the results of this section and assuming that the approximate formula (3) can be applied. Take all needed data from Fig. 2.16e and compare the calculated curve with the corresponding curve given in the figure. Comment on any differences.

---

[26] See, for example, S. Ramo, J. R. Whinnery, and T. Van Duzer, *Fields and Waves in Communication Electronics*. 2nd ed., New York: John Wiley and Sons, 1984, p. 368.

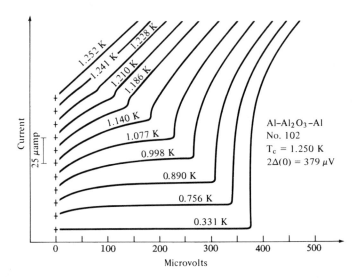

Figure 2.16e. Experimental data on an Al–Al$_2$O$_3$–Al tunnel junction. The zero points (+) are staggered for clarity.

From B. L. Blackford and R. H. March, "Temperature dependence of the energy gap in superconducting Al–Al$_2$O$_3$–Al tunnel junctions," *Canadian Journal of Physics*, Vol. 46, p. 143, 15 January 1968. Reproduced with permission of the National Research Council of Canada.

2.17. Quasiparticle Tunneling Devices for Electromagnetic Detection

The tunneling structures discussed in the preceding sections have been studied as potential detectors and mixers. The nonlinearity present in the I–V characteristic leads to frequency conversion, either to dc in the case of video detection or to the intermediate frequency for mixing. With stronger nonlinearity, the conversion is more efficient. For video detectors, the measure used for detection efficiency is the *current responsivity*, the change of dc current per unit of power absorbed:

$$R = \Delta I_{dc} / \tfrac{1}{2} V_1 I_\omega \tag{1}$$

where V_1 is the amplitude of the ac voltage applied to the device and I_ω is the dissipative-current component at the applied frequency. In the classical limit the frequency is low enough that the I–V characteristic varies slowly over a range of voltage on the order of the photon energy $\hbar\omega/e$, and the responsivity is given by

$$R = \tfrac{1}{2} \left(d^2 I_{dc} / dV_{dc}^2 \right) / \left(dI_{dc} / dV_{dc} \right) \tag{2}$$

Recent work on quantum effects in single-particle tunneling devices[27] has shown that (2) no longer applies if the conductance varies so rapidly on the photon energy scale that

$$I_{dc}(V_{dc} + \hbar\omega/e) - I_{dc}(V_{dc}) \gg I_{dc}(V_{dc}) - I_{dc}(V_{dc} - \hbar\omega/e) \qquad (3)$$

In this quantum limit, the current responsivity becomes

$$R = e/\hbar\omega \qquad (4)$$

which indicates that one additional electron flows through the barrier for each additional photon absorbed. The quantum limit is the highest possible current responsivity. It is clear that very strong nonlinearity in the $I-V$ characteristic will both increase the classical responsivity (2) and, from (3), make achievement of the quantum limit possible at lower frequencies. Similar advantages accrue with increasing curvature of the $I-V$ characteristic for a mixer in a heterodyne system, both in the classical and quantum-limited regimes.

In tunneling between normal metals and in Schottky diodes, the nonlinearity occurs on a scale of volts. Recently there has been extensive research on the use of metal–barrier–metal junctions for video and heterodyne detection of signals in the infrared and visible spectral regions, as well as on the use of Schottky diodes in the infrared. These devices have the advantages of operation at room temperature and very fast response times. Thus far, technical limitations have prevented achieving sufficient nonlinearity to approach the quantum-limited performance, but important applications in metrology and detection have been realized.

A second category of quasiparticle tunneling devices has one superconducting electrode and one normal. It is clear from Fig. 2.15e that as the bias is increased on an NIS junction with the normal metal raised in energy the number of electrons on the normal side in energy states above the level of the gap Δ of the superconductor must increase exponentially with bias. In fact, it can be shown from Eq. 2.15(4) that the current at low temperatures is given by

$$I_{dc} = I_0 \exp(eV/k_B T) \qquad (5)$$

where

$$I_0 = \tfrac{1}{2} G_n(\Delta/e)(2\pi k_B T/\Delta)^{1/2} \exp(-\Delta/k_B T) \qquad (6)$$

for $k_B T \lesssim eV \lesssim \Delta$. The strong nonlinearity is partially apparent in Fig. 2.15f. In the range of voltages below Δ/e, however, the exponential (5) is

---

[27] J. R. Tucker, "Quantum limited detection in tunnel junction mixers," *IEEE J. Quantum Electron*, Vol. QE-15, pp. 1234–1258, November 1979.

not clearly evident on the linear scale of the figure. The classical responsivity on this exponential portion of the $I-V$ characteristic may be obtained by inserting (5) into the general expression (2):

$$R = e/2k_B T \qquad (7)$$

By making T very small, extremely high responsivities can be obtained. The numerical value of (7) is $R = (5800/T)$ A/W.

There is another device, not mentioned previously in this chapter, that also depends on quasiparticle tunneling and that is very similar in principle to the NIS junction. It consists of a superconductor contact to a degenerately doped semiconductor and is called a *super-Schottky diode*.[28] A Schottky barrier forms at the surface, as shown in Fig. 2.17 for an n-type semiconductor, and the depletion region provides a tunneling barrier. The only practical differences between this and the NIS junction are in the shape of the tunnel barrier and that the super-Schottky diode contains a spreading resistance in series with the tunneling barrier as a result of the finite conductivity of the semiconductor. Calculation of the tunneling

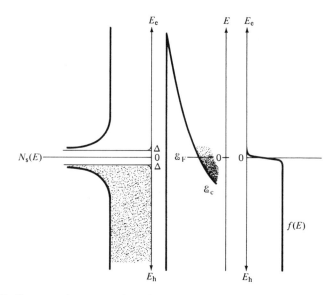

Figure 2.17. Superconductor–semiconductor contact. The central portion shows the Schottky barrier for an n-type semiconductor that is heavily degenerately doped. It is assumed that a single number can represent the density of states in the semiconductor at the edge of the barrier region.

[28] M. McColl, M. F. Millea, A. H. Silver, M. F. Bottjer, R. J. Pedersen, and F. L. Vernon, Jr., "The super-Schottky microwave mixer," *IEEE Trans. Magn.*, Vol. MAG-13, pp. 221–227, January 1977.

current leads to the same results, (5) and (6), as for the NIS junction. For either the NIS or the super-Schottky diode, criterion (3) and the $I-V$ relation (5) indicate that for frequencies such that $\hbar\omega > 2k_BT$, quantum-limited responsivity will be approached. Thus, for $T = 1$ K, the quantum limit should be attainable in these devices above about 40 GHz.

Tunneling between two superconductors at low temperatures leads to even stronger nonlinearities in the single-particle $I-V$ characteristic, as illustrated in Fig. 2.16e. Simple analytic forms are not available in this case. Quantum-limited response should be attainable for the SIS junction at even lower frequencies than in the NIS junction if effects of the Josephson pair tunneling can be made negligible.

Heterodyne detection is also predicted by the theory of photon-assisted tunneling to make a transition between classical mixing and quantum behavior at $\hbar\omega \cong 2k_BT$ for the NIS and super-Schottky diodes, and at frequencies satisfying (3) in general. For higher frequencies, the theoretical limit of detectable power in heterodyne mixing can approach $P_{\text{det}} \cong \hbar\omega B$, where B is the intermediate-frequency bandwidth. This is the limit imposed by the quantum nature of electromagnetic radiation. The quantum theory for a three-port mixer predicts conversion gain L^{-1} according to the formula

$$L^{-1} \cong 2\Delta/\hbar\omega \qquad (8)$$

A summary has been given of recent theoretical and experimental results on the use of quasiparticle tunneling devices for detection and mixing, including recent observations of conversion gain in heterodyne mixers at 36 GHz.[29]

---

[29] P. L. Richards and T. M. Shen, "Superconductive devices for millimeter-wave detecting, mixing, and amplification," *IEEE Trans. Electron Devices*, Vol. ED-27, pp. 1909–1920, October 1980.

Chapter 3

Electrodynamics of Superconductors
in Weak Magnetic Fields

3.01. Introduction

Early experiments with superconductors quickly demonstrated some un-
usual properties not observed for conduction electrons in normal metals.
Although, at first, the vanishing of the dc resistance was the most striking
feature of superconductivity, a complete characterization of the superconducting state required that other electromagnetic properties be investigated,
a task that proved to be difficult until suitable signal sources and measurement techniques become available.

   In this chapter we develop the electromagnetic equations for superconductors, emphasizing the key role played by the relation between current
and field. Our treatment identifies the important differences between electronic conduction by paired electrons and by single electrons, and demon-
strates the simplicity introduced by considering the paired-electron component of the free-electron population as a boson fluid. In the earlier sections
of this chapter, we shall study the behavior of the paired-electron component. However, at any finite temperature there are some unpaired electrons
near the Fermi surface, so there is also a current of single electrons in the
presence of time-varying fields. Later sections deal with a so-called two-
fluid model which describes currents in terms of paired-electron and
single-electron components.

   *Throughout the chapter, we assume that the magnetic fields are weak
enough that the Meissner effect (Section 1.10) applies, i.e., that the magnetic
field is excluded from the interior of the superconductor except in a thin
penetration region at the surface.* This restriction enables the presentation to
be less heavily qualified by exceptions and permits a more straightforward
account of the dynamic electromagnetic response of a superconductor. The
description of conduction phenomena in superconductors with penetrating
magnetic fields is postponed until Chapter 7, after a discussion of the
thermodynamics of magnetized systems.

   The development of solid-state electronics has traditionally benefited a
great deal from the use of models to describe observed physical effects.

Much of device research involves the refinement and testing of basic models used as working hypotheses in the absence of more complete knowledge. An essential part of this is a critical assessment of the model and a clear delineation of the limits of its applicability. For example, the conduction processes in semiconductors and normal metals have often been described in terms of free-electron flow, with the addition of collisions. There are good sound reasons for using this analogy: It is a simplification that can be justified by the need to obtain a useful picture of conduction processes without the complications of crystal structure, positive-ion background, and the rest. The standard textbook derivation of Ohm's law introduces the concepts of mean free path, mean time between collisions, and mobility without specific reference to conduction of free charges in solids. A collision-dominated electron fluid is employed for the model and suffices for most purposes. The application of a uniform magnetic field produces cyclotronic motion of the conduction electrons in vacuum and in solids. Two-particle phenomena—electrons and mobile ions in vacuum and electrons and holes in solids—can be compared usefully in the two cases. Electrons at the bottom of an empty conduction band, as in many semiconductors, can be regarded as virtually free since the effective-mass approximation takes into account the effects of the crystal lattice of positive ions. Of course, there are limits beyond which the analogy does not hold; the most striking example arising in solids is the Bragg reflection of electrons by the crystal lattice for particular values of energy and momentum.

However, it is not possible to draw such a correspondence between free electrons and the electrons responsible for superconduction. The reason is that single electrons are fermions, whereas the paired electrons behave more like bosons. The latter can have any number in the same quantum state and this leads to behavior that is quite different from that of single electrons. For example, there is no counterpart of the Meissner effect to be found outside of superconductor electrodynamics. In this chapter we introduce another distinctive property: the persistent currents induced in superconducting rings and the quantization of magnetic flux trapped within multiply connected superconductors. These phenomena also cannot be explained in terms of the properties of free electrons. On the other hand, as we show later, the assumption of a boson-fluid model for superconducting electrons leads to electrodynamic equations consistent with experimental observations. The long-range coherence of the conducting superfluid mentioned in Section 2.07, which allows a single well-defined phase angle to be meaningful over laboratory-scale dimensions, bears a closer resemblance to the properties of boson fields familiar in optics and acoustics than to those of nonsuperconducting electron fluids. The London brothers in the 1930s used the then-available experimental evidence to develop a theoretical description that is still recognized as valid, with certain restrictions. It was not found possible to derive a current–field relation for superconductors from microscopic properties until the quantum-mechanical description of the paired-electron state was developed by Bardeen, Cooper, and Schrieffer (Chapter 2). We choose to use the boson-fluid approximation even though the electrodynamic properties can be found directly from the BCS theory, since the latter requires a facility with quantum mechanics beyond that expected for this text.

3.02. Current–Field Relations

A principal task of this chapter is to develop equations that can be used to solve for the electromagnetic fields and currents within superconductors in the Meissner state. To do this we combine Maxwell's equations with a current–field relation. The latter, a so-called *constitutive relation*, is necessary in all field problems in order to solve Maxwell's equations. In normal conductors $\vec{J}$ (in $\nabla \times \vec{H} = \vec{J} + \partial\vec{D}/\partial t$) is given by Ohm's law ($\vec{J} = \sigma\vec{E}$) and in vacuum we use $\vec{J} = -n\,e\langle\vec{v}\rangle$, where n is the electron density and $\langle\vec{v}\rangle$ is the average electron velocity. We saw in Section 1.10 that assuming a superconductor to be simply a perfect conductor to get the current–field relation led to a result in conflict with the Meissner experiment.

In the next section we derive the London relations that relate the current of paired electrons (here assumed to be bosons) to field quantites. In those relations the current at a point in space is assumed to depend only on fields at that point, which is also the assumption implicit in Ohm's law. We consider later a nonlocal constitutive relation in which the current density at a point depends on the fields in a surrounding region and indicate the conditions under which this added complication is necessary.

3.03. Boson-Gas Model: London Equations

We shall not follow the historical development[1] of the physics of superconductors, preferring to use the quantum-mechanical picture at the outset in deriving the London equations for a charged boson fluid. We then proceed to show that the Meissner effect (Section 1.10) is a characteristic property of the system.

The fundamental assumption is that a macroscopic many-body wave function with a well-defined amplitude and phase angle can be used to represent the condensed electron-pair fluid. It is in fact not a proper wave function but rather, as mentioned in Section 2.07, the ensemble-average

---

[1] There are a number of excellent accounts of the history of the development of superconductivity to which we draw the reader's attention. It would be an unfortunate omission on the part of any student of superconductivity not to experience the fascinating chronicle of events that culminated in the modern theory. Among the most useful references are the following: F. London, *Superfluids*. New York: Dover Publications, 1960. K. Mendelssohn, *The Quest for Absolute Zero*. New York: McGraw-Hill, 1966.

wave function describing the condensed electron pairs. This ensemble-average function can be written as

$$\psi(\vec{r}) = |\psi(\vec{r})| e^{i\theta(\vec{r})} \tag{1}$$

Since the actual wave function representing the electron-pair fluid for any given superconductor deviates but little from the ensemble average, we can use the latter with a high degree of accuracy. (The use of the ensemble averages to represent member systems of the ensemble is the basis of statistical mechanics and thermodynamics and will be discussed further in Sections 6.02 and 6.03.) We can normalize the amplitude in (1) such that $\psi\psi^*$ equals the number density at that point in the superconductor. We then have

$$\psi(\vec{r}) = \left[n_s^*(\vec{r}) \right]^{1/2} e^{i\theta(\vec{r})} \tag{2}$$

where $n_s^*(\vec{r})$ is the density of Cooper pairs, and $\theta(\vec{r})$ is a scalar function of position. For many purposes n_s^* can be taken as spatially constant. We assume in this chapter that the fraction of electrons in the superconducting state is independent of position. Also, any accumulation of electrons relaxes exceedingly rapidly and can be ignored for time variations slower than 10^{12} Hz in superconductors.

The classical canonical momentum for a particle of charge q and mass m in the presence of a magnetic field is given by $\vec{p} = m\vec{v} + q\vec{A}$ and can be written for a pair with effective mass m^* and charge e^* as[2]

$$\vec{p} = m^*\vec{v}_s + e^*\vec{A} \tag{3}$$

Then with a density n_s^* of pairs, all having the same momentum, we can write the momentum density as

$$n_s^*\vec{p} = n_s^*\left(m^*\vec{v}_s + e^*\vec{A}\right) \tag{4}$$

The connection with the quantum-mechanical description is that $n_s^*\vec{p}$ is the expectation value of the canonical-momentum operator $-i\hbar\nabla$, operating on the pair-fluid wave function (1). Thus

$$n_s^*\vec{p} = \langle\psi| -i\hbar\nabla|\psi\rangle \tag{5}$$

Since

$$-i\hbar\nabla\psi = \hbar(\nabla\theta)\psi$$

we obtain $\vec{p} = \hbar\nabla\theta$, so (3) becomes

$$\vec{p} = \hbar\nabla\theta = m^*\vec{v}_s + e^*\vec{A} \tag{6}$$

---

[2]As would be expected from the pairing theory in Chapter 2, the pair effective mass and effective charge can be taken to be twice the values for single electrons. We take the e^* to be $-2e$, where $e = 1.6 \times 10^{-19}$ C, to agree with the usage in much of the literature.

The pair-current density is given by $\vec{J}_s = n_s^* e^* \vec{v}_s$, so we may write

$$\vec{p} = \hbar \nabla \theta = e^* \Lambda \vec{J}_s + e^* \vec{A} \tag{7}$$

with

$$\boxed{\Lambda \stackrel{\Delta}{=} m^* / n_s^* e^{*2}} \tag{8}$$

We can proceed to take the curl of both sides of (7) and obtain a relation between the current density and the magnetic field, known as the "second London equation":

$$\boxed{\Lambda(\nabla \times \vec{J}_s) + \vec{B} = 0} \tag{9}$$

where the induction $\vec{B} = \nabla \times \vec{A}$.

We should note here some properties of the canonical momentum and phase θ. First, since the curl of the gradient of a scalar is zero and $\vec{p} = \hbar \nabla \theta$,

$$\nabla \times \vec{p} = 0 \tag{10}$$

For fields in good conductors up through the microwave frequencies, one may take $\nabla \cdot \vec{A} \cong 0$. Since $\nabla \cdot \vec{J}_s = -\partial \rho / \partial t \cong 0$ assuming negligible accumulation of charge, we can conclude from (7) that

$$\nabla \cdot \vec{p} = 0 \tag{11}$$

and

$$\nabla^2 \theta = 0 \tag{12}$$

Another London equation represents the motion of the accelerated superfluid under the influence of an applied electric field

$$m^* \frac{d\vec{v}_s}{dt} = e^* \vec{E} \tag{13}$$

This may be written as

$$m^* \frac{\partial \vec{v}_s}{\partial t} = e^* \vec{E} \tag{14}$$

assuming small spatial variations of $\vec{v}_s$ in the direction of $\vec{v}_s$. Then (14) may be converted to

$$\boxed{\Lambda \frac{\partial \vec{J}_s}{\partial t} = \vec{E}} \tag{15}$$

which is the "first London equation."

Equations (9) and (15) are directly useful in solving practical problems, as we shall see later in the chapter, but cannot be applied to superconductors indiscriminately. One difficulty arises from the strong spatial variation of the magnetic induction at the surface of a superconductor. In some cases it is necessary to use Pippard's nonlocal treatment, described in Section 3.11, to obtain agreement with experimental measurements. Further, the equations apply only for weak fields and contain no portent of the disappearance of superconductivity in high magnetic fields.

In contrast with the relation between current density and electric field for a normal conductor, (9) shows immediately that it is the magnetic field that determines the current flowing in the superconductor. The electric field, if one is present, controls the time derivative of the supercurrent. For stationary currents, we see that no electric field exists at any point in the superconductor.

3.04. Gauge Transformation

It will be recalled from electromagnetic theory that the electric potential Φ and the magnetic vector potential $\vec{A}$ are not unique quantities but are only defined in terms of their derivatives. The physical quantities, electric-field intensity and magnetic induction, are derived from the potentials as follows:

$$\vec{E} = -\nabla\Phi - \partial\vec{A}/\partial t \tag{1}$$

$$\vec{B} = \nabla \times \vec{A} \tag{2}$$

Thus any transformation (called a *gauge transformation*) of the form

$$\vec{A}' = \vec{A} + \nabla\chi; \qquad \Phi' = \Phi - \partial\chi/\partial t \tag{3a; b}$$

where χ is a single-valued scalar function, leaves the field quantities unchanged. In fact, a gauge transformation must leave all measurable quantities unchanged since it is a purely mathematical operation.

In Section 3.03 we showed that the expectation value of the canonical momentum for the electron-pair wave function can be expressed as

$$\vec{p} = m^*\vec{v}_s + e^*\vec{A} \tag{4}$$

Let us make a gauge transformation of $\vec{A}$ and see how the momentum $\vec{p}$ must change in order to leave the velocity (the measurable quantity) unchanged. Substitution of (3a) into (4) shows that if the transformed momentum has the form $\vec{p}' = \vec{p} + e^*\nabla\chi$, then the velocity is still in the form of the untransformed relation (4).

Similarly we can deduce how the electron-pair wave function itself must transform in a gauge transformation by showing that if the transformed wave function has the form

$$\psi' = \psi \exp\left[(ie^*/\hbar)\chi\right] \tag{5}$$

the velocity is unaffected by the transformation. Consider the operator equivalent of (4) in the new gauge:

$$-i\hbar\nabla\psi' = (m^*\vec{v}_s + e^*\vec{A})\psi' \tag{6}$$

Substitute the transformed vector potential (3a) and wave function (5):

$$-i\hbar \, \nabla \{ |\psi| \exp[i(\theta + e^*\chi/\hbar)]\} = (\hbar \, \nabla \theta + e^* \, \nabla \chi)\psi'$$

$$= (m^* \vec{v}_s + e^* \vec{A} + e^* \, \nabla \chi)\psi' \qquad (7)$$

Comparing the coefficients in (7) and identifying $\vec{p}$ with $\hbar \, \nabla \theta$, we see that the original form (4) is unchanged. The only effect of changing gauge is to alter the local phase of the wave function.

At this point it is useful to emphasize the differences between the scalar functions θ, χ, and Φ which have been introduced:

θ is the phase angle of the macroscopic wave function for the superfluid; it exists only inside the superconductor and is possibly multiple valued.

Φ is the electrostatic potential, assumed to be zero for quasistationary or low-frequency behavior in a superconductor.

χ is a mathematical function that allows the gauge for the electromagnetic potentials to be changed and consequently must be single-valued everywhere in space.

The choice of gauge for $\vec{A}$ ultimately depends upon the nature of the problem, since the primary motivation for changing gauges is that of casting the equations in the most convenient form.

Problem

3.04. Show that the energy $\mathcal{E}$ of a stationary state satisfying Schrödinger's equation $\mathfrak{H}\Psi = \mathcal{E}\,\Psi$, where

$$\mathfrak{H} = (1/2m^*)(\vec{p} - e^*\vec{A})^2$$

is unaffected by the gauge transformations described in this section.

3.05. Gauge Selection for Simply Connected Superconductors: The London Gauge

In the solution of electrodynamics problems, simplification of the mathematics can be achieved by an appropriate choice of gauge, that is, by specification of the vector potential. By definition, the curl of $\vec{A}$ is the magnetic induction. One may also independently specify the divergence. A choice that decouples the differential equations for the electric and magnetic potentials is $\nabla \cdot \vec{A} = -\mu\varepsilon\partial\Phi/\partial t$. In superconductors, the electric potential Φ seldom has a value significantly different from zero so we may make the approximation $\nabla \cdot \vec{A} = 0$, which is the condition usually used for static-electrodynamics problems. It is a peculiar feature of the superconductor that the vector potential is directly related to the current. This allows us to specify the value of $\vec{A}$ on the superconductor boundary to simplify the form of the electrodynamics equations.

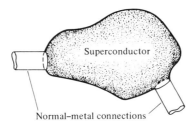

Figure 3.05. Simply connected superconductor with normal-metal connections.

Let us consider a simply connected superconducting body which may have normal-metal connections as shown in Fig. 3.05. If we choose the so-called *London gauge* to complete the specification of $\vec{A}$, we set $A_\perp = -\Lambda J_{s\perp}$, where the subscript $\perp$ signifies the normal conponent of the vectors at the boundaries. By this choice we see from Eq. 3.03(7) that $p_\perp = 0$ over the entire boundary. From Eqs. 3.03(12) and 3.03(6) we see that the phase θ satisfies Laplace's equation and $\vec{p}$ is proportional to its gradient. The specification of a vanishing normal gradient over the entire surface ($p_\perp = \hbar \nabla_\perp \theta = 0$) ensures that θ is a constant over the entire superconductor (see Problem 3.05), so $\vec{p} = 0$ throughout. Then from Eq. 3.03(7) we get

$$\boxed{\Lambda \vec{J}_s = -\vec{A}} \tag{1}$$

Note that we were able to see that the curl of (1) was true in Eq. 3.03(7) before specifying the gauge. Equation (1) is a special form of London's second equation, which is convenient for solving problems involving simply connected superconductors.

Problem

3.05. Show that the phase θ is uniquely determined except for an arbitrary additive constant throughout a simply connected superconductor when its normal gradient is specified on the boundary.

3.06. dc Electrodynamic Solutions for Superconductors Having Simple Shapes: The Meissner Effect and Penetration Depth

Although Eqs. 3.03(7) and 3.03(9) do not give a completely general picture of superconductor electrodynamics, they are adequate for many purposes and have solutions that agree reasonably well with experimental observations. In this section we establish the main features of the solutions for the simplest possible shapes. A somewhat more complex problem is analyzed in Section 3.07. It should be kept in mind that the solutions only apply for weak magnetic fields and where the fields have a slow spatial variation. The strong-field problem will be treated in Chapter 7 and the case of rapid spatial variation will be studied in Section 3.11.

We obtain the basic differential equation by combining the constitutive relation between conduction current and vector potential with Maxwell's equations for stationary currents and fields. Recall that in the dc case the electric fields in the superconductor vanish, so there are no currents of electrons in the normal state (excitations, Section 2.09) and no displacement current; thus,

$$\nabla \times \vec{H} = \vec{J}_s \tag{1}$$

where $\vec{J}_s$ is the pair current. For the present purposes, we may use the constitutive relation either in the form of Eq. 3.03(9) or Eq. 3.05(1). In either case

$$\Lambda \nabla \times \nabla \times \vec{H} = -\vec{B} \tag{2}$$

As with normal metals, the permeability of a superconductor is negligibly different from that of free space, so we can take $\vec{B} = \mu_0 \vec{H}$. Making use of this fact and a vector identity, (2) becomes

$$(\Lambda/\mu_0)\left[\nabla(\nabla \cdot \vec{B}) - \nabla^2\vec{B}\right] = -\vec{B} \tag{3}$$

But $\nabla \cdot \vec{B} = 0$ and we define

$$\lambda_L \overset{\Delta}{=} (\Lambda/\mu_0)^{1/2} = \left(m^*/\mu_0 n_s^* e^{*2}\right)^{1/2} \tag{4}$$

so (3) becomes

$$\nabla^2\vec{B} = (1/\lambda_L^2)\vec{B} \tag{5}$$

A similar equation applies for the pair current density, $\nabla^2\vec{J}_s = \vec{J}_s/\lambda_L^2$. The same form $\nabla^2\vec{A} = \vec{A}/\lambda_L^2$ applies also for magnetic vector potential, but only for simply connected bodies where $\nabla\theta = 0$ (See Prob. 3.06a).

It is important to note that the local relation, Eq. 3.05(1), and its derived results, such as (5), are good approximations to the actual electrodynamics only for materials having very small Cooper pairs.[3] In some such cases, however, the coefficient in (5) does not have the value given by (4). Also, virtues of simplicity and linearity inherent in (5) suggest using it as an approximation even for materials with larger coherence lengths. Again the coefficient in (5) is not that given by (4). For now, we replace λ_L by λ and assume (5) applies. This new coefficient is defined and evaluated in Section

---

[3] The effective pair size, or *coherence length*, is discussed in Section 3.11.

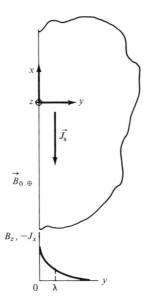

Figure 3.06a. Magnetic field applied parallel to a superconducting half space is diminished in strength to $1/e$ of its surface value B_0 in a distance of λ. The shielding of the interior of the superconductor is accomplished by a current flowing near the surface.

3.12. The differential equations become

$$\nabla^2 \vec{B} = (1/\lambda^2)\vec{B} \tag{6}$$

$$\nabla^2 \vec{A} = (1/\lambda^2)\vec{A} \tag{7}$$

$$\nabla^2 \vec{J}_s = (1/\lambda^2)\vec{J}_s \tag{8}$$

Now let us apply (6) to the superconducting half space in Fig. 3.06a with a magnetic field B_0 in the z direction at its surface ($y = 0$). In this case (6) reduces to

$$d^2 B_z / dy^2 = (1/\lambda^2)B_z \tag{9}$$

which has the solutions

$$B_z = B_0 e^{\pm y/\lambda} \tag{10}$$

Since B_z must not grow indefinitely as $y \to \infty$, only the minus sign is allowed and the dependence is as shown in Fig. 3.06a. Corresponding to B_z, we obtain the current density from (1):

$$J_{sx} = -(B_0/\lambda\mu_0)e^{-y/\lambda} \tag{11}$$

It is clear that the penetration of the external field and concomitant current is measured by λ, which accordingly is called the *penetration depth*.

The penetration depth is on the order of 50 nm, so the exponential decay of the current density and magnetic field is extremely rapid. We have the surprising result that, even for static conditions, the current and magnetic induction are confined to a very thin surface layer of a superconductor. This nearly complete flux exclusion is known as the *Meissner effect*. There is virtually no current within the bulk of the material. Although the behavior is reminiscent of the skin effect of normal metals at high frequencies, it should be kept in mind that we are concerned here with a dc

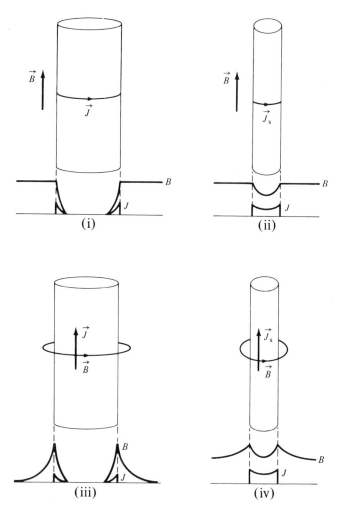

Figure 3.06b. (i) and (ii) show situations in which a magnetic field is applied to samples large and small, respectively, compared with the penetration depth λ. In (iii) and (iv), the magnetic field results from a current passed through the superconductor.

phenomenon. There is an additional high-frequency effect introduced in Section 3.15. The solution given by (10) does not, then, predict *complete* exclusion of magnetic flux from the superconductor. Rather, we see that the Meissner effect allows a small amount of penetration of magnetic flux into the superconductor. A useful approach to understanding the nature of the currents is to recognize that they are, in effect, screening currents serving to cancel the magnetic flux deep inside the superconductor. Their failure to accomplish this task completely results from the necessity for them to be distributed over a finite spatial extent, i.e., the penetration region.

The magnetic field in question may be derived from some outside source or it may be the result of a transport current driven through the superconductor by an external circuit. Figure 3.06b shows examples of the current and field distributions for superconductors of various geometries. In (i) and (ii), an external static bias field is applied, whereas the magnetic fields in (iii) and (iv) are generated by transport currents. The examples shown in (ii) and (iv) illustrate the solutions for samples where the dimensions become comparable to the penetration depth; the field and current penetrate the specimen substantially. For larger bodies the Meissner exclusion of flux may be taken as virtually complete since the region of penetration is a negligible fraction of the total volume.

The solution presented for the superconducting half space can be applied regardless of the specimen shape, provided that the significant dimensions are large compared to the penetration depth. This condition may not be met for thin-film and particle samples. We shall see later that λ may become far greater than the value calculated at 0 K near the transition temperature.[4]

Problems

3.06a. Show that the magnetic vector potential and the current density satisfy the following equations, and discuss required conditions:

$$\nabla^2 \vec{A} = (1/\lambda^2)\vec{A} \qquad \nabla^2 \vec{J}_{\mathrm{s}} = (1/\lambda^2)\vec{J}_{\mathrm{s}}$$

3.06b. Solve the London equations for an infinite superconducting plate of finite thickness $2d$, assuming a magnetic field B_0 applied parallel to both surfaces. (i) As an example, plot the current and magnetic field for a thickness $2d = \lambda$. (ii) Calculate the magnetic flux within the plate as a fraction of that which would be in the same space with the plate missing. Find the plate thickness necessary for this fraction to equal $1/100$.

---

[4]The temperature dependence of λ_{L} will be discussed in Section 3.13 with the two-fluid model.

3.07. Two-Dimensional Transition Between a Normal Conductor and a Superconductor

Figure 3.07 shows an idealization of the common situation where a normal conductor is joined to a superconductor. We shall analyze the pattern of current flow in the neighborhood of the ns junction to illustrate the use of the London equation. The equations will be simplified by assuming the system to be in two-dimensional rectangular coordinates. We consider the dc case where the superconductor is an equipotential and the current flow is uniformly distributed in the connecting normal conductor. Deep inside the superconductor, the current flow is near the surfaces at $y = \pm a$. The uniformly distributed current at $z = 0$ makes a transition in the superconductor as illustrated in Fig. 3.07. We neglect here the fact that the direct contact at the ns junction affects the density n_s^* of electron pairs in the superconductor in the immediate neighborhood of the junction; this so-called *proximity effect* is discussed in Chapter 7.

The differential equation for pair current density, Eq. 3.06(8), can be written for the y and z components:

$$\nabla^2 J_{sy} = (1/\lambda^2)J_{sy} \tag{1}$$

$$\nabla^2 J_{sz} = (1/\lambda^2)J_{sz} \tag{2}$$

The components must also satisfy the continuity equation

$$\frac{\partial J_{sy}}{\partial y} + \frac{\partial J_{sz}}{\partial z} = 0 \tag{3}$$

The boundary conditions are

$$J_{sz} = J \qquad \text{for} \quad -a \leqslant y \leqslant a, \quad z = 0 \tag{4}$$

$$\left.\begin{aligned} \partial J_{sz}/\partial y = 0 \\ J_{sy} = 0 \end{aligned}\right\} \quad \text{for} \quad y = 0, \quad 0 \leqslant z \tag{5a} \tag{5b}$$

$$J_{sy} = 0 \qquad \text{for} \quad y = \pm a, \quad 0 \leqslant z \tag{6}$$

$$J_{sy} = 0 \qquad \text{for} \quad -a \leqslant y \leqslant a, \quad z = \infty \tag{7}$$

It can be shown that solutions of (1) can be found in the product-solution form:

$$J_{sy} = (A \sin \alpha y + B \cos \alpha y)\left\{ C \exp\left[(1/\lambda)^2 + \alpha^2\right]^{1/2} z \right.$$

$$\left. + D \exp -\left[(1/\lambda)^2 + \alpha^2\right]^{1/2} z \right\} \tag{8}$$

Application of the boundary conditions (5b) and (6) reveals that $B \equiv 0$ and $\alpha = n\pi/a$, where n is an integer. The boundary condition (7) requires that $C \equiv 0$ and the general form of the solution can be written in the following

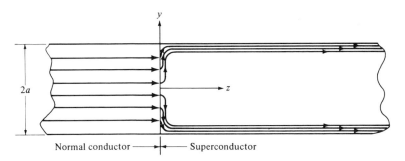

Figure 3.07. Pattern of current flow at the junction of a normal conductor and a superconductor in a two-dimensional system.

form:

$$J_{sy} = \sum_{n=1}^{\infty} A_n \sin \frac{n\pi y}{a} \exp\left\{ -\left[\left(\frac{1}{\lambda} \right)^2 + \left(\frac{n\pi}{a} \right)^2 \right]^{1/2} z \right\} \tag{9}$$

The z component is found by substituting (9) in (3), differentiating with respect to y, and integrating with respect to z:

$$J_{sz} = \sum_{n=1}^{\infty} \frac{A_n(n\pi/a)\cos(n\pi y/a)}{\left[(1/\lambda)^2 + (n\pi/a)^2 \right]^{1/2}} \exp\left\{ -\left[\left(\frac{1}{\lambda} \right)^2 + \left(\frac{n\pi}{a} \right)^2 \right]^{1/2} z \right\} + f(y) \tag{10}$$

where $f(y)$ must satisfy (2) [since all of (10) must] and be independent of z. It may be noted also that $f(y)$ must be an even-symmetric, monotonic function of y because of the boundary conditions (5a) and (4). Thus

$$f(y) = F \cosh(y/\lambda) \tag{11}$$

At $z = 0$, $J_{sz} = J$ from boundary condition (4), so (10) and (11) give

$$J - F \cosh \frac{y}{\lambda} = \sum_{n=1}^{\infty} \frac{A_n(n\pi)\cos(n\pi/a)y}{\left[(a/\lambda)^2 + (n\pi)^2 \right]^{1/2}} \tag{12}$$

To find F, integrate (12) over the range $-a \leqslant y \leqslant a$; the right side vanishes since it has no average value and

$$\int_{-a}^{a} \left(J - F \cosh \frac{y}{\lambda} \right) dy = 0 \tag{13}$$

This yields

$$F = (Ja/\lambda)/\sinh(a/\lambda) \tag{14}$$

Substituting (14) into (12), multiplying by $\cos(n\pi/a)y$, and integrating from

$- a$ to a yields the values of the coefficients A_n:

$$A_n = - \frac{2J(-1)^n}{n\pi} \frac{(a/\lambda)^2}{\left[(a/\lambda)^2 + (n\pi)^2\right]^{1/2}} \tag{15}$$

Finally, the components J_{sy} and J_{sz} are obtained by substituting (15) into (9) and (10):

$$J_{sy} = -J \sum_{n=1}^{\infty} \frac{2(-1)^n}{n\pi} \frac{(a/\lambda)^2}{\left[(a/\lambda)^2 + (n\pi)^2\right]^{1/2}} \sin \frac{n\pi y}{a}$$

$$\times \exp\left\{ -\left[\left(\frac{1}{\lambda}\right)^2 + \left(\frac{n\pi}{a}\right)^2\right]^{1/2} z\right\} \tag{16}$$

$$J_{sz} = J \left[\frac{(a/\lambda)\cosh(y/\lambda)}{\sinh(a/\lambda)} - \sum_{n=1}^{\infty} \frac{2(-1)^n(a/\lambda)^2\cos(n\pi y/a)}{(a/\lambda)^2 + (n\pi)^2} \right.$$

$$\left. \times \exp\left\{ -\left[\left(\frac{1}{\lambda}\right)^2 + \left(\frac{n\pi}{a}\right)^2\right]^{1/2} z\right\}\right] \tag{17}$$

The pattern of currents described by (16) and (17) is shown in Fig. 3.07. The summations in (16) and (17) decay rapidly for $z > \lambda$, the penetration depth, and for large z the current is essentially in the z direction only. The distance over which the transition from the uniform current distribution of the normal conductor to the surface distribution of z-directed current in the superconductor takes place would be typically in the neighborhood of 0.1–0.2 μm. It should be kept in mind, however, that we have neglected the proximity effect (Chapter 7) and this would modify the result. Also, it is virtually impossible to fabricate an ns contact in a strip if the shape of the contact is to be considered a good approximation to the ideal shape shown in Fig. 3.07, where dimensions on the order of 0.1–0.2 μm are important. The purpose of the example is to show how the equations would be used and to suggest the general nature of the transition. The method used here is that of London, who gives the solution of two related problems.[5]

Problems

3.07a. Use the method of separation of variables to derive (8) from (1). Verify that (11) has the proper form.

---

[5] F. London, *Superfluids, Macroscopic Theory of Superconductivity*, Vol. 1. New York: Dover Publications, 1960.

3.07b.   Integrate (17) over a cross section of the film (z = const) and show that the integral equals $2aJ$, the total current, independent of the value chosen for z.

3.08.   Isolated Current-Carrying Thin Strip

A common configuration in thin-film superconducting circuits is a film of width appreciably greater than its thickness carrying current along its length which is, in turn, much greater than the width. In many cases, the strip is deposited on top of a thin layer of insulation over a superconducting sheet ("ground plane"); this arrangement will be discussed in Section 3.09. Here we consider the strip of thickness b, and width w (Fig. 3.08a) to be of infinite length and to be remote from other superconductors. Such a configuration is most commonly made by depositing a film on a bulk insulator.

The exact distribution of current in the cross section of the isolated strip cannot be put in simple analytic form using London's equations. An approximate solution has been found for the case where the film thickness b is comparable with the penetration depth λ and the width w is much greater than λ, so $wb \gg \lambda^2$. By virtue of the assumption that $b \approx \lambda$, it can be assumed that the current density is uniform across the thickness of the film. The dependence of the current density on x near the center of the strip is (see Prob. 3.09a)

$$J_s(x) = J_s(0)\left[1 - (2x/w)^2\right]^{-1/2} \tag{1}$$

and the form near the edges is

$$J_s(x) = J_s(\tfrac{1}{2}w)\exp-\left[(\tfrac{1}{2}w - |x|)b/a\lambda^2\right] \tag{2}$$

where a is a constant near unity. The solutions (1) and (2) are joined at the points

$$x = \pm\left(\tfrac{1}{2}w - a\lambda^2/2b\right) \tag{3}$$

since the slopes and magnitudes of the functions are equal there. Equating (1) and (2) and substituting (3) (with + sign), one obtains a relation between the current density at the edge of the film and that at the center:

$$J_s(\tfrac{1}{2}w) = (1.165/\lambda)(wb/a)^{1/2}J_s(0) \tag{4}$$

The distribution of current density is plotted in Fig. 3.08b for a lead ($\lambda = 39$ nm) strip of thickness $b = 200$ nm and width $w = 1.5$ mm. The constant a is

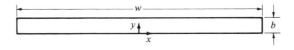

Figure 3.08a. Cross section of a thin strip carrying a current in the z direction.

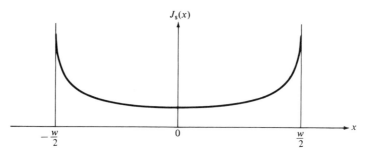

Figure 3.08b. Distribution across the width of the strip in Fig. 3.08a assuming the thickness b is less than the penetration depth so J_z is independent of y.

taken to be unity. The exponential region has a width of only about λ, so on the scale of Fig. 3.08b, (2) only serves to prevent infinite current density at $x = \pm \frac{1}{2} w$.

The y component of the magnetic field has been calculated as a function of x using the current distribution (1) and neglecting the edge correction (2) and is shown in Fig. 3.08c.[6] Also shown (by a broken line) is the magnetic field for a uniform distribution of current density. Experimental data, fitted in magnitude and x because of unknowns in the experiment, reveal that the shape of the distribution is well represented by the approximate current distribution; we take this to be a confirmation of (1). Neglect of (2) also seems to be justified for evaluation of fields not too close to the film.

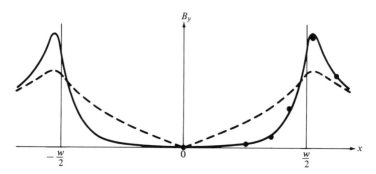

Figure 3.08c. Comparison of the theoretical and experimental values of the component of magnetic field perpendicular to the strip, B_y. The broken line shows the theoretical value obtained assuming the current to be distributed uniformly and the solid line uses (1) and neglects the end correction (2). Experimental points are shown.

[6]E. H. Rhoderick and E. M. Wilson, "Current distribution in thin superconducting films," *Nature*, Vol. 194, pp. 1167–1168, 23 June 1962.

Problems

3.08a. Rhoderick and Wilson[6] give an expression for the y component of the magnetic field in the form

$$H_y = \int_{-1}^{1} \frac{(\xi - t)\, dt}{(1 - t^2)^{1/2} \left[(\xi - t)^2 + \eta^2 \right]}$$

which is the real part of

$$\int_{-1}^{1} \frac{dt}{(1 - t^2)^{1/2}(\zeta - t)} = \pi (\zeta^2 - 1)^{-1/2}$$

In these expressions $\xi = 2x/w$, $\eta = 2y/w$, and $\zeta = \xi + i\eta$. Derive H_y from Eq. 3.08(1) and show that it is the real part of the integral in the second expression. Find the expression for H_x.

3.08b. Suppose it is desired to have a region of relatively uniform current distribution in the center of an isolated strip. What could be the width of the region of interest as a fraction of the strip width if a uniformity of 10% is required? What fraction of the total current would be in the region of interest?

3.09. Images and an Electrostatic Analogy: Application to Inductance Reduction

In this section we argue the idea of images on two different bases and show how the image concept facilitates reasoning about the magnetic fields between current-carrying superconductors. This makes clear, for example, the reduction of inductance of a superconducting loop lying parallel to a nearby superconducting plane.

Let us consider the effect of placing a differential current element near and parallel to an infinite superconducting plate. First, suppose the plate is in the normal state so its permeability is virtually μ_0. The magnetic fields resulting from the current element would be those expected in free space. In particular, in the plane of the plate surface there would be components of $\vec{B}$ both parallel and perpendicular to the plane. Now if the plate becomes superconducting, currents must flow on its surface in such a pattern as to make the internal fields zero (neglecting penetration depth λ). Just above the superconductor surface, the normal component $B_\perp = 0$ because of the requirement of continuity of normal components; the tangential component B_t must be related to the surface current according to the relation for tangential components. Since the field inside the superconductor is zero, $B_t = \mu_0 J_S$, where J_S is the surface current density. It is clear from symmetry that the requirement of zero $B_\perp$ along the surface of the plate may be satisfied by replacing the plate by an image current element. It should be located a distance below the surface plane equal to that of the given element above the plane and have a magnitude equal to and direction opposite from the given element. Thus the original problem of a current element over a superconducting plate can be replaced by the easier problem of two current elements in free space.

In the above considerations, it was assumed that vanishing of the perpendicular components $B_\perp$ at the surface of the superconductor constitutes a sufficient boundary condition. The validity of that view is most easily seen by using the fact that, in the current-free region of the given problem, the magnetic field is curl-free and therefore can be expressed as the gradient of a scalar potential. This potential satisfies Laplace's equation, and it is well known that specification of the perpendicular gradient of a function satisfying Laplace's equation is a sufficient boundary condition.

Now let us establish an analogy between the magnetic fields produced by currents on superconductors and the electrostatic fields resulting from charges on the surfaces of identically shaped conductors. A differential current element $I\,\overrightarrow{dl}$ represents a part of the surface current on a conductor lying near an infinite superconducting plane. If the current element is pointed in the z direction, the magnetic vector potential can have only a z component and therefore satisfies a scalar Laplace equation in the current-free space:

$$\nabla^2 A_z = 0 \tag{1}$$

In this analogy we use electric potential Φ as the analog of A_z; the potential also satisfies a Laplace equation. One boundary condition on electric potential at the surface of a perfect conductor is that the tangential component of its gradient be zero. In the magnetic problem the perpendicular component $B_\perp = 0$ at the superconductor surface. We must establish an identity between $B_\perp$ and the tangential component of the gradient of A_z so it will be seen to satisfy the same boundary condition as Φ.

Since $A_x = A_y = 0$ and $\vec{B} = \nabla \times \vec{A}$, $B_z = 0$ and

$$\vec{B} = \hat{x}\,\frac{\partial A_z}{\partial y} - \hat{y}\,\frac{\partial A_z}{\partial x} \tag{2}$$

The magnitude of $\vec{B}$ is thus

$$B = \left(B_x^2 + B_y^2\right)^{1/2} = \left[\left(\frac{\partial A_z}{\partial y}\right)^2 + \left(\frac{\partial A_z}{\partial x}\right)^2\right]^{1/2} \tag{3}$$

which is seen to be the magnitude of the gradient of A_z:

$$B = |\nabla A_z| \tag{4}$$

Also, by forming the scalar product of ∇A_z and $\vec{B}$, it is seen immediately that

$$\vec{B} \cdot \nabla A_z = 0 \tag{5}$$

In view of (5) and the fact that $B_\perp = 0$ at the superconductor surface, we see that the tangential component of $\nabla A_z = 0$ there.

Let us consider the relation between the flux density B and the field intensity $\vec{E}$ in the analog system. Since $E = |\nabla \Phi|$ and $B = |\nabla A_z|$, E and B have the same values if A_z and Φ do also. We know that $\vec{E}$ is parallel with $\nabla \Phi$ and, from (5), that $\vec{B}$ is perpendicular to ∇A_z, so $\vec{B}$ and $\vec{E}$ will be equal in magnitude but orthogonal at each point in the analogous fields if $A_z = \Phi$. The value of B just outside the superconductor surface is $\mu_0 J_S$, where J_S is the surface current density, and E just outside the analogous conductor surface is ρ_S / ε. Then if ρ_S in the analog system is

$$\rho_S = \mu_0 \varepsilon J_S \tag{6}$$

the magnitudes of $\vec{E}$ and Φ will be equal to those of $\vec{B}$ and A_z, respectively, and the analogy will be complete.

The idea of an image current in the case of a one-dimensional current parallel to an infinite superconducting surface is obvious with this analogy in light of the common electrostatic-image concept. Using (6) and judging from the fact that the image of a line charge in a conducting plane is a line of opposite charge located the same distance on the other side of the plane of the conductor surface, it is clear that the image of a line current is one of opposite direction located like the image charge. Note that the image method only gives correctly the fields between the current and the super-conductor in the original problem.

One useful way to use the electrostatic analogy would be to deduce the distribution of surface currents on two nearby superconductors. Consider, for example, the distribution of currents on a tunnel junction lying above a superconducting ground plane as in Fig. 3.09a(i). From the analog system [Fig. 3.09a(ii)], it is easy to deduce that charges will be distributed as shown and to conclude that surface currents will be likewise distributed.

At the beginning of this section, we gave an argument for the image concept based on a differential current element; by linearity the concept applies for any arbitrary collection of current elements. For determination of fields, however, the distribution of currents on the conductor lying above the superconducting plate must be known. This can only be found with reasonable effort in the one-dimensional case, where the vector potential satisfies a scalar Laplace equation, (1). Finally, note that all the arguments given here are based on the assumption that $B = 0$ inside the superconductor, which is approximately true if the penetration depth λ is small compared with the thickness of the superconductors and the space separating them.

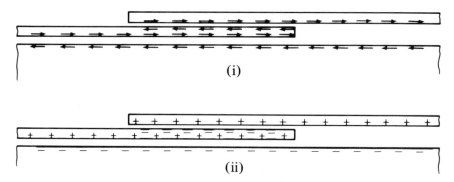

Figure 3.09a. Overlapping-electrode tunnel junction (i) and its electrostatic analog (ii). The analogy is only roughly correct in this case because the top side of the bottom junction electrode only roughly approximates an infinite plane below the currents in the top electrode. If, however, the spacing is small compared with the length of the overlap, the analogy gives a good representation of the current flow.

Current-Carrying Thin Strip over a Ground Plane

Consider a straight thin strip of thickness b_1 and width w separated from a ground plane of thickness b_2 by an insulator of thickness d, as shown in Fig. 3.09b. Use of the electrostatic analog has shown that if the current distribution as a function of x is assumed uniform, the thickness b_1 of the strip negligible, the thickness of the ground plane infinite, and the strip uniform in the direction of the current, the magnetic field varies at the edges of the strip as shown in Fig. 3.09c. Notice that the field along the bottom and top surfaces of the film strip peaks up at the edge over a distance about equal to the spacing d from the ground plane. The field at the ground plane decays appreciably over a distance of a few times d away from the strip edge. The field shown in Fig. 3.09c is normalized to the field B_0 in the center of the strip. This, in turn, can be related to the field $\mu_0 I/w$ (where I is the total current in the strip) that would exist if $(w/d) \to \infty$ by the parameter κ:

$$B_0 = \mu_0 \kappa (I/w) \tag{7}$$

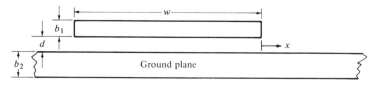

Figure 3.09b. Superconducting thin strip over a ground plane.

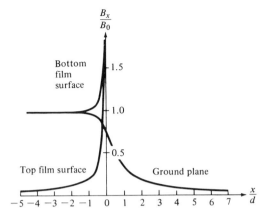

Figure 3.09c. Surface fields for a superconducting strip of width w carrying a uniformly distributed current I over an infinite superconducting ground plane. (After V. L. Newhouse, *Applied Superconductivity*. New York: John Wiley and Sons, 1964, p. 104.)

where κ has been calculated from potential theory to have the dependence on w/d shown in Fig. 3.09d.[7,8]

The current distribution has been assumed to be uniform as a function of x because the overall exact solution for field and current distribution in a strip over a ground plane has not been found. It has been estimated

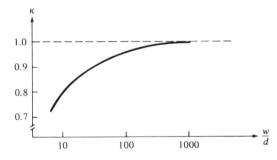

Figure 3.09d. Dependence of the uniform field at the center of a superconducting strip over a ground plane as a function of the ratio of the strip width to the strip–ground plane spacing. (After V. L. Newhouse, *Applied Superconductivity*. New York: John Wiley and Sons, 1964, p. 104.)

---

[7] V. L. Newhouse, *Applied Superconductivity*. New York: John Wiley and Sons, 1964, pp. 103–105.

[8] Recent work has given a correction factor that includes the effect of the thickness of the top film. See W. H. Chang "The inductance of a superconducting strip transmission line," *J. Appl. Phys.*, Vol. 50, pp. 8129–8134, December 1979.

theoretically that the peaking of current at the edges of the strip (analogous to Fig. 3.08b) is neither large nor extensive in the x direction.[9]

The thin strip over a ground plane constitutes a strip transmission line since the currents in the strip and the ground plane flow in opposite directions. The inductance per unit length has been found for a straight strip neglecting edge effects [the current distribution is assumed to be uniform and κ in (7) is unity]. The superconducting strip and ground plane are of finite thickness and account is taken of the penetration of magnetic field into the superconductors, as discussed in Section 3.06. In the case of the infinite parallel-plane structure, the field is zero outside the structure. It is easily verified by substitution in Eq. 3.06(6) that the magnetic field varies through each plane of thickness b according to

$$B_x(y) = (\mu_0 I/w)\sinh(y/\lambda)/\sinh(b/\lambda) \tag{8}$$

where the coordinate is inwardly directed with origin at the outer edge of the superconductor being considered. It is necessary to include in the total inductance the kinetic inductance discussed in Section 1.10, as well as the field energy $B^2/2\mu_0$. Setting the total energy equal to that defined in terms of inductance, we have

$$\frac{LI^2}{2} = \frac{1}{2\mu_0}\int_V \left[B^2 + \mu_0^2\lambda^2 J_s^2 \right] dV \tag{9}$$

where J_s is the current density in the superconductors and λ is the penetration depth appropriate to the region over which the integral is being evaluated. The volume of integration includes both superconductors and the intervening space for a unit length in the direction of current flow. Integration of (9), using (8) and taking account of the field reduction (7) for a strip of finite width, leads to

$$L = \frac{\mu_0 d\kappa}{w}\left(1 + \frac{\lambda_1}{d}\coth\frac{b_1}{\lambda_1} + \frac{\lambda_2}{d}\coth\frac{b_2}{\lambda_2} \right) \tag{10}$$

where λ_1 and λ_2 are the penetration depths in the two superconductors. The proper penetration depths to be used are those which take account of nonlocal effects (see Section 3.12). For the case where the superconductors are thick compared with their respective penetration depths, (10) reduces to

$$\boxed{L = \frac{\mu_0 d\kappa}{w}\left(1 + \frac{\lambda_1}{d} + \frac{\lambda_2}{d} \right)} \tag{11}$$

[9] E. Muchowski and A. Schmidt, "On the current distribution in a shielded superconducting film," Z. Physik, Vol. 255, pp. 187–195, 1972 (In English).

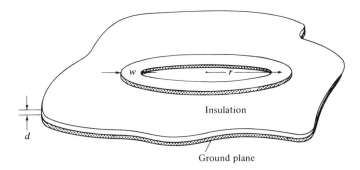

Figure 3.09e. Thin-film loop deposited on an insulated ground plane.

Problem 3.09b shows how (11) would be decreased if the kinetic inductance had not been included.

It has been assumed that the depth of penetration of the magnetic field is that appropriate to static fields. The situation is more complex at high frequencies because there the unpaired electrons also produce significant shielding of the interiors of superconductors from high-frequency fields, as will be discussed in Section 3.15. Expressions (10) and (11) can be expected to give good results, however, for temperatures below $0.95 T_c$ (where T_c is the critical temperature for either the strip or the ground plane, whichever has the lower T_c) and for frequencies below about 1 GHz.

Let us apply these considerations to the important situation of a super-conducting thin-film loop deposited on an insulator covering a supercon-ducting ground plane as shown in Fig. 3.09e. If the mean radius r of the loop is much greater than the strip width w, we can use the results (10) or (11) as good approximations. Taking the latter for simplicity, we find that the total inductance of the loop is

$$L_1 = \frac{2\pi r \mu_0 d\kappa}{w} \left(1 + \frac{\lambda_1}{d} + \frac{\lambda_2}{d} \right) \tag{12}$$

This is to be compared with the approximate expression for an isolated loop[10]

$$L_0 \simeq r\mu_0 \left[\ln(16r/w) - 2 \right] \tag{13}$$

Taking typical values of interest—$r = 0.1$ mm, $d = 300$ nm, $w = 0.01$ mm, $\lambda_1 = \lambda_2 = 50$ nm—we find that $L_1/L_0 = 0.074$. Such reduction of induc-tance is the primary reason for the use of ground planes.

[10] S. Ramo, J. R. Whinnery, and T. Van Duzer, *Fields and Waves in Communication Electrons.* New York: John Wiley and Sons, 1965, p. 311.

Problems

3.09a. Show that the assumed current density at the center of an isolated super-conducting strip, Eq. 3.08(1), is the same as the charge distribution on the surface of a thin conducting strip in the analogous electrostatic problem. Argue why that should be true. Discuss the choice of the function in Eq. 3.08(2) for the current near the edges of the strip.

3.09b. Calculate the inductance per unit length of a strip line over a ground plane, assuming both are much thicker than their respective penetration depths, the width is large enough to take $\kappa = 1$, and *neglecting the kinetic inductance contribution*. Compare the result with (11) to determine the relative values of the kinetic inductance and the component associated with the magnetic flux penetrating the superconductors. This result is modified when the film thickness is comparable to or less than the penetration depth, in which case the kinetic inductance dominates and (10) must be used.

3.10. Quantization of Magnetic Flux in a Superconducting Ring

We shall examine in this section one of the most striking demonstrations of the quantum-mechanical properties of the superconducting state. The long-range phase coherence discussed in Section 2.07 and represented by the boson wave function, Eq. 3.03(1), leads to some macroscopically observable results. One of these is a quantization of the magnetic flux in a supercon-ducting ring.

Let us integrate Eq. 3.03(7) around the contour C lying within a super-conductor and surrounding a nonsuperconducting hole as shown in Fig. 3.10:

$$\hbar \oint \vec{\nabla} \theta \cdot d\vec{l} = e^* \oint (\Lambda \vec{J_s} + \vec{A}) \cdot d\vec{l} \tag{1}$$

The phase θ of the wave function must be unique or differ by a multiple of 2π at each point; thus the integral on the left side of (1) has the value $2n\pi$, where n is an integer. The integral on the right side of (1) is London's *fluxoid*. If the contour is chosen deep inside the superconductor, $J_s \approx 0$, as

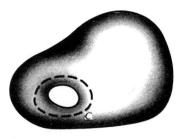

Figure 3.10. Contour of integration within a multiply connected superconductor.

shown by Eq. 3.06(11), and one may write the right side of (1) as

$$e^* \oint_C \vec{A} \cdot \vec{dl} = e^* \int_S (\nabla \times \vec{A}) \cdot \vec{dS} = e^* \int_S \vec{B} \cdot \vec{dS} = e^* \Phi_S \qquad (2)$$

where Stokes' theorem is used for the first equality and Φ_S is the total magnetic flux enclosed by the selected contour. Since the integral on the left side of (1) has the value $2n\pi$,

$$\Phi_S = nh/e^*, \qquad \text{where} \quad n = 0, 1, 2, 3, \ldots \qquad (3)$$

i.e., magnetic flux is quantized in units of $h/|e^*|$. This result was found by London in the 1930s, but with e^* replaced by $-e$, since he did not know that the basic unit of charge in the superconductor was an electron pair. Later experiments[11] found the flux quantization to involve $2e$ rather than e. The value of the basic quantum of magnetic flux is therefore

$$\boxed{\Phi_0 = h/2e = 2.07 \times 10^{-15} \text{ Wb}} \qquad (4)$$

Recent developments in experimental superconductivity have allowed flux quantization to be observed much more easily than in the pioneering experiments. The flux quantum, in fact, has become a prominant feature of superconducting science and technology.

The trapped magnetic flux is necessarily accompanied by induced persistent shielding currents, a physical state without parallel in the world of electrical science. Experimentally it has proved not to be possible to detect any decay of these currents, which have been observed to flow for several years at a constant amplitude. The persistence of currents in a closed loop is used in the practical application of superconducting magnet coils. A current is initiated in the coil and then a superconducting short circuit is placed across the terminals to put the magnet in the *persistent-current mode*. Persistent currents are also used in microscopic loops as memory elements for computer circuits.

Problems

3.10a. A ring having 10-μm inside diameter and a thickness of 1.0 μm is formed of a material having $\lambda = 50$ nm at the temperature under consideration. Find the current density (A cm^{-2}) at the inner surface of the ring when the ring contains one flux quantum.

3.10b. Consider a rod of diameter 5×10^{-2} mm thickly coated with a superconducting material. Make a plot of the enclosed flux that you would expect if you did the flux-trapping experiment in which the temperature is raised, a small increment of B is made, and then the temperature is lowered below

[11] B. S. Deaver, Jr., and W. M. Fairbank, "Experimental evidence for quantized flux in superconducting cylinders," *Phys. Rev. Lett.*, Vol. 7, pp. 43–46, 15 July 1961. R. Doll and M. Näbauer, "Experimental proof of magnetic flux quantization in a superconducting ring," *Phys. Rev. Lett.*, Vol. 7, pp. 51–52, 15 July 1961.

T_c. Consider a small range in the neighborhood of 1 G. What is the fractional change at the step nearest to 1 G? How low would you have to reduce the field to exclude all the flux from the rod?

3.10c. One may test the validity of the assumption of zero resistivity by producing a circulating current and observing the reduction of current with time. Suppose that a circulating current were set up in a lead tube 1 cm in diameter and 10 cm in length with a 0.05-cm wall thickness. If after one year, a current set up in this tube had decayed by no more than 0.5%, what is the largest possible value of the bulk resistivity of the material? Neglect end effects, assume that the current is entirely circumferential, use the long-solenoid relation for the magnetic field inside the tube, and neglect fields outside the tube. Take $\lambda_{Pb} = 39$ nm. Compare the calculated σ to that of typical copper at 4.2 K which is $\approx 3 \times 10^{10}$ $(\Omega \text{ m})^{-1}$.

3.11. Nonlocal Field–Current Relation: Pippard Coherence Length

There are three serious criticisms that can be applied to the London electrodynamic equations obtained for the boson superfluid:

   a. They are local relations between fields and currents and therefore must be called into question for situations where sharp spatial variations are predicted.
   b. They do not take account of the presence of normal electrons (quasiparticles).
   c. They apply only for a rigid wave function, the magnitude of which is independent of the strength of the magnetic field.

Point b is answered by the introduction of the two-fluid model which allows for a normal component of the conducting fluid. We shall use this approach in dealing with time-varying phenomena in Section 3.13. Point c can only be removed by a full consideration of the behavior of superconductors in strong magnetic fields. This will be left to Chapter 7 since there are many situations where the rigid wave function is a good approximation

The difficulties raised by the use of local electrodynamic equations become apparent in the extremely rapid decay of the magnetic field and current obtained as solutions for bulk superconductors. If the effective size of the superfluid particles (electron pairs) is greater than the distance over which the vector potential varies significantly, it is clear that the local relation Eq. 3.03(9) requires modification. The size of the particles is called the *coherence length* since this is the spatial range of phase coherence in the wave function for the particle. The penetration depth introduced in Section 3.06 is smaller than the coherence length for many superconductors, so it is clear that the London theory requires modification. The apparent similarity between the London relation $\Lambda \vec{J}_s = -\vec{A}$ and Ohm's law $\vec{J}_n = \sigma \vec{E}$ for normal metals, and the use of a nonlocal theory for the latter in a situation where the spatial variation of $\vec{E}$ is rapid, suggested to Pippard[12] that a similar nonlocal theory could be used for the superconductor.

where the spatial variation of E is rapid, suggested to Pippard[12] that a similar nonlocal theory could be used for the superconductor.

In the normal metal, it is at frequencies where the field varies significantly in a distance comparable to the electronic mean free path that deviations from the classical skin-effect behavior are observed. The result is called the *anomalous skin effect*. The electrons contributing to the conduction current at any point carry with them the momentum acquired from the field at earlier times in other places. As a result, the current is not determined simply by the value of the electric field at a point. Since the field varies strongly with distance, it becomes essential to account for the contributions from the region surrounding the observation point. Mathematically an integral relation is employed, as was discussed in Section 3.02. In Fig. 3.11a a pictorial representation of the nonlocal relation is shown; it is clear from this diagram that if the mean free path became extremely small, perhaps by the introduction of defects or impurities into the metal, a local formulation of the current–field relation would be appropriate.

The superconductor, as we have emphasized throughout this chapter, cannot be described in terms of a collision-dominated electron gas. The conducting superfluid is comprised of boson-like particles that are assumed to scatter neither from each other nor with other agents important in the

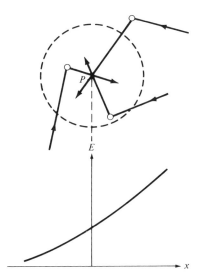

Figure 3.11a. Anomalous skin effect. Where the electric field $\vec{E}$ varies appreciably in a mean-free-path length, the electrons contributing to the current density at P have experienced values of $\vec{E}$ in addition to that at P.

[12] A. B. Pippard, "An experimental and theoretical study of the relation between magnetic field and current in a superconductor," *Proc. Roy. Soc.* (*London*), Vol. A216, pp. 547–568, 24 February 1953.

normal metal. However, because of the finite spatial extent of the Cooper pairs noted above, we cannot assume that the fluid is capable of responding to arbitrarily sharp variations of electromagnetic field. The current response of the pair fluid at a given point must depend on the value of the vector potential at all points within a distance of about a coherence length, since pairs contributing to the current at the given point are large enough to be affected by vector potentials that far away (see Fig. 3.11b). It was clear to Pippard that although the problem of rapid field variations in the supercon-ductor and the normal metal are physically different, the formal similarity could be useful. Some details are given in Section 3.12.

Recognizing the coherence length as the range of phase coherence in a Cooper pair, it would be surprising if it were independent of the physical state of the superconductor. Pippard deduced from microwave surface-impedance measurements that the intrinsic coherence length was reduced by the presence of impurities. He suggested an empirical relation for the coherence length:

$$\boxed{\frac{1}{\xi} = \frac{1}{\xi_0} + \frac{1}{\alpha l}} \tag{1}$$

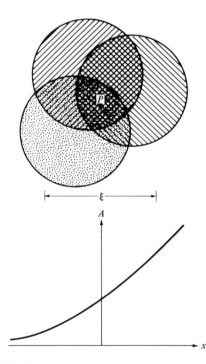

Figure 3.11b. Nonlocal influence on current density at point P in a superconductor with a spatially rapid variation of vector potential.

where ξ_0 is known as the intrinsic coherence length, l is the electron mean free path, and α is a constant on the order of unity. The microscopic theory gives the value[13]

$$\xi_0 = 0.18\hbar v_F / k_B T_c \tag{2}$$

where v_F is the electron velocity at the Fermi surface. The numerical values are roughly 1 μm, but there is a wide range of both v_F and T_c in the various superconductors.

In physical terms we have a picture in which the mean free path limits the range of pair interaction, and therefore the distance over which the superfluid parameters are correlated. Pippard realized that, although impurities introduced on a small scale, say a few percent, do not have a pronounced effect on the transition temperature, their effect on his microwave measurements was a direct result of the coherence phenomenon.

Problem

3.11. Calculate and plot the dependence of the coherence length ξ for Sn and Pb at $T = 0$ on the mean free path, assuming α in Eq. 3.11(1) to be 0.8. Take $\xi_0(\text{Sn}) = 250$ nm, $\xi_0(\text{Pb}) = 83$ nm, and use a range of mean free paths from 10 to 500 nm.

3.12. Penetration Depths for Pure and Impure Materials at $T = 0$

In this section we shall examine Pippard's modification of the London current–vector-potential relation and discuss its effect on the penetration depth. Pippard's measurements on microwave absorption in alloys of tin at 9.4 GHz showed that the penetration depth λ was noticeably dependent upon the impurity content. For example, a 3% content of indium in tin increased the penetration depth by a factor of 2 over the pure-tin value. The number density of pairs and the effective mass could only be weak functions of the impurity concentration; thus the London penetration-depth expression could not account for the effect. As discussed in Section 3.11, Pippard formulated a nonlocal theory to relate current density and vector potential to allow the mean free path to be included through its effect on the coherence length. The relation, which replaces London's $\vec{J}_s(\vec{r}) = -(1/\Lambda)\vec{A}$, was written in a form analogous to the current–field relation that arises in anomalous skin-effect calculations:

$$\vec{J}_s(\vec{r}) = -\frac{3}{4\pi\xi_0\Lambda}\int_{V'}\frac{(\vec{r}-\vec{r}')\left[(\vec{r}-\vec{r}')\cdot\vec{A}(\vec{r}')\right]\exp\left[-|\vec{r}-\vec{r}'|/\xi\right]}{|\vec{r}-\vec{r}'|^4}dV' \tag{1}$$

[13] J. Bardeen, L. N. Cooper, and J. R. Schrieffer, "Theory of superconductivity," *Phys. Rev.*, Vol. 108, pp. 1175–1204, 1 December 1957.

The range of effectiveness of the vector potential $\vec{A}(\vec{r'})$ about the point $\vec{r}$ is on the order of ξ, so that where ξ is reduced by the effect of a short mean free path, (1) becomes a more nearly local relation. With this relation one can investigate the penetration depth for various situations. Let us classify materials in the following way:

  a. Pure superconductors with large intrinsic coherence lengths ξ_0 (large Fermi velocities or low transition temperatures) such as aluminum.
  b. Impure superconductors with ξ virtually controlled entirely by the mean free path l, so that $\xi \simeq l$.
  c. Pure superconductors with small ξ_0.

Pure materials with large coherence lengths require a full nonlocal treatment and are therefore sometimes called *Pippard superconductors*. It can be shown[14] that under these conditions, which can be formally expressed by the relation $\xi^3 \gg \xi_0 \lambda_L^2$, and assuming diffuse reflection of electrons at the superconductor surface,[15] the penetration depth is

$$\boxed{\lambda/\lambda_L = 0.65(\xi_0/\lambda_L)^{1/3}} \qquad \text{for} \quad \xi^3 \gg \xi_0 \lambda_L^2 \tag{2}$$

The ratio ξ_0/λ_L is sometimes quite large and λ can be appreciably larger than λ_L.

Note that in this case there is not a simple proportionality between $\vec{J}$ and $\vec{A}$, so the decay of magnetic induction from the plane surface of a superconductor is not exponential. However, it can be used as a measure of the total flux in the superconductor by using the definition

$$\lambda \overset{\Delta}{=} \frac{1}{B(0)} \int_0^\infty B(x)\,dx \tag{3}$$

where $B(0)$ is the induction at the surface. This relation clearly yields the usual value of λ where $B(x)$ is exponential.

For impure materials and alloys, the electronic mean free paths (mfp) are much smaller than ξ_0. The mfp is determined largely by the distribution of physical defects and foreign atoms and by boundaries in samples with small dimensions. This condition is known as the *London limit* or *dirty limit*, for which $\xi \to l$ and $\xi \ll \xi_0$. If one assumes random scattering of electrons from the superconductor surface and requires the formal condition $\xi^3 \ll \xi_0 \lambda_L^2$, one obtains from (1) a local form of the $\vec{J}-\vec{A}$ relation:

$$\Lambda \vec{J_s} = -(\xi/\xi_0)\vec{A} \qquad \text{for} \quad \xi^3 \ll \xi_0 \lambda_L^2 \tag{4}$$

---

[14] M. Tinkham, *Introduction to Superconductivity*. New York: McGraw-Hill, 1975, Section 3-1.

[15] In the study of electron dynamics, there are two different assumptions that can be made about the trajectory of an electron incident on the surface. It can be assumed to come off at the same angle from the normal as the incident path (*specular scattering*) or to be randomized by surface irregularities (*diffuse scattering*).

which can easily be seen to be equivalent to a reduction of the effective number of pairs by the reduced coherence range. The direct use of (4) in the derivation in Section 3.06 leads to a penetration depth:

$$\lambda = \lambda_L(\xi_0/\xi)^{1/2} \approx \lambda_L(\xi_0/l)^{1/2} \qquad \text{for} \quad \xi^3 \ll \xi_0\lambda_L^2 \qquad (5)$$

which can give values of λ as much as an order of magnitude greater than λ_L in the extreme impurity limit.

Finally, some pure materials have values of ξ_0 so small that $\xi_0 \ll \lambda_L$. In this case the spatial variation in the penetration zone is slow enough compared with ξ_0 that London's local relation $\vec{J} = -(1/\Lambda)\vec{A}$ holds and the penetration depth is λ_L. But if the mean free path is also very small, (4) and (5) should be used.

Figure 3.12 shows, as an example, the dependence of penetration depth on mfp for tin. The London value is seen to lie below the lowest value for

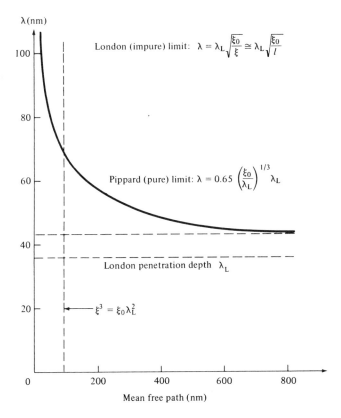

Figure 3.12. Penetration depth at $T = 0$ as a function of mean free path for tin dilutely alloyed with indium. Limits for very large and very small mean free paths are shown.

very pure material (Pippard limit) by a factor of ≈ 1.2. As we have seen in this section, that is a result of the nonlocality of the $\vec{J}-\vec{A}$ relation. At the other end of the curve, in the extremely impure case (London limit), the $\vec{J}-\vec{A}$ relation becomes local, but there is a large reduction of the effective number of pairs as a result of the reduced coherence range and the penetration increases appreciably.

The phenomenological approach of Pippard has since been confirmed by the microscopic theory based on the BCS work described in Chapter 2. Note that we have not yet said anything about the temperature dependence of penetration depth. This will be discussed in the following section.

3.13. Temperature Dependences of Carrier Densities and Penetration Depths

Long before the BCS theory established the concept of a fluid of electron pairs coexistent and intermingled with a fluid of single electrons (quasiparticle excitations, discussed in Section 2.09), attempts had been made to formulate a two-fluid theory to explain the known properties of superconductors. The most successful was that developed by Gorter and Casimir in 1934.[16] They assumed that the fraction of the conduction electrons in the superfluid state n_s varies from unity at $T = 0$ to zero at the temperature of transition to the completely normal state T_c.[17] They found that the best agreement with the *thermal* properties of superconductors was obtained when this fraction was chosen to have the form

$$\boxed{n_s/n = 1 - (T/T_c)^4}\tag{1}$$

It gave, for example, very close agreement with the temperature variation of electronic specific heat ($\approx T^3$) except at the lowest temperatures, where the existence of the energy gap at the Fermi energy leads to an exponential dependence of the specific heat on inverse temperature (see Prob. 1.06b).

A formulation of the ac electrodynamics of superconductors for nonzero temperatures has also been based on this two-fluid model. It assumes that those electrons not in the superconducting fluid behave according to the electrodynamics of normal electrons and the paired electrons satisfy the London equations. Some measure of success in describing the performance

---

[16] See D. Shoenberg, *Superconductivity*. Cambridge, England: Cambridge University Press, 1965, pp. 194–196.

[17] Note that n_s is the number of paired electrons, so $n_s = 2n_s^*$. Also n_s is not the number of electrons held in the paired state by the attractive potential discussed in Section 2.05 but more nearly includes those that are only mathematically paired, so that at low temperatures $n_s \cong n$. When $T \cong T_c$, the normal component in this model nearly equals n, so in that case the electrons well below the Fermi surface are a part of the normal component.

of high-frequency superconductive devices has been achieved with this two-fluid model.

Using (1) in Eq. 3.06(4), one sees that the temperature dependence of the London penetration depth is given by

$$\lambda_L(T) = \lambda_L(0)\left[1 - (T/T_c)^4 \right]^{-1/2} \tag{2}$$

Likewise, the penetration depths discussed in Section 3.12, which involve the London penetration depth, should employ (2) for temperatures other than $T = 0$. We see that the London penetration depth is infinite at the transition temperature but that it differs from its $T = 0$ value by only several percent at $T/T_c = 0.5$. Various other expressions for the temperature dependence of penetration depth have been derived. These have the largest fractional differences close to T_c.[18]

Problem

3.13. Calculate the penetration depth in the Pippard limit for lead at $T = 6$ K, using the data on the inside back cover. Assume the addition of a small amount of impurities that lowers the mfp to 10 nm and find the new value of λ at 6 K.

3.14. Complex Conductivity

The aim of this and the following sections is to provide formulations for the study of the properties of high-frequency superconductive structures such as wave-guiding systems and resonant cavities. The first step is to find the relation between current and electric field, the conductivity, which will be seen to be complex and dependent on temperature, frequency, and material properties. We shall derive an expression for the complex conductivity using the two-fluid model since it is simple and reveals some of the important behavioral properties. Mattis and Bardeen[19] developed a microscopic theory that is more complicated and contains the effect of the energy gap as well as a more correct way of handling the paired and unpaired electrons. We shall present only the results of their analysis here and in the following sections. Its application in the calculation of surface impedance and wave propagation on transmission lines will be discussed.

As discussed in the previous section, the two-fluid model for a superconductor postulates that a fraction of the conduction electrons is in the lowest-energy, or superconducting, state with the remainder in the excited,

---

[18] See Tinkham (footnote 14).
[19] D. C. Mattis and J. Bardeen, "Theory of anomalous skin effect in normal and superconducting metals," *Phys. Rev.*, Vol. 111, pp. 412–417, 15 July 1958.

or normal, state. The electron pairs are assumed to be immune from collisions. The dynamics of the pair fluid are studied here using the "first London equation," Eq. 3.03(15), and a momentum relaxation equation is used for the normal component to account for the effect of collisions. These are, respectively,

$$m \frac{d\vec{v}_s}{dt} = -e\vec{E} \tag{1}$$

$$m \frac{d\langle \vec{v}_n \rangle}{dt} + m \frac{\langle \vec{v}_n \rangle}{\tau} = -e\vec{E} \tag{2}$$

where $\vec{v}_s$ and $\vec{v}_n$ are the particle velocities for the pair (superconducting) fluid and quasiparticle (normal) fluid and τ is the momentum relaxation time. [Note that factors of 2 cancel in (1), so m^* and e^* could be replaced by m and $-e$.] The corresponding current densities are

$$\vec{J}_s = -n_s e \vec{v}_s \tag{3}$$

$$\vec{J}_n = -n_n e \langle \vec{v}_n \rangle \tag{4}$$

where n_s and n_n are the number densities of electrons in the paired and unpaired states.

Making the usual assumption that the total time derivatives in (1) and (2) can be replaced by partial time derivatives [see comment after Eq. 3.03(14)], and assuming an electric field in the form $\vec{E}e^{j\omega t}$, we obtain the following for the total current density responding to the field:

$$\vec{J} = \vec{J}_n + \vec{J}_s = (\sigma_1 - j\sigma_2)\vec{E} \tag{5}$$

where

$$\sigma_1 = \frac{n_n e^2 \tau}{m(1 + \omega^2 \tau^2)} \quad \text{and} \quad \sigma_2 = \frac{n_s e^2}{m\omega} + \frac{n_n e^2 (\omega \tau)^2}{m\omega(1 + \omega^2 \tau^2)} \tag{6}$$

Here we see that the real part of the conductivity involves only the normal fluid, whereas the imaginary part includes contributions from both fluids. An equivalent circuit representing the components of conductivity is shown in Fig. 3.14a. The term σ_2 in (6) is the sum of σ_{2s} and σ_{2n} in Fig. 3.14a.

Assuming frequencies low enough that $\omega^2 \tau^2 \ll 1$ (typically for $f < 10^{11}$ Hz) and using Eq. 3.06(4), (6) gives the effective conductivity in the form

$$\sigma_{eff} = \sigma_1 - j\sigma_2 \cong \sigma_n(n_n/n) - j(1/\omega\mu_0\lambda^2) \tag{7}$$

where n is the total density of conduction electrons and σ_n is the conductivity in the normal state, $ne^2\tau/m$.[20]

---

[20]We omit the subscript on λ_L here and in the following sections since the results of the two-fluid model are quite approximate and comparably accurate results will be obtained if the λs of Section 3.12 are used.

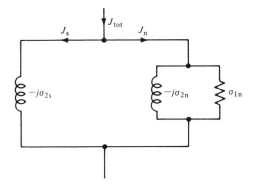

Figure 3.14a. Equivalent circuit for the admittance of a unit cube of superconductor in the two-fluid model.

The temperature dependences of the components of conductivity result from the temperature dependences of the proportions of the total number of conduction electrons that are in the normal and superconducting states [Eq. 3.13(1)]. The general forms of the real and imaginary parts of the conductivity (7) as a function of temperature are shown in Fig. 3.14b. The real part of the conductivity is reduced below the normal-state conductivity σ_n by the ratio n_n/n and decreases rapidly below T_c. This leads to lower RF losses because the shunting effect of the inductive branch becomes stronger.

The Mattis–Bardeen analysis of the conductivity of superconductors assumes the extreme anomalous limit where the field penetration into a

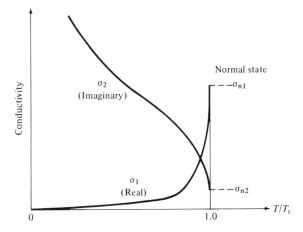

Figure 3.14b. Real and imaginary components of conductivity as functions of temperature.

surface is much smaller than the intrinsic coherence length. They find

$$\frac{\sigma_1}{\sigma_n} = \frac{2}{\hbar\omega} \int_\Delta^\infty \left[f(E) - f(E + \hbar\omega) \right] g(E)\, dE$$

$$+ \frac{1}{\hbar\omega} \int_{\Delta - \hbar\omega}^{-\Delta} \left[1 - f(E + \hbar\omega) \right] g(E)\, dE \tag{8}$$

and

$$\frac{\sigma_2}{\sigma_n} = \frac{1}{\hbar\omega} \int_{\Delta - \hbar\omega, -\Delta}^\Delta \frac{\left[1 - 2f(E + \hbar\omega) \right]\left[E^2 + \Delta^2 + \hbar\omega E \right]}{\left[\Delta^2 - E^2 \right]^{1/2}\left[(E + \hbar\omega)^2 - \Delta^2 \right]^{1/2}}\, dE \tag{9}$$

where $f(\eta)$ is the Fermi function, Eq. 2.10(2),

$$f(\eta) = \frac{1}{1 + e^{\eta/k_B T}} \tag{10}$$

and

$$g(E) = \frac{E^2 + \Delta^2 + \hbar\omega E}{(E^2 - \Delta^2)^{1/2}\left[(E + \hbar\omega)^2 - \Delta^2 \right]^{1/2}} \tag{11}$$

The first integral in (8) represents the effect of the thermally excited quasiparticles ("normal-state electrons" in the present context). The second integral in (8) accounts for the contribution of photon-excited quasiparticles and is zero for $\hbar\omega < 2\Delta$. The inertial term (9) includes only the effect of paired electrons and its lower limit is taken as $-\Delta$ if $\hbar\omega > 2\Delta$. The gap parameter depends on temperature, as described in Section 2.11.

3.15. Surface Impedance

The propagation properties of transmission lines and the quality factors of resonant cavities depend on the surface impedance of the metals forming the structures. In this section we use the complex conductivity presented in the preceding section to obtain expressions for the surface impedance in the two-fluid model and make a comparison with numerical results obtained by means of the Mattis–Bardeen expressions, Eqs. 3.14(8)–(11).

In the usual manner for analysis of the surface impedance of a material,[21] we assume a plane surface of a half space of that material and determine the ratio E/H there for fields uniform in the surface coordinates. The displacement currents in a superconductor can be neglected as usual for a "good" conductor, so the form of the results for the latter can be adopted. There is a skin depth for the superconductor, for which we can use the general form derived for conductors, making use of the complex

---

[21] See Ramo et al. (footnote 10), pp. 249–254.

conductivity derived in Section 3.14. These forms are derived for a plane half space but can be accurately applied wherever the thickness and radius of curvature of the conductor are large compared with the skin depth.

Making use of the usual expression for skin depth

$$\delta = (2/\omega\mu_0\sigma)^{1/2} \tag{1}$$

and inserting the two-fluid expression for the effective conductivity, Eq. 3.14(7), one can obtain

$$\delta = \sqrt{2}\,\lambda/\left[\omega\tau(n_n/n_s) - j\right]^{1/2} \tag{2}$$

As frequency is reduced to zero, we should expect the field to penetrate the superconductor according to the static formulas of Section 3.06. Setting $\omega = 0$ in (2) and substituting the result, $\delta = \sqrt{2j}\,\lambda$ into the classical expression for field penetration, we find

$$B = B_0 e^{-(1+j)z/\delta} = B_0 e^{-z/\lambda} \tag{3}$$

It is clear from (2) that as frequency is increased, the magnitude of the skin depth decreases. Thus the maximum $1/e$ distance is the penetration depth, which is typically some tens of nanometers and, therefore, much smaller than typical values of skin depth for normal metals, even for high microwave frequencies. The reduction of the penetration in the superconducting state is a result of the reactive current of the electron pairs.

The formula for surface impedance of a good conductor

$$Z_S = (j\omega\mu_0/\sigma)^{1/2} \tag{4}$$

may also be adopted. Using the two-fluid relation, Eq. 3.14(7), for the complex conductivity, this becomes

$$Z_S \cong j\omega\mu_0\lambda\left[1 - j\tfrac{1}{2}\omega\tau(n_n/n_s)\right] \tag{5}$$

where a binomial expansion has been used. This can also be written as

$$Z_S = (\omega^2\mu_0^2\lambda^3 n_n\sigma_n/2n) + j\omega\mu_0\lambda$$

$$= R_S + j\omega L_S \tag{6}$$

The imaginary term represents the surface inductive reactance of the superconductor and the real part R_S gives the surface losses per unit area per unit surface current-density amplitude.

The variation of Z_S with temperature on the basis of the two-fluid model is shown in Fig. 3.15.[22] It can be seen that the phase angle of the surface impedance varies from 90° leading at $T = 0$ when $n_n = 0$ to 45° leading at $T = T_c$, assuming that $\omega\tau \ll 1$. The losses increase as the square of the

---

[22] J. I. Gittleman and B. Rosenblum, "Microwave properties of superconductors," *Proc. IEEE*, Vol. 52, pp. 1138–1147, October 1964.

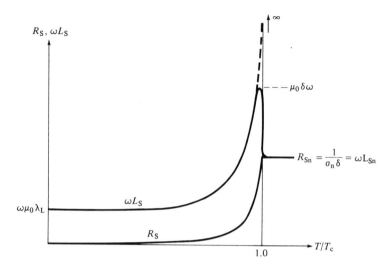

Figure 3.15. Temperature dependence of the resistive and reactive components of the surface impedance of a superconductor.

frequency in this model, whereas for normal conductors the losses increase only as the square root of the frequency.

Improvements on the Two-Fluid Model

Throughout this section we have treated only London superconductors and have made no use of the BCS theory or considerations of nonlocal behavior. In spite of this considerable simplification, the results obtained give a reasonably accurate picture of the RF behavior of superconductors. However, care must be exercised in the extreme anomalous limit, encountered at microwave frequencies above 10 GHz for very pure superconductors, where considerable deviations from the results obtained above for R_S occur. The mean free path l for normal electrons can become much larger than the penetration depth under these conditions and, as in the case of the anomalous skin effect in normal metals, this results in a large increase in microwave absorption.[23]

An empirical formula proposed by Pippard which agrees very closely with experiment gives

$$R_S = A(\omega)t^4(1 - t^2)/(1 - t^4)^2 \tag{7}$$

---

[23] P. B. Miller, "Surface impedance of superconductors," *Phys. Rev.* Vol. 118, pp. 928–934, 15 May 1960.

where $t = T/T_c$, the reduced temperature. This is similar to the two-fluid London result above, which can be written as

$$R_S = \frac{A(\omega)t^4}{\left(1 - t^4\right)^{3/2}} \qquad (8)$$

if the temperature dependences are inserted in (6).

It would be expected that the incorporation of the energy gap would improve the temperature dependence predicted by the two-fluid model. For microwave frequencies ω much less than $\Delta(T)/\hbar$ and temperatures below $0.5T_c$, the BCS theory of electromagnetic absorption in bulk superconductors leads to an approximate relation for surface resistance[24]:

$$R_S = \left(C\omega^{3/2}/T\right)\exp\left[-\Delta(T)/k_BT\right] \qquad (9)$$

where C is a constant and $\Delta(T)$ is the temperature-dependent energy-gap parameter discussed in Section 2.11.

The above treatments of surface resistance differ from experimental results by an additive factor that is temperature independent. This "residual" surface resistance is strongly dependent on surface preparation and is not well understood.[25]

To summarize, the two-fluid model gives a useful qualitative picture of the RF and microwave behavior of superconductors. It is less successful when judged on a quantitative basis, but even the Mattis–Bardeen theory is unable to achieve reliable estimates of losses in many practical situations. The frequency and temperature dependences of the two-fluid approach are close to the experimental behavior. However, at higher microwave frequencies (above 10 GHz), especially for pure superconductors, appreciable deviations occur. Fortunately, in many practical applications the superconductors are well described by local electrodynamics and, if the appropriate penetration depth is used, fairly good agreement is obtained. As a result many circuit and waveguide calculations are based on the two-fluid approach.

3.16. Superconducting Transmission Lines

There are two basic reasons why superconductors are of importance in the transmission of electrical power and communications signals: they offer a means of reducing losses to very low, perhaps negligible, levels and they

---

[24] J. Halbritter, "On the surface resistance of superconductors," *Z. Physik*, Vol. 266, pp. 209–217, 1974 (In English).

[25] W. H. Hartwig, "Superconducting resonators and devices," *Proc. IEEE*, Vol. 61, pp. 58–70, January 1973.

make possible the transfer of large amounts of electrical power in very compact geometries.

At power frequencies, i.e., 50 or 60 Hz, the frequency is so low that the losses calculated on the basis of the two-fluid model are quite negligible, even close to the transition temperature. In fact, because power transmission inevitably involves large-amplitude currents and attendant magnetic fields, the principal source of power dissipation is hysteresis loss. In this frequency range, it is therefore more useful to abandon the two-fluid model and to treat the superconductor as a lossy magnetic material. We shall consider this problem in Chapter 8 in dealing with the behavior of superconductors in high magnetic fields.

Commonly used coaxial lines, strip lines, and hollow waveguides using normal-metal conductors at room temperature all have usefully low losses at RF and microwave frequencies up to 10 GHz. They are generally acceptable in this respect except for special applications such as input lines for ultra-low-noise amplifiers of the maser and parametric-amplifier types. However, there are two important applications for which the normal loss does cause severe problems: very long delay lines ($\tau_{\text{del}} > 1$ μs) and wideband lines carrying short pulses.

We shall examine in some detail superconducting two-conductor transmission lines. As seen in the preceding section, the RF surface impedance of a superconductor is not'zero as it is assumed to be for a "perfect conductor." This comes about because of the substantial inertia of the electron-pair fluid and leads to the existence of a nonvanishing RF electric field within the skin depth at the superconductor surface. This field is required to drive the RF supercurrents that flow in a transmission line. Thus, the lowest mode in a two-conductor line is not a pure transverse-electromagnetic (TEM) wave, as is the case for perfect conductors, but rather a transverse-magnetic (TM) mode. However, the z component of the electric field is small, as suggested in Fig. 3.16a, and the formulas for TEM waves on two-conductor lines can be used.

The TEM wave on a two-conductor line has a z dependence of $e^{-\gamma z}$ with

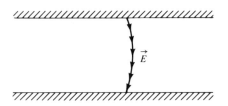

Figure 3.16a. Schematic representation of the electric field in a parallel-plane superconducting transmission line. Even in the absence of losses (ideal case) a z component of field is required at the superconductors.

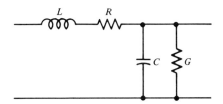

Figure 3.16b. General transmission-line equivalent circuit.

the propagation constant and characteristic impedance given by

$$\gamma = \alpha + j\beta = \left[(R + j\omega L)(G + j\omega C)\right]^{1/2} \tag{1}$$

and

$$Z_0 = \left[(R + j\omega L)/(G + j\omega C)\right]^{1/2} \tag{2}$$

where α is the attenuation constant, β is the phase constant, and R, G, L, and C are the distributed constants shown in Fig. 3.16b. The series inductance L includes contributions from the surface impedance as well as that related to the magnetic flux in the space surrounding the conductors. The capacitance C is the per-unit-length ratio of charge on one conductor to the voltage between conductors. The line losses are represented by G and R; the losses in the dielectric are represented by G and are usually less important than the losses in the conductors, represented by R. The latter can cause significant attenuation in long lines and, more importantly, introduce dispersion. (As a result, very short pulses cannot be transmitted without appreciable distortion over long transmission lines using normal conductors.)

Let us consider a parallel-plane line (Fig. 3.16c). We assume the width w to be much greater than the spacing d in order to neglect fringing fields and thus simplify the relations. The most commonly encountered lines of this type are fabricated with thin films, the thicknesses of which are often at least three penetration depths. Thus, the bulk surface-impedance relation

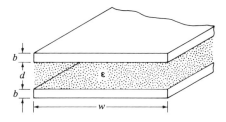

Figure 3.16c. Parallel-plane transmission line.

[Eq. 3.15(6)] applies. The total series impedance per unit length is

$$R + j\omega L = (2Z_S/w) + j\omega L_{ext} \tag{3}$$

where L_{ext} is the inductance associated with the magnetic flux external to the conductors (between them). We use the first term of Eq. 3.09(11) with $\kappa = 1.0$ for L_{ext}; the other two terms are included in Z_S. Then using Eq. 3.15(6) and Eq. 3.09(11) in (3), we get

$$R + j\omega L = \left(\omega^2\mu_0^2\lambda^3 n_n\sigma_n/nw\right) + j\left[\omega\mu_0(d + 2\lambda)/w\right] \tag{4}$$

Using (4) in (1) and taking the shunt conductance G to be negligible, we obtain for the propagation constant:

$$\gamma = \left[-\omega^2\mu_0\varepsilon\frac{d + 2\lambda}{d} + j\frac{\omega^3\mu_0^2\varepsilon\lambda^3 n_n\sigma_n}{nd}\right]^{1/2} \tag{5}$$

where ε is the permittivity of the dielectric between the superconductors.

From (5) one can find the attenuation constant α and phase constant β, but the expressions are in general quite complicated. One important simplification is the case where the second term is small but not negligible (low frequencies and temperatures well below T_c). The expressions for α and β are given for this approximation in Table 3.16. One can readily obtain relations for the phase and group velocities from $v_{ph} = \omega/\beta$ and $v_{gr} = \partial\omega/\partial\beta$ and these also are given in Table 3.16.

The slowing of the wave is accentuated as the films are made thinner (b comparable to λ); this is sometimes desirable, as in compact delay lines, and sometimes undesirable, as in pulse propagation in high-speed computer circuits. Neglecting effects of R_S, the wave velocities are given by

$$v_{ph} = v_{gr} = (\mu_0\varepsilon)^{-1/2}\left[1 + (2\lambda/d)\coth b/\lambda\right]^{-1/2} \tag{6}$$

for a line consisting of two planar thin superconductors, each of thickness

Table 3.16. Parameters for Quasi-TEM Waves in Superconducting Parallel-Plane Transmission Lines[a]

$$\beta = \omega[\mu_0\varepsilon(1 + 2\lambda/d)]^{1/2}[1 + R_S^2/2\omega^2\mu_0^2(d + 2\lambda)^2]$$

$$\alpha = (R_S/d)[\varepsilon/\mu_0(1 + 2\lambda/d)]^{1/2}$$

$$v_{ph} = \{[\mu_0\varepsilon(1 + 2\lambda/d)]^{1/2}[1 + R_S^2/2\omega^2\mu_0^2(d + 2\lambda)^2]\}^{-1}$$

$$v_{gr} = \{[\mu_0\varepsilon(1 + 2\lambda/d)]^{1/2}[1 - R_S^2/2\omega^2\mu_0^2(d + 2\lambda)^2]\}^{-1}$$

$$Z_0 = (d/w)\{(\mu_0/\varepsilon)[1 + (2\lambda/d) - j(2R_S/\omega d\mu_0)]\}^{1/2}$$

[a] Low-loss, low-frequency approximation. Both electrodes thick and of identical material.

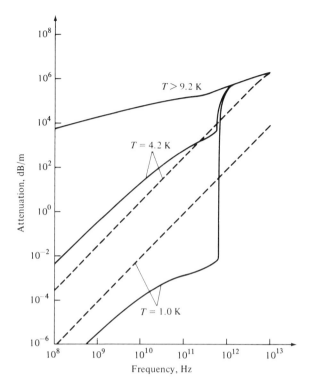

Figure 3.16d. Attenuation of waves on a Nb–Nb$_2$O$_5$–Pb–In parallel-plane transmission line. Solid lines show calculations using Mattis–Bardeen formulation and broken lines represent the two-fluid model. (From R. L. Kautz, "Picosecond pulses on superconducting striplines," *J. Appl. Phys.*, Vol. 49, p. 310, January 1978.)

b. Slowing factors of at least 10 are feasible for very thin films separated by a thin high-permittivity insulator.

An informative analysis has been made of propagation on a parallel-plane transmission line using both the two-fluid model and the Mattis–Bardeen formulation.[26] One plate is Nb and the other a Pb-In-Au alloy [with $\lambda(0) = 127$ nm]. The dielectric is Nb$_2$O$_5$ with $\varepsilon_r = 29$ and 0.1-μm thickness. Figure 3.16d shows attenuation as a function of frequency for three different temperatures. The solid lines show the attenuation found from the Mattis–Bardeen complex conductivity; it is seen that a large step increase occurs at the gap frequency when the temperature is below the transition temperature, 9.2 K. The attenuation below the gap frequency (which is seen to depend slightly on temperature between 1 and 4.2 K)

[26] R. L. Kautz, "Picosecond pulses on superconducting striplines," *J. Appl. Phys.*, Vol. 49, pp. 308–314, January 1978.

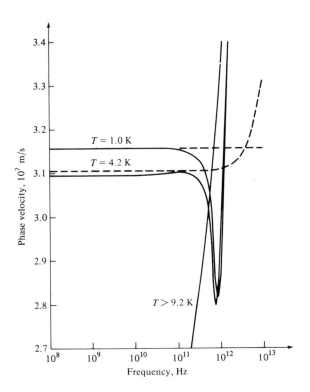

Figure 3.16e. Phase velocity of waves on a Nb–Nb$_2$O$_5$–Pb–In parallel-plane transmission line. Solid lines show calculations using Mattis–Bardeen formulation and broken lines represent the two-fluid model. (From R. L. Kautz, "Picosecond pulses on superconducting striplines," *J. Appl. Phys.*, Vol. 49, p. 311, January 1978.)

decreases appreciably with decreasing temperature. The broken lines show the corresponding two-fluid results, where the equivalence of materials for the two calculations is set by equating the dc values of zero-temperature penetration depth in the two-fluid and Mattis–Bardeen formulations:

$$\lambda(0) = \left[\hbar / \pi \mu_0 \sigma_n \Delta(0) \right]^{1/2} \tag{7}$$

Figure 3.16e shows phase velocity as a function of frequency for three different temperatures. Above $T_c = 9.2$ K, there is a strong dependence on frequency and, therefore, a large dispersion. At both 4.2 and 1.0 K there is very little dispersion for frequencies well below the gap frequency in either of the Mattis–Bardeen (solid lines) and two-fluid (broken lines) models.

Problem

3.16. Design a parallel-plane superconducting niobium transmission line using SiO$_2$ insulation ($\varepsilon_r = 3.9$) such that the zero-temperature values of the characteristic impedance and phase velocity are 5 Ω and 0.8 × the speed of light in SiO_2, respectively. Neglect losses and consider the niobium films to be much thicker than the penetration depth; use the λ_L zero-temperature value of 39 nm. Use the two-fluid model. Integrated-circuit technology will soon routinely use ≈ 1.0-μm linewidths. Find the characteristic impedance of this transmission line if the width is 1.0 μm.

3.17. Superconducting Microwave Cavities

The possibility of circuits having Q values as high as 10^{11} has motivated repeated efforts to produce superconducting resonators. The earliest work concentrated on resonant circuits for stabilization of standard-frequency oscillators, but more recently the possibility of achieving continuous operation of high-energy microwave linear accelerators has focused attention on superconducting microwave cavities.[27]

As in the case of low-loss delay lines, it is the surface-impedance function that provides the foundation for the approach to the ultimate in attainable Q values. However, the calculation of surface resistance and hence absorption using the results presented in Section 3.15 becomes much less reliable as the losses are progressively reduced because of the presence of the so-called *residual losses*. The surface resistance in microwave cavities can be adequately represented for pure superconductors by

$$R_S = \frac{C\omega^{3/2}}{T} \exp\left(-\frac{\Delta(T)}{k_B T}\right) + R_0(\omega) \tag{1}$$

where R_0 is the residual resistance. Although it is not entirely clear where the residual losses originate, it has been determined experimentally that trapped flux and impurities are principal causes. During the cooling of the superconductor through the transition temperature the presence of a weak ambient magnetic field can produce trapped flux. Impurities, especially magnetic impurities, cause the energy gap to vary locally, perhaps to the point of driving isolated regions normal. A further source of additional loss is imperfection of the surface of the superconductor, which may not be perfectly flat or may contain mechanically damaged layers as a result of initial processing. The presence of roughness, even on a microscopic scale, can cause difficulties. The sharp contours raise the level of the magnetic field locally, above the average surface value, perhaps beyond the critical value. Irreversible magnetic behavior occurs on a microscopic scale in these circumstances so that the maximum allowable stored energy for a given Q value is reduced. These irregularities also act as sources for field emission of electrons, resulting from the enormous peak RF electric fields generated in high-Q accelerators and other high-power applications.

---

[27] See Hartwig (footnote 25) and J. P. Turneaure, "The status of superconductivity for RF applications," *Proc. of the 1972 Applied Superconductivity Conf.*, 1–3 May 1972. IEEE Pub. No. 72CH0682-5-TABSC, pp. 621–630.

These factors ultimately limit the maximum possible Q value for a given geometry. Inevitably, the small-signal Q values exceed those obtainable under high-power conditions. A considerable amount of research has been conducted on the effect of residual losses in high-Q resonators, with strong emphasis on the processing of the superconductor metal. Both electroplated films and bulk metals have been used in practice, although only bulk materials are used in high-power applications.

Solid niobium cavities have been used for accelerator resonators. The requirement of a longitudinal axial electric field determines the choice of (transverse-magnetic) mode, TM_{010}, for which Q values in excess of 10^{10} have been measured.

For small-signal applications such as oscillator stabilization, the TE_{011} mode is more appropriate, yielding Q values of 10^{11} at 10 GHz, an improvement of 10^6 over room-temperature copper cavities.

The Q values of resonant circuits are proportional to $\omega^{1/2}$ for normal metals in the classical skin-effect regime, since the surface resistance is proportional to $\omega^{1/2}$, whereas the stored energy density increases as ω. This favors the choice of a high frequency to obtain the maximum possible Q. We have seen earlier that the superconducting losses, ignoring residual losses, increase approximately as $\omega^{3/2}$, so that Q values are roughly inversely proportional to $\omega^{1/2}$. This suggests that lower frequencies are favored for the highest Q values.

The temperature dependence of the conduction losses dictates that high-Q resonators must be operated as far below the critical temperature as possible. However, there is clearly no point in reducing the conduction losses much below the level of residual losses. Thus, the lowest temperatures used in practice are just below the λ point for superfluid helium,[28] where considerable refrigeration advantages are obtainable.

---

[28] At temperatures below the λ point (2.17 K), He^4, the common cryogen, is a thermal superconductor.

Chapter 4

Josephson Tunnel Junctions

4.01. Introduction

A broad area of applications has developed around the peculiar properties of tunneling between superconductors. We have already discussed single-particle tunneling in Sections 2.15 and 2.16. In 1962, B. D. Josephson[1] published a suggestion that it should be possible for electron pairs to tunnel between closely spaced superconductors even with no potential difference. An observation of the effect was made by Anderson and Rowell [2] in 1964.

A simple quantum-mechanical derivation of the Josephson relations is given. The pair-tunneling current is seen to depend on the difference of phases of the effective wave functions (introduced in Section 2.07) on the two sides of the junction. The phase difference across the barrier is seen to be both temporally and spatially variable. It is used as the variable in a macroscopic quasiclassical theory for the electrodynamics of the junction. We study the effects of magnetic fields in the junction, both fields applied externally and those resulting from the currents in the junction.

In Chapter 5 we shall point out that the Josephson tunnel junction is but one member of a larger family of Josephson junctions which have as their common feature a weak connection between two superconducting regions. It turns out that the Josephson relations developed in the present chapter for tunnel junctions apply also to the general junction. We shall reserve discussion of applications of Josephson junctions for Chapter 5 because in some cases the purpose is better served by a junction of other than the tunnel variety.

[1] B. D. Josephson, "Possible new effects in superconductive tunneling," *Phys. Lett.*, Vol. 1, pp. 251–253, July 1962. P. W. Anderson, "How Josephson discovered his effect," *Phys. Today*, Vol. 23, pp. 23–29, November 1970.

[2] P. W. Anderson and J. M. Rowell, "Probable observation of the Josephson superconducting tunneling effect," *Phys. Rev. Lett.*, Vol. 10, pp. 230–232, 15 March 1963.

4.02. Pair Tunneling: The Josephson Relations

In Section 2.16 we discussed the tunneling of quasiparticles between two superconductors. Here we introduce the concept of tunneling of Cooper pairs. Unlike quasiparticle tunneling, pair tunneling does not involve excitations and can occur even without bias across the junction. Thus one could connect a current source to a junction and, for currents less than a certain critical value, no voltage would be developed if the current were carried across the insulator by Cooper pairs.

Let us first consider qualitatively the effect on the pair wave functions in two superconductors that are brought close together. Remember that if the separation between the superconductors is large, the pairs in each can be described by a macroscopic wave function

$$\psi = |\psi(\vec{r})| \exp\{ i[\theta(\vec{r}) - (2\mathcal{E}_F/\hbar)t] \}$$

as discussed in Section 2.07; the phases of the two wave functions are unrelated and, in fact, are only definable to within arbitrary additive constants. As the separation of the superconductors is reduced, the wave functions penetrate the barrier sufficiently to couple and the system energy is reduced by the coupling. When the energy associated with the coupling exceeds the thermal fluctuation energy, the phases become locked and pairs can pass from one superconductor to the other without energy loss. We shall see that pair tunneling can also take place when there is a voltage; in that case the phases of the wave functions are not locked together but rather slip relative to each other at a rate that is precisely related to the voltage.

We now give a simple derivation of the Josephson relations.[3] The time evolution of the wave functions of the superconductors on each side of a coupled Josephson junction can be described by

$$i\hbar \frac{\partial \psi_1}{\partial t} = U_1 \psi_1 + K \psi_2$$
$$i\hbar \frac{\partial \psi_2}{\partial t} = U_2 \psi_2 + K \psi_1$$

$$(1)$$

The Us are the energies of the wave functions for the two superconductors and K is a coupling constant that measures the interaction of the two wave functions. It is assumed that a voltage source is applied between the two sides; a difference of energy $e^*(V_2 - V_1) = e^*V$ is imposed between the two sides so that $U_2 - U_1 = e^*V$. For convenience, the zero of energy can

[3] R.P. Feynman, R. B. Leighton, and M. Sands, *The Feynman Lectures on Physics*, Vol. III, Reading, Massachusetts: Addison-Wesley, 1965, p. 21-14. A more detailed treatment is given by B. D. Josephson, "Weakly coupled superconductors," in *Superconductivity*, Vol. I (R. D. Parks, Ed.). New York: Marcel Dekker, 1969.

be taken midway between the energies U_1 and U_2. Then equations (1) become

$$ i\hbar \frac{\partial \psi_1}{\partial t} = -\frac{e^* V}{2} \psi_1 + K\psi_2 $$

$$ i\hbar \frac{\partial \psi_2}{\partial t} = \frac{e^* V}{2} \psi_2 + K\psi_1 \tag{2} $$

It is convenient to express the wave functions in terms of the pair density as in Eq. 3.03(2),

$$ \psi_k = (n_{sk}^*)^{1/2} e^{i\theta_k} \tag{3} $$

where k is 1 or 2. Substituting (3) into (2), separating real and imaginary parts, and introducing the phase difference across the junction as $\phi = \theta_2 - \theta_1$, we find the following:

$$ \frac{\partial n_{s1}^*}{\partial t} = \frac{2}{\hbar} K (n_{s1}^* n_{s2}^*)^{1/2} \sin \phi \tag{4} $$

$$ \frac{\partial n_{s2}^*}{\partial t} = -\frac{2}{\hbar} K (n_{s1}^* n_{s2}^*)^{1/2} \sin \phi \tag{5} $$

$$ \frac{\partial \theta_1}{\partial t} = -\frac{K}{\hbar} \left(\frac{n_{s2}^*}{n_{s1}^*} \right)^{1/2} \cos \phi + \frac{e^* V}{2\hbar} \tag{6} $$

$$ \frac{\partial \theta_2}{\partial t} = -\frac{K}{\hbar} \left(\frac{n_{s1}^*}{n_{s2}^*} \right)^{1/2} \cos \phi - \frac{e^* V}{2\hbar} \tag{7} $$

From (4) and (5) we see that the rate of decrease of pair density in one superconductor is the negative of that in the other. This rate of change represents only a tendency to change. There cannot be an actual change of pair density since that would create a charge imbalance between the electrons and the background of ions; the imbalance is avoided by the currents that flow in the circuit connected to the junction. Thus, the tendency toward rate of change of pair charge density $e^* n_s^*$ times the thickness of the junction electrodes is the density of current flowing from one electrode to the other.

The sign of the current density can be deduced from a comparison with the phenomena in a bulk superconductor. There the current density $\vec{J}$ is in the opposite direction from that of the gradient of phase $\nabla \theta$, as seen from Eq. 3.03(7). In the Josephson junction, $\phi > 0$ corresponds to a positive gradient of phase from 1 to 2. Therefore, current density from 2 to 1 is positive when $\phi > 0$. Since there must be a transfer of electrons from 1 to 2 for this current polarity, then $\partial n_{s2}^*/\partial t > 0$. Therefore, K is a negative quantity. Equation (4) gives, for the current density from 2 to 1:

$$ \boxed{J = J_c \sin \phi} \tag{8} $$

where the constant J_c is the *critical current density* whose value must be found by more sophisticated means, and is presented below. Note that J_c cannot be evaluated from the above analysis since we have given no indication of the value of K. Subtracting (6) from (7) and equating n_{s1}^* and n_{s2}^* gives the time evolution of the difference of phase across the junction at any point[4]:

$$\boxed{\frac{\partial \phi}{\partial t} = \frac{2e}{\hbar} V}$$
(9)

where G_n is the tunneling conductance for $V \gg 2\Delta/e$ and A is the junction area. Figure 4.02a shows the I–V characteristic of a tunnel junction at $T = 0$. The critical current I_c is J_c times the area, assuming the coupling energy is constant over the junction surface. Notice that I_c equals the tunneling current that would have existed in the absence of pairing at a voltage of about three-quarters ($\pi/4$) of the *gap voltage* $V_g = 2\Delta/e$. Figure 4.02b shows the effect of temperature on lead–insulator–tin and tin–insulator–tin Josephson junctions, as calculated using (11) and from experiment.[7] The insulators are oxides of the first-mentioned metal.

$$E_c = (\hbar I_c/2e)\cos \phi$$
(10)

Here I_c is the critical current in the junction.[5] When $\phi = 0$, the current density is zero and the coupling energy has its maximum value. As the current density is raised to its maximum, $\phi \to \pi/2$ and the coupling energy is reduced to zero. For higher currents, the wave functions become uncoupled and begin to slip relative to each other at a rate determined by (9).

The general expression for the maximum zero-voltage current density, the critical current density, in a tunnel junction has been derived from microscopic theory[6]:

$$\boxed{J_{ctu} = \frac{G_n}{A}\left(\frac{\pi\Delta(T)}{2e}\right)\tanh\frac{\Delta(T)}{2k_B T}}$$
(11)

where G_n is the tunneling conductance for $V \gg 2\Delta/e$ and A is the junction

---

[4] We take $n_{s1}^* = n_{s2}^*$ for simplicity but the analysis can be extended. See H. Ohta, "A self-consistent model of the Josephson junction," in *SQUID, Superconducting Quantum Interference Devices and Their Applications* (H. D. Hahlbohm and H. Lübbig, Eds.). Berlin and New York: Walter de Gruyter, 1977, pp. 35–50.

[5] M.Tinkham, *Introduction to Superconductivity*. New York: McGraw-Hill, 1975, pp. 209–212.

[6] V. Ambegaokar and A. Baratoff, "Tunneling between superconductors," *Phys. Rev. Lett.*, Vol. 11, p. 104, 15 July 1963 (Erratum of *Phys. Rev. Lett.*, Vol. 10, pp. 486–491, 1 June 1963).

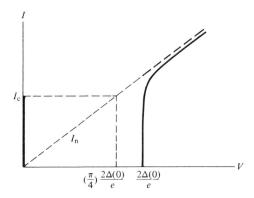

Figure 4.02a. $I-V$ characteristic for a Josephson junction at $T = 0$. The maximum zero-voltage current is equal to the normal-state current at $\pi/4$ of the quasiparticle tunneling gap.

area. Figure 4.02a shows the $I-V$ characteristic of a tunnel junction at $T = 0$. The critical current I_c is J_c times the area, assuming the coupling energy is constant over the junction surface. Notice that I_c equals the tunneling current that would have existed in the absence of pairing at a voltage of about three-quarters $(\pi/4)$ of the *gap voltage* $V_g = 2\Delta/e$. Figure 4.02b shows the effect of temperature on lead–insulator–tin and tin–insulator–tin Josephson junctions, as calculated using (11) and from experiment.[7] The insulators are oxides of the first-mentioned metal.

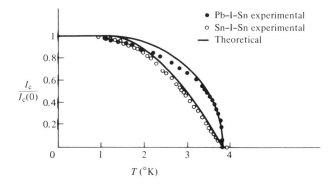

Figure 4.02b. Temperature dependence of the maximum zero-voltage current from experiment (Fiske, footnote 7) and from the theory of Ambegaokar and Baratoff (footnote 6). (From M. Fiske, *Rev. Mod. Phys.*, Vol. 36, p. 222, January 1964.)

---

[7] M. Fiske, "Temperature and magnetic field dependences of the Josephson tunneling current," *Rev. Mod. Phys.*, Vol. 36, pp. 221–222, January 1964.

ac Effects

If a dc voltage V is applied to a junction, integration of (9) shows that

$$\phi = \phi_0 + (2e/\hbar)Vt \tag{12}$$

If this is substituted into (8) one obtains the result

$$I = I_c \sin(\omega_J t + \phi_0) \tag{13}$$

so there is an ac current at the frequency

$$f_J = \frac{\omega_J}{2\pi} = \left(\frac{1}{2\pi}\right)\frac{2e}{\hbar} V \tag{14}$$

The coefficient in the last term in (14) is 483.6×10^{12} Hz/V. It has been shown that I_c is frequency dependent; thus the amplitude of the current oscillations varies with frequency. Riedel[8] predicted the form shown in Fig. 4.02c and this has been verified experimentally.[9] One important aspect of this result is that substantial ac pair currents flow even when the junction voltage exceeds the gap by several times.

It is of interest to make an observation here about the I–V characteristic in Fig. 4.02a. There it appears that it is possible to increase the current along the ordinate from zero to I_c without developing any voltage. That is not exactly true, as can be seen from (9), where the voltage is related to the change of phase difference required by (8) to effect a change of current. At I_c the phase difference is $\pi/2$, and it is easy to see from (9) that this phase difference can be caused by a voltage of 1 μV applied for 0.5 ns. Although this is very small, it could be significant in some high-speed switching applications (Section 5.12).

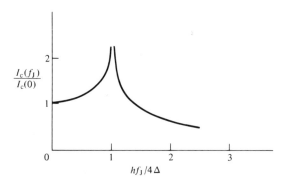

Figure 4.02c. Dependence of the critical current I_c on the Josephson frequency. The peak occurs where the applied dc voltage is $2\Delta/e$.

---

[8] E. Riedel, "Zum Tunneleffekt bei Supraleitern im Mikrowellenfeld," *Z. Naturforsch.*, Vol. 19a, pp. 1634–1635, 15 December 1964.

[9] C. A. Hamilton, "Frequency dependence of the Josephson current," *Phys. Rev. B.*, Vol. 5, pp. 912–913, 1 February 1972.

Problems

4.02a. For applied dc voltages in excess of several millivolts, a tin–tin oxide–tin tunnel junction was observed to have a resistance $R_n = 1 \; \Omega$. The transition temperature of tin is 3.72 K. Sketch the I–V characteristics for $T = 0$ and $T = 3.2$ K, making appropriate allowance for the effect of the change of gap with temperature on both the pair and quasiparticle tunneling. Give numerical values where possible.

4.02b. Find the critical current for which the coupling energy at $I = 0.9I_c$ equals the thermal energy $k_B T$ at $T = 4.2$ K. Discuss how a junction with that I, I_c, and T would be expected to behave.

4.02c. Show that the results (8) and (9) are valid even if the zero of energy is displaced so that $U_2 = U + \frac{1}{2}e^*V$ and $U_1 = U - \frac{1}{2}e^*V$, where U is arbitrary.

4.02d. Estimate the frequencies at which the ac Josephson current amplitudes for niobium and lead junctions fall to 0.5 of the very-low-frequency values. Comment on the values in light of the difference of transition temperatures.

4.03. Gauge Invariance: Effect of a Magnetic Field

We saw in Eq. 4.02(8) that the current is directly related to the phase difference. In this section we shall see how to redefine the phase difference in such a way that the choice of mathematical formulation for any magnetic field that may be present will not affect the value of current. That is, we shall ensure that the current is gauge invariant as we did in Chapter 3.

Consider two points on opposite sides of the barrier in a Josephson junction as shown in Fig. 4.03a. Recall from Section 3.04 that if a gauge change is made so that

$$\vec{A}' = \vec{A} + \nabla\chi \tag{1}$$

where χ is an arbitrary scalar function, the phases at the two points become

$$\theta_1' = \theta_1 - (2e/\hbar)\chi_1$$
$$\theta_2' = \theta_2 - (2e/\hbar)\chi_2 \tag{2}$$

Let us define the phase difference between points 1 and 2 to be

$$\phi = \theta_2 - \theta_1 + \frac{2e}{\hbar} \int_1^2 \vec{A}(x,t) \cdot \vec{dl} \tag{3}$$

We can easily see by substitution of (1) and (2) that ϕ is independent of the choice of gauge, i.e., the choice of χ. This modified definition of ϕ does not

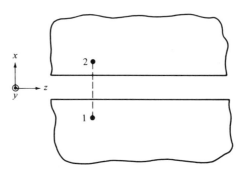

Figure 4.03a. Points on opposite sides of a tunneling junction for consideration of gauges.

affect its being canonically conjugate to the number of pairs transferred, so the Josephson relations still apply.

Now let us use (3) to develop a relation between the phase difference and the magnetic field passing through a junction in the plane of the barrier. Consider two pairs of points Q_1, Q_2 and P_1, P_2 at two different positions along the junction as in Fig. 4.03b. The choice of gauge is arbitrary, so let us choose the London gauge (Section 3.05) in which $\nabla\theta$ is zero inside each of the two electrodes. Then θ_2 is the same at P and Q, and likewise for θ_1. Using (3), we can form

$$\phi(P) - \phi(Q) = \frac{2e}{\hbar} \left[\int_{P_1}^{P_2} \vec{A}'(P,t) \cdot \vec{dl} - \int_{Q_1}^{Q_2} \vec{A}'(Q,t) \cdot \vec{dl} \right] \qquad (4)$$

The outward-directed magnetic flux through the rectangular contour in

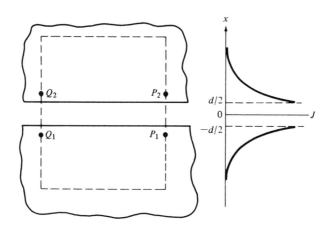

Figure 4.03b. Integration path to relate flux in a junction and the phase difference along the junction. Current density in the bounding superconductors.

Fig. 4.03b is

$$\Phi_y = \int_S \vec{B} \cdot \vec{dS} = \oint \vec{A'} \cdot \vec{dl} = \int_{Q_2}^{Q_1} \vec{A'} \cdot \vec{dl} + \int_{Q_1}^{P_1} \vec{A'} \cdot \vec{dl} + \int_{P_1}^{P_2} \vec{A'} \cdot \vec{dl} + \int_{P_2}^{Q_2} \vec{A'} \cdot \vec{dl}$$

$$(5)$$

It can readily be argued as follows that the second and fourth integrals on the right side of (5) are negligible if the superconductors are much deeper than the penetration depth. As we saw in Section 3.04, the canonical momentum in the transformed gauge is $\vec{p'} = e^* \Lambda \vec{J}_s + e^* \vec{A'}$ and $\vec{p'} = \hbar \nabla \theta'$. Since the gauge was chosen so $\nabla \theta' = 0$ in the superconductors, then $\Lambda \vec{J}_s = -\vec{A'}$. The integrals in (5) are equivalent to integrals of current density. The current is predominantly parallel to the junction surface, so those portions of the contour that are perpendicular to the surface make no significant contribution to the integrals in (5). We have located the portions of the contours lying parallel to the surface deep enough (appreciably beyond one penetration depth) within the superconductor that the current is essentially zero there, as illustrated in Fig. 4.03b. Therefore, the Q_1–P_1 and P_2–Q_2 integrals may be neglected. What remains in (5) are the same two integrals that appear in (4), so we obtain

$$\phi(P) - \phi(Q) = (2e/\hbar)\Phi_y \qquad (6)$$

The difference of the phase differences between two points along a junction is simply proportional to the magnetic flux passing through the junction between the points including that in the penetration depths of the superconductors.

It is useful to obtain a differential equation for the phase difference. Suppose the points P and Q are separated by a differential distance dz. The flux in that distance will be $B_y^0 \, dz(\lambda_1 + \lambda_2 + d)$, where B_y^0 is the flux density in the barrier, λ_1 and λ_2 are the penetration depths in the two superconductors, and d is the barrier thickness. Then, letting $d' = \lambda_1 + \lambda_2 + d$, (6) becomes

$$\frac{\partial \phi}{\partial z} = \frac{2ed'}{\hbar} B_y^0 \qquad (7)$$

where we have used partial-derivative notation to take account of the fact that there can also be a component of $\vec{B}$ in the z direction leading to

$$\frac{\partial \phi}{\partial y} = -\frac{2ed'}{\hbar} B_z^0 \qquad (8)$$

Combining (7) and (8) we can write the gradient of the phase difference in the plane of the junction as

$$\nabla \phi = (2ed'/\hbar)(\hat{n} \times \vec{B}^0) \qquad (9)$$

where $\hat{n}$ is the unit vector directed from superconductor 1 toward super-conductor 2.

4.04.   Wave Equation for a Josephson Tunnel Junction

In Section 4.02 we referred to the phase difference ϕ across the junction without explicit account being take of the fact that it can differ at different points in the junction. Here we shall derive an equation that relates the spatial and temporal changes of ϕ to the Josephson tunneling current density. It is in the form of a wave equation; it will be used in this section to study waves and in later sections to analyze the current-density distribution in large junctions.

For simplicity we shall assume identical superconductors that are much thicker than the penetration depth so the results of the preceding section can be applied.[10] The model for the analysis is shown in Fig. 4.04a. The broken line will be a path of integration that extends deep enough into the superconductors so the fields are zero along the segments of dz length parallel to the junction surface. We shall take account of the magnetic-field penetration into the superconductors and assume that the electric field normal to the superconductors penetrates a negligible distance.[11]

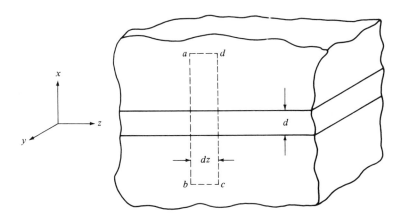

Figure 4.04a. Model for the analysis of a Josephson junction waveguide.

---

[10] The problem of the junction bounded by superconductors not much thicker than the penetration depth has been treated by C. S. Owen and D. J. Scalapino, "Inductive coupling of Josephson junctions to external circuits," *J. Appl. Phys.*, Vol. 41, pp. 2047–2056, April 1970.

[11] The penetration of the magnetic field into the superconductor is treated here in the low-frequency approximation. At very high frequencies, the penetration must be corrected as in Section 3.15. The normal electric-field penetration is just the Thomas–Fermi screening length (see Section 2.04), typically less than 0.1 nm in metals.

To apply Faraday's law, let us first integrate $\nabla \times \vec{E}$ over the $abcd$ surface in Fig. 4.04a:

$$\int_S (\nabla \times \vec{E}) \cdot \overrightarrow{dS} = \oint \vec{E} \cdot \overrightarrow{dl} = d\left[E_x^0(z + dz) - E_x^0(z) \right] = d \frac{\partial E_x^0}{\partial z} dz \qquad (1)$$

where the superscript 0 is used to signify the value of quantities in the insulating layer. Integrating $-\partial \vec{B}/\partial t$ over the same area gives

$$- \frac{\partial \vec{B}}{\partial t} \cdot \overrightarrow{dS} = - \frac{\partial B_y^0}{\partial t} (2\lambda + d) \, dz \qquad (2)$$

Equating (1) and (2) and operating on the results with $\partial/\partial z$, we obtain

$$\frac{\partial^2 E_x^0}{\partial z^2} = - \left(\frac{2\lambda + d}{d} \right) \frac{\partial^2 B_y^0}{\partial t \, \partial z} \qquad (3)$$

If we take a similar surface, normal to the z axis, and follow the above procedure, we find

$$\frac{\partial^2 E_x^0}{\partial y^2} = \left(\frac{2\lambda + d}{d} \right) \frac{\partial^2 B_z^0}{\partial t \, \partial y} \qquad (4)$$

Now we operate with $\partial/\partial t$ on the x component of Maxwell's $\nabla \times \vec{H}$ equation and obtain the following in the insulating region:

$$\frac{1}{\mu} \left(\frac{\partial^2 B_z^0}{\partial y \, \partial t} - \frac{\partial^2 B_y^0}{\partial z \, \partial t} \right) = \frac{\partial J_x}{\partial t} + \varepsilon \frac{\partial^2 E_x^0}{\partial t^2} \qquad (5)$$

Substituting the derivatives of B^0 from (3) and (4) and rearranging, we find

$$\left(\frac{\partial^2}{\partial y^2} + \frac{\partial^2}{\partial z^2} - \frac{1}{v_{ph}^2} \frac{\partial^2}{\partial t^2} \right) E_x^0 = \frac{1}{\varepsilon v_{ph}^2} \frac{\partial J_x}{\partial t} \qquad (6)$$

where

$$\boxed{v_{ph} = (\mu\varepsilon)^{-1/2} [d/(2\lambda + d)]^{1/2}} \qquad (7)$$

It is easily seen that, if $\partial J_x/\partial t = 0$, (6) describes a TEM wave propagating between parallel plates with properties different from a normal-metal structure. Here, the effect of the deeper penetration of the magnetic field can be understood conveniently by thinking of the structure as a parallel-plane transmission line. The inductance per unit length of such a line is proportional to the spacing through which the magnetic field passes, so $L \propto (2\lambda + d)$. The capacitance per unit length is inversely proportional to the spacing for the electric field, so $C \propto (1/d)$. The phase velocity $v_{ph} = (LC)^{-1/2}$ or $v_{ph} \propto [d/(2\lambda + d)]^{1/2}$ as in (7). The oxide thickness and penetration depth typically are 2.5 and 50 nm, respectively, so the phase velocity is slowed by a factor of about 6 by the term $[d/(2\lambda + d)]^{1/2}$. As $T \to T_c$, the penetration increases appreciably so the slowing further increases. Waves satisfying (6) with $J_x = 0$ (that is, for a superconducting guide with no Josephson current) are called *Swihart modes.*[12]

Now we shall convert (6) into a wave equation for the junction phase difference ϕ. Taking the top plate as positive, we have from Eq. 4.02(9)

$$\frac{\partial \phi}{\partial t} = \frac{2eV}{\hbar} = -\frac{2eE_x^0 d}{\hbar} \tag{8}$$

Solving this for E_x^0 and substituting it in (6) with $J_x = -J_c \sin \phi$, we obtain [13]

$$\left(\frac{\partial^2}{\partial y^2} + \frac{\partial^2}{\partial z^2} - \frac{1}{v_{ph}^2} \frac{\partial^2}{\partial t^2} \right) \frac{\hbar}{2ed} \frac{\partial \phi}{\partial t} = \frac{J_c}{\varepsilon v_{ph}^2} \frac{\partial(\sin \phi)}{\partial t} \tag{9}$$

in which ϕ is a function of y and z, as is E_x^0 in (6). If we take our time reference where $\phi = 0$, we have by integration, at any point (y, z),

$$\left(\frac{\partial^2}{\partial y^2} + \frac{\partial^2}{\partial z^2} - \frac{1}{v_{ph}^2} \frac{\partial^2}{\partial t^2} \right) \phi = \frac{\sin \phi}{\lambda_J^2} \tag{10}$$

where

$$\boxed{\lambda_J^2 = \hbar/2eJ_c \mu(2\lambda + d)} \tag{11}$$

The quantity λ_J is called the *Josephson penetration depth*; we shall see the reason for this name in Section 4.05. For practical orientation, note that a typical value for $2\lambda \cong 2\lambda + d$ is 90 nm. Using this value, $\lambda_J \cong 5$ μm if $J_c = 10^4$ A/cm^2 and $\lambda_J = 50$ μm if $J_c = 10^2$ A/cm^2.

Let us now consider a linearization of (10) for small phase variations with time, about a possibly spatially dependent time-average $\phi_0(y, z)$:

$$\phi(y, z, t) = \phi_0(y, z) + \phi_1(y, z, t) \tag{12}$$

Substituting (12) into (10), assuming $\cos \phi_1 \cong 1$, and subtracting out time-average quantities, we get

$$\left(\frac{\partial^2}{\partial y^2} + \frac{\partial^2}{\partial z^2} - \frac{1}{v_{ph}^2} \frac{\partial^2}{\partial t^2} \right) \phi_1 = \left(\frac{\cos \phi_0}{\lambda_J^2} \right) \phi_1 \tag{13}$$

Let us consider the situation where $\phi_0(y, z)$ is constant.[14] Then a

---

[12] J. C. Swihart, "Field solution for a thin-film superconducting strip transmission line," *J. Appl. Phys.*, Vol. 32, pp. 461–469, March 1961.

[13] The current J_x may be generalized to include the single-particle tunneling. See B. D. Josephson, "Supercurrents through barriers," *Advan. Phys.*, Vol. 14, pp. 419–451, October 1965.

[14] If the spatial gradient of $\phi_0(y, z)$ is small compared with β, the dispersion relation (15) is approximately valid.

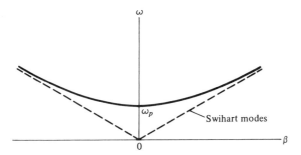

Figure 4.04b. Dispersion relation in a Josephson junction waveguide. The Swihart modes exist in the absence of Josephson tunneling current.

solution of (13) can be written in the form

$$\phi_1 = e^{-i(\omega t - \vec{\beta} \cdot \vec{r})} \tag{14}$$

where $\vec{r}$ is in the plane of the junction. Substitution of (14) into (13) leads to a dispersion relation:

$$\omega^2 = \beta^2 v_{ph}^2 + \omega_p^2 \tag{15}$$

where ω_p is given by

$$\boxed{\omega_p^2 = \left(\frac{v_{ph}}{\lambda_J} \right)^2 \cos \phi_0} \tag{16}$$

This relation is shown in Fig. 4.04b. It is seen that no propagating waves exist below ω_p. It should also be noted that ω_p can be reduced to near zero by raising the phase difference ϕ_0 to near $\pi/2$. The dc critical current has its maximum at $\phi_0 = \pi/2$ so there is little change of current for small perturbations ϕ_1.

Where $\beta = 0$, there are no RF magnetic fields present and there is a periodic exchange of energy between the electric field and the coupling energy. The similarity with oscillations of a cold plasma have led to ω_p being called the *plasma frequency* of a Josephson junction. It is the natural frequency of oscillation of a $\beta = 0$ perturbation in a junction.

Problem

4.04. The derivation given in this section was designed to show first the wave equation for the RF electric field and from that, the wave equation (10) for the phase difference ϕ. Show that the latter may be derived more directly by substituting appropriate results from Sections 4.02 and 4.03 into Maxwell's $\nabla \times \vec{H}$ equation.

4.05. Dependence of Maximum Zero-Voltage Current on Magnetic Field

In Section 4.03 we saw that a magnetic field passing through the gap between two superconductors produces a variation of the phase difference across the gap as a function of the distance perpendicular to the magnetic field and to the superconductors. Section 4.02 showed how the maximum zero-voltage current (*critical current*) depends on the phase difference across the junction. There it was assumed that the phase difference is the same at all points along the junction. However, it can vary along the junction by virtue of the presence of a magnetic field passing through the junction. We should then apply the results of Section 4.02 to each point in the junction and use the local value of phase difference. The Josephson relation, Eq. 4.02(8), will be written as

$$J(y, z) = J_c(y, z)\sin \phi(y, z) \tag{1}$$

where ϕ is a function of the space coordinates in the plane of the junction. (ϕ is also a function of time, but we shall not write it explicitly here.)

For generality, let us consider a junction of arbitrary shape and find the dependence of the maximum zero-voltage current on the intensity of a uniform magnetic field passing through the junction, as shown in Fig. 4.05a. In this section, we assume that the magnetic field produced by the tunneling current is negligible. The effects of self-induced field are treated in Section 4.06. The magnetic field is in the y direction, so that the gradient of the phase given by Eq. 4.03(9) has only a z component, which is given by

$$\frac{\partial \phi}{\partial z} = \frac{2ed'}{\hbar} B^0 \tag{2}$$

where B^0 is the magnetic induction in the insulator region in the junction. Here $d' = d + 2\lambda$, where d is the insulator thickness and λ is the penetration depth. Then making use of the uniformity of B^0 with respect to z, we have

$$\phi(z) = (2ed'/\hbar)B^0 z + \phi(0) \tag{3}$$

where $\phi(0)$ is a constant of integration that will be determined below. There is no variation of phase along the magnetic field, and we shall find it convenient to define an integral over the length of the junction along the magnetic field. All the current components along the path of the integral are determined by the same phase ϕ. Figure 4.05b shows a possible dependence of critical current density on the coordinates of the junction plane (y, z), with the integral along the y coordinate shown by crosshatching. After performing the integration we are left with a current density that depends only on z and has the units of A/m:

$$J(z) = J_c(z)\sin \phi(z) \tag{4}$$

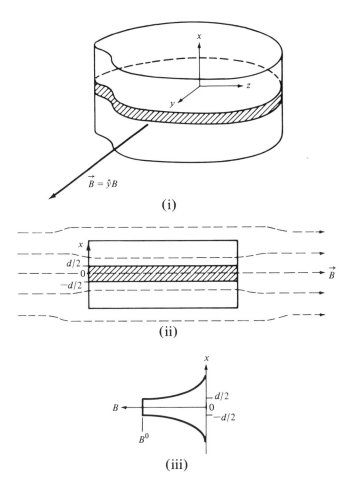

$$\vec{B} = \hat{y}B$$

(i)

(ii)

(iii)

Figure 4.05a. (i) Magnetic-field penetration through a tunnel junction of arbitrary cross section. Part (ii) shows how the field must be distorted around the junction. (Thickness of the oxide is not to scale.) Part (iii) shows the magnitude of $\vec{B}$ including its penetration into the superconducting films.

where

$$J_c(z) = \int J_c(y, z)\, dy \tag{5}$$

Keep in mind that the integrand in (5), which is the quantity plotted in Fig. 4.05b, is the maximum zero-voltage current density that can pass through the junction at (y, z).

Combining (3) and (4) we have the expression for the current per meter width of the junction in the presence of a uniform magnetic field:

$$J(z) = J_c(z)\sin\left[\frac{2ed'B^0}{\hbar} z + \phi(0)\right] \tag{6}$$

$J_c(y, z)$

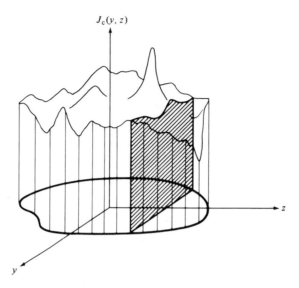

Figure 4.05b. Dependence of the maximum zero-voltage current density on the coordinates in the plane of the junction. The crosshatched plane represents the integral $J_c(z)$ [Eq. 4.05(5)].

The total current in the junction is the integral of (6) over z:

$$I(B^0) = \int_{-\infty}^{\infty} J_c(z)\sin\left[\frac{2ed'B^0}{\hbar} z + \phi(0)\right] dz \tag{7}$$

We shall later return to the junction of general shape, but let us first take an important special case—the rectangular junction having a uniform critical current density shown in Fig. 4.05c. The integral in (5) is simply a multiplication by W, and (7) becomes

$$I(B^0) = WJ_c \int_{-L/2}^{L/2} \sin\left[\frac{2ed'B^0}{\hbar} z + \phi(0)\right] dz \tag{8}$$

Integrating and making use of a trigonometric identity, we obtain

$$I(B^0) = (\hbar WJ_c/ed'B^0)\sin \phi(0)\sin(ed'B^0L/\hbar) \tag{9}$$

The maximum value of the current is that for which $\phi(0) = \pm\pi/2$. Making that choice and rearranging (9), we have

$$I_c(B^0) = I_c(0)\left| \frac{\sin(ed'LB^0/\hbar)}{(ed'LB^0/\hbar)} \right| \tag{10}$$

where $I_c(0) = WLJ_c$ is the total critical current with zero magnetic field. Since the current source has only one polarity, $\phi(0)$ flips from $+\pi/2$ to $-\pi/2$ and back as necessary to keep $I_c(B^0)$ positive. We can put (10) in another useful form by noting that $(e/\hbar) = \pi/\Phi_0$, where Φ_0 is the flux

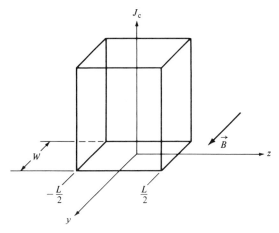

Figure 4.05c. Uniform distribution of the maximum zero-voltage current density.

quantum $(2.07 \times 10^{-15}$ Wb) and expressing the total flux through the junction as $\Phi = d'LB^0$:

$$I_c(\Phi) = I_c(0) \left| \frac{\sin(\pi\Phi/\Phi_0)}{(\pi\Phi/\Phi_0)} \right| \tag{11}$$

This result is plotted in Fig. 4.05d; it is a commonly used criterion for the uniformity of tunneling current in a Josephson junction. One measures the maximum zero-voltage current as the magnetic field is varied, and the extent to which the dependence fits (11) is a measure of the uniformity. It should be pointed out that this test only measures the uniformity of the integral shown in (5) and in Fig. 4.05b as a function of z; thus small-scale irregularities would average out in the integration. Also, recall that fields produced by tunneling currents are neglected, so the test only applies for small $I_c(0)$ (see Section 4.06).

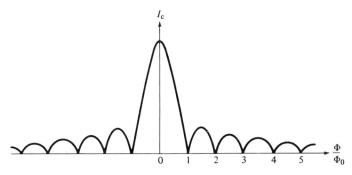

Figure 4.05d. Dependence of the maximum zero-voltage current in a junction with a current density of the form in Fig. 4.05c as a function of the flux linking the junction.

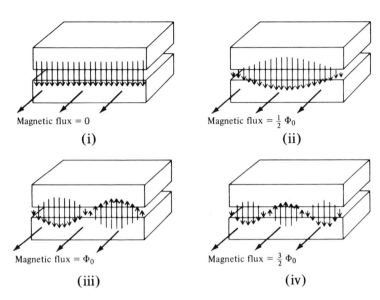

Magnetic flux = 0
(i)

Magnetic flux = $\frac{1}{2}\Phi_0$
(ii)

Magnetic flux = Φ_0
(iii)

Magnetic flux = $\frac{3}{2}\Phi_0$
(iv)

Figure 4.05e. The effect of the magnetic field on the tunneling currents in a uniform junction. In each case the current is adjusted to its maximum value. As the enclosed magnetic flux in the junction increases, the resulting phase shifts along the junction lead to a reduction of the maximum zero-voltage current up to $\Phi/\Phi_0 = 1$. There are subsequent periodic variations as shown in Fig. 4.05d. (From D. N. Langenberg, D. J. Scalapino, and B. N. Taylor, "The Josephson Effects," *Scientific American*, Vol. 214, p. 36, May 1966. Copyright © 1966 by Scientific American, Inc. All rights reserved.)

To see physically what is happening to cause the maximum zero-voltage current to fall to zero, refer to Fig. 4.05e. In part (i) there is no applied field so the flux threading the junction is zero. In this case, the maximum zero-voltage current is the integral of the maximum zero-voltage current density over the junction. In part (ii) the magnetic field is such that the flux in the junction is one-half of a flux quantum. This causes a variation of the phase difference $\phi(z)$ along the junction so that when the phase constant $\phi(0)$ in (9) is adjusted for maximum current, the phase differences at the two ends of the junction are zero; thus, according to (1), the current density at the ends is zero as shown in Fig. 4.05e(ii). Clearly, the total maximum zero-voltage current when the junction contains magnetic flux is reduced, as shown in Fig. 4.05d. When the junction contains a full flux quantum (or any multiple thereof) the maximum zero-voltage current is zero regardless of the adjustment of the phase constant $\phi(0)$. As shown in Fig. 4.05e(iii), the phase differences are such that just as much current is flowing upward as downward. The currents are circulating in the junction. The variation of current density with z increases as shown in Fig. 4.05e(iv) and as described by (6).

One practical point should be made here. A typical junction width is 20 μm and a typical penetration depth (say, for Pb) is 39 nm. Assuming an oxide thickness of 2.5 nm, we find that the junction contains one flux quantum when the magnetic field in the junction $B^0 = 12.9 \times 10^{-4}$ Wb/m^2 (or 12.9 G).

In the general case, we note that we can write (7) in the form

$$I(B^0) = \text{Im}\left[e^{i\phi(0)} \int_{-\infty}^{\infty} J_c(z) e^{i\beta z}\, dz \right] \tag{12}$$

where $\beta = (2ed'/\hbar)B^0$. Thus, $I_c(B^0)$ is the magnitude of the complex Fourier transform of the y-integrated current density (5); that is,

$$I_c(B^0) = \left| \int_{-\infty}^{\infty} J_c(z) e^{i\beta z}\, dz \right| \tag{13}$$

It is of interest that this can be used to design junctions to give some desired dependence of the critical current on magnetic field. An example in which the aim was to get $I_c(B^0)$ to approximate the form of a rectangular pulse is shown in Fig. 4.05f. By shaping the tunneling region,

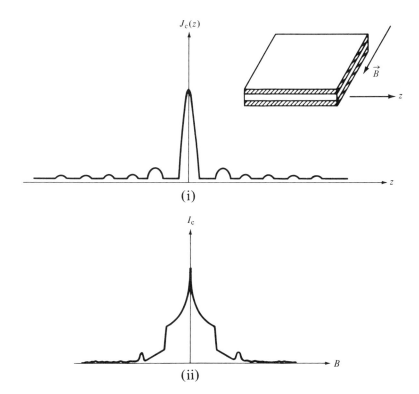

Figure 4.05f. (i) Current density vs distance perpendicular to magnetic field and (ii) the corresponding dependence of maximum zero-voltage current on magnetic field.

we can control the y-integrated current density $J_c(z)$. It is not possible to get every desired $I_c(B^0)$ because it is the *magnitude* of the transform and not the transform itself. For example, to get a rectangular shape of $I_c(B^0)$ would require $J_c(z)$ to be in the form $(\sin x)/x$; but $J_c(x)$ can only be positive, whereas $(\sin x)/x$ must be negative in some places.

Finally, it should be recalled that we have not accounted for the magnetic field produced by the tunneling current itself. The way the connections are made to the junction and the presence of a ground plane (Section 3.09) strongly affect these self-magnetic fields.

Problems

4.05a. Determine the $I_c(B^0)$ relation for a junction having a circular tunneling region of radius a and assuming a uniform $J_c(y, z)$.

4.05b. Determine the $I_c(B^0)$ relation for a junction having a diamond-shaped tunneling region. The tunneling region lies in the range $-a \leqslant z \leqslant a$ and has its maximum y dimension at $z = 0$. The maximum range of y is $-b \leqslant y \leqslant b$. The magnetic field is in the y direction and $J_c(y, z)$ is uniform.

4.05c. Suppose a junction of width L (as in the junction represented by Fig. 4.05c) is made too thick for Josephson tunneling and has two very weak shorts at $y = 0$, $z = \pm L/2$. Treat the shorts as δ functions with critical currents I_s and find the dependence of I_c of the junction on B^0. Repeat for three shorts located at $y = 0$, $z = 0$, $\pm L/2$.

4.06.   Self-Field Effects: Dependence of I_c on Shape and Size of Junction

In Section 4.05 we discussed the dependence of the maximum zero-voltage current that can be passed through a junction on the strength of a magnetic field threading through the insulating layer in the junction. We neglected entirely the fact that the tunneling current can also produce a magnetic field that affects the behavior of the junction. Two important symptoms of the effect of the self-field are

  a. the current passed by a junction does not increase indefinitely as the size of the junction is increased and
  b. there are no values of applied field for which the maximum zero-voltage current is zero, as was the case in Fig. 4.05d.

The analysis of this situation involves nonlinear mathematics and is necessarily numerical. Two similar junction configurations have been

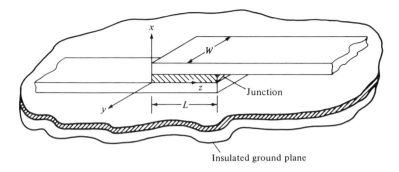

Figure 4.06a. In-line Josephson junction.

analyzed[15,16]; the results have been applied approximately to other junction shapes with some success.[17] The basic shape is the in-line junction shown in Fig. 4.06a; analyses have been done with and without the ground plane (cf. Section 3.09). The effect of the image current in the ground plane is to cancel the magnetic field produced in the junction area by the lower electrode. It also makes uniform, in the y direction, the z-directed current in the junction electrodes, which would otherwise be peaked at their edges. We shall see below the effect of the ground plane on the tunneling current.

We seek information about the distribution of the tunneling current in the junction and its maximum value as functions of the strength of the field applied in the plane of the junction (see Fig. 4.05a). We restrict attention to the z dimension, assuming that there is no variation in the y direction. As will become clear later, neglect of y variation can be justified when the width w is comparable to or less than the Josephson penetration depth λ_J [see Eq. 4.04(11)]. To analyze the junction currents, we employ the one-dimensional, time-independent form of the wave equation for the phase difference ϕ, Eq. 4.04(10):

$$\frac{\partial^2 \phi}{\partial z^2} = \frac{\sin \phi}{\lambda_J^2} \tag{1}$$

and the integral of Eq. 4.05(4) in which $J_c(z)$ is assumed to be a con-

[15] C. S. Owen and D. J. Scalapino, "Vortex structure and critical currents in Josephson junctions," *Phys. Rev.*, Vol. 164, pp. 538–544. 10 December 1967.

[16] S. Basavaiah and R. F. Broom, "Characteristics of in-line Josephson tunneling gates," *IEEE Trans. Magn.*, Vol. MAG-11, pp. 759–762. March 1975.

[17] K. Schwidtal, "Type-I and type-II superconductivity in wide Josephson junctions," *Phys. Rev. B*, Vol. 2, pp. 2526–2532, 1 October 1970.

stant J_1:

$$I\left(B_y^0\right) = J_1 \int_{-\infty}^{\infty} \sin \phi(z)\, dz \tag{2}$$

These equations are numerically evaluated using boundary conditions that can be derived from Eq. 4.03(7):

$$\left.\frac{\partial \phi}{\partial z}\right|_{z=0,L} = \left(\frac{2ed'}{\hbar}\, B_y^0\right)_{z=0,L} \tag{3}$$

where the values of B_y^0 at the two ends of the junction are different depending on whether or not there is a ground plane; it is in the boundary conditions that the differences of the calculated results originate. With or without the ground plane, the fields at the two ends of the junction must differ by the amount of the current (the tunneling current) enclosed. Thus

$$W\left[B_y^0(0) - B_y^0(L)\right] = \mu_0 I \tag{4}$$

For the junction *without* a ground plane, the applied B_y^0 is decreased by the field of the tunneling current as much on one end of the junction as it is increased on the other end, so the average is the applied field:

$$\tfrac{1}{2}\left[B_y^0(0) + B_y^0(L)\right] = \mu_0 H_{ex} = B_{ex} \tag{5}$$

For the junction *with* a ground plane, the tunneling current flows into the junction through the lower electrode and the field at the $z = 0$ end of the junction is canceled by the field of the image current in the ground plane. Thus the induction at $z = 0$ is just the applied value B_{ex},

$$B_y^0(0) = B_{ex} \tag{6}$$

Solving (4)–(6) for $B_y^0(0)$ and $B_y^0(L)$ and substituting them into (3) gives the boundary conditions to be applied in the solution of (1) and (2).

Let us look first at the calculated distribution of tunneling-current density in the absence of an externally applied field. Figure 4.06b shows that the distribution in the case without a ground plane is symmetric, which would be expected from the symmetry of the structure. The distribution in Fig. 4.06c for the junction with a ground plane reflects the asymmetry it imposes. The most striking feature in these diagrams is that when the junction length is much greater than the Josephson penetration depth λ_J, there is very little current in the center. This occurs because the tunneling current produces a magnetic field which causes a decrease in the phase difference in the center, according to (3). The Josephson penetration depth plays a role similar to that of the London penetration depth for bulk superconductors. There is one significant difference which is most obvious in Figs. 4.06b, c for the longest junctions. The peak of the current density is not at the edge of the junction but is positioned where needed to maximize

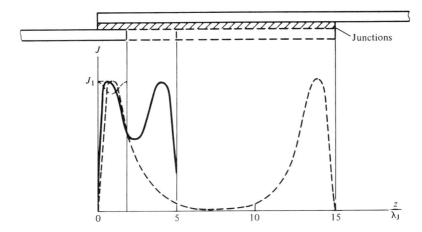

Figure 4.06b. Distribution of Josephson tunneling currents in in-line junctions of three different normalized lengths ($L/\lambda_J = 2, 5$, and 15) without a ground plane (after Owen and Scalapino, footnote 15).

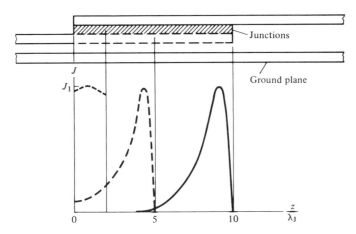

Figure 4.06c. Distribution of Josephson tunneling currents in in-line junctions of three different normalized lengths ($L/\lambda_J = 2, 5$, and 15) with a ground plane (after Basavaiah and Broom, footnote 16).

the total current. The total critical current as obtained by (2) is the area under the curves in Figs. 4.06b, c and is shown on Fig. 4.06d. We notice that the current saturates at a length of 3–4 times the Josephson penetration depth at values of $2\lambda_J J_1$ or $4\lambda_J J_1$ depending on whether or not there is a ground plane, respectively. Thus there is a limit to how much current can be obtained by increasing the junction size.

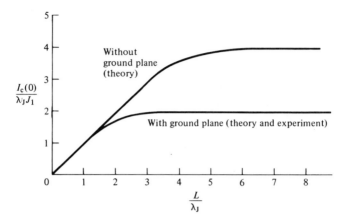

Figure 4.06d. Maximum zero-voltage current as a function of length for in-line junctions with (from Basavaiah and Broom, footnote 16) and without (from Owen and Scalapino, footnote 15) an underlying ground plane.

Now let us consider the effect of an applied external field. For very small junctions (compared with the Josephson penetration depth) the self-field is negligible and the Fraunhofer pattern in Fig. 4.05d results, but for larger junctions this becomes distorted. Figure 4.06e shows theoretical and experimental curves of dependence on applied flux for the junction with a ground plane for three different lengths. (The curves for the case without a ground plane are symmetrical but otherwise similar.) It is to be noticed that I_c does not reach zero for any value of B_{ex}. To understand this situation, refer back to Fig. 4.05e(iii); with an applied magnetic flux of one flux quantum Φ_0 there is only a circulation of the supercurrent in the junction—this circulation is called a *vortex*. Equal positive and negative currents flow through the junction so there is zero net current. The critical value of current density exists at two points. Since any net current would raise the current density above the critical value at some point in the junction, the net critical current for the junction is zero, as shown in Fig. 4.05d. Increasing the applied flux as in Fig. 4.05e(iv) so there are between one and two vortices in the junction leads to a pattern of currents such that they do not cancel out and a nonzero net current can exist. When more than one flux quantum is present in the junction, there are corresponding loops of circulating current and it is said to be in the *vortex state*. The difference produced by nonvanishing self-fields is that there is more than one vortex state that can exist for some values of applied flux density B_{ex}. This is suggested by the broken (theoretical) line in the middle part of Fig. 4.06e; the small hump corresponds to the first small hump on the right side of Fig. 4.05d. As in the latter situation, the junction contains between one and two

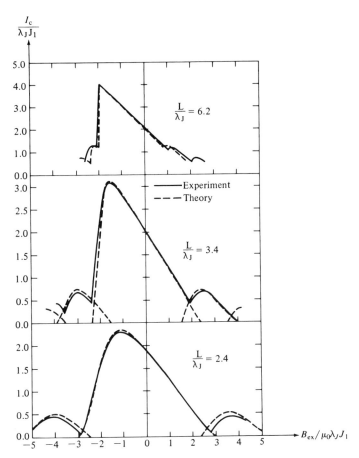

Figure 4.06e. Dependence of the maximum zero-voltage current in an in-line junction with a ground plane on applied external flux. (From S. Basavaiah and R. F. Broom, footnote 16. Copyright © IEEE. Reprinted, with permission, from Basavaiah and Broom, IEEE *Transactions on Magnetics*, p. 762.)

vortices while on that part of the characteristic. The difference here is that the curve for less than one vortex overlaps that for one-to-two vortices; two distinct states are possible there. The idea is illustrated by the states shown in Fig. 4.06f; both are possible at the same value of applied flux. The state of the junction depends on the history and value of the junction current and the applied field B_{ex}. It should be noted that the maximum zero-voltage current occurs at a negative applied flux in Fig. 4.06e; for long junctions, the value attained there is the same as for the junction without a ground plane with zero applied flux.

In attempting to apply these results to other junction shapes, one must

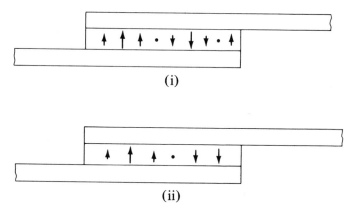

Figure 4.06f. Two different states having about the same net current, which could exist at the same applied flux lying in the region of overlap of the main hump and the smaller hump on the right side of the middle graph in Fig. 4.06e. The state in (i) has more than one vortex and belongs to the smaller hump; that in (ii) has less than one vortex and is described by the larger hump.

take care that the boundary conditions (4)–(6) and the requirement that $\partial^2\phi/\partial y^2 = 0$ are satisfied. This has been done with a narrow rectangular junction between crossed superconducting strips with good results[18] and also with more complex shapes.[19]

---

[18] See Schwidtal, footnote 17.

[19] A. Moser, "Logic gates with shaped Josephson junctions," *IEEE J. Solid-State Circuits*, Vol. SC-14, pp. 672–679, August 1979.

Chapter 5

The General Josephson Junction: Circuit Applications

5.01. Introduction

The special form of the Josephson junction discussed in Chapter 4, in which tunneling takes place through an insulating barrier between two superconductors, reveals the important dc and ac Josephson effects. In this chapter we shall see that the insulator-barrier junction is just one of a family of devices that exhibit these effects; for some applications, it does not have the most desirable properties. In general, it is only necessary that there be a geometrically small region where the superconductor pair wave function is weakened connecting larger unweakened regions. We shall see various device configurations in which this result is achieved.

Device models will be discussed to lay the groundwork for circuit applications in generation, detection, mixing, amplification, magnetometry, and switching. The device modeling also suggests mechanical analogs which can be used to gain insight into the complex nonlinear dynamics of Josephson junction circuits. It will be seen that the Josephson junction has the potential to be a voltage-tunable RF source or an excellent low-noise detector or mixer; in the latter applications, gain can be simultaneously achieved. We shall examine the use of a Josephson junction to achieve low-noise parametric amplification for receiver application.

The application of a magnetic field to a Josephson junction was seen in Fig. 4.05e to cause the current at one point in a tunnel junction to have its polarity different from that at another point and thus to interfere. This interference leads to a reduction of the maximum zero-voltage current. We consider here parallel arrays of junctions interconnected by superconductors wherein the threading of a magnetic field through the array causes interference of the currents through the junctions comprising it. This interference effect is used in a device called a superconducting quantum interference device (SQUID) which has important applications in the measurement of extremely weak magnetic fields and, thereby, of small voltages and currents. It also is used in certain kinds of logic devices.

The potentially most important application of Josephson junctions is in digital circuits. We shall see that individual junctions can switch from a zero-voltage state to a nonzero-voltage state in times as small as several picoseconds with the switching limited by the RC time constant of the junction. These junctions can also be used in memory cells and logic circuits and the times are limited by the inductances and capacitances in the circuits. Memory cells with state changes well below 100 ps and similar performance of logic circuits have been demonstrated. The high speed and low power of these circuits make their eventual use in high-performance computers and signal processors highly likely.

5.02. The General Josephson Junction: Equivalent Circuits

In Chapter 4 we derived the Josephson relations for an oxide-barrier tunnel junction; the basic results were that (a) the current density depends on the difference of phases of the wave functions across the junction and (b) the phase difference advances in time according to the instantaneous voltage across the junction. Thus, the Josephson relations of Eqs. 4.02(8) and 4.02(9), upon integration of the current density over the junction surface, become

$$I = I_c \sin \phi \tag{1}$$

$$\frac{\partial \phi}{\partial t} = \frac{2e}{\hbar} V \tag{2}$$

The total critical current I_c will depend on an applied magnetic field if one is present, e.g., according to Eq. 4.05(10); in that case ϕ is the phase difference at the center of the junction if the junction characteristics are spatially uniform. It should be kept in mind that (1) and (2) describe only that current which is carried by the electron pairs. From the sandwich configuration of the oxide-barrier junction, it should be clear that a displacement current will parallel the pair current. We also saw in Section 2.16 that, where $V, T \neq 0$, there is also a quasiparticle current in parallel with the pair current. Also, if the oxide is not a perfect insulator, there will be an additional component of single-particle current. Representing the displacement current by a capacitor, and the sum of the quasiparticle tunneling and insulator leakage currents by a voltage-dependent conductance, we can devise an equivalent circuit for the junction as shown in Fig. 5.02a. The voltage dependence of the shunt conductance can be determined from $I-V$ characteristics such as those in Fig. 2.16e. The solution of circuit problems using this equivalent circuit can be quite complicated; since ϕ must be obtained from (2), it depends on the voltage. This, in turn,

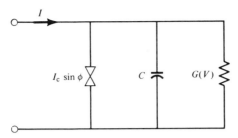

Figure 5.02a. Equivalent circuit for a Josephson junction.

depends on the impedance of the circuit into which the device is connected, as well as on C and $G(V)$.[1]

There is a whole family of devices that have in common the existence of a pair current that satisfies the Josephson relations (1) and (2), though the periodic relation between I/I_c and ϕ may not in all cases be a sine function. The factor necessary for the existence of the Josephson effects is a weak connection between two superconducting regions. As in the case of the tunnel junction (Section 4.02), the system energy is reduced below the uncoupled value by coupling through the junction. As the current is increased from zero, the phase difference likewise increases and the coupling energy decreases. When the current reaches a certain value, which we denote as I_c, the coupling energy reaches zero. For larger currents, the phases of the wave functions on the two sides begin to slip with respect to one another, with the rate of slippage given by (2).

Some members of the Josephson junction family are shown in Figs. 5.02b–d. One set of devices has a sandwich configuration as in Fig. 5.02b, where the coupling is through a layer of insulation (normally an oxide) about 2.5 nm thick, a film of degenerate semiconductor typically about 0.1 μm thick, or a metal layer typically about 0.5 μm thick. In another set of device configurations, the superconducting electrodes are coplanar, as seen in Fig. 5.02c, and are separated by a gap, usually of submicron length (in the direction of current flow). Coupling may be provided by a variety of means. The variables in the construction of the coupling are

   a. the type of material, which may be a superconductor, normal metal, semimetal, or semiconductor,

   b. the thickness of the material, and

---

[1] This model is not sufficient to explain all observed effects. See A. Baratoff and L. Kramer "Order parameter relaxation and Josephson effects in superconducting weak links," in *SQUID, Superconducting Quantum Interference Devices and Their Applications* (H. D. Hahlbohm and H. Lübbig, Eds.). Berlin and New York: Walter de Gruyter. 1977.

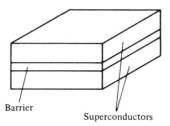

Barrier

Superconductors

Figure 5.02b. Sandwich-type Josephson junction in which the barrier may be ≈ 2.5 nm of insulator, ≈ 0.1 μm of degenerate semiconductor, or ≈ 0.5 μm of normal metal.

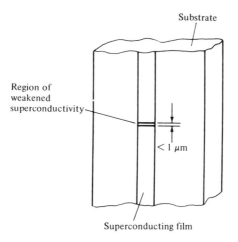

Substrate

Region of weakened superconductivity

< 1 μm

Superconducting film

Figure 5.02c. Josephson junction formed by providing a narrow strip of weakened superconductivity.

    c. the width, which may be equal to or less than the width of the superconducting electrodes.

    In the structures where an insulator is the coupling medium, the process is by tunneling, as discussed in Chapter 4. Where the coupling material is a weak superconductor, normal metal, or semimetal, the coupling is by means of the so-called *proximity effect* in which there is a leakage of the pair wave function from a superconductor into another contiguous medium having free carriers. The description of this type of coupling depends on the theoretical foundation laid in Chapter 7, so its treatment will be found there. The process in semiconductor coupling is a combination of tunneling through the Schottky barriers that form at the interface between the superconductor and the semiconductor and pair leakage through the degenerate region between the Schottky barriers. Finally, there is the point contact shown in Fig. 5.02d in which the coupling is either through an

Figure 5.02d. Point-contact Josephson junction formed by sharpening one wire to a fine point (typically $\leqslant$ 1-μm-radius tip) and adjusting the pressure of the contact to the flattened end of a second wire.

oxide barrier or one or more microscopic projections on the end of the point. The strength of the coupling is readily adjusted by changing the pressure on the point. Some applications of the Josephson effects have been demonstrated most ably with point contacts and efforts have been made to eliminate the need for readjustment. Recent presentations of fabrication technology are given elsewhere.[2,3]

There have been a number of different proposals of equivalent circuits, most of which contain an inductance in some position; these have met with some success in explaining certain features of measured properties, but only the one in Fig. 5.02a has been used very extensively.

Problems

5.02a. It is desired to find the capacitance for the junctions of the type shown in Figs. 5.02c. Neglect the material coupling the electrodes. Take the gap to be of length L and the length of each electrode to be a. Assume a dielectric of permittivity $\varepsilon_r\varepsilon_0$ surrounding the electrodes. By the method of conformal transformation, it can be shown that the capacitance between infinite coplanar strip electrodes for a unit length along the direction of the narrow dimension of the gap is given by

$$C = 2\varepsilon_r\varepsilon_0 K(k)\Big/K\big(\sqrt{1 - k^2}\,\big)$$

[2] T. Van Duzer, "Junction fabrication techniques," in *SQUID, Superconducting Quantum Interference Devices and Their Applications*, (H. D. Hahlbohm and H. Lübbig, Eds.). Berlin and New York: Walter de Gruyter, 1977. B. T. Ulrich and T. Van Duzer, "Fabrication of Josephson junctions," in *Superconductor Applications: SQUIDs and Machines* (B. B. Schwartz and S. Foner, Eds.). New York: Plenum Press. 1977.

[3] See several papers in special publications on Josephson devices, circuits, and systems: B. S. Deaver, Jr., C. M. Falco, J. H. Harris, and S. A. Wolf (Eds.) *Future Trends in Superconductive Electronics*. New York: American Institute of Physics, 1978. *IBM J. Res. and Dev.*, Vol. 24, March 1980; *IEEE Trans. Electron Devices*, Vol. ED-27, October 1980.

where $k = a/(a + L)$. The quantity $K(k)$ is the complete elliptic integral of the first kind.

   i. Argue the required change in the above expression if the electrodes are deposited on a substrate of relative permittivity ε_{rs} with air above the substrate. Take the substrate to fill the half space below the electrodes.
   ii. As a typical example, take the electrode lengths to be 1 mm and widths to be 25 μm with a gap of 0.3 μm and find the capacitance. Comment on the effect of fringing that occurs in this example because of the finite (25-μm) electrode widths. Take $\varepsilon_r = 4$.

5.02b. Calculate the capacitance of a sandwich-type junction in which the barrier is 2.5 nm of Nb_2O_5, the relative dielectric constant of which can be taken to be 29 if the junction size is 100 μm^2. Compare the result with the capacitance found in Prob. 5.02a.

5.03. Static $I-V$ Characteristics with a dc Source

In this section we shall study the equivalent circuit shown in Fig. 5.02a with G constant following the analyses of Stewart[4] and McCumber.[5] It is assumed that the circuit is driven by a dc current source; one could also study how to modify the results for a source with a finite internal impedance. The differential equation for the circuit and source is[6]

$$I = I_c \sin \phi + GV + C \frac{dV}{dt} \tag{1}$$

By making use of Eq. 5.02(2), the right side of (1) can be put entirely in terms of ϕ:

$$I = \frac{\hbar C}{2e} \frac{d^2\phi}{dt^2} + \frac{\hbar G}{2e} \frac{d\phi}{dt} + I_c \sin \phi \tag{2}$$

If (2) is divided by I_c and t is replaced by a new time variable,

$$\theta \stackrel{\Delta}{=} \omega_c t \stackrel{\Delta}{=} (2e/\hbar)(I_c/G)t \tag{3}$$

we obtain

$$\frac{I}{I_c} = \beta_c \frac{d^2\phi}{d\theta^2} + \frac{d\phi}{d\theta} + \sin \phi \tag{4}$$

---

[4] W. C. Stewart, "Current–voltage characteristics of Josephson junctions," *Appl. Phys. Lett.*, Vol. 12, pp. 277–280, 15 April 1968.

[5] D. E. McCumber, "Effect of ac impedance on dc voltage–current characteristics of superconductor weak-link junctions," *J. Appl. Phys.*, Vol. 39, pp. 3113–3118, June 1968.

[6] There is properly another term in (1) which represents an interference between the pair current and the quasiparticle current. It does not seem to affect applications and is normally omitted. For a recent discussion of the term, see K. K. Likharev, A. B. Zorin, I. O. Kulik, and J. R. Schrieffer, "On the sign of the quasiparticle-pair interference current in superconducting tunnel junctions," *Sov. J. Low Temp. Phys.*, Vol. 5, No. 10, 1979.

where

$$\boxed{\beta_c \overset{\Delta}{=} \frac{\omega_c C}{G} = \left(\frac{2e}{\hbar}\right)\left(\frac{I_c}{G}\right)\frac{C}{G}} \tag{5}$$

Notice that ω_c is the Josephson angular frequency [see Eq. 4.02(14)] for a voltage corresponding to the maximum zero-voltage current I_c and the conductance G. Also, note that β_c is the ratio of the capacitive susceptance at that frequency to the shunt conductance.

The aim is to find the average value of voltage $V = \langle(\hbar/2e)d\phi/dt\rangle$ with a given constant applied current. In the simplest case, where $C = 0$ and hence $\beta_c = 0$, (4) can be integrated directly (see Prob. 5.03a), and we obtain for positive current

$$V = 0 \qquad\qquad \text{for} \quad I < I_c$$
$$V = (I_c/G)\left[(I/I_c)^2 - 1\right]^{1/2} \quad \text{for} \quad I > I_c \tag{6}$$

This parabolic dependence for $I > I_c$ and $\beta_c = 0$ is shown in Fig. 5.03a, where normalized voltage GV/I_c is plotted as a function of normalized current I/I_c.[7] We see that for each value of current there is a unique value of voltage. The line marked $\beta_c = \infty$ in Fig. 5.03a describes the relation

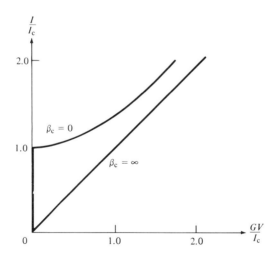

Figure 5.03a. Normalized I–V characteristics for a Josephson junction described by the equivalent circuit of Fig. 5.02a for cases of negligible ($\beta_c = 0$) and dominating ($\beta_c = \infty$) capacitance.

---

[7] It should be kept in mind that the Josephson junction is a symmetric device, so all I–V characteristics have symmetry about the origin. In this text we show only the positive portion for economy of space.

between I and V for a constant conductance G by itself. It is clear that an appreciable amount of dc current is flowing through the Josephson junction at low voltages for $\beta_c = 0$. If the voltage across the junction were dc only, there would be only a sinusoidal ac current, according to Eq. 4.02(13), with a zero average value. Actually, the ac current through the junction must pass through the shunt conductance as the source has infinite impedance; it thus produces an alternating voltage across the junction, so the rate of change of phase is no longer constant. The result is a complex temporal variation of current with periodicity equal to the Josephson frequency equivalent of the average voltage. Figure 5.03b shows how the current becomes increasingly nonsinusoidal as the voltage approaches zero. It is the average value of this wave that adds to the current through the conductance to give the $\beta_c = 0$ curve in Fig. 5.03a.

The situation becomes appreciably more complex when the capacitance is not negligible ($\beta_c \neq 0$). For $I > I_c$ there is again a unique value of V for each I. However, there is a range of current $I_{min} \leqslant I \leqslant I_c$ in which there are two values of voltage, $V = 0$ and $V \neq 0$. Also, below I_{min} the voltage is zero. To obtain the actual relation between the (normalized) average voltage and the constant applied current, (4) must be integrated numerically. The result for $\beta_c = 4$ is shown in Fig. 5.03c. If a junction with $\beta_c = 4$ were connected to a dc current source and the current raised from zero, the I–V characteristic would be traced out as shown by the arrows. When the current reaches I_c, an abrupt jump to a finite voltage occurs and upon subsequent reduction of the current, the voltage returns to zero along a different path. Here, as in the $\beta_c = 0$ case, the ac current in the junction has an average value which contributes to the total dc current, so that $I > GV$.

One can repeat the calculations for various β_c and find the $(I/I_c)_{min}$ and, hence, the amount of hysteresis in each case. Figure 5.03d shows the

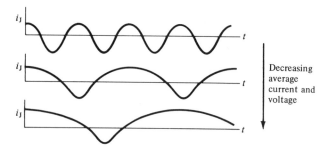

Decreasing average current and voltage

Figure 5.03b. Time dependence of current through the Josephson junction in the circuit of Fig. 5.02a for small β_c at three different points on the I–V characteristic. The average values of these functions measure the difference of the I–V characteristic from that for $\beta_c = \infty$, where only the current through G determines the average voltage.

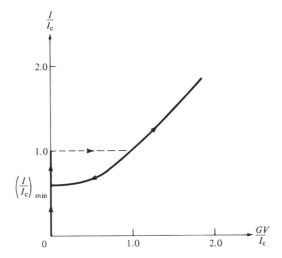

Figure 5.03c. Normalized $I-V$ characteristic for a junction represented by the circuit of Fig. 5.02a with $\beta_c = 4$.

dependence of $(I/I_c)_{min}$ on β_c as originally found independently by Stewart and McCumber. The case of $\beta_c \cong \infty$ is where the capacitive susceptance at frequency ω_c [Eq. (3)] is very much larger than the conductance. One finds that, for $\beta_c = \infty$, the current rises to I_c and then makes an abrupt transition to the straight line in Fig. 5.03a. Subsequent decrease of current follows the straight line to the origin because $(I/I_c)_{min} = 0$. In this

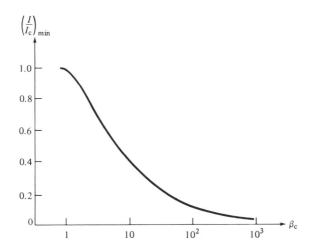

Figure 5.03d. Dependence of the minimum current (when current is decreased from values greater than I_c) in the shunt–GC equivalent circuit in Fig. 5.02a on the admittance ratio β_c.

case the ac current in the junction (Fig. 5.03b) is shunted through the capacitance and does not develop an ac voltage. Thus the current in the junction is purely sinusoidal and does not contribute a dc component to the total current.

For junctions of the coplanar type (Fig. 5.02c), the capacitance is very small and $\beta_c \approx 0$ under almost all circumstances. In the sandwich-type junctions shown in Fig. 5.02b, there is a substantial amount of capacitance, and significant amounts of hysteresis can often be seen in the $I-V$ characteristics. In all existing data on junctions with normal-metal coupling, the low resistance of the metal leads to nonhysteretic $I-V$ characteristics ($\beta_c \approx 0$). At the other extreme in the insulating-barrier junctions, it is nearly impossible to get tunneling conductances high enough to avoid hysteresis. The semiconductor-coupled junctions have been made both with hysteretic and nonhysteretic $I-V$ characteristics. Point contacts typically have $0 < \beta_c < 10$.

We note that the shape of the $I-V$ characteristic for $\beta_c = \infty$ (Fig. 5.03a) is quite different from that given by the solid line in Fig. 4.02a for a tunnel junction. The reason for this discrepancy is that the shunt conductance in a tunnel junction is actually far from constant. Reasonably good calculations of the $I-V$ characteristics can be made by putting in a voltage-dependent conductance determined from the quasiparticle tunneling $I-V$ characteristic.

Problems

5.03a. Integrate (4) to show that the $I-V$ characteristic for $\beta_c = 0$ has the parabolic form given by (6) for $I > I_c$.

5.03b. Junctions with $\beta_c \cong 0$ are used in certain applications where the dynamic impedance of the junction is an important factor. Assuming $\beta_c = 0$, derive an expression for the dynamic impedance of the junction at low frequencies where the slope of the $I-V$ characteristic can be used. If a dc constant-current source is used to bias the junction at the point where the low-frequency dynamic resistance is $5/G$, where G is the junction shunt conductance, what is the highest frequency for which you would feel justified to use the slope of the $I-V$ characteristic? State your reasoning. Illustrate numerically using the typical value $I_c/G = 1$ mV.

5.03c. Estimate the average power supplied to a junction by an ideal ac current source operating at a low frequency. Assume that the junction shunt resistance is 1 Ω, $\beta_c = 4.0$, the peak current is 1.0001 I_c, and the average current is zero. Note that the $I-V$ characteristics given in this section also apply to negative currents. The latent heat of vaporization of liquid helium is 0.605 kcal/l. Calculate the time required for the heat generated by cycling this junction to evaporate one liter of liquid helium.

5.03d. A small-area Josephson junction is supplied with a constant current much less than the critical current in the period $-\infty < t \leqslant 0$. At $t = 0$ the source current is reduced to zero. Linearize the differential equation describing the junction behavior and find the solution. Show that in the case of negligible losses, the frequency of oscillation is given by $\omega_p = (2eI_c/\hbar C)^{1/2}$ and that for a small junction, this is the same as the "plasma oscillation" frequency introduced in Eq. 4.04(16). Note that the time for a decay by $1/e$ in the presence of losses is $2C/G$.

5.04. Analogs of Small-Area Josephson Junctions

There are two different kinds of mechanical analog for the Josephson junction which have proved to be of immense value in understanding the complex nonlinear phenomena that take place in a junction both when it is acting alone and when connected to some kind of outside circuit such as a resonant cavity. The first is a driven pendulum—many of these have been used to gain insights that do not come from studying calculated numerical results. The second is used almost exclusively for thought experiments—it is not convenient for use as a real experiment, since it involves a ball rolling down a corrugated slope which must, perforce, be of limited length.

In addition to the mechanical analogs, two different electronic analogs have been developed.[8] These do not share with the mechanical analogs the advantage of easy visualization but rather provide a means for readily evaluating changes in the parameters of the simulated junction or the circuit to which it is attached. The simulated results suffer somewhat in accuracy but facilitate the determination of ranges of parameters that are of interest for more precise numerical calculations or experiments. We shall concentrate here on the mechanical analogs because of their importance in visualizing the complex behavior of the Josephson junction.

In this section we shall study the application of these analogs to junctions small enough to ensure that internal inductances can be neglected. To illustrate the point, consider a junction of the sandwich type to be divided into two halves, as shown by the broken line in Fig. 5.04a. Each half could be represented by an equivalent circuit of the type in Fig. 5.02a. A consideration of the loop shown by dotted lines in Fig. 5.04a suggests that there is a certain inductance associated with the loop. Thus the equivalent circuit for the junction could take the form in Fig. 5.04b. We shall assume that the inductive reactances are negligible with respect to the impedances of the shunt circuits; thus the junction can be represented by a single shunt circuit. This does not require the current to be uniform in the

[8] C. A. Hamilton, "Analog simulation of a Josephson junction," *Rev. Sci. Instrum.*, Vol. 43, pp. 445–447, March 1972. C. K. Bak and N. F. Pedersen, "Josephson junction analog and quasiparticle-pair current," *Appl. Phys. Lett.*, Vol. 22, pp. 149–150, 15 February 1973.

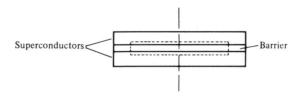

Figure 5.04a. Josephson junction showing a possible subdivision (by dashed line) for equivalent circuit purposes. The dotted line is a loop along which an inductance can be defined.

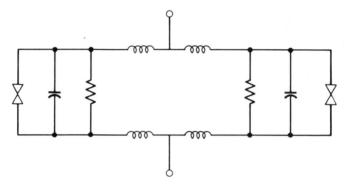

Figure 5.04b. Equivalent circuit for the subdivided junction shown in Fig. 5.04a.

junction and the critical current may depend on an applied magnetic field as mentioned in connection with Eqs. 5.02(1) and 5.02(2).

Driven-Pendulum Analog

The fundamental equation for a pendulum relates the torque to the angular acceleration:

$$T = \mathfrak{M} \, d^2\phi/dt^2 \tag{1}$$

The constant $\mathfrak{M}$ is the moment of inertia of the pendulum. The torque T consists of

a. the applied torque T_a;
b. the gravitationally produced restoring torque, $mgl \sin \phi$, where m is the mass of the pendulum bob, g is the gravitational acceleration, l is the length of the pendulum arm (assumed weightless), and ϕ is the angle from the vertical shown in Fig. 5.04c;
c. the damping torque $D \, d\phi/dt$, where D is a damping constant.

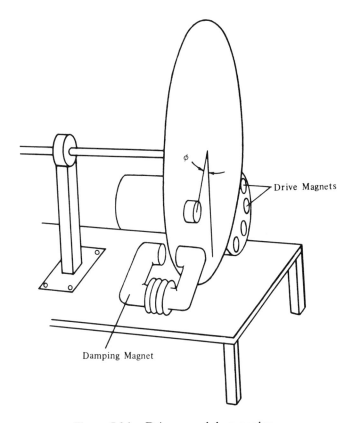

Figure 5.04c. Driven-pendulum analog.

Combining these, we get

$$\mathfrak{M} \frac{d^2\phi}{dt^2} + D \frac{d\phi}{dt} + mgl \sin \phi = T_a \tag{2}$$

This is to be compared with Eq. 5.03(2):

$$\frac{\hbar C}{2e} \frac{d^2\phi}{dt^2} + \frac{\hbar G}{2e} \frac{d\phi}{dt} + I_c \sin \phi = I \tag{3}$$

By comparing (2) and (3), we see that

a. the angle ϕ is the analog of the phase difference ϕ,
b. the angular velocity is the analog of voltage,
c. the moment of inertia is the analog of capacitance,
d. the damping constant is the analog of conductance,

e. the maximum gravitational torque is the analog of the maximum zero-voltage current, and

f. the applied torque is the analog of the source current.

The actual form of an analog of this type is shown in Fig. 5.04c. The mass m of the pendulum bob is attached to the large disk at a distance l from its center. The moment of inertia $\mathfrak{M}$ includes all the parts that rotate with the disk (pendulum bob, axle, bearings). The damping D is provided in part by the friction in the system but also by the field of an electromagnet that induces eddy currents in the disk which react, in turn, on the field. The applied torque T_a is provided by a disk of spinning permanent magnets which also induce eddy currents that interact with the field of the magnets producing the currents.

By setting a low rate of rotation of the motor turning the disk containing the permanent magnets, the pendulum mass is moved to an angle ϕ off the vertical; this corresponds to an equal amount of phase difference across the junction. When ϕ exceeds $90°$, the restoring torque decreases and the pendulum disk goes into rotation. This transition corresponds to that shown in Fig. 5.03c by the broken line. A steady average rate of rotation $d\phi/dt$ is reached and this average corresponds to the average voltage where the broken line joins the solid line in Fig. 5.03c. Since the disk carries an eccentric mass m, the rate of rotation is not uniform; rather it increases where the gravitational torque is aiding the applied torque and decreases where gravity opposes the applied torque. Likewise, the instantaneous voltage differs from the average voltage in the actual junction. Subsequent increase of the applied torque increases the average angular velocity. Upon decreasing the applied torque, a different torque–velocity locus is traced out. The inertia of the disk (and associated elements) keeps it rotating for applied torques lower than that required to initiate rotation, which is mgl. An experimental torque–velocity relation for an analog of the type discussed here is shown in Fig. 5.04d. The analog equivalent of β_c is

$$\mathfrak{B}_c = mgl\left(\mathfrak{M}/D^2\right) \tag{4}$$

By taking the ratio T_a/mgl at the point where the decreasing torque characteristic joins the $d\phi/dt = 0$ axis and applying the curve in Fig. 5.03d, we find that $\mathfrak{B}_c \cong 6.5$ for the example in Fig. 5.04d.[9] One can easily change $\mathfrak{B}_c$ by changing the current in the damping electromagnet.

This analog has been very fruitfully employed to study complex situations including the coupling of a Josephson junction to a resonant cavity.

---

[9] D. B. Sullivan and J. E. Zimmerman, "Mechanical analogs of time dependent Josephson phenomena," *Am. J. Phys.*, Vol. 39, pp. 1504–1517, December 1971. (The value of β_c found in this reference was based on measurements of the parameters of the mechanical system.)

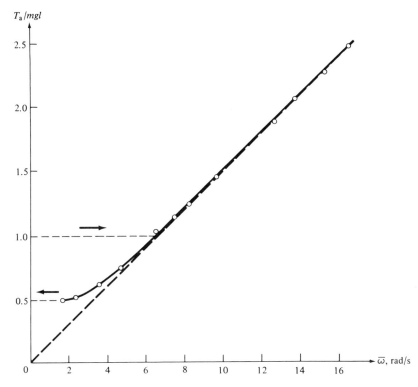

Figure 5.04d. Relation between the (normalized) torque and average rate of rotation obtained on a driven-pendulum analog. (From D. B. Sullivan and J. E. Zimmerman, *Am. J. Phys.*, Vol. 39, p. 1510, December 1971.)

"Washboard" Analog

The equation of motion for a ball rolling down a washboard-like hill as shown in Fig. 5.04e can be cast into the form of (3) so a formal analogy can be established. The average slope of the hill corresponds to the source current and the ripples on the hill are analogous to the current $I_c \sin \phi$ through the ideal Josephson element. The mass of the ball corresponds to the capacitance and is the energy-storage factor. The ball is assumed to be moving in a viscous fluid and the drag thereby imposed corresponds to the conductance in an actual junction.

If the ball is initially at rest, the average slope of the washboard is zero (corresponding to zero source current), and the slope is gradually increased, the ball will shift to a new position within one ripple. When the average slope is increased sufficiently, the slope at every point on the board will be negative and the ball will start rolling. This occurs at a slope corresponding to the critical current. The ball will reach some average

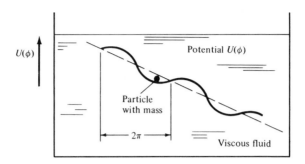

Figure 5.04e. Washboard analog of the Josephson junction.

velocity which is the analog of the dc voltage. If the board is then lowered gradually past the slope where the ball started to roll, the ball will not stop because its inertia will carry it over the places at each ripple where it must go uphill. However, if the viscosity of the fluid is sufficient, the ball will stop when the average slope is reduced to that at which rolling started. Thus different amounts of viscosity (corresponding to conductance) can lead to average slope-vs-velocity relations with differing amounts of hysteresis, as in the curves for the actual junction in Section 5.03. One advantage of this kind of analog is that it facilitates consideration of the effect of different kinds of functional relationship between the Josephson current and the phase difference by imagining ripples of different shapes.

We have given only a superficial treatment of analogs for small junctions and have not discussed analogs for large and coupled junctions. For an extended discussion of mechanical analogs, see Fulton.[10]

Problem

5.04. A disc analog made as shown in this section exhibited oscillations of velocity about the average value. These oscillatitons increased in amplitude as the average velocity decreased. Discuss this phenomenon in terms of physical quantities in a junction.

5.05. RF Effects in Josephson Junctions

The intent of this section is to show the effect of driving a Josephson junction simultaneously by both dc and ac sources, which is the usual situation in detection applications. Typically, the junction is connected to a dc bias source through an impedance and the RF signal is impressed on

---

[10] T. A. Fulton, "Equivalent circuits and analogs of the Josephson effect," in *Superconductor Applications: SQUIDs and Machines* (B. B. Schwartz and S. Foner, Eds.). New York: Plenum Press, 1977.

the junction by placing it in a microwave waveguide or cavity. For optimum matching to the microwave system, the source impedance must equal the conjugate of that of the junction. The analysis of the situation of matched impedance would be quite complex; instead we look at two limiting cases which give important insight into the RF operation of a junction. The first employs dc and ac voltage sources (zero internal impedance) and the second uses dc and ac current sources (infinite internal impedance). The former permits analytic results which can be qualitatively adjusted to explain important features of the $I-V$ characteristic. Results with the current-source model can only be obtained numerically but correspond more closely to experimental data.

Voltage-Source Model

Here we assume that both the dc and ac sources have zero internal impedance as shown in Fig. 5.05a. We use the shunt GC equivalent circuit (with constant G) for the junction since it gives good agreement in many cases. By combining Eqs. 5.02(1) and 5.02(2), the current through the ideal Josephson element becomes

$$i_J(t) = I_c \sin\left[\int_0^t \frac{2ev(t')}{\hbar} dt' + \phi_0\right] \tag{1}$$

Taking the voltage to be $V + V_S \cos \omega_S t$, the current (1) becomes

$$i_J(t) = I_c \sin\left[(2eV/\hbar)t + (2eV_S/\hbar\omega_S)\sin \omega_S t + \phi_0\right] \tag{2}$$

where ϕ_0 is a constant of integration. Using standard trigonometric identities and the Bessel function relations,[11]

$$\cos(X \sin \theta) = \sum_{n=-\infty}^{\infty} J_n(X) \cos n\theta \tag{3}$$

$$\sin(X \sin \theta) = \sum_{n=-\infty}^{\infty} J_n(X) \sin n\theta \tag{4}$$

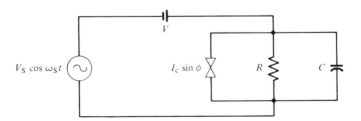

Figure 5.05a. Equivalent circuit for a Josephson device connected to dc and ac voltage sources.

[11] M. Abramowitz and I. A. Stegun (Eds.) *Handbook of Mathematical Functions.* Washington, DC: National Bureau of Standards, U.S. Government Printing Office, 1964.

where J_n is an nth order Bessel function of the first kind, the current (2) can be put in the form

$$i_J(t) = I_c \sum_{n=-\infty}^{\infty} (-1)^n J_n\left(\frac{2eV_s}{\hbar\omega_s}\right) \sin\left[(\omega_J - n\omega_s)t + \phi_0\right] \tag{5}$$

where $\omega_J = 2eV/\hbar$, the Josephson oscillation frequency. From this result we see that at values of average voltage V such that $\omega_J = n\omega_s$ or

$$V = \frac{n\hbar\omega_s}{2e} \tag{6}$$

there are current spikes in the $I-V$ characteristic that have maximum heights $I_c J_n(2eV_s/\hbar\omega_s)$, where the phase $\phi_0 = \pi/2$. For each value of dc voltage there is also a dc current through the conductance $I_G = GV$. The sum of the dc currents is then as shown in Fig. 5.05b by the solid lines. The dependences of the various spike heights on the ac voltage amplitude are shown on Fig. 5.05c.

Actual measurements do not reveal these spikes in the $I-V$ characteristics, because the junctions usually have resistances low enough that the sources act more like current sources. As a result, increasing the dc current source from zero raises the operating point along a step-like locus somewhat as shown by the arrows in Fig. 5.05b. With this qualitative modification of the voltage-source model, we find reasonable corroboration by experimental data.

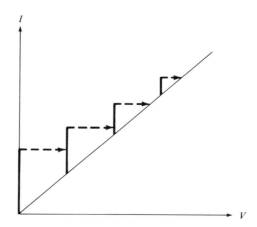

Figure 5.05b. $I-V$ characteristics for the circuit of Fig. 5.05a. In the voltage-source model, spikes in the dc current occur at voltages $V = n\hbar\omega_s/2e$. Measurements are usually made with sources that do not have zero impedances; steps, rather than spikes, are observed (broken lines).

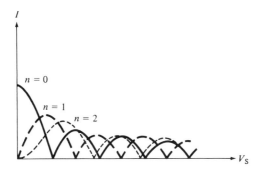

Figure 5.05c. Dependences of the spike heights in Fig. 5.05b on the amplitude of the ac source voltage for the first three spikes. Dependences are Bessel function magnitudes; only positive values are allowed because the source has a fixed polarity, so the sign of ϕ_0 adjusts accordingly.

Current-Source Model

It has been found that the step structure suggested by Fig. 5.05b actually occurs in practice, but the dependences of the various step heights on the ac signal amplitude are different from the Bessel function dependences found for the voltage-source model. It is found that the current-source model (Fig. 5.05d) is a better representation. Figure 5.05e shows a set of I–V characteristics calculated[12] using the current-source model for a zero-capacitance junction where the signal frequency ω_S is 0.16 ω_c, with ω_c given by Eq. 5.03(3). Experimental data for a point-contact junction is shown for comparison and it is clear that the model gives quite accurate results. Figure 5.05f shows the theoretical and experimental values of the step heights at voltages for which $n = 0$, 1 in (6).

It should be pointed out here that the step-height measurement is a fairly sensitive test for the Josephson effect. For example, measurements

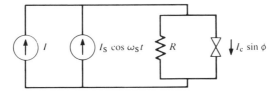

Figure 5.05d. An extensively used current-source model for low-capacitance Josephson devices.

---

[12] Y. Taur, P. L. Richards, and F. Auracher, "Application of the shunted junction model to point-contact Josephson junctions," in *Low Temperature Physics—LT-13* (K. D. Timmerhaus, W. J. O'Sullivan, and E. F. Hammel, eds.), Vol. 3. New York: Plenum Press, 1974, pp. 276–280.

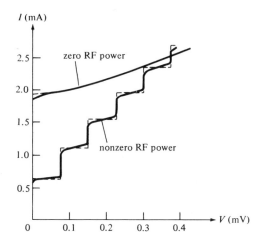

Figure 5.05e. *I–V* characteristics for a point-contact junction with 35 GHz applied RF power. Solid lines show experimental results. Broken lines give results of calculations without noise. With 100 K thermal noise assumed in the calculations, a very close fit to the experimental results is achieved. (Data from Y. Taur et al., footnote 12.)

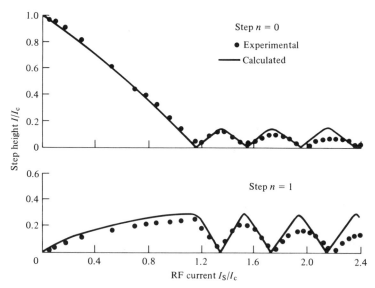

Figure 5.05f. Experimentally determined dependences of the zeroth and first steps for the data in Fig. 5.05e in comparison with theoretical calculations made with the current-source model. (From Y. Taur, P. L. Richards, F. Auracher, in *Low Temperature Physics—LT-13* (K. D. Timmerhaus, W. J. O'Sullivan, and E. F. Hammel, Eds.), Vol. 3. New York: Plenum Press, 1974, p. 278.)

on constricted thin films (Fig. 5.02c) give results that agree resonably well with the theory only for constrictions with very small lengths and widths. For larger constictions, the connection is too strong and Josephson effects do not appear.

RF Junction Impedance (Current-Source Model)

Calculations have been made of the RF impedance of a zero-shunt-capacitance junction driven by an ideal current source. Let us first consider two simple situations. For vanishingly small signal amplitudes,[13] the junction impedance for zero-dc-voltage operation can be expressed analytically. Finding $d\phi/dt$ from Eq. 5.02(1) as $d\phi/dt = (I_c \cos\phi)^{-1} dI/dt$ and substituting in Eq. 5.02(2), we can identify an equivalent nonlinear inductance:

$$L_J = \hbar/2eI_c\cos\phi_0 \qquad (7)$$

where ϕ_0 is the phase angle imposed by the dc bias current. The equivalent circuit is just this inductance in parallel with the shunt conductance G.

Another simple situation is where the bias voltage is not zero, the signal frequency is much smaller than the Josephson frequency ($\omega_S \ll \omega_J$), and the signal amplitude is small ($I_S \ll I_c$). Under these conditions, the junction responds quasistatically to the RF signal and the impedance Z_S is real and simply equals the reciprocal of the slope of the $I-V$ charcteristic at the operating bias point. To keep a perspective on the requirement on signal frequency and amplitude, note that $\omega_J/2\pi \cong 48$ GHz for $V = 100\mu V$ and I_c is typically in the range 100 μA to 1 mA.

For larger signals and higher frequencies, the dependences of the impedance of a junction driven by a current source becomes quite complicated. The calculation of its impedance requires a numerical solution of the nonlinear equation for the junction voltage with subsequent Fourier analysis to pick out the voltage component at the signal frequency.[14] A typical form of the variation of this impedance with dc current bias is shown in Fig. 5.05g. The real and imaginary parts are plotted separately and are normalized to the shunt resistance. The abscissa is normalized to the value of critical current I_{c0} that exists in the absence of an RF signal. It is characteristic that the imaginary component is zero between current steps. Notice also here that the RF resistance is negative at the bottom of the dc

---

[13] This gives agreement to within a few percent with numerically calculated results for signal amplitudes such that $I_S \lesssim 0.2 I_c$.

[14] F. Auracher and T. Van Duzer, "rf impedance of superconducting weak links," *J. Appl. Phys.*, Vol. 44, pp. 848–851, February 1973. For a recent analytical approach to the impedance of a Josephson junction for small signals, see C. V. Stancampiano, "Microwave theory of Josephson oscillators," *IEEE Trans. Electron Devices*, Vol. ED-27, pp. 1934–1944, October 1980.

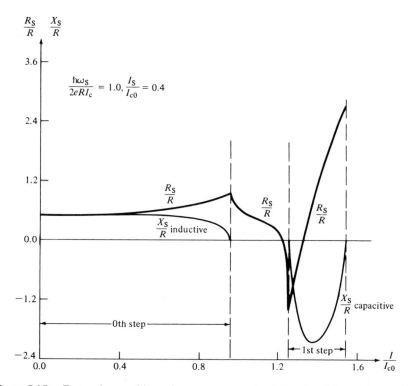

Figure 5.05g. Dependence of impedance components at the signal frequency on the dc current. Impedance components are normalized to the value of the resistor in the equivalent circuit and current is normalized to the maximum zero-voltage current in the absence of applied RF current I_{c0}. (From F. Auracher and T. Van Duzer, *J. Appl. Phys.*, Vol. 44, p. 849, 1973.)

current step; this allows the junction to supply power to a circuit (such as a microwave cavity) coupled to it. The variation of impedance with current depends strongly on the frequency and amplitude of the signal.

Voltage–Frequency Relation

We have seen that the behavior of the Josephson junction with an applied rf signal can be quite complex, with considerable qualitative variations that depend on source impedance and signal amplitude and frequency. However, one characteristic that pervades is the existence of steps in the dc I–V characteristic which occur at the voltages

$$V = (n\hbar/2e)\omega_S \tag{8}$$

Frequency can be measured with great precision so, given the ratio of fundamental constants $2e/h$, voltage can be measured with similar precision. It is the present practice of the U.S. National Bureau of Standards[15] to use the steps in the Josephson junction I–V characteristic to maintain the U.S. legal volt.[16] The most accurate available value of $2e/h$ is that chosen by NBS on the basis of (8) and the average voltage of an array of standard cells. This value was established on 1 July 1972 and has been subsequently treated as a constant:

$$\frac{2e}{h} = 483593.420 \text{ GHz/V}_{\text{NBS}} \tag{9}$$

Problems

5.05a. Show that (5) follows from (2) using (3) and (4).

5.05b. The voltage across a junction with a shunt resistance R connected to an ideal dc current source I can be written as $v(t) = R(I - I_c \sin \phi)$. Show that for $I > I_c$ this leads to

$$v(t) = \frac{RI\left[1 - \left(\dfrac{I_c}{I}\right)^2\right]}{1 + \left(\dfrac{I_c}{I}\right)\sin(\omega_0 t + \phi_0)}$$

where $\omega_0 = 2eV/\hbar$ and $V = R(I^2 - I_c^2)^{1/2}$.

5.05c. From $v(t)$ given in Problem 5.05b, find the current through the Josephson element, $i_J(t) = I_c \sin \phi$. Plot the result as a function of time for $R = 0.5\ \Omega$, $V = 0.1$ mV, and $I_c = 1.0$ mA.

5.05d. Show that the average value of $i_J(t)$ in Prob. 5.05c is

$$(i_J)_{av} = \left[I_c^2 + (V/R)^2\right]^{1/2} - V/R$$

Show an appropriate I–V characteristic and display the role of $(i_J)_{av}$

5.05e. Show that $v(t)$ in Prob. 5.05b can be expanded in a Fourier series (making an adjustment of the phase ϕ_0) of the form

$$v(t) = V\left(1 + \sum_{m=1}^{\infty} a_m \cos m\omega_0 t\right)$$

with

$$a_m = 2\left\{\frac{I}{I_c} - \left[\left(\frac{I}{I_c}\right)^2 - 1\right]^{1/2}\right\}^m$$

V and ω_0 are as defined in Prob. 5.05b.

---

[15] B. F. Field, T. F. Finnegan, and J. Toots, "Volt maintenance at NBS via $2e/h$: A new definition of the NBS volt," *Metrologia*, Vol. 9, pp. 155–166, 1973.
[16] Other national standards laboratories are also adopting this maintenance standard.

5.06. Fluctuations (Noise) in Josephson Junctions

Fluctuations of the current and voltage in a Josephson junction are of importance to applications in a variety of ways. The ac current that results when a voltage exists across a junction has a rather broad spectrum mainly because of the fluctuations of the (frequency-determining) voltage. Also, thermal fluctuations lead to a rounding of the $I-V$ characteristics and therefore to a reduction of the dynamic resistance $R_D = dV/dI$, which will be seen in the next section to play a prominent role in the properties of detectors and mixers. The fluctuations also enter directly into applications such as mixing and detection and sensitive measurements where there is a competition between noise and the desired signal. Neither all types of Josephson junction nor all operating situations have been analyzed, and some of the predicted results have not yet been confirmed experimentally, so the theory must be used in a patchwork manner.

AC Current Fluctuations

The most extensively developed theory is that for tunnel junctions. A detailed work on this subject has been published by Rogovin and Scalapino.[17] They have given expressions for the power spectra of current fluctuations $[P(\omega) = \langle i(\omega)^2 \rangle]$ for the quasiparticle current, the pair current, and the interference pair-quasiparticle current (see Section 5.03). We shall give the results here only for those operating conditions that are important in applications and where appreciable simplification is achieved. The magnitude of the interference term is small enough to justify its neglect. The components of the noise currents with frequencies such that $\omega \ll eV/\hbar$ and $\omega \ll k_B T/\hbar$, where V is the dc voltage bias, can be expressed as

$$\langle i^2(\omega) \rangle = \frac{e}{\pi}\left[I_{qp}(V)\coth\left(\frac{eV}{2k_B T} \right) + 2I_p(V)\coth\left(\frac{eV}{k_B T} \right) \right] \quad (1)$$

Thus, in this extreme low-frequency limit, the currents are of the shot-noise form. The factor $\coth(eV/k_B T)$ enters because the currents involved flow in two directions. Note that $k_B T/e = 0.36$ mV, where $T = 4.2$ K, so for bias voltages greater than about 1 mV, the coth terms are almost unity and (1) takes on the usual shot-noise form (footnotes 2 and 3) with pairs having a charge of $2e$.

On the other hand, when the voltage is low enough that $eV \ll k_B T$, (1) becomes

$$\langle i^2(\omega) \rangle \cong \left(\frac{1}{2\pi} \right) \frac{4k_B T}{R_T} \quad (2)$$

---

[17] D. Rogovin and D. J. Scalapino, "Fluctuation phenomena in tunnel junctions," *Ann. Phys.*, Vol. 86, pp. 1–90, July 1974.

so, in this limit, the result is the same as Johnson noise[18] across the dc junction resistance $R_T = V/(I_p + I_{qp})$.

The only kind of Josephson junction other than the tunneling device for which any noise theory exists is the metallic connection with dimensions less than the coherence length. It is assumed that the only source of fluctuations is the normal resistance R_n of the weak connection, and the power spectrum of the current is found to be[19]

$$\langle i^2(\omega) \rangle = \frac{\hbar\omega}{\pi R_n} \coth(\hbar\omega/2k_B T) \tag{3}$$

which, for low frequencies such that $\hbar\omega \ll k_B T$, is

$$\langle i^2(\omega) \rangle \cong \left(\frac{1}{2\pi} \right) \frac{4k_B T}{R_n} \tag{4}$$

The difference between (2) and (4) lies in the fact that R_T is the resistance at the operating point and R_n is the asymptotic resistance at voltages well beyond the gap voltage.

Essentially all direct measurements of the current or voltage fluctuations produced by Josephson junctions have been made on point contacts. These structures are rather complicated in that their physical configuration is not well defined. In some cases, there is evidence of an energy gap and the Riedel singularity (see Section 4.02), so the coupling process is probably tunneling; in other cases, the coupling is probably by metallic contact. There may even be situations where some electrons are transferred both by metallic contact and parallel tunneling. One set of measurements[20] showed good agreement with the bias-voltage dependence expected on the basis of (1). In this work, voltage fluctuations were measured and use was made of the fact that they are related to the current fluctuations by

$$\langle v^2(\omega) \rangle = \frac{\langle i^2(\omega) \rangle R_D^2}{(1 + \omega^2\tau^2)} \tag{5}$$

where τ is the circuit time constant associated with the capacitance and normal resistance of the junction. In mixing experiments,[21] the observed noise for point contacts was more nearly the lower, thermal value predicted on the basis of (3). The former probably corroborates the predictions of the tunneling theory and the latter suggests that point contacts can behave more like metallic contacts in some circumstances.

---

[18] M. Schwartz, *Information Transmission, Modulation and Noise*, 2nd Edition. New York: McGraw-Hill, 1970.

[19] K. Likharev and V. K. Semenov, "Fluctuation spectrum in superconducting point contacts," *JETP Lett.*, Vol. 15, pp. 442–445, 20 May 1972.

[20] H. Kanter and F. L. Vernon, Jr., "Current noise in Josephson point contacts," *Phys. Rev. Lett.*, Vol. 25, pp. 588–590, 31 August 1970.

[21] Y. Taur, J. H. Claassen, and P. L. Richards, "Josephson junctions as heterodyne detectors," *IEEE Trans. Microwave Theory Tech.*, Vol. MTT-22, pp. 1005–1009, December 1974.

Radiation Linewidth

With a junction biased to an average voltage V, one would expect an ac Josephson current having a frequency $f_0 = 2eV/h$. If, in addition to the applied bias, there are fluctuations of the voltage, the frequency also fluctuates and the result is a broadened line of radiation. The voltage fluctuations are reflected in changes of the frequency of the ac Josephson current through integration of $\dot{\phi} = 2ev(t)/\hbar$. High-frequency fluctuations are therefore less effective in producing changes of frequency than are low-frequency components of the same amplitude. The result is that the significant frequency-modulating voltages themselves have frequency components in the range $0-\Delta\omega$, where $\Delta\omega \ll \omega_0$ and $\omega_0 = 2eV/\hbar$. Following through the analysis,[22] one finds that the fluctuating ac Josephson current has a Lorentzian spectrum given by

$$\langle i^2(\omega)\rangle = \tfrac{1}{2} I_c^2 \left\{ \tfrac{1}{2}\Delta\omega / \left[(\omega - \omega_0)^2 + \left(\tfrac{1}{2}\Delta\omega\right)^2 \right] \right\} \tag{6}$$

The full width of the radiation line at the half-power points is

$$\Delta\omega = \left(\frac{2e}{\hbar} \right)^2 R_D^2 e \left[I_{qp}(V)\coth\frac{eV}{2k_BT} + 2I_p(V)\coth\frac{eV}{k_BT} \right] \tag{7}$$

Effect on I–V Characteristics

Ambegaokar and Halperin[23] have analyzed the effect of thermal fluctuations on the $I-V$ characteristics of a highly damped Josephson junction where the McCumber parameter $\beta_c \ll 1$. They used the model for the junction shown in Fig. 5.02a with a constant-current dc source and a parallel noise-current source. Consideration was restricted to the condition that $eV \ll k_BT$ so, as was pointed out in connection with (2), the noise can be considered to be purely thermal. Here the resistance is taken as the shunt R [which is somewhat different from that in (2) and more nearly like that in (4)]. They defined a parameter γ that is proportional to the ratio of the Josephson coupling energy $\hbar I_c/2e$ (see Section 4.02) to the thermal energy k_BT:

$$\gamma = \frac{\hbar I_c}{ek_BT} \tag{8}$$

As would be expected, the smaller the Josephson coupling compared with

---

[22] See Rogovin and Scalapino (footnote 17).

[23] V. Ambegaokar and B. I. Halperin, "Voltage due to thermal noise in the dc Josephson effect," *Phys. Rev. Lett.*, Vol. 22, pp. 1364–1366, 23 June 1969.

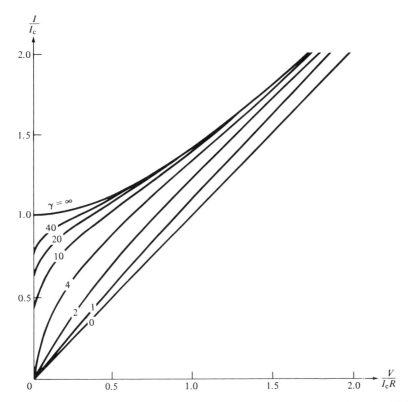

Figure 5.06a. Effect of thermal fluctuations on the $I-V$ characteristics of a highly damped Josephson junction. The parameter γ is proportional to the ratio of the Josephson coupling energy to the thermal energy. (From C. M. Falco, W. H. Parker, S. E. Trullinger, and P. K. Hansma, *Phys. Rev. B*, Vol. 10, p. 1867, 1 September 1974.)

the thermal energy, the more the $I-V$ characteristics are affected. These are shown for various values of γ in Fig. 5.06a; the corresponding normalized dynamic resistances are shown in Fig. 5.06b. These curves have been experimentally corroborated both for constricted thin films[24] as in Fig. 5.02c and for shunted $\beta_c \ll 1$ tunnel junctions. In the former case, there was quantitative agreement except for some small discrepancies; in the latter there was complete quantitative agreement. Falco et al.[25] also extended the Ambegaokar and Halperin analysis to include appreciable

[24] M. Simmonds and W. H. Parker, "Thermal fluctuations in superconducting weak links," *Phys. Rev. Lett.*, Vol. 24, pp. 876–879, 20 April 1970.
[25] C. M. Falco, W. H. Parker, S. E. Trullinger, and P. K. Hansma, "Effect of thermal noise on current–voltage characteristics of Josephson junctions," *Phys. Rev. B*, Vol. 10, pp. 1865–1873, 1 September 1974.

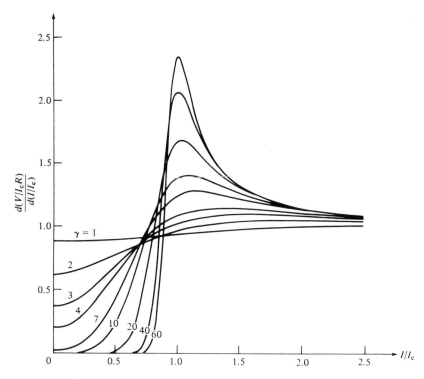

Figure 5.06b. Normalized dynamic resistance as a function of current with dependence on the parameter γ, which is proportional to the ratio of the Josephson coupling energy to the thermal energy. (From C. M. Falco, W. H. Parker, S.E. Trullinger, and P. K. Hansma, *Phys. Rev.B*, Vol. 10, p. 1867, 1 September 1974.)

shunt capacitance so the McCumber parameter β_c had values of 1 and 4, and obtained some measure of experimental corroboration.

Problems

5.06a. Estimate the fluctuation-induced percentage reduction of the dynamic resistance of a junction biased with a dc current to a point 10% above I_c if the junction is operated at $T = 4.2$ K, has a critical current 1 μA, and $\beta_c \ll 1$.

5.06b. Consider the use of a Josephson junction as a conveniently tunable RF signal source. Suppose the junction is to be operated at 4.2 K and that the dc voltage $V \cong I_c R \cong 2$ mV. For simplicity, take $R_D \cong R$, the quasiparticle currents to be I_c, and the pair current to be $\frac{1}{2}I_c$. Find R and I_c necessary to have $\Delta\omega/\omega_0 = 0.01$. Evaluate the effect of this amount of noise on the $I-V$ characteristic and show the operating point on a sketch of the $I-V$ characteristic.

5.07. Detection and Mixing

There are various ways of using Josephson junctions for detection of signals on electromagnetic waves[26]; we shall discuss here two of the simplest and potentially most useful. These are video square-law detection and heterodyne mixing. Both depend on the sensitivity of the maximum zero-voltage current shown in Figs. 5.05c, e, f. The basic idea is shown in Fig. 5.07a in which the details of the process are shown in the inset. With the application of an RF signal to the junction, a displacement of the $I-V$ characteristic approximately parallel to itself will result. The maximum zero-voltage current increases and decreases as the amplitude of the RF signal decreases and increases, respectively. We consider the junction to be biased at a point slightly above the maximum zero-voltage current as shown. The dc voltage across the junction varies with the changes of the position of the $I-V$ characteristic and therefore measures the modulation of the RF signal. This varying junction voltage is the detector output.

Let us consider the factors important to all kinds of detection and mixing employing Josephson effects.[27] Some of these can be seen from Fig. 5.07a. It is, first of all, important that there be no hysteresis in the $I-V$ characteristic. The amount of voltage output for a given input RF signal will depend on the sensitivity of the maximum zero-voltage current to RF signal. Also, the output voltage will be larger the greater the dynamic resistance dV/dI at the operating point. As in all types of detector or mixer, parallel capacitance (Fig 5.02a) is disadvantageous since it shunts the RF current around the Josephson element. The capacitive shunt will be negligible compared with the resistive shunt if the angular frequency ω_S of the RF signal is low compared with $(RC)^{-1}$. It can be shown that with $I \approx 0$ and the junction in the zero-voltage state, the normalized frequency, defined by

$$\Omega \overset{\Delta}{=} \frac{\omega_S}{(2eI_cR/\hbar)}$$

is the ratio of the current in the resistor to that in the Josephson element (Prob. 5.07). Therefore, a greater part of the ac source signal I_S is useful if

---

[26] Summaries of this work have been published: P. L. Richards, "The Josephson junction as a detector of microwave and far infrared radiation," in *Semiconductors and Semimetals*, Vol. 12, *Infrared Detectors II* (R. K. Willardson and A. C. Beer, Eds.). New York: Academic Press, 1972. R. Adde and G. Vernet, "High frequency properties and applications of Josephson junctions from microwaves to far-infrared," in *Superconductor Applications: SQUIDs and Machines* (B. B. Schwartz and S. Foner, Eds.). New York: Plenum Press, 1977.

[27] Tunnel junctions used as resistive detectors and mixers (Section 2.17) have different criteria. A comparison of mixing effectiveness of superconductive tunnel junctions and Josephson junctions is made by P. L. Richards and T.-M. Shen, "Superconductive devices for millimeter-wave detection, mixing, and amplification," *IEEE Trans. Electron Devices*, Vol. ED-27, pp. 1909–1920, October 1980.

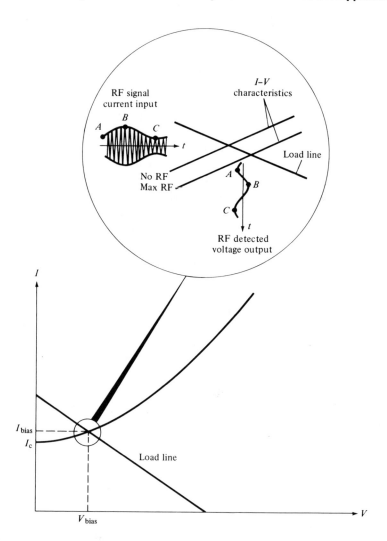

Figure 5.07a. Basic detection and mixing operation of a Josephson junction. The position of the $I-V$ characteristic is shifted by the applied RF signal. With a fixed bias, the voltage variation measures the modulation. ©1973 IEEE. Reprinted, with permission, from P. L. Richards, F. Auracher, and T. Van Duzer, *Proceedings of the IEEE*, Vol. 61, p. 39, January 1973.

Ω is small. It is believed that this is roughly true also in the nonzero-voltage state where detectors are actually operated. Thus, to avoid wasting the RF signal through the shunt resistance, one should have $\Omega < 1$. So for a given operating frequency, it is advantageous to have as high an $I_c R$ product as possible. To optimize the operation of the mixer or detector, it is generally necessary to use a step-down impedance transformer between the feed system and the junction. The transformer can have a larger bandwidth if the junction resistance is larger. However, noise increases with junction resistance, so there is a trade-off between bandwidth and noise.

Video Detection

In this case we shall be interested in the output voltage from a Josephson junction that is subjected to a chopped single-frequency signal as shown in Fig. 5.07b. The detected voltage is the difference between the dc voltages with and without the RF signal present. We assume, for analytical convenience, that the maximum zero-voltage current varies with signal amplitude V_S in the manner described by the voltage-source model presented in Section 5.05. From Eq. 5.05(5), with $n = 0$, we see that

$$I_c \cong I_c(0)\left[1 - \left(\frac{eV_S}{\hbar\omega_S}\right)^2\right] \tag{1}$$

This turns out to be a good approximation also for the case with an ideal current source for high normalized frequencies ($\Omega > 1$). The most desirable way to operate a detector is to match it to the source for maximum power transfer, so the dependence of I_c on the signal level then differs from that for either a voltage or a current source. Nonetheless, we shall use (1) to find a simple expression for the *responsivity* of the detector.

The equivalent circuits for the source and load circuits are shown in Fig. 5.07c. The source circuit can be treated separately because the load circuit

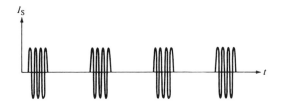

Figure 5.07b. Type of signal assumed in the video-detection analysis.

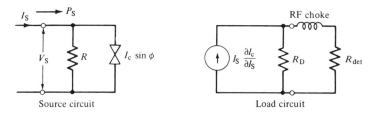

Figure 5.07c. Source and load circuits assumed for the video-detection analysis.

is assumed to be separated from the junction by an RF choke with a very high impedance at the signal frequency. The load circuit is shown separately because it is assumed to be matched to the dynamic resistance R_D of the junction, which includes the effect of the source resistance. The actual impedance of the junction is a complicated function of the bias point and other factors, as shown in Fig. 5.05g, but we shall simplify the analysis by assuming it is simply the shunt resistance R in the junction equivalent circuit.

Let us obtain an expression for the *coupled-power responsivity* which relates the voltage output from the junction to the signal power P_S actually supplied to the junction:

$$S \overset{\Delta}{=} \frac{V_{det}}{P_S} = \frac{2 V_{det}}{I_S^2 R} \tag{2}$$

We rewrite (1) in terms of the RF current I_S and the junction resistance:

$$I_c = I_c(0)\left[1 - \left(\frac{e R I_S}{\hbar \omega_S} \right)^2 \right] \tag{3}$$

or

$$I_c = I_c(0)\left[1 - \gamma I_S^2 \right] \tag{4}$$

where

$$\gamma = \left(\frac{eR}{\hbar \omega_S} \right)^2 = \left(\frac{1}{2 I_c(0)\Omega} \right)^2 \tag{5}$$

It can be seen from Fig. 5.07a that the detected voltage is

$$V_{det} = - \frac{\partial I_c}{\partial I_S} I_S \frac{R_D}{2} \tag{6}$$

where it is assumed that the load resistance is matched to the dynamic resistance of the junction. Using (4) and (5), the detected voltage (6) becomes

$$V_{det} = \gamma I_S^2 R_D I_c(0) = \frac{I_S^2 R_D}{4 I_c(0)\Omega^2} \tag{7}$$

Then the responsivity (2) is

$$S = \frac{R_D}{2 I_c(0)\Omega^2 R} \tag{8}$$

which can be shown to be valid even for Ω somewhat smaller than unity. The important point to notice in (8) is that the responsivity is inversely proportional to Ω^2, so a lower normalized frequency raises the responsivity.

More thorough analyses show that (8) only applies for a bias low enough that $f_J = 2eV/h$ is much less than the signal frequency f_S. For example, the dc voltage at the bias point must be appreciably less than 75 μV for a signal frequency of 36 GHz. It is also shown that, for $f_J \gg f_S$, the responsivity becomes that of the usual nonlinear detector wherein the important factor is the curvature of the $I-V$ characteristic. Also, the RF impedance of the junction approaches the dynamic resistance and the responsivity can be shown to be

$$S \approx \frac{1}{2R_D} \frac{d^2V}{dI^2} \tag{9}$$

Expressions for the *noise equivalent power* (NEP), one of the appropriate measures of the noise properties of video detectors, have been derived for the two above-mentioned modes of operation.[28] For the small-bias mode for which the responsivity is given by (8), the result is

$$\text{NEP} = n(8e)^{1/2}I^{3/2}R\Omega^2 \tag{10}$$

in which n is a small factor expressing the uncertainty in the relative contributions to the noise currents from pair-current fluctuations and quasiparticle-current fluctuations ($n \geqslant 1$). For the large-bias mode corresponding to (9), the result is

$$\text{NEP} = n(8eI)^{1/2}R_D\left(\frac{d^2V}{dI^2}\right)^{-1} \tag{11}$$

Heterodyne Detection (Mixing)

In heterodyne detection the signal is mixed in a nonlinear device with the output of a *local oscillator* (LO) usually having a frequency nearly equal to that of the signal.[29] There results a set of frequencies, one of which is the difference between the signal and local-oscillator frequencies. This is called the intermediate-frequency (IF) signal; it is amplified in a narrow-band amplifier prior to video detection, which derives the modulation from the IF signal. We shall take the intermediate frequency ω_{IF} to be much smaller than the signal and local-oscillator frequencies, ω_S and ω_{LO}, respectively. We further assume the amplitude of the signal current I_S to be much smaller than the local-oscillator current I_{LO}. With these assumptions, one can show that the sum $I_S + I_{LO}$ can be represented as a current at the local-oscillator frequency with an intermediate-frequency amplitude modu-

---

[28] H. Kanter and F. L. Vernon, Jr., "High-frequency response of Josephson point contacts," *J. Appl. Phys.*, Vol. 43, pp. 3174–3183, July 1972.

[29] Although the oscillating Josephson current may be used as the local oscillator, the linewidth of the oscillation (Section 5.06) is too wide for low-noise mixing. We shall therefore concentrate on junctions used with external oscillators.

lation having a magnitude determined by the signal amplitude. Such a
signal is suggested in Fig. 5.07a; its peak value varies by $2I_S$.

As in the above analysis of video detection, the studies that have been
made of mixing have assumed that the reactance of the shunt capacitance
(Fig. 5.02a) at the RF frequencies used is appreciably higher than the
shunt resistance, so the capacitance can be neglected.[30–32] The load circuit
for this analysis is the same as that in Fig. 5.07c for video detection, but
the source circuit is different (see Fig. 5.07d). The bias is selected to have
the operating point halfway between zero voltage and the first RF-induced
step (Fig. 5.05e), here caused by the local oscillator. We shall see the
reason below. The maximum sensitivity of the $I-V$ characteristic to a
change of RF current amplitude is obtained by setting I_{LO} at a value
sufficient to reduce the maximum zero-voltage current to $0.1I_c(0) < I_c <
0.5I_c(0)$, as may be appreciated from Fig. 5.05f. The intermediate-
frequency voltage V_{IF} is determined by the amount of variation of the
maximum zero-voltage current as the applied RF signal varies between its
minimum and maximum amplitudes.

When the junction is connected to a matched load, the condition that is
illustrated in Fig. 5.07a, the IF voltage is

$$V_{IF} = \frac{R_D I_S}{2} \frac{\partial I_c}{\partial I_{LO}} \qquad (12)$$

where I_S and I_{LO} are the peak values of the source currents shown in Fig.
5.07d, not the values of signal and local-oscillator currents in the junction.

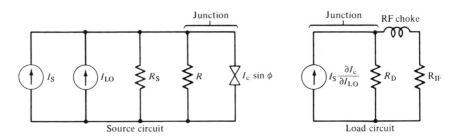

Figure 5.07d. Source and load circuits for a Josephson junction operated in the
heterodyne mixing mode. The source is here assumed to be broadband.

[30] F. Auracher and T. Van Duzer, "Numerical calculations of mixing with superconducting
weak links," *Proc. 1972 Applied Superconductivity Conf.*, Annapolis, Maryland, May 1972,
IEEE Publ. No. 72CH0682-5-TABSC.
[31] Y. Taur, J. H. Claassen, and P. L. Richards, "Josephson junctions as heterodyne
detectors," *IEEE Trans. Microwave Theory Tech.*, Vol. MTT-22, pp. 1005–1009, December
1974.
[32] M. T. Levinsen and B. T. Ulrich, "Perturbation treatment of mixing in Josephson
junctions," *IEEE Trans. Magn.*, Vol. MAG-11, pp. 807–810, March 1975.

The conversion efficiency is the ratio of the power actually coupled into the IF amplifier to the *available power*[33] from the signal source. Assuming a coupling efficiency C_{IF} between the mixer and the IF amplifier, the conversion efficiency can be written as

$$\eta = \frac{C_{IF} P_{IF}}{P_S} \qquad (13)$$

where P_{IF} and P_S are available powers. The available IF power is

$$P_{IF} = \frac{V_{IF}^2}{2R_D} = \frac{R_D I_S^2}{8} \left(\frac{\partial I_c}{\partial I_{LO}} \right)^2 \qquad (14)$$

and the available signal power is $P_S = \frac{1}{8}(I_S^2 R_S)$. Then (13) can be written as

$$\eta = C_{IF} \frac{R_D}{R_S} \left(\frac{\partial I_c}{\partial I_{LO}} \right)^2 \qquad (15)$$

It is convenient to have this expressed in terms of experimentally measurable quantities. If the waveguide leading from the local oscillator to the mixer is matched to the former, the power flow toward the mixer is the available local-oscillator power $P_{LO} = \frac{1}{8}(I_{LO}^2 R_S)$. This can be measured conveniently, so we replace I_{LO} by $(8P_{LO}/R_S)^{1/2}$:

$$\eta = C_{IF} \frac{R_D}{8} \left[\frac{\partial I_c}{\partial(P_{LO}^{1/2})} \right]^2 \qquad (16)$$

The overall receiver noise temperature is a common way of specifying the sensitivity in the frequency range where Josephson junctions are most likely to be used (30–300 GHz). This is determined by the mixer and the IF amplifier following it and can be written as

$$T_R = T_M + \frac{T_{IF}}{\eta} \qquad (17)$$

where T_M is the mixer noise temperature and T_{IF} is the noise temperature of the IF amplifier. The second term in (17) can dominate, so there is a premium placed on high conversion efficiency. A value of η greater than unity was reported in an experiment at 36 GHz.[34] In general, one would vary the source resistance seen by the junction to maximize η. This process is complicated because variation of the source resistance changes both the dependence of I_c on the RF power P_{LO} and also the dynamic resistance R_D. A recent study has given optimization procedures.[35]

---

[33] *Available* power is that which can be absorbed from a source when the load impedance is matched to it.

[34] Taur et al. (footnote 31).

[35] Y. Taur, "Josephson junction mixer analysis using frequency-conversion and noise-correlation matrices," *IEEE Trans. Electron Devices*, Vol. ED-27, pp. 1921–1928, October 1980.

The mixer noise temperature T_M has been calculated using thermal noise in the junction resistance. In general, all calculations must be made on a computer. The results show that the noise is minimized by biasing at a point midway between the zeroth and first steps, which is where the conversion efficiency is also best, at least for normalized frequency $\Omega < 1$. For $\Omega > 1$ the situation changes somewhat.

The first experimental evidence of conversion gain in mixing with a Josephson junction gave $\eta = 1.3$ at $f = 36$ GHz with $T_M = 53$ K.[36] Recent results and comparison with achievements in mixing with quasiparticle tunneling devices (Section 2.17) have been summarized.[37]

Problem

5.07. Assume a Josephson junction to be driven only by a small-signal current source $I_S \ll I_c$ and represent the Josephson current by its equivalent inductance, Eq. 5.05(7). Neglect the shunt capacitance in the McCumber–Stewart model. Show that the normalized frequency Ω is the magnitude of the ratio of the current through the resistor to that through the Josephson inductance. This shows that a larger fraction of the source signal is wasted through the shunt resistor for larger Ω.

5.08. Parametric Interactions

In Section 5.07 we discussed mixing of two high-frequency signals in a Josephson device to give an intermediate-frequency signal. Here we consider more general combining of signals where the interaction comes about because of the nonlinear reactance of the Josephson device. The many possible types of interaction fall into the categories of *parametric amplification* and *parametric frequency conversion*. A variety of nonsuperconducting devices can be used for parametric interactions and these are discussed at length in other texts.[38] In order to achieve parametric interaction, it is necessary to have a time-dependent impedance. This is usually achieved by applying a sinusoidal *pump* signal to a nonlinear device, giving an impedance whose value varies at the pump frequency and/or its harmonics. Here we make use of the fact that the supercurrent in a Josephson junction is inductive and has a value that depends on the applied current, as given by Eq. 5.05(7).

In situations where the nonlinear impedance is a pure reactance, the Manley–Rowe equations provide relations between the powers and frequencies of the various frequency components that can exist across the nonlinear element. They can be used, for example, to predict the condi-

---

[36] Taur et al. (footnote 31).

[37] Richards and Shen (footnote 27).

[38] See, for example, D. P. Howson and R. B. Smith, *Parametric Amplifiers*. New York: McGraw-Hill, 1970.

tions for a negative resistance at the signal frequency and, thus, reflective amplification. Extended Manley–Rowe equations have been derived for the ideal Josephson element ($I = I_c \sin \phi$) but predictions made from them must be held questionable since the shunt conductance shown in Fig. 5.02a is an important factor in the circuit. It now appears necessary to solve each interaction situation individually in the case of a real Josephson junction. The most important interactions are

a. those leading to amplification of a signal without changing its frequency and

b. frequency down-conversion.

The former, called *parametric amplification*, could be used in the first stage of a receiver preceding a mixer and would determine the noise temperature of the system if it had sufficient gain. The down-converter (mixer) with possible gain was discussed in Section 5.07. Parametric amplification has been analyzed and observed experimentally.[39]

The basic idea of the parametric amplifier can be illustrated as in Fig. 5.08. A nonlinear impedance element (here a Josephson junction) is located in a tuned circuit (here a microwave resonator) which presents a significant impedance only to selected frequencies. A large pump power is coupled through a circulator from port 1 to port 2 and drives the nonlinearity at the frequency ω_p. A small-amplitude signal is applied to the same port and is coupled into the nonlinear element. If all parameters are correctly selected, the admittance Y_1 has a negative real part so there is a reflected signal of larger amplitude than the applied signal. Because of the nature of the circulator, the reflected signal power is coupled to port 3 where the load is connected. The pump power is similarly coupled to the output port. Subsequent detection must separate the amplified signal from the pump. The interaction of the signal power with the nonlinear impedance varying at the pump frequency leads to the generation of an *idler* signal and a variety of harmonic signals, all of which must be correctly treated.

Feldman et al.[40] have studied a parametric amplification scheme in which there are three frequencies involved: a pump, an idler, and the signal. The arrangement is referred to as *four-photon* or *four-wave* amplification because the relation between the frequencies is $\omega_s + \omega_i = 2\omega_p$ so there are two photons (or two waves) at the pump frequency. In the analysis three sinusoidal voltages closely spaced in frequency are impressed across the junction. It is assumed that the junction is placed in a resonant stripline circuit with the three frequencies lying within the circuit

[39] A review of this work is found in A. N. Vystavkin, V. N. Gubankov, L. S. Kusmin, K. K. Likharev, V. V. Migulin, and V. K. Semenov, "S–c–S junctions as nonlinear elements of microwave receiving devices," *Rev. Phys. Appl.*, Vol. 9, pp. 79–109, January 1974.

[40] M. J. Feldman, P. T. Parrish, and R. Y. Chiao, "Parametric amplification by unbiased Josephson junctions," *J. Appl. Phys.*, Vol. 46, pp. 4031–4042, September 1975.

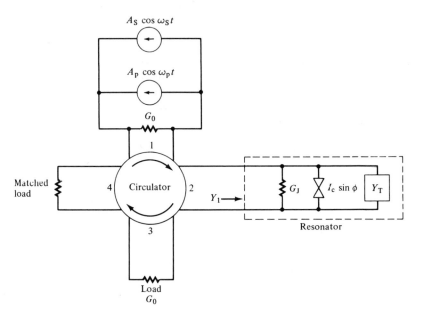

Figure 5.08. Circuit model for Josephson junction reflection parametric amplifier. The admittance Y_T is used to tune out the shunt capacitance of the junction.

resonance (so-called *doubly degenerate* operation) at roughly the same finite impedance. It is further assumed that the circuit properties are such that a short-circuit load is presented to signals at all other frequencies, so that no power flows except at ω_s, ω_i, and ω_p. The maximum square-root gain–bandwidth product was calculated.

In a 10-GHz experiment with unbiased junctions, a gain of 12 dB, a bandwidth of 1 GHz, and a noise temperature of less than 20 K were observed. Similar results have also been achieved at 33 GHz. The noise temperatures are appreciably better than uncooled or cooled varactor parametric amplifiers and very little local-oscillator power is required.

The noise temperature of the Josephson junction parametric amplifier now appears to be proportional to its gain Thus, the expected achievement of photon-noise-limited performance may not be possible. This consideration and the current state of analysis and measurement have recently been reviewed.[41]

5.09.   RF Signal Generation

We have seen before (Sections 4.02, 5.03, and 5.05) that an RF Josephson current passes through a junction if there is a nonvanishing voltage across it. This suggests the use of a Josephson junction as a voltage-tunable signal

---

[41] Richards and Shen (footnote 27).

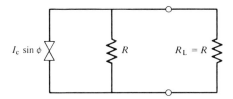

Figure 5.09a. Equivalent circuit used for the calculation of power radiated from a Josephson junction.

source; the possibilities are explored in this section. We shall determine the power that can be produced and the inherent frequency modulation, and comment on some of its potential advantages over other voltage-tunable sources.

We assume that the junction can be represented as in Fig. 5.09a by a resistively shunted Josephson element driven by a dc current source and connected to a load of the same resistance as that of the junction, so as to effect maximum power transfer from the junction to the load. We assume, for simplicity, that any shunt capacitance may be neglected at the frequencies of interest. In practice, the junction could be located in some kind of resonant structure which would be designed to couple the maximum possible energy out of the junction. The load could therefore be a tuned circuit, but that refinement is neglected here. It has been shown that the voltage appearing across the junction (and load) in this equivalent circuit is (see Prob. 5.05e)[42]

$$v(t) = V\left(1 + \sum_{m=1}^{\infty} a_m \cos m\omega_J t\right) \tag{1}$$

where the average voltage V is given by Eq. 5.03(6):

$$V = (I_c/G)\left[(I/I_c)^2 - 1\right]^{1/2}$$

Here the total shunt conductance G is $(R_L + R)/R_L R = 2/R$ since it is assumed that the load is matched to the junction resistance. The coefficient a_m is given by Fourier analysis as (Prob. 5.05e)

$$a_m = 2\left\{\frac{I}{I_c} - \left[\left(\frac{I}{I_c}\right)^2 - 1\right]^{1/2}\right\}^m \tag{2}$$

We shall concern ourselves here only with the component at ω_J (i.e., $m = 1$); Fig. 5.09b shows the normalized magnitude of that component of the voltage as a function of the dc voltage V. The power in the load at the frequency ω_J is $P_{L1} = V_1^2/2R$ (since $R_L = R$) and can be expressed in

[42] L. G. Aslamazov and A. I. Larkin, "Josephson effect in superconducting point contacts," *Sov. Phys. JETP Lett.*, Vol. 9, pp. 87–93, January 1969.

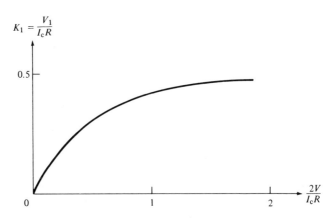

Figure 5.09b. Normalized amplitude of the fundamental frequency component of ac voltage across a Josephson junction with a matched load as shown in Fig. 5.09a.

terms of the normalized V_1, which is $K_1 \overset{\Delta}{=} V_1/I_c R$:

$$P_{L1} = \tfrac{1}{2} K_1^2 I_c^2 R \tag{3}$$

Let us consider a typical situation of interest to see the order of magnitude of the power in the load. Take as typical $I_c R = 1$ mV and $I_c = 1$ mA, and assume the junction is biased so $V = \tfrac{1}{2} I_c R$. The fundamental frequency of oscillation is 242 GHz and $R = 1\Omega$, $K_1 = 0.41$, so the power in the load is, from (3), 0.84×10^{-7} W. But for comparison with certain experiments which were done at 10 GHz, take the bias voltage to be 21 $\mu V = 0.042 \, (I_c R/2)$. Then $K_1 = 0.042$ and $P_{L1} = 0.88 \times 10^{-9}$ W. Actual measurements of radiated power have been made on point contacts, tunnel junctions, and thin-film constrictions; the highest measured power to date was 10^{-9} W, both in the range 60 GHz $< f <$ 400 GHz and at 9 GHz.[43, 44]

It is easy to see from circuit considerations that output power to a load R_L across a series of N phase-locked Josephson junctions can, under some circumstances, increase as the square of the number of junctions. In one case, if the sum of the junction resistances NR is always much smaller than the load, the RF voltage developed across each junction is independent of the presence of the others. Since the junctions are phase-locked, the voltages add directly and the power in the load increases as N^2. Unfortunately, in this scheme the power coupled to the load from each junction is only a small fraction of the power available; even with N junctions the

[43] R. K. Elsley and A. J. Sievers, "Millimeter and submillimeter wave radiation generated by a Josephson junction," *Proc.* 1972 *Appl. Superconductivity Conf.*, IEEE Publ. No. 72CHO 682-5-TABSC, pp. 716–718.

[44] T. F. Finnegan and S. Wahlsten, "Observation of coherent microwave radiation emitted by coupled Josephson junctions," *Appl. Phys. Lett.*, Vol. 21, pp. 541–544, 1 December 1972.

power out is less than from a single matched junction. Alternatively, one might take the view that the phase-locked string of junctions should always be matched to the load resistor for optimum coupling. If one then asks how the power output changes as the number of junctions in the series changes, the following considerations apply. The junction resistance will vary inversely with the number N, so that $R = R_L/N$. Since $I_c R$ can be considered constant for a given type of junction, $(I_c)_N = (I_c)_1 N$, and the voltage V_1 across each junction is $K_1 I_c R$, the same as if $N = 1$. Since there are N junctions in series, the total RF voltage is N times larger than with one junction. Thus the load power is N^2 times that obtained if one junction were used to match the same load resistance.

Another important property of an oscillator is its spectral linewidth. This question has already been addressed in the study of noise in Section 5.06. Equation 5.06(7) showed that the linewidth is proportional to the square of the dynamic resistance of the junction, so a narrow linewidth could be achieved by using a junction with a low dynamic resistance, and therefore, with a low resistance R. Fractional linewidths $\Delta\omega/\omega$ as small as 10^{-7} have been reported. If a single junction is used, the junction resistance usually must be on the order of 10 Ω for good output matching. This gives a linewidth too great for most applications. On the other hand, a series of phase-locked junctions with the total resistance NR matched to the load could achieve a sufficiently narrow linewidth. It can be seen from Eq. 5.06(7) that the linewidth $\Delta\nu \propto R$. For a given R_L, $R = R_L/N$ so $\Delta\nu \propto N^{-1}$. Additionally, phase-locking N identical junctions leads to a linewidth narrower by a factor N than that of one of the junctions. The result is a factor of N^2 narrower linewidth if N junctions are used for a given load resistance.[45]

The Josephson junction RF source can provide power levels well above that required from local oscillators in heterodyne systems using either quasiparticle diodes (Section 2.17) or Josephson junctions (Section 5.07) and could easily be integrated on the same chip. In the use as a voltage-tuned oscillator, the Josephson junction has the advantage of having an oscillation frequency that is exactly proportional to voltage. The frequency can also be changed with great rapidity.

Problems

5.09a. Find the ratio of the power in the load at $2\omega_J$ to that at ω_J if $I_c R = 1$ mV, $I_c = 1$ mA, and $V = \frac{1}{2} I_c R$. Qualitatively, how does this ratio vary with bias? Relate your comments to Fig. 5.03b.

[45] C. Varmazis, R. D. Sandell, A. K. Jain, and J. E. Lukens, "Generation of coherent tunable Josephson radiation at microwave frequencies with narrowed linewidth," *Appl. Phys. Lett.*, Vol. 33, pp. 357–359, 15 August 1978.

5.09b. Show that the voltage amplitude at ω_J in the circuit of Fig. 5.09a is $V_1 \cong 2V$ for $V \to 0$ and that, in the next order of approximation, $V_1 \cong 2V(1 - 2V/I_c R)$. Check this result against Fig. 5.09b.

5.10. Quantum Interference in Parallel Arrays of Junctions

We introduce here the basic methods and concepts involved in studying interference of wave functions in parallel arrays of Josephson junctions as it affects the dependence of the maximum zero-voltage current on the magnetic field applied to the array. Concentration will be on the simplest possible array, one with just two junctions, so the principles can be most easily understood. Techniques are available for analysis of larger arrays and we shall comment briefly on them.

In the array shown in Fig. 5.10a, there is a common electron-pair wave function throughout the upper superconductor and another throughout the lower one; these are weakly connected through the junctions. For a symmetrical array, the gauge-invariant phase difference is the same across both junctions in the absence of a magnetic field. When a magnetic field is applied perpendicular to the plane of the array, it causes the phase differences at the junctions to differ. The result is that the maximum zero-voltage current that can be passed through the array depends on the magnetic field. We shall make the simplification that the individual junctions are small enough that they never contain a significant fraction of a flux quantum and shall point out how the results are modified when this condition is not met.

General Relationships

Let us first relate the phase differences in the two junctions ϕ_1 and ϕ_2 to one another through the magnetic vector potential existing in the loop. We integrate the gradient of the phase of the pair wave function, Eq. 3.03(7), around the path shown in Fig. 5.10a. Inside the superconductors, we employ the London gauge in which the canonical momentum $\vec{p} = \nabla\theta$ is zero (cf. Section 3.05). Thus, the integral, taken in the clockwise direction, reduces simply to the integrals across the junctions

$$\oint \nabla\theta \cdot \vec{dl} = 2n\pi = (\theta_a - \theta_d) + (\theta_c - \theta_b) \tag{1}$$

where the $2n\pi$ result derives from the uniqueness of θ. Making use of the gauge-invariant phase defined in Eq. 4.03(3) and assuming the superconductors are large enough that paths exist from a to b and from c to d along which the current density is zero and therefore $\vec{A} = -\Lambda\vec{J}_s = 0$, we can write (1) as

$$\phi_2 = \phi_1 + \frac{2e}{\hbar} \oint \vec{A} \cdot \vec{dl} - 2n\pi \tag{2}$$

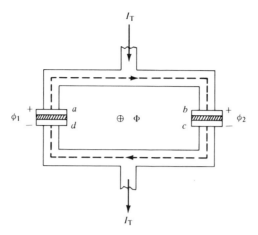

Figure 5.10a. Two-junction parallel array with symmetrical feed. The integration path for the analysis is shown by the broken line.

The $2n\pi$ will hereafter be disregarded since the current through junction 2 ($I_{c2}\sin\phi_2$) is independent of factors of 2π added to the phase difference. Also, using Stokes' theorem, the integral of the vector potential can be put in terms of the flux inward through the loop and (2) becomes

$$\phi_2 = \phi_1 - (2\pi\Phi/\Phi_0) \tag{3}$$

where $\Phi_0 = h/2e$, the flux quantum. If the superconducting circuit cannot be assumed thick enough such that $\vec{J}_s = 0$ inside, these conclusions must be modified. The total current through the parallel junctions is

$$I_T = I_1 + I_2 = I_{c1}\sin\phi_1 + I_{c2}\sin\phi_2$$
$$= I_{c1}\sin\phi_1 + I_{c2}\sin\left(\phi_1 - \frac{2\pi\Phi}{\Phi_0}\right) \tag{4}$$

where the critical currents I_{c1} and I_{c2} of the two junctions are assumed to be generally unequal.

Self-Induced Flux Neglected

The analysis of the critical current of the array is greatly simplified by neglecting the fact that the currents flowing in the loop produce flux in the loop in addition to that of the externally applied field. With that assumption, we denote Φ in (4) as Φ_{ex} and treat it as an independent parameter. The maximum zero-voltage current is found by maximizing (4) with respect to ϕ_1; the result is

$$I_{Tc}(\Phi_{ex}) = \left[(I_{c1} - I_{c2})^2 + 4I_{c1}I_{c2}\cos^2(\pi\Phi_{ex}/\Phi_0)\right]^{1/2} \tag{5}$$

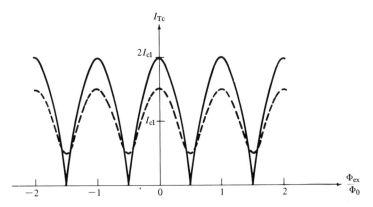

Figure 5.10b. Dependence of the critical current for a two-junction parallel array on the applied flux where the self-induced flux is neglected. Solid line for symmetrical array ($I_{c1} = I_{c2}$) and broken line for asymmetrical array with $I_{c1} = 2I_{c2}$. (Data from R. de Bruyn Ouboter and A. Th. A. M. de Waele, Footnote 46.)

If the critical currents of the two junctions are equal, (5) becomes

$$I_{Tc}(\Phi_{ex}) = 2I_{c1} \left| \cos \frac{\pi \Phi_{ex}}{\Phi_0} \right| \tag{6}$$

This dependence of the total critical current on the magnetic field is shown by the solid line in Fig. 5.10b. Notice that this is identical with the interference pattern found for waves that have passed through two identical narrow slits.

Let us consider how the magnetic field affects the I–V characteristic of a typical junction pair. We assume the junctions to be of the type having a high conductance. Figure 5.10c shows the two extreme forms of the

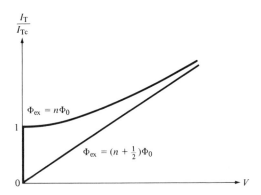

Figure 5.10c. I–V characteristics for the array described by the solid line in Fig. 5.10b for integer and half-integer multiples of the flux quantum in the loop. (Data from R. de Bruyn Ouboter and A. Th. A. M. de Waele, footnote 46.)

characteristic when the loop contains either a whole number of flux quanta or a half-integral number. In the latter case the total supercurrent for the two junctions is completely suppressed because that in junction 1 is oppositely directed and of equal magnitude to that in junction 2.

If the critical currents of the two junctions are not equal, there is incomplete cancellation and the minimum total critical current is not zero, as shown by the broken line in Fig. 5.10b. If $I_{c1} = \alpha' I_{c2}$, where $\alpha' > 1$, it may readily be shown that

$$(I_{Tc})_{max}/(I_{Tc})_{min} = (\alpha' + 1)/(\alpha' - 1) \tag{7}$$

The broken line in Fig. 5.10b obtains for the case where $I_{c1} = 2I_{c2}$.

The variation of the individual currents with magnetic field when the total current is set to its maximum value can be determined from the ϕ_1 required to maximize (4). This is left as a problem for the reader (Prob. 5.10b).

Symmetrical Array with Self-Induced Flux

Let us first consider a two-junction array in which the feed points for the current I_T are symmetrically placed as in Fig. 5.10a and the individual critical currents are equal. Later we shall consider the effect of asymmetries. If the current I_T divides equally between the two junctions in the symmetrical system, the fluxes in the loop produced by the two currents will cancel. In the more general situation, when $I_1 \neq I_2$ (when an applied flux is present), one can define a circulating current $I_{circ} = \frac{1}{2}(I_2 - I_1)$ which, when added to the $\frac{1}{2} I_T$ of the balanced case, gives the currents in the two junctions. Since there is no net magnetic flux in the loop in the balanced case, all the flux in the unbalanced case can be attributed to I_{circ}. The definition of inductance requires that the self-induced flux be

$$\Phi_s = L I_{circ} \tag{8}$$

This can more usefully be expressed in terms of the currents in the junctions:

$$\Phi_s = \frac{1}{2} L(I_2 - I_1) = \frac{1}{2} L I_{c1}(\sin\phi_2 - \sin\phi_1) \tag{9}$$

The total flux in the loop is then the sum of the applied flux Φ_{ex} and that which is self-induced:

$$\Phi = \Phi_{ex} + \frac{1}{2} L I_{c1}(\sin\phi_2 - \sin\phi_1) \tag{10}$$

The phase difference in junction 2 is related to that in junction 1 by (3), which becomes here an implicit relation between ϕ_2 and ϕ_1:

$$\phi_2 = \phi_1 - (2\pi/\Phi_0)\left[\Phi_{ex} + \frac{1}{2} L I_{c1}(\sin\phi_2 - \sin\phi_1)\right] \tag{11}$$

Solution of (11) for ϕ_2 in terms of ϕ_1 and Φ_{ex} allows determination of the total flux (10) and, therefore, the total current (4) as functions of the same

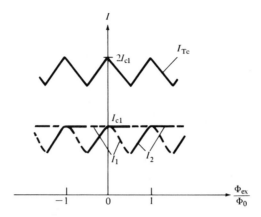

Figure 5.10d. Total critical current and individual junction currents in a two-junction parallel symmetrical array with self-induced fields included. (Data from R. de Bruyn Ouboter and A. Th. A. M. de Waele, footnote 46.)

variables. For each value of applied flux Φ_{ex}, the current I_T is maximized with respect to ϕ_1. This must be done numerically and the resulting relation I_{Tc} vs Φ_{ex} for a sample case with $LI_{c1} = (5/\pi)\Phi_0$ is shown by the solid line in Fig. 5.10d.[46] The dashed and solid lines show the currents through the individual junctions and it is seen that I_{Tc} is their sum. Notice that, for applied flux in the range $0 < \Phi_{ex} < \frac{1}{2}\Phi_0$, the maximum zero-voltage current I_{Tc} is limited by the current in junction 2, which stays at its critical value. At $\Phi_{ex} = \frac{1}{2}\Phi_0$ a step change in the flux occurs and the circulating current reverses. For $\frac{1}{2}\Phi_0 < \Phi_{ex} < \Phi_0$ the maximum zero-voltage current I_{Tc} is limited by the current in junction 1, which remains at its critical value. The flux for the same case is shown in Fig. 5.10e. The ordinate is the total flux in the loop (10) and the abscissa is the applied flux Φ_{ex}. The deviations of this relation from a 45° line are caused by Φ_s, the flux generated by circulating currents. At $(n + \frac{1}{2})\Phi_0$ the circulating current reaches a value for which a step increase of included flux is energetically advantageous. The circulating currents try but fail to keep the flux in the loop at multiples of a flux quantum. The loop switches when one state requires less circulating current than the neighboring state. This behavior should be compared with the superconducting loop in which there is no junction, where the flux in the loop can only be in exact multiples of the flux quantum.

---

[46] R. de Bruyn Ouboter and A. Th. A. M. de Waele, "Superconducting point contacts weakly connecting two superconductors," in *Progress in Low Temperature Physics*, Vol. VI, C. J. Gorter (Ed.), Amsterdam: North Holland, and New York: American Elsevier, 1970.

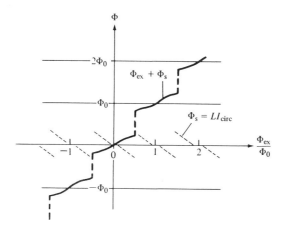

Figure 5.10e. Dependence of total flux in the loop and the self-induced flux on the applied flux for the same array as in Fig. 5.10d ($LI_{c1} = 5\Phi_0/\pi$). (Data from R. de Bruyn Ouboter and A. Th. A. M. de Waele, footnote 46.)

The depth of modulation of I_{Tc} by the magnetic field is an important factor in practical applications. Its dependence on LI_{c1} in the symmetrical two-element array is shown in Fig. 5.10f. Notice that $(I_{Tc})_{min}/(I_{Tc})_{max} < 0.5$ (i.e., 50% modulation) if $LI_{c1} \lesssim \frac{1}{2}\Phi_0$. Let us consider some numerical values. To achieve 50% modulation with junctions having $I_{c1} = 0.1$ mA,

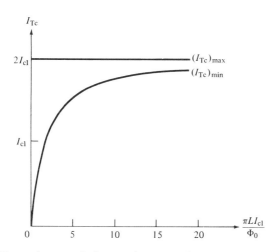

Figure 5.10f. Dependences of the maximum and minimum values of the total critical current on the loop inductance and single-junction critical current. The difference between these curves measures the modulation of I_{Tc} achievable with an applied magnetic field.

$L \lesssim 10^{-11}$ H. A thin-film loop having a mean diameter of 50 μm and a strip width of 10 μm (dimensions convenient with photolithographic techniques) has an inductance of 5×10^{-11} H. If it is separated from a ground plane (see Section 3.09) by 0.2 μm of insulation, $L \cong 3-4 \times 10^{-12}$ H. Thus, we see that it is possible to get 50% modulation with critical currents as high as 0.1 mA.

Note that there are two different reasons for $(I_{Tc})_{min}$ being larger than zero—asymmetry and nonvanishing self-induced flux. In experiments, these two effects can be separated by measuring the effect of changing the temperature. By approaching the critical temperature, the critical currents of the junctions can be reduced to values where LI_c becomes small. The modulation depth should follow the dependence in Fig. 5.10f if the array is symmetrical. If there is a residual limit to the depth of modulation as $LI_{c1} \rightarrow 0$, the asymmetry of critical currents can be determined from (7).

Asymmetrical Array with Self-Induced Flux

Two kinds of asymmetry are possible. In one case the connections to the loop may be displaced from the center so the flux produced by a given current in one side of the loop produces less flux linking the loop than the same current in the other side. If so desired, this asymmetry can be avoided in fabrication. The second type is where the critical currents are

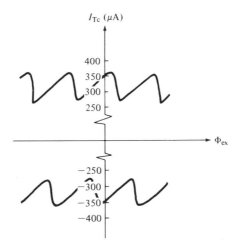

Figure 5.10g. Dependences of the positive and negative total maximum zero-voltage currents on applied flux found experimentally for an asymmetric parallel two-junction array of tin–tin oxide–tin junctions. The periodicity of applied flux density is 12.7 mG and the deduced inductance is 15.7×10^{-12} H. (Data from T. A. Fulton et al., footnote 47.)

unequal; this is less easily controlled in fabrication. In either case, when self-induced flux must be taken into account, the dependence of I_{Tc} (and other quantities) on the applied flux cannot be found analytically. Graphical[47] and numerical[48, 49] techniques have been developed and solutions for a variety of cases have been found. The shapes of the critical-current dependence on applied flux are varied and complex. A typical result for a two-element array of tin–tin oxide–tin junctions having both structural and critical-current asymmetries is shown in Fig. 5.10g.

Effect of Finite Junction Size

Throughout this section we have assumed the junctions to contain a negligible amount of flux. Where the junction size is significant compared with the size of the loop, this assumption cannot be made in determining the I_{Tc}-vs-Φ_{ex} dependence. By analogy with wave interference using two slits of finite width, one would expect the loop pattern determined as discussed above to be modulated by the envelope appropriate to the junctions.[50] For example, if the self-inductance of the loop can be neglected and the junctions have identical uniform properties as a function of distance perpendicular to the magnetic field and the direction of current flow, the I_{Tc}-vs-Φ_{ex} curve will be the product of (6) and Eq. 4.05(11):

$$I_{Tc} = 2I_{c1} \left| \cos \frac{\pi\Phi_{ex}}{\Phi_0} \left[\frac{\sin(\pi\Phi_{Jex}/\Phi_0)}{\pi\Phi_{Jex}/\Phi_0} \right] \right| \qquad (12)$$

where Φ_{Jex} is the applied flux that passes through each of the junctions.

Figure 5.10h shows the effect of finite junction size for two different loop sizes.[51] In each case the junctions are oxide-barrier sandwich types. Sample A has a loop inductance and junction critical current such that $LI_{c1} \lesssim \frac{1}{6}\Phi_0$, whereas for B, $LI_{c1} \approx \Phi_0$. It is expected from Fig. 5.10f that we should see nearly 100% modulation (and we do) in the I_{Tc}-vs-B_{ex} curve for sample A. Likewise, the partial modulation seen for sample B is also to

[47] T. A. Fulton, L. N. Dunkleberger, and R. C. Dynes, "Quantum interference properties of double Josephson junctions," *Phys. Rev.* B., Vol. 6, pp. 855–875, 1 August 1972. (See also earlier papers referenced therein.)

[48] W.-T. Tsang and T. Van Duzer, "dc analysis of parallel arrays of two and three Josephson junctions," *J. Appl. Phys.*, Vol. 46, pp 4573–4580, October 1975.

[49] B. S. Landman, "Calculation of threshold curves for Josephson quantum interference devices," *IEEE Trans. Magn.*, Vol. MAG-13, pp. 871–874, January 1977.

[50] S. Ramo, J. R. Whinnery, and T. Van Duzer, *Field and Waves in Communication Electronics*. New York: John Wiley and Sons, 1965, p. 675.

[51] R. C. Jaklevic, J. Lambe, J. E. Mercereau, and A. H. Silver, "Macroscopic quantum interference in superconductors," *Phys. Rev.*, Vol. 140, pp. A1628–A1637, 29 November 1965.

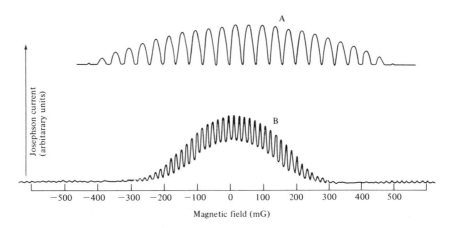

Figure 5.10h. Total maximum zero-voltage current for a two-element parallel array employing junctions of finite size. In experiment A, the self-induced flux is negligible. The sample used in experiment B has a larger loop and larger self-induced flux. (From R. C. Jaklevic, J. Lambke, J. E. Mercereau, and A. H. Silver, *Phys. Rev.*, Vol. 140, p. A1634, 1965.)

be expected from the curves in Fig. 5.10f. Sample A appears to give the dependence predicted by (12).

Parallel Arrays of Three or More Junctions

The methods discussed above have been extended to arrays of three or more junctions and the calculations have become correspondingly more complex. In one method the total zero-voltage current of the array is determined as the sum of the individual junction currents. Constraint equations are set up using Lagrange multipliers that relate the phases of the various junctions in terms of the self- and mutual inductances of the array and the externally applied flux. Then the total zero-voltage current is maximized to obtain the dependence of the total critical current I_{Tc} on the applied flux. One can also obtain the individual junction currents and the relation between the internal loop fluxes and the applied field, corresponding to the relations shown in Figs. 5.10d, e under the conditions where $I_T = I_{Tc}$.

Both the two- and three-junction arrays (referred to as *interferometers*) are finding application in digital circuits (Sections 5.12–5.14). One particularly useful configuration has critical currents in a three-junction interferometer with ratios 1:2:1 in the three junctions. Figures 5.10i, j show calculated dependences of critical current on magnetic flux, expressed in terms of the current producing the flux, for selected values of Φ_0/LI_0. All

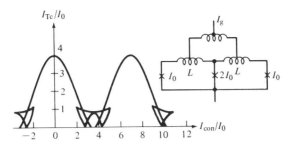

Figure 5.10i. Threshold characteristics for a three-junction interferometer with symmetrical supply-current connections; $\Phi_0/LI_0 = 7$. (©1977 IEEE. Reprinted, with permission, from H. H. Zappe, *IEEE Transactions on Magnetics*, Vol. MAG-13, p. 43, January 1977.)

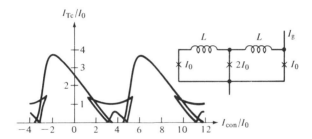

Figure 5.10j. Threshold characteristics for a three-junction interferometer with asymmetric supply-current connections; $\Phi_0/LI_0 = 8$. (©1977 IEEE. Reprinted, with permission, from H. H. Zappe, *IEEE Transactions on Magnetics*, Vol. MAG-13, p. 43, January 1977.)

currents are normalized to the critical current of one of the smaller junctions.[52]

Problems

5.10a. Show that the ratio of the maximum to minimum critical current for the two-junction array with negligible self-induced flux is given by (7). If the junctions in the array can be made reproducibly to ±10%, what is the maximum depth of modulation that can be guaranteed (neglect self-induced flux)?

[52] H. H. Zappe, "Josephson quantum interference computer devices," *IEEE Trans. Magn.*, Vol. MAG-13, pp. 41–47, January 1977.

5.10b. For the two-junction array with negligible self-induced flux, plot the dependence on magnetic field of the currents in the individual junctions with the total current set to a maximum. Assume $I_{c1} = I_{c2}$.

5.11. SQUID Magnetometers

In this section we shall study the application of quantum interference effects for the sensitive detection of extremely weak quasistatic magnetic fields. The term SQUID is an acronym for Superconducting QUantum Interference Device and is usually used to refer to a loop of small inductance containing either one or two Josephson junctions. We shall see two different kinds of SQUID system: one employs a SQUID containing two junctions and depends on the dc interference effects seen in Section 5.10; the other depends on variation of properties of a SQUID containing one junction when an RF magnetic flux is applied. Both kinds of SQUID system have been used for measurement of changes in quasistatic magnetic fields that are orders of magnitude weaker than can be detected by the best nonsuperconductive device. The systems can also be configured to measure magnetic-field gradients, voltages, currents, and susceptibilities.

All commercial SQUID systems to date are of the RF type, partly for historical reasons. Nonetheless, we shall describe the dc system in more detail since it is easier to understand.

dc SQUID

The method of detection is somewhat similar to that used for electromagnetic detection and mixing, which was discussed in Section 5.07. It requires that the two Josephson junctions used in the SQUID loop be non-hysteretic, as in Fig. 5.03a for $\beta_c = 0$. It was seen in Fig. 5.10d that the total critical current for a pair of junctions in parallel, as in Fig. 5.10a, is modulated by an applied external magnetic flux and has a repetitive variation with a period Φ_0. The depth of modulation of I_{Tc} for the pair depends on the inductance L of the loop and the critical current I_c of the junctions, as shown in Fig. 5.11a. As will be discussed below, it is advantageous to choose $LI_c/\Phi_0 \approx 1$. With this choice, one obtains half of the maximum ΔI_{Tc}, or $\Phi_0/2L$. As the external magnetic flux is changed, and I_{Tc} is thereby modulated, it causes, in turn, a modulation of the voltage across the SQUID equal approximately to the dynamic resistance R_D times the modulation of the critical current, $\Delta V \cong R_D \Delta I_{Tc}$, as seen in Fig. 5.11b.

The modulation of I_{Tc} leads to a change of shape of the $I-V$ characteristic, as seen in Fig. 5.11b, as a result of circulating currents flowing at the Josephson frequency and its harmonics. There is appreciable attenuation of the currents by the inductance and resistance of the loop if the

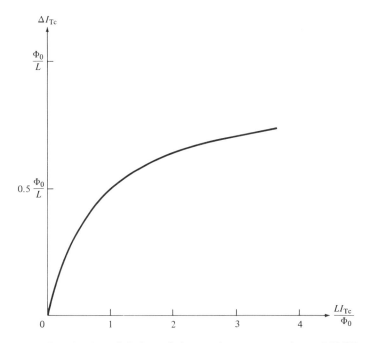

Figure 5.11a. Depth of modulation of the maximum zero-voltage SQUID current in a two-junction SQUID.

Josephson frequency $f_J > 2R_D/\pi L$ and there is little modification of I. To get the desired modulation of the $I-V$ characteristic so the maximum possible ΔV is achieved, it is necessary to set the current bias so the average voltage satisfies

$$V < \frac{2\Phi_0 R_D}{\pi L} \tag{1}$$

for all Φ_{ex}.

An upper bound can be set on the allowed values of L on the basis of noise considerations. The thermal noise power in the SQUID is $\frac{1}{2}k_BT/\text{Hz}$ and the mean energy/Hz in an inductor is $\frac{1}{2}LI_N^2$, so $I_N^2 = k_BT/L$. The corresponding flux noise is $\Phi_N^2 = L^2 I_N^2 = Lk_BT$, and this should be less than the square of one-half of a flux quantum. Thus

$$L < \frac{\Phi_0^2}{4k_BT} \tag{2}$$

from which one sees that $L < 10^{-8}$ H at $T = 4$ K. Typically, $L \approx 10^{-9}$ H since there is other noise present, such as external RF pickup or noise currents fed down the leads from room-temperature circuits.

Another important parameter is the LI_c product. We saw in connection

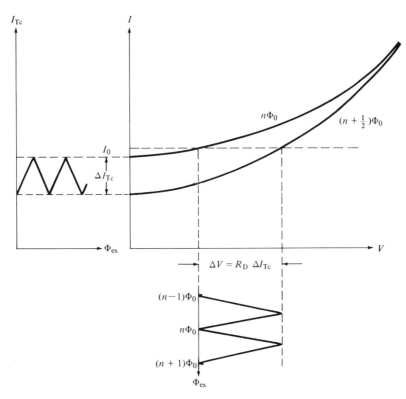

Figure 5.11b. Voltage variations across the dc SQUID resulting from modulation of the maximum zero-voltage current by an externally applied flux through the SQUID loop. (From J. Clarke, W. M. Goubau, and M. B. Ketchen, *J. Low Temp. Phys.*, Vol. 25, Nos. 1/2, p. 103, October 1976.)

with Fig. 5.11a that one usually chooses $LI_c/\Phi_0 \approx 1$. There is a rather limited range of values of L that are possible; it is bounded from above by noise, as discussed above, and from below by magnetic-flux input coupling. Let us consider, then, changes that can be made with I_c. If I_c is increased, LI_{Tc}/Φ_0 increases and greater ΔI_{Tc} is obtained; however, above $LI_{Tc}/\Phi_0 = 1$, the rate of increase of ΔI_{Tc} is slow. At the same time, to avoid hysteresis one must keep McCumber's parameter $\beta_c < 1$, and this requires reducing R and therefore also R_D; this, in turn, reduces the voltage signal ΔV. On the other hand, reduction of I_c reduces the ΔI_{Tc} and also leads to reduction of R_D because of noise rounding of the I–V characteristic (Fig. 5.06b). Thus, one usually chooses $LI_{Tc}/\Phi_0 \approx 1$.[53]

---

[53] Sensitivity falls off rapidly as LI_{Tc}/Φ_0 is reduced below unity but only slowly as it is increased above unity.

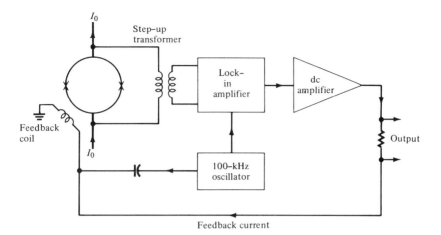

Figure 5.11c. Simplified diagram of the circuit used to measure the voltage across the SQUID loop. The output voltage is proportional to the feedback current which keeps the total quasistatic flux in the loop at the value $\Phi_q = n\Phi_0$, thus minimizing the 100-kHz component into the lock-in amplifier, as explained in connection with Fig. 5.11d. The output voltage is, therefore, proportional to the externally applied flux to be measured.

The most successful type of dc SQUID loops made to date have employed oxide-barrier junctions, resistively shunted to make them non-hysteretic.[54] Improvements have been made [55] by using reduced-area junctions to increase their resistance or to use another type of junction which does not have to be shunted to make it nonhysteretic.

The readout system for a dc SQUID is shown in Fig. 5.11c. The coil on the left side applies both a dc and a 100-kHz flux to the SQUID loop; the dc flux cancels the flux being measured and the 100 kHz is used to facilitate a narrowband, lock-in type of measurement. The output is proportional to the feedback current and, hence, to the amount of flux required to cancel the measured flux. Figure 5.11d illustrates the basic idea of the measurement scheme. The modulation of the voltage across the SQUID loop by the applied external flux has a sawtooth form with a period of Φ_0. If the dc bias point, determined by the combination of external and feedback fluxes, is at $n\Phi_0$ and the 100-kHz flux of magnitude $\approx \frac{1}{4} \Phi_0$ is superimposed, the voltage coupled into the lock-in amplifier is of

[54] J. Clarke, W. M. Goubau, and M. B. Ketchen, "Tunnel junction dc SQUID: Fabrication, operation, and performance," *J. Low Temp. Phys.*, Vol. 25, Nos. 1/2, pp. 99–144, October 1976.

[55] J. Clarke, "Advances in SQUID magnetometers," *IEEE Trans. Electron Devices*, Vol. ED-27, pp. 1896–1908, October 1980.

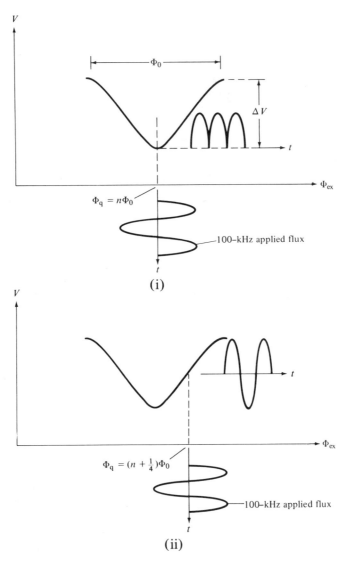

Figure 5.11d. Dependence of the voltage across the SQUID on the quasistatic applied external flux: (i) where $\Phi_q = n\Phi_0$, the voltage has no component at 100 kHz; (ii) where $\Phi_q = (n + \frac{1}{4})\Phi_0$, the voltage has only a component at 100 kHz. (From J. Clarke, W. M. Goubau, and M. B. Ketchen, *J. Low Temp. Phys.*, Vol. 25, Nos. 1/2, p. 104, October 1976.)

the form shown in Fig. 5.11d(i); it has no component at 100 kHz. On the other hand, if the bias is changed to $(n + \frac{1}{4})\Phi_0$ and the signal level kept $< \frac{1}{4}\Phi_0$, the voltage coupled to the lock-in amplifier is a sinusoid at 100 kHz. This behavior is the same for all n. The lock-in amplifier measures the component at 100 kHz and provides a detected output, which is fed back to the SQUID in such a way as to keep the 100-kHz signal at the minimum possible value. The current fed back to the coil coupled to the SQUID is thus a measure of the applied external flux that would try to drive the operating point away from $n\Phi_0$.

RF SQUID

The basic principle of operation of the RF SQUID is that when a superconducting loop containing a Josephson junction as shown in Fig. 5.11e is coupled to a tuned circuit driven by an RF current source and the quasistatic applied flux is changed, there is a periodic variation of the loading on the tank circuit and, therefore, of the RF voltage across the tank circuit, by the SQUID loop as a function of applied flux. As in the case of the dc SQUID system, a feedback arrangement is used and is based on the periodic dependence of a SQUID property on applied flux.[56]

Of fundamental importance to understanding the operation of the RF SQUID is the relation of the flux actually passing through the SQUID loop Φ_i to that applied externally to the loop Φ_{ex}. The flux produced by the current through the loop is just the difference between Φ_{ex} and Φ_i, so $I = (\Phi_{ex} - \Phi_i)/L$. The phase difference across the junction can be related to the flux Φ_i by Eq. 5.10(3), which, specialized to one junction, becomes $\phi = 2\pi\Phi_i/\Phi_0$. The voltage across the junction is given by Faraday's Law, $V = d\Phi_i/dt$. Substituting these relations into Eq. 5.03(1), we obtain

$$\Phi_{ex} = \Phi_i + LI_c \sin\frac{2\pi\Phi_i}{\Phi_0} + GL\frac{d\Phi_i}{dt} + LC\frac{d^2\Phi_i}{dt^2} \tag{3}$$

Equation (3) describes a complex dynamic behavior that can be solved for

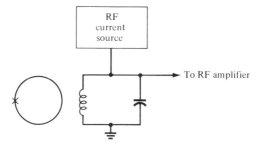

Figure 5.11e. Basic circuit of the RF SQUID.

---

[56] For more details and references see A. H. Silver and J. E. Zimmerman, "Josephson weak-link devices," in *Applied Superconductivity*, Vol. I, V. L. Newhouse (Ed.). New York: Academic Press, 1975.

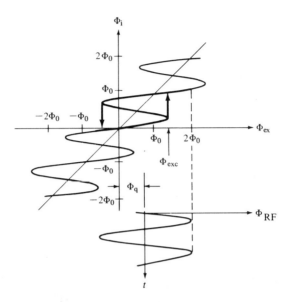

Figure 5.11f. Relation between the flux inside the SQUID loop as a function of external flux in the loop area for $LI_c/\Phi_0 > 1/2\pi$. With sufficient applied RF flux, a lossy hysteretic path is followed. The quasistatic flux applied to the loop causes an offset and leads to switching at Φ_{exc} with a lower level of RF flux. (Data from L. D. Jackel and R. A. Buhrman, footnote 57.)

a detailed understanding of the RF SQUID. A useful understanding of the operation can be achieved in terms of the solutions of the quasistatic simplification of (3):

$$\Phi_i = \Phi_{ex} - LI_c \sin \frac{2\pi\Phi_i}{\Phi_0} \qquad (4)$$

There are two different modes of operation of the RF SQUID which can be defined in terms of the solutions of (4). One, called *hysteretic*, exists when $2\pi LI_c/\Phi_0 > 1$, in which case the $\Phi_i - \Phi_{ex}$ relation has regions of negative slope. The portions of that curve with negative slope are unstable; thus, as the external flux is varied (e.g., sinusoidally as shown in Fig. 5.11f), the internal flux follows a path only along portions of the curve with positive slope and the path is hysteretic. The other mode is called *non-hysteretic* or *inductive* and results where $2\pi LI_c/\Phi_0 \leqslant 1$, in which case the deviations from a diagonal straight line are smaller and there are no portions of the curve with negative slope. We shall discuss the mechanisms involved in SQUID operation in these two modes.

Operation in the hysteretic mode depends on the periodic dependence of the losses in the SQUID loop on the magnitude of the applied quasistatic magnetic field.[57] Figure 5.11f shows the locus of points traced out on the Φ_i-vs.-Φ_{ex} curve for an assumed magnitude of RF applied flux Φ_{RF}. At Φ_{exc}, the current in the junction reaches I_c and during the upward transition a flux quantum enters the loop; a flux quantum leaves the loop at the downward transition. The energy dissipation per cycle is approximately $\Phi_0 I_c$. The amount of RF flux needed to cause the transitions responsible for energy losses depends on the quasistatic applied flux Φ_q. In the usual method of operation, the RF current in the coil which applies flux is set to a large enough value that the SQUID loop would be driven around a hysteretic and lossy path on the Φ_i-vs-Φ_{ex} curve. However, once a lossy transition is made, the level of the oscillations in the tuned circuit decreases and it must then grow enough to make another transition. The fractional energy lost from the tuned circuit is very small and the growth is slow, so the oscillation amplitude is kept at the threshold of the value needed to cause transitions. That amplitude depends on the quasistatic applied flux, as illustrated in Fig. 5.11g; the shape of that dependence is optimized (made triangular) by adjusting the coupling between the tuned circuit and the SQUID loop.

The other mode of operation (*nonhysteretic* or *inductive*) results where $LI_c/\Phi_0 < 1/2\pi$ and the Φ_i-vs-Φ_{ex} relation is single-valued.[58,59] In this case the Josephson junction remains in the zero-dc-voltage state and there are

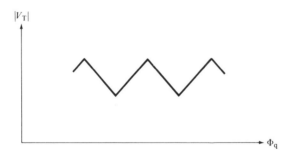

Figure 5.11g. Amplitude of the RF voltage in the tank circuit in the RF SQUID as a function of the applied quasistatic flux.

[57] For a more complete description of this mode of operation, see J. Clarke, "Superconducting quantum interference devices for low frequency measurements," in *Superconductor Applications: SQUIDS and Machines*, B. B. Schwartz and S. Foner (Eds.). New York: Plenum Press, 1977; and L. D. Jackel and R. A. Buhrman, "Noise in the RF SQUID," *J. Low Temp. Phys.*, Vol. 19, Nos. 3/4, pp. 201–246, 1975.

[58] P. K. Hansma, "Observability of Josephson pair–quasiparticle interference in superconducting interferometers," *Phys. Rev. B.* Vol. 12, pp. 1707–1711, 1 September 1975.

[59] S. N. Erné, H. -D. Hahlbohm, and H. Lübbig, "Theory of RF-biased superconducting quantum interference device for nonhysteretic regime," *J. Appl. Phys.*, Vol. 47, pp. 5440–5442, December 1976.

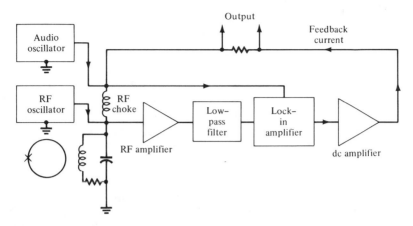

Figure 5.11h. Simplified diagram of the system used to measure the dependence of the magnitude of the RF voltage in a tank circuit coupled to a SQUID loop on the quasistatic applied magnetic flux to be measured. Amplitude modulation by the audio oscillator is used to facilitate the use of lock-in, narrowband detection. The feedback current and, hence, the output voltage are proportional to the measured flux. (From J. Clarke, "Superconducting quantum interference devices for low frequency measurements," in *Superconductor Applications: SQUIDS and Machines*, B. B. Schwartz and S. Foner (Eds.). New York: Plenum Press, 1977, p. 98.)

no important losses in the SQUID loop. There is, however, a periodic variation of the SQUID-loop reactive loading on the tuned circuit (Fig. 5.11e) as the applied quasistatic flux Φ_q through the SQUID loop is varied linearly. This variation of the reactive loading can be ascribed to the Josephson inductance, Eq. 5.05(7), the variation of which during an RF cycle depends on the quasistatic flux Φ_q. The analytical treatments consider the effect from the point of view of the dependence on Φ_q of the current induced in the SQUID loop by the current in the tuned circuit. The SQUID-loop current produces a reaction on the RF tuned circuit through the mutual inductance and thus affects the voltage across the tuned circuit.

The circuit controlling the RF SQUID for either mode is shown in Fig. 5.11h. A low-frequency modulation (typically, 10 kHz) is used in the same way that was described for the dc SQUID in connection with Fig. 5.11d. The RF signal frequency is typically 30 MHz, though sensitivity can be improved with higher frequencies provided the RF amplifier noise does not increase proportionately.

Flux Transformer

It is generally advantageous to use a superconducting flux transformer to couple the flux to be measured into the SQUID loop. The configuration of such a transformer is shown schematically in Fig. 5.11i. The small loop that couples to the SQUID loop is shielded from the measured fields.

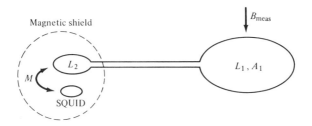

Figure 5.11i. Transformer used to enhance the sensitivity of a SQUID. The SQUID loop may contain one or two junctions for use in RF or dc systems.

When a field B_{meas} is applied (assumed perpendicular for simplicity) to the large loop of area A_1, a current I flows in the loop as needed to keep the flux inside the superconducting transformer at zero (flux quantization). The total flux applied from a measured field that must be compensated by the current is $B_{meas}A_1$. The total flux produced by the transformer $(L_1 + L_2)I$ must just cancel the applied flux, so

$$(L_1 + L_2)I = B_{meas}A_1 \tag{5}$$

The flux coupled into the SQUID loop from L_2 can be expressed in terms of mutual inductance M between them ($\Phi = MI$). The currents flowing in the two coils are the same, so

$$\Phi = \frac{MB_{meas}A_1}{L_1 + L_2} \tag{6}$$

One would judge from (6) that very large increases in sensitivity could be achieved by adjusting the parameters; in practice, a factor of about 10 can be obtained.

Gradiometer

If the transformer arrangement is modified to that shown in Fig. 5.11j, wherein the two coils called L_{11} and L_{12} are as precisely as possible equal

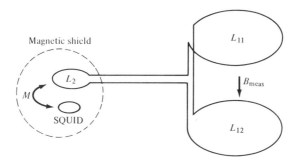

Figure 5.11j. Gradiometer arrangement of flux transformer. Currents induced in L_{11} and L_{12} cancel each other if B_{meas} is a uniform field.

and parallel to one another and are wound with opposite senses, one obtains a current in L_2 that is a measure of the gradient of the magnetic field. There are many applications in which it is possible to eliminate the interference of distant field sources since their gradients are very small compared with the field from the nearby source of interest as, for example, in the measurements of fields produced by the human body.

Figure of Merit

In order to compare the sensitivity of various kinds of SQUIDs, a figure of merit has been devised. It can be shown to be a general measure by comparing separate analyses of various kinds of SQUIDs. It is the least energy per hertz that can be resolved, and is given by

$$S_E = L \frac{(\Delta I)^2}{2} \tag{7}$$

where ΔI is the noise current in loop 2 in Fig. 5.11i and L is the inductance of the SQUID loop. This can be expressed in terms of the spectral density S_Φ of flux noise, which is shown in Fig. 5.11k, as

$$S_E = \frac{S_\Phi}{2M^2/L_2} = \frac{S_\Phi}{2\alpha^2 L} \quad \text{joules/hertz} \tag{8}$$

where $M = \alpha(LL_2)^{1/2}$, so α is a measure of the coupling.

The best value of this parameter obtained to date in a practical configu-

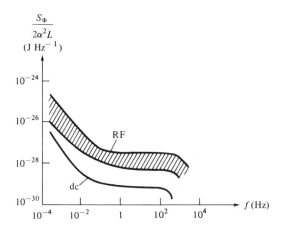

Figure 5.11k. Noise power spectra (plotted as energy resolution) for a dc SQUID and for two commercial RF SQUIDs. The cross-hatched region represents a typical range of value of the noise in commerical RF SQUIDs.

ration is 1.2×10^{-33} J/Hz for a dc SQUID.[60] Recent results on RF SQUIDs are reported elsewhere.[61]

5.12. Single Josephson Junctions and Interferometers as Switches

A single Josephson junction or interferometer (Section 5.10) can be switched between zero-voltage and nonzero-voltage states in times approaching several picoseconds with an extremely low energy. In order to appreciate the motivation for developing the use of Josephson digital circuits, we refer to Fig. 5.12a, a so-called *delay-power graph* which is a commonly used guide for comparison of logic gates based on various technologies. The diagonal lines can be interpreted as the energy required per switching event, which is roughly the product of power and the length of the switching delay through a logic circuit. It is clear that the Josephson logic gates require several orders of magnitude lower switching energy than silicon gates and about two orders of magnitude less than recent results on GaAs gates. In order to take advantage of the very fast switching, it is necessary to have extremely densely packed circuits. The low power levels of Josephson circuits make the required dense packing possible.[62]

A junction may be driven into the nonzero-voltage state by raising the gate current beyond the critical current or by reducing the critical current below the gate current by application of a magnetic field. An interferometer can be treated (from the terminal point of view) as a single junction and likewise be driven into the $V \neq 0$ state by overdriving or by application of a magnetic field to reduce its critical current. The latter was discussed in Section 5.10.

There is a sense in which all switching into the $V \neq 0$ state is by overdrive. In an interferometer, for example, the application of a magnetic field causes a circulating current which adds to the total current passed through the interferometer. Thus, in the circuit shown in Fig. 5.10a, a circulating current following the path shown by a broken line is produced by an applied magnetic field. This current, added to the current I_T, will cause the right-hand junction to have a higher current. If I_T is near $2I_c$ before application of the field so that the current in the right-hand junction is near I_c, the additional current resulting from applying the magnetic field

---

[60] R. R. Voss, R. B. Laibowitz, S. I. Raider, and J. Clarke, "All-Nb low noise dc SQUID with 1 μm tunnel junctions," *J. Appl. Phys.*, Vol. 51, pp. 2306–2309, 1980. See also footnote 55.

[61] J. N. Hollenhorst and R. P. Giffard, "High sensitivity microwave SQUID," *IEEE Trans. Magn.*, Vol. MAG-15, pp. 474–477, January 1979.

[62] The current state of a large portion of the work in this field is described in detail in a special issue of the *IBM J. Res. Dev.*, Vol. 24, March 1980, and in a special issue of the *IEEE Trans. Electron Devices*, Vol. ED-27, October 1980.

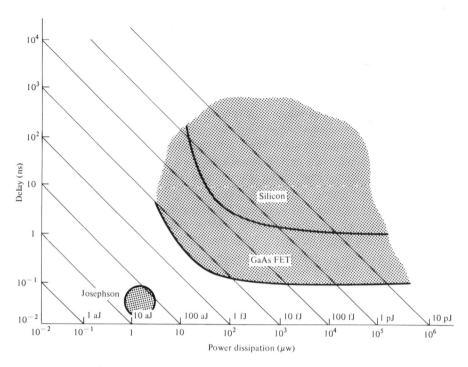

Figure 5.12a. Delay-power chart showing the advantage of Josephson digital logic gates over semiconductor gates. The oblique lines are loci of constant energy per switching event; it is seen that the Josephson devices require orders of magnitude less energy than their semiconductor counterparts. (©IEEE. Reprinted, with permission, from T. Van Duzer, *IEEE Transactions on Microwave Theory and Techniques*, Vol. MTT-28, p. 491, May 1980.)

may be sufficient to make the current through that junction greater than I_c and, therefore, necessarily switch it to the $V \neq 0$ state. The voltage developed will cause a transfer of current to the junction on the left side and it, too, will switch to the $V \neq 0$ state. The entire interferometer is then in the $V \neq 0$ state. In Section 5.04 it was pointed out that a single junction can be represented by a multiplicity of junctions representing portions of a larger junction and interconnected by inductances (shown in Fig. 5.04b as a subdivision into two smaller junctions). This equivalent circuit is useful for understanding the switching event in a single junction upon application of magnetic field, since it makes the junction equivalent to the interferometer we just discussed. Upon application of a magnetic field, the current density at one edge of a junction will exceed the local critical current density and the resultant switching to the $V \neq 0$ state there will redirect currents and drive the rest of the junction into the V $\neq$ 0 state.

To avoid excess complexity in the discussions of this and the following

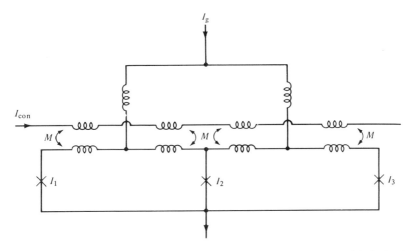

Figure 5.12b. Equivalent circuit of a three-junction interferometer with inductive coupling to the control line.

two sections, we shall treat interferometers as single devices and distinguish switching by application of a magnetic field from that caused by supplying excess current from the external circuit. For switching by magnetic induction, a thin-film control line is placed over, and insulated from, the junction or interferometer. In the case of a single junction, current in the control line produces a magnetic field that passes through the junction barrier. For interferometers, there is an inductive coupling between the control line and the strips making up the interferometer, as shown in the equivalent circuit of Fig. 5.12b. (Both two- and three-junction interferometers are being applied in digital circuits.) One can make a diagram showing the dependence of the critical current of a junction or of an entire interferometer on the current through the control line. These are the kinds of graph shown in Section 5.10 with magnetic flux replaced by control current. They are usually called *threshold characteristics* for devices in digital circuit applications.

A tunnel junction or an interferometer employing tunnel junctions has a static $I-V$ characteristic like that shown in Fig. 5.12c, and switching occurs either along $A-B$ or $A'-B'$ when the junction is overdriven or magnetically controlled, respectively. In the case of overdriving, the slope of the line $A-B$ depends on the rate of increase of the gate current during switching. For magnetic control, the current through the junction or interferometer, called *gate current* I_g, is set to the level marked A' somewhat below the critical current. With control current applied, the critical current is lowered below the gate current and switching to B' occurs.

The various delays in switching a junction are illustrated in Fig. 5.12d,

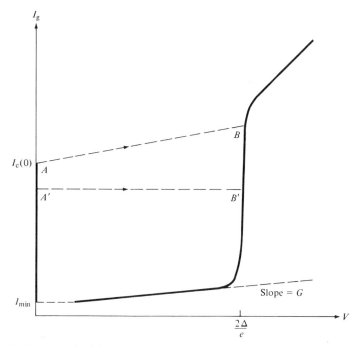

Figure 5.12c. A typical hysteretic $I-V$ characteristic for a Josephson junction or interferometer suitable for switching applications. The broken line $A-B$ represents the transition from the $V = 0$ state to the $V \neq 0$ state with gate-current overdrive. The $A'-B'$ line shows the switching trajectory with a constant-current source and magnetic depression of the critical current.

which shows a small junction switched to the $V \neq 0$ state by the overdrive described by the inset. Subsequent reduction of the gate current allows the junction to return to the $V = 0$ state if the current is below an amount called I_{min} (Fig. 5.12c). The reason is that the average voltage at that point is sufficiently small that, with the superposed oscillating voltage, the total can reach zero. Once that happens, the junction returns to the zero-average-voltage state. It is instructive to consider the behavior of the pendulum analog (Section 5.04). If the analog has been spinning (corresponding to the $V \neq 0$ state), its average angular velocity corresponds to the average voltage. Because of the mass of the pendulum bob, the angular velocity is modulated and it reduces as the bob is rising against gravity. At some value of drive torque, corresponding to I_{min}, the weight of the bob brings the pendulum to zero angular velocity before it reaches the top. The pendulum then falls into decaying oscillations about the $\phi = 0$ position. These are the plasma oscillations discussed in Section 4.04 and Problem 5.03d. They should be allowed largely to die out before a subsequent switching; the time required to decay by a factor of $1/e$ is $2RC$.

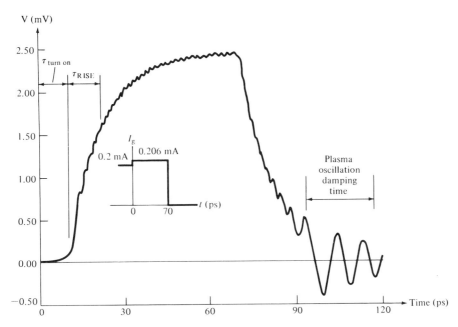

Figure 5.12d. Typical switching of a Josephson junction from $V = 0$ state to $V \neq 0$ state and return by stepping the junction current. $I_c = 0.2$ mA, $C = 1$ pF, and $R = 12\ \Omega$, where R is the subgap resistance. (©1980 IEEE. Reprinted, with permission, from T. Van Duzer, *IEEE Transactions on Microwave Theory and Techniques*, Vol. MTT-28, p. 492, May 1980.)

The various delays in Fig. 5.12d include the so-called *turn-on delay*[63] that results as the initial overdrive currents go into raising the rate of change of the junction phase. During this period, the voltage does not increase much. The length of this delay, measured as the time taken for the phase to reach $\approx 3\pi/2$, depends on the capacitance as $\tau \propto C^{1/2}$. The turn-on delay is worsened for interferometers by the larger time required to redistribute current after one junction switches to $V \neq 0$.

The time required for charging the capacitance is found as follows. First note that the capacitor largely shorts out the ac Josephson current, so the supply current can be considered to be driving a parallel G–C circuit. The conductance is the subgap ($V < 2\Delta/e$) value, so the capacitor charges toward I_A (or $I_{A'}$) times $1/G$. This is much higher than $2\Delta/e$, so the rise is

---

[63] E. P. Harris, "Turn-on delay of Josephson interferometer logic devices," *IEEE Trans. Magn.*, Vol. MAG-15, pp. 562–565, January 1979. D. G. McDonald, R. L. Peterson, C. A. Hamilton, R. E. Harris, and R. L. Kautz, "Picosecond applications of Josephson junctions," *IEEE Trans. Electron Devices*, Vol. ED-27, pp. 1945–1965, October 1980.

nearly linear in this approximation. It is easily seen that the rise time is nearly $(2\Delta/e)C/I_A$.

It is clear from the above that all delays increase with increasing capacitance. This suggests that circuits of the highest speed may require a different kind of junction from the oxide-barrier tunnel junction used almost exclusively to date. Semiconductor- and semimetal-coupled junctions, possibly of the form in Fig. 5.02c, may find use for this purpose.

The earliest measurements of switching speed were made by Matisoo in 1966.[64] He showed that the voltage rise-time depends on capacitance and gave an upper bound of 800 ps. Since then, fabrication of small, high-current-density junctions have made possible much shorter times. The values seemed to be in the tens of picoseconds but could not be measured accurately. An entire simple logic gate based on an interferometer has been made with a delay time of 13 ps; this will be discussed in Section 5.14.

Problems

5.12. Assume a junction is connected to a current source I_A and the critical current I_c is reduced below I_A. Show that the time required for the junction voltage to rise to $2\Delta/e$, the gap voltage, is given by

$$\tau = -\frac{C}{G}\ln\left(1 - \frac{2\Delta G}{eI_A}\right) \approx \frac{2\Delta}{e}\frac{C}{I_A}$$

where G and C are the subgap conductance and capacitance of the junction. This requires the neglect of the Josephson current (assuming that the Josephson frequency becomes large enough to be filtered out by C as the voltage rises). Find the rise time for an oxide-barrier junction having the I–V characteristic in Fig. 5.12c with $I_c(0) = 1$ mA and $2\Delta/e = 2 \times 10^{-3}$ V. Assume the following: area = 10 μm^2; oxide thickness = 2 nm; oxide dielectric constant $\varepsilon_r = 9$; supply current $I_A = 0.8$ mA; $T \ll T_c$.

5.13. Memory Cells

Superconductive loops containing Josephson junctions can be used to store circulating currents and their associated magnetic flux and can therefore act as memory cells. These cells are advantageous because there is no power dissipated during storage, very small energy ($\approx 10^{-18}$ J) is required for switching from one logic state to the other, high-speed switching ($< 10^{-10}$ s) is obtained, and the memory is nonvolatile as long as the cell stays in the superconducting state.[65]

---

[64] J. Matisoo, "Subnanosecond Pair-Tunneling to Single-Particle Tunneling Transitions in Josephson Junctions," *Appl. Phys. Lett.*, Vol. 9, pp. 166–168, 15 August 1966.

[65] A recent summary of the state of work on superconductive memory cells is given in H. H. Zappe, "Memory cell design in Josephson technology," *IEEE Trans. Electron Devices*, Vol. ED-27, pp. 1870–1882, October 1980.

Memory cells that have been reported can be divided into two main categories. A cell with the capability of nondestructive readout is suitable for a cache memory, where speed is of utmost importance. The second category is a cell that can be packed more densely but is read destructively so its contents require refreshing after reading. Such a cell is suitable for a main memory, where density is at a premium.

Memory Cell with Nondestructive Readout

The earliest memory cell (Fig. 5.13a) employing Josephson junctions had nondestructive readout and was originally proposed by Anacker.[66] Details of its behavior were worked out subsequently by Zappe.[67] It contained two write junctions which could be used with various combinations of word currents passing through the loop and bit currents controlling the states of the junctions in such a way as to set up circulating currents in either clockwise or counterclockwise directions to represent 0s and 1s. The circulating currents persist after removal of the driving currents and provide the memory. The read gate was designed such that in the presence

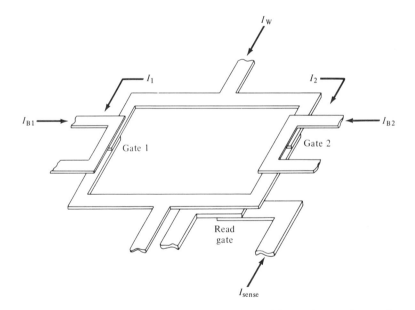

Figure 5.13a. Multiple-flux-quanta memory loop with nondestructive readout.

[66] W. Anacker, "Potential of superconductive Josephson tunneling technology for ultrahigh performance memories and processors," *IEEE Trans. Magn.* Vol. MAG-5, pp. 968–975, December 1969.

[67] H. H. Zappe, "A subnanosecond Josephson tunneling memory cell with nondestructive readout," *IEEE J. Solid-State Circuits*, Vol. SC-10, pp. 12–19, February 1975.

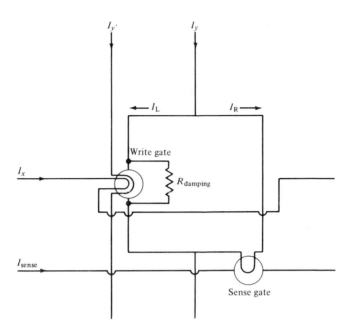

Figure 5.13b. NDRO memory cell. (From S. M. Faris, W. H. Henkels, E. A. Valsamakis, and H. H. Zappe, *IBM J. Res. Dev.*, Vol. 24, No. 2, p. 146, March 1980. Copyright 1980 by International Business Machines Corporation; reprinted with permission.)

of a clockwise circulating current, the junction would switch to the $V \neq 0$ state upon application of the sense current; the appearance of a voltage on the sense line indicated the presence of a **1** in the cell. A possible ternary operation of the cell has been analyzed in which the three states are those mentioned above plus zero circulating current.[68]

A more recent configuration for the nondestructive-readout cell contains only one write cell and thereby has the advantage of reduced size.[69] A schematic is shown in Fig. 5.13b. The cell uses a three-junction interferometer (Fig. 5.10i) as the write gate and an asymmetrically fed two-junction interferometer as the read gate. The two states of the cell are zero circulating current, which represents the logical **0**, and a clockwise current to represent the **1**.[70]

---

[68] H. W. Chan, T. Van Duzer, and S. N. Erné, "A tri-stable-state Josephson device memory cell," *IEEE Trans. Magn.*, Vol. MAG-15, pp. 1928–1932, November 1979.

[69] P. Wolf, "Two-junction Josephson memory," *IBM Tech. Discl. Bull.* Vol. 16, p. 214, June 1973.

[70] W. H. Henkels, "Fundamental criteria for the design of high-performance Josephson nondestructive readout random access memory cells and experimental confirmation," *J. Appl. Phys.*, Vol. 50, pp. 8143–8168, December 1979.

To write a **1** regardless of the initial state, a supply current I_y is first applied. It splits up into currents in the two legs in such a way as to keep the total flux in the loop at zero. Thus, the branch currents are determined by $I_L L_L = I_R L_R$, where L_L and L_R are the inductances of the left and right branches of the loop, respectively. We shall assume $L_R = L_L$ so the current I_y splits symmetrically. The currents I_x and $I_{y'}$ are applied to the cell after the current I_L is established in the write gate. The gate switches to the $V \neq 0$ state and the current I_L is thereby driven to the right-hand branch. On removal of all drive currents, a clockwise circulating current representing a **1** is left in the loop. (This is understood more easily if the state before removal of I_y is considered to be the superposition of I_y split symmetrically between the two legs plus a clockwise circulating current of $I_y/2$.)

A **0** is written in a cell with an initial **1** state by dissipating the circulating current. This is accomplished by switching the write gate to the $V \neq 0$ state by coincident application of I_x and $I_{y'}$. Of course, if the initial state is **0**, nothing happens.

The cell is read nondestructively by coincident application of I_y and I_{sense}. If a **0** had been stored, the current through the control line of the sense gate would be $I_y/2$ and this is insufficient to switch the sense gate. If a **1** had been stored, the circulating $I_y/2$ is supplemented by an additional $I_y/2$ and the sum is sufficient to switch the sense gate. When made with 2.5-μm minimum linewidths, the switching time of the cell is 120 ps. It is to be imbedded in a memory unit containing drivers, decoders, and sensing with an access time of < 500 ps for a $4 \times 1\text{K}$ chip.[71]

This type of cell has been operated satisfactorily with as little as one flux quantum stored, in which case the stored energy was only 6×10^{-20} J.

Memory Cell with Destructive Readout

This cell consists of a single two-junction interferometer designed in such a way as to maintain itself stably in either of two states. The chosen states are those with either zero or one flux quantum in the interferometer loop. The threshold characteristic shown in Fig. 5.13c is similar to that in Fig. 5.10d, but here we are interested in the structure below the upper envelope. The region under the curve marked $n = 0$ defines the range of values of gate and control currents for which there can be zero flux inside the loop, and the loop may be entirely in the superconducting state. Under the $n = 1$ curve there can be one flux quantum in the loop, and the loop again may be superconductive. As a result of the self-fields, there is an overlapping of the various states. Where they overlap, there is more than one possible

---

[71] S. M. Faris, W. H. Henkels, E. A. Valsamakis, and H. H. Zappe, "Basic design of a Josephson cache memory," *IBM J. Res. Dev.*, Vol. 24, pp. 143–154, March 1980.

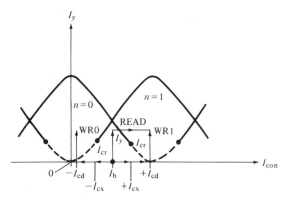

Figure 5.13c. Threshold characteristic of the single-flux-quantum memory cell. Properties of the cell are chosen to overlap the modes with zero and one flux quantum in the loop. (© 1979 IEEE. Reprinted with permission, from R. F. Broom et al., *IEEE Journal of Solid-State Circuits*, p. 692.)

state of the loop. In particular, at control current I_b in Fig. 5.13c, the loop may contain either zero flux or one flux quantum. The state with zero flux is considered to represent a stored **0** and that with one flux quantum represents **1**. We shall see that it is possible to switch from one state to the other. It is also possible to detect which state exists by means of an external circuit.

The basic cell is shown in Fig. 5.13d; the one control line shown represents the three that are actually used. For both writing and reading, the bias current I_b is continuously applied. In order to write a **1** in an

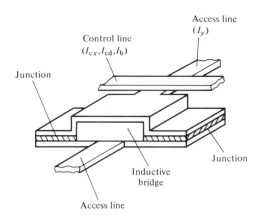

Figure 5.13d. Single-flux-quantum memory cell. Single control line shown here represents three lines in actual device. (© 1979 IEEE. Reprinted, with permission, from R. F. Broom et al., *IEEE Journal of Solid-State Circuits*, p. 692.)

initially empty cell, I_{cx} and I_{cd} are first applied, and then I_y. This takes the loop into the $n = 1$ state below a certain critical current I_{cr} and the transition is made without significant voltage perturbations being generated.[72] A flux quantum has been introduced into the cell and it remains there after the currents I_{cx} and I_{cd} are removed. If the cell initially contains one flux quantum and a **0** is to be written, the driver currents must have the opposite polarity, so $-I_{cx}$ and $-I_{cd}$ are applied, and then I_y. This carries the cell into the $n = 0$ state below the critical current I_{cr} and the flux is removed from the cell without significant voltage perturbations. It remains in that state when $-I_{cx}$ and $-I_{cd}$ are removed.

For reading, the currents are applied in opposite order and always with positive drive currents. Suppose the cell is in the **0** state initially. First I_y is applied and then I_{cx} and I_{cd}; this carries operation across the state boundary above the current I_{cr} and the loop enters the voltage state. On the other hand, if the loop had been in the **1** state when the read-sequence currents were applied, there would be no state change and no voltage developed. This permits determination of the state but destroys the information upon reading. The information is restored by a write cycle generated on-chip.

A model 16K random-access memory chip with a 15-ns access time has been tested and shown to be feasible.[73]

Problem

5.13. Follow through the operation of the memory cell in Fig. 5.13b to show that the writing of a **1** works as described in the text regardless of the initial state.

5.14. Logic Circuits

Several families of logic circuits using Josephson junctions have been demonstrated since the earliest one was reported by Herrell in 1974.[74] Switching time has decreased from about 200 ps to tens of picoseconds— including one measurement of a 13-ps OR gate. Both latching and non-latching circuits have been reported. The earlier types used magnetic control of the junctions; more recent ones have made use of current overdrive. The circuits have almost exclusively used tunnel junctions. The important criteria applied to logic circuits are usually the following:

---

[72] Fulton et al. (footnote 47).

[73] R. F. Broom, P. Guerét, W. Kotyczka, Th. O. Mohr, A. Moser, A. Oosenbrug, and P. Wolf, "Model for a 15 ns 16K RAM with Josephson junctions," *IEEE J. Solid-State Circuits*, Vol. SC-14, pp. 690–699, August 1979.

[74] D. J. Herrell, "Femtojoule Josephson tunneling logic gates," *IEEE J. Solid-State Circuits*, Vol. SC-9, pp. 277–282, October 1974.

a. gain (output current exceeds required input),
b. low power (for dense packing),
c. smallest possible size (for dense packing),
d. fast switching,
e. design margins adequate to allow for component variability,
f. impedance matching to small transmission lines, and
g. high reliability.[75]

The first logic circuit reported was based on switching of a single large in-line junction by magnetic fields produced by two or three overlying control lines. The various gates were designed to be fed in series. The output is taken from across the junction on a matched transmission line, which also serves as the control line for several succeeding stages of logic in a series fan-out arrangment (see Fig. 5.14a). By proper design of the threshold characteristic (I_c vs I_{con}) of the junction and appropriate selection of control-current polarities, it is possible to achieve the needed OR, AND, and INVERT functions. With the output line matched and of not very low impedance, the circuit latches and it is necessary to pulse the power

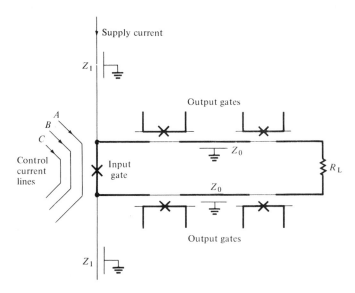

Figure 5.14a. Early Josephson logic circuit with a fan-in of three and fan-out of four. The supply lines and other control lines are not shown for the output gates.

---

[75] More complete reviews of work on Josephson logic circuits may be found in T. Van Duzer, "Josephson digital devices, circuits, and systems," *IEEE Trans. Microwave Theory Tech.*, Vol. MTT-28, pp. 490–500, March 1980; T. R. Gheewala, "Josephson logic devices and circuits," *IEEE Trans. Electron Devices*, Vol. ED-27, pp. 1857–1869, October 1980.

supply to reset the gates after each operation. With a number of gates in series, the resetting time is disadvantageously long. By changing the impedance presented by the load transmission line, the circuit could be operated in a nonlatching mode. The large single junction does not scale well to narrower linewidths and has rather large capacitance. These facts suggested the eventual change to the use of interferometers as the switching elements.

The development of an on-chip powering scheme[76] and the transition to the use of magnetically controlled interferometers led to a new logic family. In this powering scheme it is recognized that the symmetry of the Josephson junction $I-V$ characteristic permits a bipolar clock to be used. A sinusoidal signal is inductively coupled onto the chip and distributed to small clipping circuits consisting of a series of junctions, as shown in Fig. 5.14b. The resulting clipped voltage level is sufficient that logic circuits can

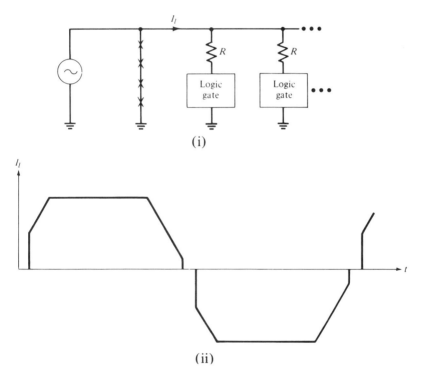

Figure 5.14b. (i) ac power source with regulation by a series of Josephson junctions. (ii) Current waveform supplied to logic gates. (After P. G. Arnett and D. J. Herrell, footnote 76.)

[76] P. G. Arnett and D. J. Herrell, "Regulated AC power for Josephson interferometer logic circuits," *IEEE Trans. Magn.*, Vol. MAG-15, pp. 554–557, January 1979.

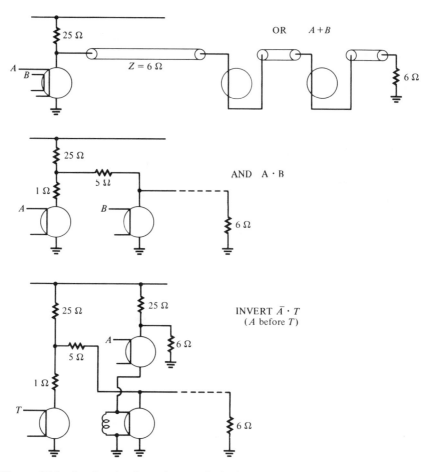

Figure 5.14c. Logic circuits using a clocked ac power supply. (© 1978 IEEE. Reprinted, with permission, from M. Klein and D. J. Herrell, *IEEE Journal of Solid-State Circuits*, p. 579.)

be driven through isolation resistors so that switching transients in one gate do not affect another.

The circuits shown in Fig. 5.14c all use three-junction symmetrical interferometers of the type in Fig. 5.10h and have one or two control lines.[77] The circuits are powered by the ac source circuit in Fig. 5.14b, are of the latching type, and use serial fan-out. When made in 5-μm line-widths, the average logic delays are 58 ps for a fan-out of one, with an added delay of 14 ps for each additional fan-out gate.

---

[77] M. Klein and D. J. Herrell, "Sub-100 ps experimental Josephson interferometer logic gates," *IEEE J. Solid-State Circuits*, Vol. SC-13, pp. 577–583, October 1978.

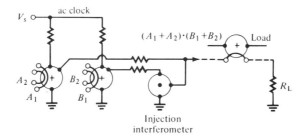

Figure 5.14d. Two-input AND gate with two magnetically coupled isolation interferometers and one direct-coupled interferometer. (© 1979 IEEE. Reprinted, with permission, from T. R. Gheewala, *IEEE Journal of Solid-State Circuits*, p. 787.)

In another ac-powered latching logic family, magnetic control was combined with direct injection of current into the interferometer switches.[78] The two-input OR circuit is the same as in the last-discussed family except for the order of applying currents, which here allows overdriving for speed. Inductive coupling is used in all logic states to achieve isolation. The two-input AND gate shown in Fig. 5.14d employs two interferometers to provide isolation of the input control lines from the output. The outputs of these isolation interferometers are combined by direct injection into a third interferometer shown in Fig. 5.14e. This injection interferometer contains two junctions in a single loop and is fed in such a way as to maximize gain. This leads to small logic delays, wide margins, and parallel fan-out. To give wide margins for the injection

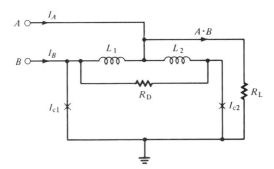

Figure 5.14e. Injection interferometer. (© 1979 IEEE. Reprinted, with permission, from T. R. Gheewala, *IEEE Journal of Solid-State Circuits*, p. 788.)

---

[78] T. R. Gheewala, "A 30-ps Josephson current injection logic (CIL)," *IEEE J. Solid-State Circuits*, Vol. SC-14, pp. 787–793, October 1979.

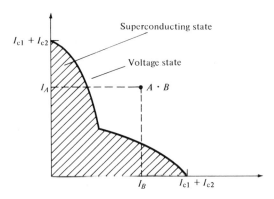

Figure 5.14f. Threshold characteristic of the injection interferometer. (© 1979 IEEE. Reprinted, with permission, from T. R. Gheewala, *IEEE Journal of Solid-State Circuits*, p. 788.)

currents, the inductances and critical currents are chosen to satisfy

$$L_1 I_{c1} = L_2 I_{c2} \quad \text{and} \quad (L_1 + L_2) I_{c2} = \Phi_0$$

where Φ_0 is the flux quantum. The former condition ensures that the current I_A acting alone must reach $I_{c1} + I_{c2}$ to switch the interferometer into the $V \neq 0$ state. The latter condition ensures that I_B alone would have the same requirement. However, with I_A and I_B present simultaneously each must be only about one-third of $I_{c1} + I_{c2}$. Minimization of the threshold values of the injection currents I_A and I_B is achieved by choosing the ratio of critical currents $(I_{c2}/I_{c1}) \approx 3$. The result is the threshold characteristic in Fig. 5.14f which shows, by the region without cross-hatching, the allowed ranges of the injection currents. This logic family has the properties of high gain and wide operating margins. The high gain results from the fact that the AND circuit (and also the four-input OR) diverts two units of current (both I_A and I_B) to its output. The gain permits the use of parallel fan-out to reduce fan-out delays and overdrive to reduce switching delays.

The experimental results on this logic family [Current Injection Logic (CIL)], when fabricated with 2.5-μm linewidths, showed a nominal logic delay of 36 ps per gate with an average fan-in of 4.5 and fan-out of 3; the power dissipation per gate was 3.4 μW.

It is possible to make logic gates that have isolation between input and output without magnetic coupling. Isolation can be achieved with series junctions in the $V \neq 0$ state. One type of gate[79] employs two junctions and a resistor as shown in Fig. 5.14g. Fan-in for an AND circuit is achieved by

[79] T. A. Fulton, S. S. Pei, and L. N. Dunkleberger, "A Josephson logic design employing current-switched Josephson gate," *Appl. Phys. Lett.*, Vol. 34, pp. 709–711, 15 May 1979.

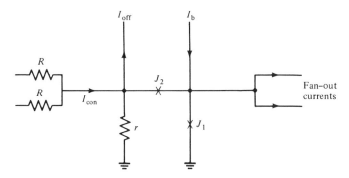

Figure 5.14g. Current-switched logic circuit. (After Fulton et al., footnote 79.)

direct connection. The gates can be combined to achieve other logic functions and their performance can be improved with additions of another resistor and junction. The circuit is most conveniently used as a latching gate, so an ac power source is needed.

Let us review the operation of the basic circuit. The bias current I_b and an additional bias I_{off} are supplied by current sources, and the current I_{con} is from the merged fan-out lines of one or more preceding gates. The fan-out lines contain resistances R much greater than the shunt resistance r. Initially, the junctions J_1 and J_2 are in the $V = 0$ state and the currents flowing are I_b and I_{off}, with possibly some subthreshold value of control current I_{con1}. These currents flow through J_1 and J_2 with levels $I_b - I_{off} + I_{con1}$ and $I_{off} - I_{con1}$, respectively, and the junctions are designed not to switch with these levels. The control current I_{con1} may be one of the two inputs of a two-input AND gate. When the second input is added, I_{con} rises so that the current in J_1 exceeds its critical current and J_1 switches to the $V \neq 0$ state. The resulting voltage in the J_1–J_2–r loop rises, and this tends to reduce the current in J_1 and increase that in J_2 and r. The current level in J_2 approaches I_b and exceeds the design critical current I_{c2} so that it too switches to the $V \neq 0$ state. The lowest resistance path for I_b then becomes the fan-out line. The currents I_{off} and I_{con} are then diverted to ground through the small resistor r, and only a small disturbance is produced on the input line. The switching speed of the basic circuit has been demonstrated to be less than 30 ps. These circuits have a size advantage over those with magnetically coupled switching elements.[80]

A variety of other kinds of logic circuit have been devised to serve

---

[80] Another family of direct coupled logic has been reported recently. See T. R. Gheewala and A. Mukherjee, "Josephson direct coupled logic," *Proc. 1979 Int. Electron Devices Meeting,* Washington, DC, IEEE No. 79, CHI504-ED, 3–5 December 1979. See also T. R. Gheewala, footnote 75.

special purposes such as the latches required for synchronization of logic signals, the driving, sensing, and decoding circuits for memories, shift registers, and samplers for analog-to-digital conversion.

Problems

5.14a. Where a control line passes over a junction or interferometer, an inductance L_c is added to the control line. Compensation may be made by a shunt capacitance $C = L_c/Z_0^2$ across the line, where Z_0 is the characteristic impedance of the control line. This avoids reflections otherwise resulting from L_c for pulses with rise times $t_r > 3 L_c/Z_0$. Show that the L_c-C combination acts as a section of transmission line with delay $t_c = L_c/Z_0$. Explain why the above rise-time restriction applies.

5.14b. i. Explain how the order of currents should be selected in the OR gate in Fig. 5.14c to permit arbitrary overdrive of the gate current.
   ii. For the same logic family, analyze the operation of the INVERT circuit.

Chapter 6

Fundamental Thermodynamic
and Magnetic Considerations

6.01. Introduction

A substantial and powerful body of theory of superconductivity has thermodynamics as its basis. In particular, the equilibrium state of a superconducting body, with its dependence on various parameters such as temperature or magnetic field, is found by minimization of the free energy. The pervasiveness of this technique in the literature of superconductivity requires the student of the subject to have an understanding of the concept of free energy and a familiarity with the difference between the two kinds of free energy. Other areas of solid-state theory lean little on the thermodynamics of systems with magnetic fields, so the reader is unlikely to be familiar with the subtleties involved.

The special use of the magnetization vector in the theory of superconductors is introduced. A simple approach to finding magnetic fields inside samples of a variety of shapes in uniform external fields then follows.

Subsequent to the general study of the thermodynamics of systems with a magnetic field, we turn our attention to superconductors. Materials that can become superconductors undergo a transition from the normal phase to the superconducting phase at a temperature that depends on the magnetic field in the same way that the phase transistion of water between its liquid and vapor phases depends on the pressure. After discussion of the Ehrenfest scheme for classification of phase transitions, some characteristics of the superconducting transition are derived.

6.02. Fundamental Concepts in Statistical Thermodynamics

The intent of this section is to provide a brief review of the development of some important concepts in thermodynamics, starting from a basic postulate of statistical mechanics. Our discussions will be limited to systems in equilibrium, which include those where time variations of parameters take place slowly compared with the time required for the systems to relax to an equilibrium state. The effects of magnetic field will be treated in some detail in later sections of this chapter since most readers will need an introduction rather than a review for that aspect of thermodynamic theory.

We are interested in systems containing a large number of interacting particles. An exact dynamical treatment of such a system, taking account of all the forces involved and solving the equations of motion of all particles, would be an impossible task for a typical system of interest. It would also give a great deal of information about the positions and velocities of the particles that would not interest us; our interest lies rather in the macroscopic parameters that we can observe. The theory of statistical mechanics provides a means for making powerful statements about some macroscopic parameters (such as magnetization and pressure) when other parameters of the system (such as its total energy, the applied magnetic field, the number of particles, or the volume) are specified.

One imagines an ensemble of an infinite number of systems prepared with identical specified parameters, say, volume and energy. The members of the ensemble are said to be in the same *macrostate*. Some unspecified parameter of the system, say, pressure, taken as an average over all the members of the ensemble, can be calculated by statistical means. Although, by definition of the ensemble, each member has the same macrostate, the detailed arrangement of the particles of the systems changes with time, as do the unspecified macroscopic parameters. The *state* or *microstate* of a system, in a quantum-mechanical description, is the quantum state of the entire system of particles, which is a function of the position and momentum coordinates of each particle. Microstates are described in classical mechanics in terms of locations in a phase space of dimensionality equal to six times the number of particles in the system—there is one dimension for each of the position and momentum coordinates of each particle.

As indicated above, we shall be concerned only with systems in equilibrium. We assume that if something has occurred to the systems of the ensemble to disturb their equilibria (such as a sudden increase in the volume of a vessel containing a gas, where the added volume was initially empty), a sufficient time has elapsed for the systems to reach their new equilibrium states. The basic postulate of the theory is that, *in equilibrium, a system has equal probability of being in any of the microstates that are accessible to it for a given set of macroscopic parameters.*

Now suppose we wish to determine the probability of finding a member of the ensemble with a particular value of some macroscopic parameter which was not specified. For example, in an ensemble of containers of gas for which the volume and total energy of each container is specified, the pressure at each instant will differ from container to container. The probability of finding a member of the ensemble with a particular selected value of pressure is proportional to the number of microstates for which the system will have that value of presssure (i.e., the number of *accessible* states). This is a result of the fact that the system has equal likelihood of being in any microstate consistent with the specified parameters (volume and energy in this case). For pressure near the average, there are a great number of different values that the positions and momenta of the particles can assume (microstates), whereas in other pressure ranges there are fewer possible arrangements. Therefore, the probability of finding a system in the ensemble with pressures near the average will be a maximum. The actual peak in the probability curve depends on the number of particles in the system in a way to be described in Section 6.03 and is extremely sharp in usual systems of interest. The peak value can be taken as the ensemble average and for usual systems this is equal to the time average for each member of the ensemble. Thus the probability of finding a system in the ensemble with a pressure much different from the average value is extremely small. Therein lies the value of statistical mechanics in predicting the behavior of a single real system. The relations of thermodynamics are justified by statistical mechanics, so their application to a particular system is also validated by the fact that the parameters of an individual system do not differ much from their ensemble averages.

6.03. Interacting Systems

The central concern of thermodynamics is the interaction between different systems. One might, for example, be concerned with the energy transfer between a system and a constant-temperature reservoir such as a superconducting sample and a bath of liquid helium in which it is immersed. In this section we shall review the relations of thermodynamics dealing with such interacting systems.

Let us begin by seeing how the internal energy U of a system can be changed. One way is to do work on the system by changing one of its external parameters. Imagine an ensemble of cylinders containing gas held under pressure by pistons, as shown for one member of the ensemble in Fig. 6.03a. The change of volume caused by depressing the piston changes the microstates available to the system. We define the work $\mathcal{W}$ done in this process as the change of the mean energy of the systems in the ensemble, assuming that the walls of the cylinders and the pistons are thermally insulated. Thus

$$\mathcal{W} = \Delta \overline{U}$$

In another type of system, one in which the particles have magnetic moments, work could be done by applying a magnetic field. The resulting alignment of the magnetic moments by the magnetic field changes the mean internal energy by an amount equal to the work done by the field. In all situations where work is done, the energy is changed by changing the microstates available for occupancy by the members of the ensemble.

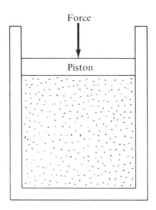

Figure 6.03a. Mechanical work done by changing the volume against the pressure of the gas in the cylinder.

It is also possible to change the energy of a system by thermal interaction with some other system. In this case, the mean internal energy changes as a result of a change in the distribution of the systems in the ensemble over the existing available microstates. We use the increase of the mean energy with purely thermal interaction as a definition of the transfer of heat to the system. Thus

$$\Delta \overline{U} = Q$$

If we consider an infinitesimal change of the energy resulting from an infinitesimal amount of work done on the system and an infinitesimal amount of heat added to the system, we can write the basic thermodynamic relation as

$$d\overline{U} = dQ + d^{\circ}\mathfrak{W}$$

or, calling the work done *by* the system $dW = -d^{\circ}\mathfrak{W}$, this can be written as

$$dQ = d\overline{U} + dW \tag{1}$$

where the symbols dQ and dW are used to signify that heat and work are not quantities that can be changed by differential amounts and are therefore not exact differentials. Rather, they are characteristic of a process that carries the system from one macrostate to another (defined by the mean internal energy and the external parameters) and their values do, in general, depend on the nature of the process. Equation (1) constitutes a statement of the *first law of thermodynamics*.

If these changes are made sufficiently slowly, the system will remain in equilibrium. Each system has some characteristic time in which it can relax to the equilibrium situation of equal probability of occupancy of the accessible states after being disturbed. We shall be concerned with so-called *quasistatic* systems which have relaxation times much shorter than times during which changes of the system parameters are made and can therefore be considered to be in equilibrium at all times.

Now let us consider two systems placed in contact and the combined system isolated from everything else so the energy of the combined system is a constant. Consider, for example, a superconducting rod in a helium bath in a perfectly insulated vessel (the practical approximation is called a *dewar*). The probability that one of them, say, the superconducting rod, has an energy U within a range δU is proportional to the number of microstates accessible to the entire system when the rod has energy U and the bath has the remaining energy $U_{tot} - U$, where U_{tot} is the fixed energy of the total system. We denote the number of states for the rod in the range δU at energy U by $\Omega(U)$. For each accessible state for the rod, there are $\Omega'(U_{tot} - U)$ states for the bath, so the total number of states for the combined system with this distribution of energy between the rod and the bath is

$$\Omega_{tot}(U) = \Omega(U)\Omega'(U_{tot} - U) \tag{2}$$

As we indicated earlier, the probability of finding any system (here the rod plus dewar of helium) in a particular macrostate is proportional to the number of microstates accessible to the system in that macrostate. Thus the probability of the rod having an energy in the range δU at energy U is

$$P(U) = C\Omega(U)\Omega'(U_{tot} - U) \tag{3}$$

where C is a proportionality constant. What is the most probable value for the energy of the rod? It can be argued that the number of states available in the range δU increases very strongly with energy (number is proportional to U^f, where f is the number of degrees of freedom) in typical systems where there are a large number of degrees of freedom. Therefore, $\Omega(U)$ is a very rapidly increasing function of U, and $\Omega'(U_{tot} - U)$ is a very rapidly decreasing function of U. The product (3) is therefore a strongly peaked function as shown in Fig. 6.03b. We shall call the value of energy at the peak $\tilde{U}$. In the equilibrium condition, the probability distribution is Gaussian so the peak and mean values of energy are equal, i.e., $\tilde{U} = \overline{U}$. The width of the region ΔU in which $P(U)$ has appreciable magnitude is extremely small. It can be shown to be

$$(\Delta U / \overline{U}) \approx f^{-1/2} \tag{4}$$

Recall our earlier comments to the effect that other macroscopic parameters also have sharply peaked probability distributions about the mean value. It is the sharpness of the peaks at the ensemble averages that allows us to use the ensemble-average behavior to predict the behavior of a single real system in the laboratory.

We can introduce the important concepts of entropy and temperature from the basic statistical relation for interacting systems (3). Let us set the derivative of the logarithm (for convenience) of (3) to zero to find the

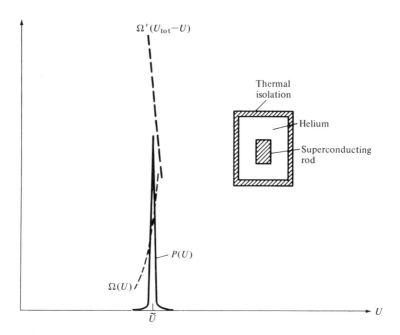

Figure 6.03b. Probability distribution of energy in an ensemble of isolated systems represented by the example in the insert. The rapidly increasing and decreasing quantities Ω and Ω' are the accessible states for the superconducting rod and the helium, respectively. The product is the probability distribution.

conditions for the peak of probability distribution, i.e., the most probable energy. The result is

$$\frac{\partial\left[\ln \Omega(U)\right]}{\partial U} = \frac{\partial\left[\ln \Omega'(U')\right]}{\partial U'} \tag{5}$$

where U' is $U_{\text{tot}} - U$, the energy of the bath. Then defining

$$\beta(U) \overset{\Delta}{=} \frac{\partial\left[\ln \Omega(U)\right]}{\partial U} \tag{6}$$

we have

$$\beta(\tilde{U}) = \beta'(\tilde{U}') \tag{7}$$

at the energy of the most probable state. For systems in equilibrium, their mean energies attain the peak values, so we can then also write

$$\beta(\overline{U}) = \beta'(\overline{U}') \tag{8}$$

The quantity β is a useful thermometric parameter in that two systems in equilibrium are characterized by the same value of the parameter, as shown by (8). In practice, it is more convenient to use the dimensionless quantity

$$T \overset{\Delta}{=} 1/k_B \beta(\overline{U})   \tag{9}$$

as the "absolute temperature," where k_B is Boltzmann's constant.

The quantity "entropy" is defined as

$$S \overset{\Delta}{=} k_B \ln \Omega(U)   \tag{10}$$

and we note from (6), (9), and (10) that it is related to the temperature by

$$\frac{1}{T} = \left(\frac{\partial S}{\partial U} \right)_{U = \overline{U}}   \tag{11}$$

From (5) and (10) we see that, at equilibrium, the total entropy $S + S'$ is a maximum and the temperatures of the two systems T and T' are equal.

One can show that, for any quasistatic process in which the parameters are changed by an infinitesimal amount, a differential change of entropy of a system is related to the heat added by

$$dS = dQ/T   \tag{12}$$

where dS is an exact differential relating the entropies of a system in two infinitesimally different macrostates.[1] This relation is true even if the external parameters are changed so work is done on the system, as long as the changes are quasistatic. Equation (12) and the fact that entropy is a maximum at equilibrum constitute the *second law of thermodynamics*.

For a system where the work done is $p\, dV$ (pressure times a change of volume) and the process can be considered quasistatic, the first law of thermodynamics (1) can be converted, with the help of (12), to the fundamental thermodynamic relation

$$T\, dS = dU + p\, dV   \tag{13}$$

Throughout the remainder of this text the averaging bar will be omitted from macroscopic quantities and the ensemble average is to be assumed.

Problems

6.03a. The purpose of this problem is to develop an order-of-magnitude argument to show the validity of the statement in the text that the number of states of a system in an energy interval δU increases as a function of total system energy U according to U^f, where f is the number of degrees of freedom in the system. We assume that we are considering a system not near its ground state and with a large number of degrees of freedom, on the order of Avogadro's number ($f \approx 10^{24}$).

---

[1] See, for example, F. Reif, *Fundamentals of Statistical and Thermal Physics*. New York: McGraw-Hill, p. 115, 1965.

i. Assume that the total energy U is roughly evenly divided among the f degrees of freedom and that, for any degree of freedom, the number of states n_1 with energy equal to or less than U/f is proportional to U/f. Argue that the total number of states in the system for a total energy of U or less is $\mathfrak{N}(U) \propto (U/f)^f$.

ii. The number of states in an energy interval U to $U + \delta U$ is given by $\Omega(U) = [\partial \mathfrak{N}(U)/\partial U]\,\delta U$, assuming δU to be much greater than the spacing between states. Evaluate $\Omega(U)$, take its logarithm, and use order-of-magnitude arguments to pick out the dominant term, assuming that $n_1 \gg 1$. Use the result to argue that the dependence of $\Omega(U)$ on U is proportional to U^f.

6.03b. Equation 6.03(4) indicated the range over which the probability distribution of energy has an appreciable magnitude. The purpose of this problem is to derive Eq. 6.03(4). Expand the logarithms $\ln \Omega(U)$ and $\ln \Omega'(U')$ in Taylor series about the peaks of the energy $\tilde{U}$ and $\tilde{U}'$ of the two systems in contact (neglecting derivatives above second-order).

i. Invoke the conservation of energy to show that

$$P(U) = P(\tilde{U})\exp\left[-(1/2)\lambda_0(U - \tilde{U})^2\right]$$

$$\lambda_0 \overset{\Delta}{=} -\frac{\partial^2[\ln \Omega'(U')]}{\partial U'^2}$$

ii. Note that this result implies that the peak and mean values of energy are equal ($\tilde{U} = \bar{U}$) and derive Eq. 6.03(4).

iii. Estimate $\Delta U/U$ for 1 mm^3 of a typical solid.

6.03c. We have assigned the number of states accessible to a system of energy U to be the number in the energy interval U to $U + \delta U$, where $\delta(U)$ is small compared with any contemplated measurement, and called this $\Omega(U)$. The entropy then clearly depends on the choice of δU. Assuming a given density of states $d\Omega(U)/dU$, show that the effect on the entropy of making two different choices of $\delta(U)$ is entirely negligible by using the fact that the entropy is of the order $k_B f$, where f is the number of degrees of freedom.

6.04. Helmholtz and Gibbs Free Energies

Central to the application of thermodynamics are various functions that are constants of different types of process. For example, an isolated system has the total internal energy U as a constant of the process. If the process has, as independent variables, the entropy S and the pressure p rather than S and the volume V, it is convenient to use a quantity called *enthalpy*, defined as $H \overset{\Delta}{=} U + pV$, instead of the energy. The enthalpy is used, for example, in the analysis of throttling processes where it, rather than the energy, is conserved. If the independent variables are temperature T and volume V, the *Helmholtz free energy* is used, and if the variables are T and p, the useful function is the *Gibbs free energy* (also called *Gibbs potential*).

The "free energies" are of central importance to the macroscopic theory of superconductivity. We develop ideas here for nonmagnetic systems and then, in Section 6.08, see how they are modified to include magnetic-field effects. The Helmholtz free energy is defined by

$$F \overset{\Delta}{=} U - TS \qquad (1)$$

and the Gibbs free energy is

$$G \overset{\Delta}{=} U - TS + pV \qquad (2)$$

In a thermally isolated system, the maximum work that can be done by the system is equal to the internal energy. That is, $\Delta U = -W$ since the heat transfer Q is zero by definition. We shall see that, for a system in thermal contact with a reservoir at constant temperature and pressure (or volume), one of the free energies equals the maximum available work that can be done by the system. It is this fact that led to the name *free energy*.

Helmholtz Free Energy

Let us consider a system A in thermal contact with a reservoir R as shown in Fig. 6.04a. We shall examine the equilibrium condition where the reservoir is at a constant temperature T_R and is large enough that it can transfer heat to system A without affecting its own temperature. The

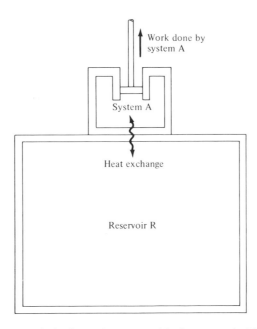

Figure 6.04a. System A is in thermal contact with the reservoir. The total system is isolated from other energy sources.

changes in the reservoir can be considered as quasistatic even though those in A may not be.

The combined system, to which we refer by the subscript "tot", is to be considered isolated, therefore, for any spontaneous process (except for random fluctuations) that takes place in it, $\Delta S_{tot} \geqslant 0$. The change of total entropy is the sum of the changes of entropy of the two systems:

$$\Delta S_{tot} = \Delta S_A + \Delta S_R \geqslant 0 \qquad (3)$$

An exchange of heat Q_A from R to A leads to a decrease of the entropy of the reservoir $\Delta S_R = -Q_A/T_R$, where T_R is the temperature of the reservoir. This exchange of heat combined with the work W_A done by A causes a change of its internal energy ΔU_A equal to $Q_A - W_A$. Then the entropy change of the combined system becomes

$$\Delta S_{tot} = \Delta S_A - \frac{Q_A}{T_R} = \frac{T_R \Delta S_A - (\Delta U_A + W_A)}{T_R}$$

$$= \frac{-\Delta(U_A - T_R S_A) - W_A}{T_R} \geqslant 0 \qquad (4)$$

Now we introduce the definition

$$F_0 \overset{\Delta}{=} U_A - T_R S_A \qquad (5)$$

which differs from the Helmholtz free energy of A by virtue of use of the temperature of the reservoir. Equation (4) becomes

$$\Delta S_{tot} = (-\Delta F_0 - W_A)/T_R \geqslant 0 \qquad (6)$$

In thermal equilibrium, the temperature of system A equals that of the reservoir T_R and (5) becomes the Helmholtz free energy of A. We see from (6) that the requirement of increasing entropy ensures that the work done by A cannot exceed the magnitude of the change of F_0; that is, $W_A \leqslant |\Delta F_0|$. The maximum work is obtained in a quasistatic process, where the equal sign applies. That is, in a quasistatic process, the temperatures of the reservoir and of system A are always equal and the changes of their individual entropies are equal and of opposite sign, so $\Delta S_{tot} = 0$. Then $|\Delta F| = W_A$.

We can also make the important deduction from (6) that if the external parameters of A are fixed and it therefore does no work W, $\Delta F_0 \leqslant 0$. Changes in F_0 are always negative until stable equilibrium is reached. *The equilibrium is therefore characterized by the condition that F_0 is a minimum, and equals the Helmholtz free energy* (1).

Gibbs Free Energy

Now let us consider a somewhat different pair of systems as shown in Fig. 6.04b. As before, there is a reservoir at constant temperature; but here we allow the volume of system A to change and require that the change of

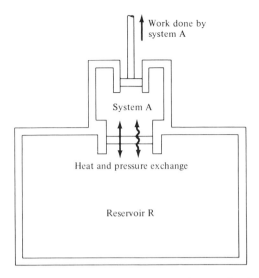

Figure 6.04b. System A is in contact with reservoir R, allowing interchange of thermal and mechanical energy. The total system is thermally isolated but system A may do work W_A^*.

volume thereby imposed on the reservoir is small enough compared with the size of the reservoir that the pressure of the latter can be considered to be unchanged. Again the combined system is isolated, so $\Delta S_{tot} \geqslant 0$. In this case the change of internal energy of A can be expressed as

$$\Delta U_A = Q_A - p_R \Delta V_A - W_A^* \qquad (7)$$

where the last two terms represent the work done *by* A: $p_R \Delta V_A$ is the mechanical work done against the constant pressure of the reservoir and W_A^* refers to other work done by A.

Following the line of reasoning used above for the Helmholtz free energy, one can show that

$$\Delta S_{tot} = \left[-\Delta (U_A - T_R S_A + p_R V_A) - W_A^* \right] / T_R \geqslant 0 \qquad (8)$$

We introduce now the definition of an approximate Gibbs free energy

$$G_0 \overset{\Delta}{=} U_A - T_R S_A + p_R V_A \qquad (9)$$

which is the ordinary Gibbs free energy (2) in the situation when the temperature and pressure of the reservoir equal those of system A. Equation (8) becomes

$$\Delta S_{tot} = (-\Delta G_0 - W_A^*)/T_R \geqslant 0 \qquad (10)$$

From this we can see that the maximum work W_A^* that can be done by the system A is done under quasistatic conditions, where the equal sign in (10) applies and T_R and p_R equal T_A and p_A, respectively; it is equal to the magnitude of the change of the Gibbs free energy.

If $W_A^* = 0$, the approximate Gibbs free energy G_0 can only decrease until at equilibrium it equals the true Gibbs free energy. *Thus the stable equilibrium of a system in contact with a reservoir of constant temperature and pressure with its external parameters fixed so it can only do mechanical work against the pressure of the reservoir is characterized by a minimum value of the Gibbs free energy.*

6.05. Magnetization

The concept of magnetization is used extensively in superconductivity so it is important that we define it carefully here. When the microscopic form of Maxwell's equations, which explicitly includes the free and bound charges and currents in a material body, are averaged over a region large enough to contain many atoms but small compared with positional accuracy in any intended measurement, one obtains the macroscopic form of the equations.[2] Here we are concerned with the differential relations for magnetic-field quantities, so we have

$$\nabla \cdot \vec{B} = 0 \tag{1}$$

$$\nabla \times \frac{\vec{B}}{\mu_0} = \frac{\partial(\epsilon_0 \vec{E} + \vec{P})}{\partial t} + \vec{J} + \langle \rho \vec{v} \rangle_{bound} \tag{2}$$

where $\vec{B}$ is the average value of the magnetic field over the small region and is called the magnetic induction or flux density, $\vec{E}$ is the average value of the electric field, $\vec{P}$ is the average electric-dipole density, $\vec{J}$ is the flow of free electrons, and the last term represents the internal motion of the electronic charge in the atoms and includes the orbital and spin effects. It is convenient to introduce a quantity called *magnetization* to represent the bound currents, where

$$\langle \rho \vec{v} \rangle_{bound} = \nabla \times \vec{M} \tag{3}$$

and the electric flux density $\vec{D} = \epsilon_0 \vec{E} + \vec{P}$. Then (2) becomes

$$\nabla \times \left(\frac{\vec{B}}{\mu_0} - \vec{M} \right) = \frac{\partial \vec{D}}{\partial t} + \vec{J} \tag{4}$$

We define a local macroscopic field intensity $\vec{H}$ by

$$\vec{H} \overset{\Delta}{=} (\vec{B}/\mu_0) - \vec{M} \tag{5}$$

---

[2] In the literature on superconductivity, the terms *microscopic* and *macroscopic* are used differently. *Microscopic* refers to variations of fields, currents, and the Cooper pair density on a size scale of about 1 μm (10^{-6}m), which is some 3–4 orders of magnitude larger than the dimensions involved in the use of the term for electromagnetic equations in solids. *Macroscopic* is used for treatments where the micron-size variations are averaged out.

and (4) can be written in the familiar form

$$\nabla \times \vec{H} = \frac{\partial \vec{D}}{\partial t} + \vec{J} \qquad (6)$$

The definition of $\vec{M}$ used above has general currency in the treatment of nonsuperconducting materials such as ferromagnetics, but the effect of the bound currents (paramagnetic and diamagnetic responses) in metals is very small except at extremely high magnetic fields. It is common in the field of superconductivity to include the circulating currents in the definition of $\vec{M}$. Note that the total free current in a superconductor may consist of two components. One is the circulating current $\vec{J}_{int}$ which results from the superconductor's response to a magnetic field as in the Meissner effect discussed in Section 3.06. The other component $\vec{J}_{ext}$ is a current which is supplied to the superconductor from outside as in Fig. 3.07; this component is not included in the modified definition of $\vec{M}$:

$$\langle \rho \vec{v} \rangle_{bound} + \vec{J}_{int} = \nabla \times \vec{M} \qquad (7)$$

We should keep in mind that this magnetization in a superconductor arises mainly from the circulating currents. With this definition of $\vec{M}$, (6) can be written as

$$\nabla \times \vec{H} = \frac{\partial \vec{D}}{\partial t} + \vec{J}_{ext} \qquad (8)$$

As an example of the use of the above meanings of $\vec{M}$, let us consider a thin slab of superconductor subjected to a small dc parallel magnetic field as shown in Fig. 6.05a. If the applied magnetic field is $\vec{H}_0 = \hat{y}H_{0y}$, current will flow as shown and will have the value found in Prob. 3.06b:

$$J_z(x) = \frac{H_0}{\lambda} \frac{\sinh(x/\lambda)}{\cosh(a/\lambda)} \qquad (9)$$

where a is the half-width of the slab and λ is the penetration depth. If we assume that the magnetic response of the bound currents in (2) is negligible, that there are no time variations, and that $\vec{J}$ represents the circulating currents flowing in response to the applied magnetic field, we can calculate the magnetic induction using (2) and (9):

$$B_y(x) = \mu_0 H_0 \frac{\cosh(x/\lambda)}{\cosh(a/\lambda)} \qquad (10)$$

In this treatment we have not used the concept of magnetization and the currents are taken into account explicitly. Since $\vec{M}$ is zero (we are neglecting the small effect of the bound currents), (5) gives the magnetic field $\vec{H}$ as $\vec{B}/\mu_0$, so $\vec{H}$ varies inside the slab in the same manner as $\vec{B}$.

Now let us consider the approach where we replace the circulating

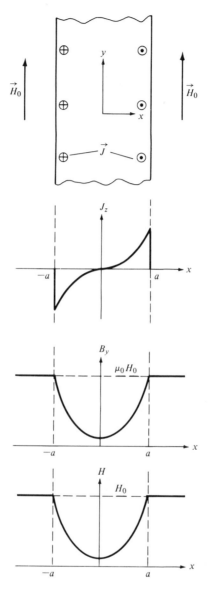

Figure 6.05a. Current, induction, and magnetic-field intensity in a superconducting slab in the formalism in which magnetization does not include the circulating currents.

currents by an equivalent magnetization as in (7). Now we must use (8); we see that $\nabla \times \vec{H} = 0$ inside the slab. Thus it can readily be seen that, with this usage, $\vec{H}$ is constant in the slab. Since $\vec{H}$ is continuous at the boundaries, it is uniform throughout the region. Neglecting the bound currents, the magnetization can be calculated from the known current

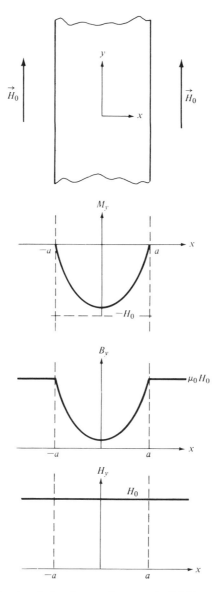

Figure 6.05b. Magnetization, induction, and magnetic-field intensity in a superconducting slab using the formalism in which a magnetization represents the circulating currents.

distribution. Thus from (7), we get

$$M_y(x) = H_0\left(\frac{\cosh(x/\lambda)}{\cosh(a/\lambda)} - 1 \right) \tag{11}$$

Then, by using (5), we obtain $\vec{B}$ with the same value as in (10). The magnetization given by (11) depends on position in the slab (see Fig. 6.05b).

One also may refer to the *average magnetization*, by which is meant the average of $\vec{M}$ over the body. It is easy to show that the average magnetization of the slab in the above example has the magnitude

$$M = H_0\left[(\lambda/a)\tanh(a/\lambda) - 1\right] \tag{12}$$

This average magnetization is shown as a function of thickness in Fig. 6.05c. In the Meissner state, the average magnetization is usually considered to be $-\vec{H}_0$ for a body of this shape or others in which the external field is not disturbed. However, it is clear that this is an approximation which is accurate only if the transverse dimensions of the body are much larger than the penetration depth λ.

The shape of the sample was chosen in the above example to simplify the problem. Long rods parallel to the field are also convenient. For other shapes, the internal $\vec{H}$ is not equal to the external value and the field outside the body is distorted; this complicates the problems somewhat, but they can be treated using demagnetization factors, as discussed in the next section.

Problem

6.05. Consider a thin circular superconducting rod lying with its axis parallel to an applied field $\vec{H}_0$. Calculate the current distribution and the equivalent distribution of magnetization. Find an expression for the average magnetization and plot the result as a function of the rod diameter, normalized to the penetration depth.

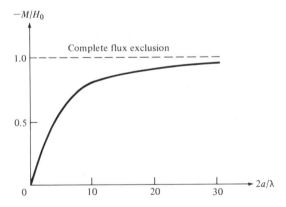

Figure 6.05c. Average magnetization in the superconducting slab in Fig. 6.05b as a function of slab thickness, normalized to the penetration depth. It is common convention to consider the magnetization to be negative if it is directed in the direction opposite to the applied magnetic field.

6.06. Demagnetization Factors

In this section we introduce a method for calculation of $\vec{H}$, $\vec{M}$, and $\vec{B}$ inside a sample having the shape of an ellipsoid of revolution and dimensions one or two orders of magnitude larger than the size of any magnetization variations. This theory was not developed specifically for superconductors but can be so applied. For example, if the diameter of a superconducting sphere located in a sufficiently weak magnetic field is greater than, say, 30 times the penetration depth, the magnetization varies only close to the surface and the theory of this section can be applied with a reasonable degree of accuracy. Later, we shall encounter other situations in superconductors wherein the magnetization has many variations inside a sample, not just at the surface. In such cases, the analysis requires a magnetization that is an average over a distance large compared with the fine-grain variations. Likewise, we shall be concerned with a similarly averaged $\vec{B}$. Such averaging allows the use of the constitutive relation $\vec{B} = f(\vec{H})$ for the averaged quantities with the effect of the free supercurrents represented by the relationship. In an ellipsoid of sufficient size (as discussed above) located in a uniform field, these average quantities are constants; the average field is *uniform inside the sample* even though the sample distorts the field around it.[3, 4]

The internal field can be determined for an ellipsoidal sample using a *demagnetization factor*, which relates the internal field to the applied, external field and the (averaged) magnetization. We shall consider the simple, but useful, situation in which the sample is an ellipsoid of revolution (spheroid) and the magnetic field is parallel to one of its axes. The demagnetization factor is a scalar and it relates the internal field to the applied field $\vec{H}_0$ by the relation

$$H_i = H_0 - \mathfrak{D}_i M_i \qquad \text{where} \quad i = x, y, z \qquad (1)$$

Equation (1) is written as a scalar equation as all vectors are parallel. Results of the analysis when the magnetic field is applied along the axis of revolution, as shown in Fig. 6.06a, are plotted in Fig. 6.06b. It is seen there that for the long, thin (prolate) spheroid, the demagnetization factor approaches zero so the internal field is approximately equal to the applied field. Therefore, the long prolate spheroid can be used as a model of a cylindrical rod.

A disk with a normal magnetic field can be modeled by a flattened (oblate) spheroid. We might note, because of its usefulness, that the

---

[3] J. A. Osborn, "Demagnetizing factors of the general ellipsoid," *Phys. Rev.*, Vol. 67, pp. 351–357, 1–15 June 1945.

[4] E. C. Stoner, "The demagnetizing factors for ellipsoids," *Phil. Mag.*, Vol. 36, pp. 803–820, December 1945.

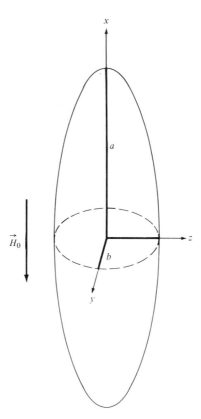

Figure 6.06a. Spheroidal sample with magnetic field applied along the axis of revolution (polar axis).

demagnetization factor in this case has the simple approximate form

$$\mathfrak{D} = 1 - \pi a / 2b \tag{2}$$

where a is the polar semiaxis and b is the equatorial semiaxis, as shown in Fig. 6.06a.

The sum of the demagnetization factors for the three axial orientations of magnetic field is unity, so

$$\mathfrak{D}_y = \mathfrak{D}_z = \tfrac{1}{2}(1 - \mathfrak{D}_x) \tag{3}$$

Since the two equatorial axes are identical, so are their demagnetization factors. One easily sees from (3) that the demagnetization factor is $1/3$ for the sphere (as is also seen in Fig. 6.06b). Since $\mathfrak{D}_x$ approaches zero for the long prolate spheroid, the demagnetization factors with the field applied along the equatorial axes are $\mathfrak{D}_y = \mathfrak{D}_z \cong 1/2$.

The problem of finding the internal field H is obviously not finished with knowledge of the demagnetization factors (except in the special cases

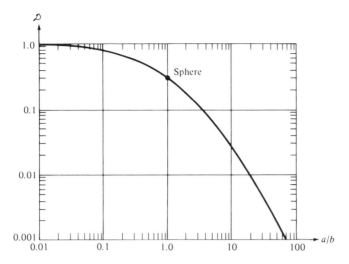

Figure 6.06b. Demagnetization factor for an ellipsoid of revolution vs ratio of polar semiaxis to equatorial semiaxis with magnetic field applied parallel to the polar axis.

where they are zero) since one must also know the magnetization. We can recast (1), using Eq. 6.05(5), in the form

$$H = (H_0 - \mathcal{D} B/\mu_0)/(1 - \mathcal{D}) \tag{4}$$

The determination of H in (4) depends on the induction B. The relation between B and H is called the *constitutive relation* and is determined by the nature of the material of the sample and not by its shape.

In a superconductor with a perfect Meissner effect (total flux exclusion), $B = 0$ and we see that

$$H = H_0/(1 - \mathcal{D}) \tag{5}$$

Problems

6.06a. For the sample shapes listed below, make plots of H existing inside a perfectly diamagnetic superconducting body as functions of applied field H_0 for the range of H_0 from zero up to the value where $H = H_c$, where H_c is the field at which superconductivity is destroyed.

  i. Sphere;

  ii. Long circular rod with applied field parallel to its axis;

  iii. Long circular rod with field applied perpendicular to the rod axis.

6.06b. The requirement that $B \equiv 0$ inside a perfectly diamagnetic superconductor forces certain conditions on the external field. Sketch the magnetic-field lines around a perfectly diamagnetic sphere. Find the functional form of the tangential component of the external field at the surface of the sphere.

6.07. Energy in Magnetic Fields

Consider a body of material in which a magnetization can arise. We select a region of interest to be of very small cross-sectional area A and of length l sufficient that $l \gg A^{1/2}$. All dimensions of the region are much smaller than the distances over which variations of the magnetization take place but large enough to include an appreciable number of atoms, so macroscopic field concepts can be applied. We imagine the region of interest to be enclosed by a long, thin solenoid (Fig. 6.07) to which can be applied the formula of an infinite solenoid. As the current in the N-turn solenoid is increased, a counter electromotive force v is induced in its windings. The energy source must provide a voltage equal to the emf to make the current flow. The work done by the source in a time dt is

$$d \mathcal{W}' = vi \, dt \tag{1}$$

The induced emf v is expressed in terms of the rate of change of flux linkage through the coil which is

$$v = NA \, dB/dt \tag{2}$$

where B is the flux density. Assuming fields as in an infinite solenoid, the magnetic field is expressed in terms of the current i as

$$H = Ni/l \tag{3}$$

Substituting (2) and (3) in (1), the work done by the source can be written

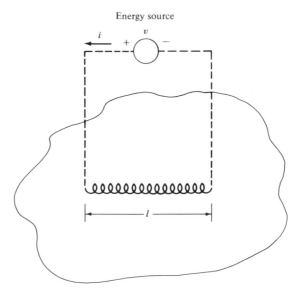

Energy source

Figure 6.07. Imaginary solenoid surrounding a macroscopically small region in a body of magnetizable material.

in terms of the magnetic field quantities as

$$d^{\circ}\!\mathcal{W}' = V\vec{H} \cdot d\vec{B} \tag{4}$$

where $V = Al$ is the volume of the solenoid. Using Eq. 6.05(5) we can recast (4) in the form

$$d^{\circ}\!\mathcal{W}' = \mu_0 V d(H^2/2) + \mu_0 V \vec{H} \cdot \overrightarrow{dM} \tag{5}$$

Writing (5) on a per-unit-volume basis, we have

$$d^{\circ}\!\mathcal{W} = \mu_0 d(H^2/2) + \mu_0 \vec{H} \cdot \overrightarrow{dM} \tag{6}$$

We can clarify the meaning of the terms in (6) by using

$$d(\vec{M} \cdot \vec{H}) = \vec{H} \cdot \overrightarrow{dM} + \vec{M} \cdot \overrightarrow{dH} \tag{7}$$

to replace $\vec{H} \cdot \overrightarrow{dM}$. The work per unit volume is then

$$d^{\circ}\!\mathcal{W} = \mu_0 d(H^2/2) + \mu_0 d(\vec{M} \cdot \vec{H}) - \mu_0 \vec{M} \cdot \overrightarrow{dH} \tag{8}$$

The work done by the source has been divided into three components. The first of these is the energy required to establish the magnetic field in the volume V, assuming no magnetic reaction of the material, and is given by the first term on the right side of (8). One frequently has occasion to express the energy in a magnetic field in a normal metal and uses this form. It is usually assumed that the small paramagnetic response of the metal atoms can be neglected in comparison with the much stronger diamagnetic behavior of a superconductor, which was discussed in Section 6.05. The last term in (8) can be identified as the energy per unit volume required to increase the magnetic field on a magnetization of fixed strength M. The term $\mu_0 d(\vec{M} \cdot \vec{H})$ is the total interaction energy between the coil producing the field and the magnetization. It would be the work done by the source driving a solenoid if the magnetic material were brought into an already existing field H that vanishes at infinity and if the magnetization M were a function of H at each point, being zero at infinity.

Finally, we should note that it is the work done *by* a system that appears in the thermodynamic relations we developed earlier in this chapter; this is the negative of (8):

$$dW = -\mu_0 d(\tfrac{1}{2} H^2) - \mu_0 d(\vec{M} \cdot \vec{H}) + \mu_0 \vec{M} \cdot \overrightarrow{dH} \tag{9}$$

6.08. Thermodynamic Relations for Magnetic Systems

In this section we shall point out some of the various conventions that are used in the thermodynamic treatment of magnetic systems and present some important relations. It is perhaps the succinctness of thermodynamics that leads to the confusion resulting when different conventions are used. The correct final results can be obtained with different usages as long as they are internally consistent. The difficulties arise when one reads different references and finds the same problem couched in different terms.

The difficulties hinge around the choice of quantities to be included in the internal energy of the system of interest. Suppose, for example, the system consisting of a piece of magnetizable material in a solenoid. We see from Eq. 6.07(4) that the work per unit volume done by the source for a differential change of the induction $\vec{B}$ in a magnetic field $\vec{H}$ is

$$d\mathcal{W} = \vec{H} \cdot d\vec{B} \tag{1}$$

As seen from Eq. 6.07(5), this work can be divided into two terms: one that represents the energy required to fill the space in the solenoid with field, assuming no magnetic reaction of the material, and another that represents the energy required to produce the magnetization of the material. In one convention[5] the internal energy includes neither of these. This usage appears little or never in the literature of superconductivity. Another choice would be to include the energy involved in magnetizing the material but not that which would be required even without the material present, $\mu_0 H^2/2$. One does find this usage. We choose to include in the internal energy the entire energy given by (1).

Helmholtz Free Energy

Consider a system A in thermal contact with a reservoir of fixed temperature as shown in Fig. 6.04a. There is a magnetic field $\vec{H}$ present in A and if the induction changes so $d\vec{B} \neq 0$, there will be work done, according to (1). This work can be considered a part of W_A in Eq. 6.04(4), in addition to the work $p\,dV$ suggested by Fig. 6.04a. The arguments relating to Eq. 6.04(6) all apply in the case where W_A includes magnetic field. If $d\vec{B} = 0$ and there is also no mechanical work, the parameters of the system will adjust themselves to minimize the free energy F. Thus, one may determine the equilibrium conditions where $\vec{B}$ is a constant (as well as volume) by minimizing the free energy.

The free energy is given by

$$F = U - TS \tag{2}$$

and, with magnetic field, the basic thermodynamic relation Eq. 6.03(13) becomes

$$dU = T\,dS + \vec{H} \cdot d\vec{B} - p\,dV \tag{3}$$

so we can find the differential change of free energy as

$$dF = -S\,dT + \vec{H} \cdot d\vec{B} - p\,dV \tag{4}$$

---

[5] See C. Kittel, *Statistical Physics*. New York: John Wiley and Sons, 1958, p.77.

Since we are dealing in this text with solids, dV can be taken to be zero, and the form that we find of use is

$$dF = -S\, dT + \vec{H} \cdot \overrightarrow{dB} \qquad (5)$$

Gibbs Free Energy

A more common physical situation is one in which the magnetic field $\vec{H}$ is held constant by virtue of fixed current in the coils producing the field. We can consider the applied field as a reservoir field H_R for the purposes of the present argument, as shown in Fig. 6.08. We write the change of internal energy per unit volume from Eq. 6.04(7) as

$$\Delta U_A = Q_A - p_R \Delta V_A + \vec{H}_R \overrightarrow{\Delta B}_A - W_A^{**}$$

where the work W_A^{**} done by the system excludes the magnetic and

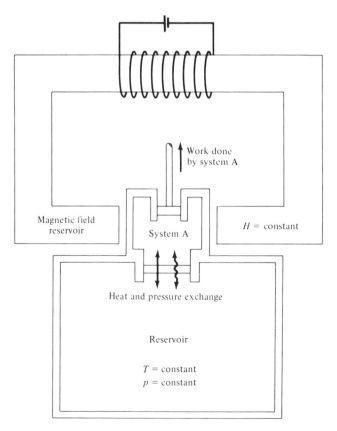

Figure 6.08. System A in contact with reservoirs of constant temperature, pressure, and magnetic field. Total system is isolated but A may do work W^{**}.

mechanical work done on the reservoir. Keeping the pressure and the magnetic field of the reservoir constant, one finds

$$\Delta S_{tot} = (-\Delta G_0 - W_A^{**})/T_R \geqslant 0 \tag{6}$$

where

$$G_0 \triangleq U - T_R S_A + p_R V_A - \vec{H}_R \cdot \vec{B}_A \tag{7}$$

Since $\Delta S \geqslant 0$ in any spontaneous change, we have

$$-\Delta G_0 \geqslant W_A^{**} \tag{8}$$

where the equal sign applies under quasistatic conditions. If the physical constraints on the system are such that no work can take place except that associated with ΔV_A and $\overrightarrow{\Delta B_A}$, the work $W_A^{**} = 0$ so $\Delta G_0 \leqslant 0$. Thus the Gibbs free energy can only decrease for spontaneous changes. Under the conditions of constant pressure, temperature, and applied field, the equilibrium state is characterized by a minimum value of the Gibbs free energy.

In equilibrium, the temperature, pressure, and magnetic field in the system of interest are equal to the reservoir quantities T_R, p_R, and $\vec{H}_R$. Thus we write the Gibbs free energy per unit volume as

$$\begin{aligned} G &= U - TS - \vec{B} \cdot \vec{H} + pV \\ &= F - \vec{B} \cdot \vec{H} + pV \end{aligned} \tag{9}$$

Making use of (3), the differential change of the Gibbs free energy per unit volume is found to be

$$dG = -S \, dT - \vec{B} \cdot \overrightarrow{dH} + V \, dp \tag{10}$$

For use in the study of solids, we can take $dp = 0$, so the useful form of (10) is

$$dG = -S \, dT - \vec{B} \cdot \overrightarrow{dH} \tag{11}$$

These expressions are used later in the analysis of superconductive phenomena.[6]

---

[6] In another convention, the internal energy includes the work required to magnetize the material but does not account for the change of energy stored in the field as $\vec{H}$ is raised from zero. In that case (neglecting volume changes), the following relations apply:

$$dU = T \, dS + \mu_0 \vec{H} \cdot d\vec{M} \tag{f1}$$

$$F = U - TS \tag{f2}$$

$$dF = -S \, dT + \mu_0 \vec{H} \cdot d\vec{M} \tag{f3}$$

$$G = U - TS - \mu_0 \vec{H} \cdot \vec{M} \tag{f4}$$

$$dG = -S \, dT - \mu_0 \vec{M} \cdot d\vec{H} \tag{f5}$$

6.09. Phase Transitions

It is common experience that materials undergo profound changes of state under certain conditions. Thus a disordered collection of molecules in a liquid will solidify into a regular crystalline array when the temperature drops below some critical value or the pressure is raised beyond some value. Another well-known state change is the ordering of the electronic spins in a ferromagnetic material below the Curie temperature. These are examples of *phase transitions*. Under the right conditions of temperature and magnetic field, the electrons in certain materials form pairs and a long-range ordering takes place, as discussed in Chapter 2. The thermodynamics of this superconducting phase transition will be the subject of the next section. Here we shall present some general considerations regarding phase transitions.

Assume a system in contact with a reservoir of constant temperature, pressure, and magnetic field. The system contains a single kind of substance, a part of which may be in one phase and part in another. In equilibrium the total Gibbs function for the system, Eq. 6.08(9), including contributions from the portions in each phase, is a minimum.

The choice between the Helmholtz and Gibbs free energies is made on the basis of the quantities that are constant in the reservoir. It is common to assume a constant-pressure reservoir for phase transitions in general since the atmosphere constitutes that aspect of the reservoir. We can write the total as

$$G = \nu_1 g_{m1} + \nu_2 g_{m2} \tag{1}$$

where $\nu_{1,2}$ is the number of moles of the material present in phase 1 or 2, respectively, and $g_{m1,2}$ is the Gibbs free energy *per mole* of the substance in phase 1 or 2, respectively. Since the total number of moles of the substance is constant, $-d\nu_2 = d\nu_1$ and we can form the following from (1):

$$dG = (g_{m1} - g_{m2})\, d\nu_1 \tag{2}$$

But since the total Gibbs function (1) is a minimum in equilibrium, $dG = 0$ and

$$g_{m1} = g_{m2} \tag{3}$$

It is clear from (1) that if one of the molar Gibbs functions is less than the other, the system will choose to be entirely in that phase. Then (3) marks the boundary between phases (the *phase-equilibrium line*) as shown in Fig. 6.09a.

The importance of the Gibbs function for systems with constant temperature, pressure, and magnetic field suggests its use for a classification of various types of phase transformation. Ehrenfest used the terms *first order* and *second order* to describe various phase changes in terms of the first-

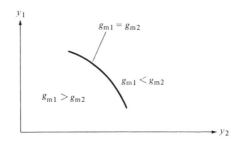

Figure 6.09a. Phase boundary in a space of two of the three variable parameters (p, T, H).

and second-order derivatives of the total Gibbs function. In first-order phase transitions, there are step changes of the entropy, volume, and magnetic induction, which are the following partial derivatives of the Gibbs function:

$$S = -\left(\frac{\partial G}{\partial T} \right)_{p, H} \tag{4}$$

$$V = \left(\frac{\partial G}{\partial p} \right)_{T, H} \tag{5}$$

$$B = -\left(\frac{\partial G}{\partial H} \right)_{p, T} \tag{6}$$

This is illustrated in Fig. 6.09b, where the continuous nature of the Gibbs function itself is seen. The parameter y represents any one of T, p, or H.

In a second-order transition, as originally defined by Ehrenfest, the first derivatives of the Gibbs function are continuous and finite-step discontinuities occur in the second derivatives as illustrated in Fig. 6.09c.

The *latent heat of transformation* is defined as the heat absorbed by the system from the reservoir as a transformation takes place from phase 1 to phase 2. We see from Eq. 6.03(12) that, at constant temperature, the heat

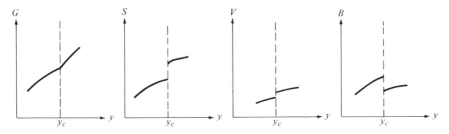

Figure 6.09b. Schematic representation of a first-order phase transition ($y = p, T$, or H).

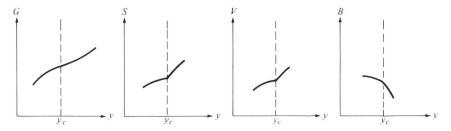

Figure 6.09c. Schematic representation of a second-order phase transition ($y = p$, T, or H).

added to the system is

$$L_{12} = Q = T(S_2 - S_1) \tag{7}$$

and this can be put in terms of the Gibbs functions using (4):

$$L_{12} = T[(\partial G/\partial T)_1 - (\partial G/\partial T)_2]_{p,H} \tag{8}$$

The continuity of the first derivatives implies zero latent heat of transformation in a second-order transition.

The *specific heat* is defined in terms of the change of temperature of a given quantity of the material in question when heat is added and other external parameters are kept constant. The specific heat per unit volume is

$$c_y \overset{\Delta}{=} (1/v)(dQ/dT)_y \tag{9}$$

where y denotes the quantities held constant and dQ is added to v moles. Then we can employ the second law of thermodynamics, $dQ = vT\,ds_m$ where s_m is the entropy of a mole of the substance, to recast (9) into the form

$$c_y = T(\partial s_m/\partial T)_y \tag{10}$$

Furthermore, we replace the molar entropy with the expression (4), modified to use the molar Gibbs function g_m, with the result

$$c_y = -T(\partial^2 g_m/\partial T^2)_y \tag{11}$$

Thus we see that a discontinuity of the specific heat is characteristic of second-order transitions.

6.10. The Superconducting–Normal Phase Transition

Up to this point we have assumed that the body under consideration is either normal or superconducting (Meissner state); now let us examine the transition between these two states. It is only under special circumstances that there is a direct transition from one of these two states to the other. We shall see in Chapter 7 that superconductors can be categorized as type

I or type II, depending on certain magnetic properties. It is only the type I material which makes a direct magnetic transition from the Meissner state to the normal state. (The type I classification includes all elemental superconductors except vanadium and niobium, whereas all superconducting compounds and alloys are in the type II category.) We note further that even if the material is type I, it must have the sample shape and field orientation with zero demagnetization factor (Section 6.06) in order to make a direct transition from Meissner to normal states. For all other cases the results of this section *do not apply*; the cases in which a mixed or intermediate state lies between the Meissner state and the purely normal state will be treated in later chapters.

Let us consider a superconductor at some temperature below its transition temperature. As we have seen earlier (Section 6.05) the application of a magnetic field stimulates the flow of a current in the superconductor, which can be represented by an equivalent magnetization; energy is added to the superconductor, as given by Eq. 6.07(5). At some value of magnetic field, the energy of the magnetization is larger than the condensation energy Eq. 2.08(8), so it is more favorable for the body to be in the normal state. Since the condensation energy depends on temperature, the critical value of magnetic field H_c does also. The relation between H_c and T is shown in the phase diagram in Fig. 6.10. Its shape is known experimentally to follow to within a few percent the relation:

$$H_c(T) = H_c(0)\left[1 - (T/T_c)^2\right] \qquad (1)$$

Equation (1) is consistent with the two-fluid model of Gorter and Casimir[7] (Section 3.13).

Though we consider that, for parameters in the region below the $H_c(T)$ curve in Fig. 6.10, the body is in the superconducting phase, it should be kept in mind that at any nonzero temperature the total electronic fluid is a mixture of a paired portion and excitations. With $H = 0$ the fraction in the paired state gradually diminishes to zero as $T \to T_c$. At other values of magnetic field below H_c, there is still a decrease of paired electrons as the temperature is raised, but their number does not approach zero as $T \to T_c(H)$, the transition temperature at that magnetic field. We consider there to be a phase transition because, even when most of the electrons are unpaired, the character of the electronic fluid is strongly affected by the presence of the small number of paired electrons. The mixture of paired and unpaired electrons below $H_c(T)$ is represented by a molar Gibbs free energy g_{ms} at the $H_c(T)$ phase boundary. The normal phase is likewise

[7] See D. Schoenberg, *Superconductivity*. Cambridge, England: Cambridge University Press, pp. 194–196, 1965.

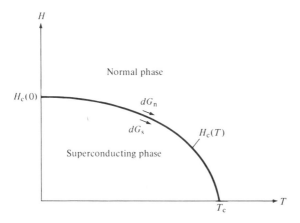

Figure 6.10. Phase diagram for a type I superconductor with a zero demagnetization factor.

represented by a molar Gibbs free energy g_{mn}. As we saw in Section 6.09, these must be equal at a phase boundary [here $H_c(T)$]. Since a unit volume contains the same number of moles regardless of whether it is in the normal or superconducting phase, the Gibbs free energies per unit volume of the two phases must also be equal on the phase boundary.

$$G_n(T, H_c) = G_s(T, H_c) \tag{2}$$

Let us now consider a differential change of position along the $H_c(T)$ curve. Since (2) applies for any point along the curve, we have

$$dG_n(H_c) = dG_s(H_c) \tag{3}$$

for the differential changes indicated in Fig. 6.10. If we now replace the differential changes of the Gibbs function by Eq. 6.08(11), we obtain

$$- S_n \, dT - B_n \, dH_c = - S_s \, dT - B_s \, dH_c \tag{4}$$

Rearranging, we have

$$(S_n - S_s) \, dT = (B_s - B_n) \, dH_c \tag{5}$$

Now making use of the fact that $B_s = 0$ and $B_{cn} = \mu_0 H_c$, this becomes

$$S_n - S_s = \mu_0 H_c (dH_c / dT) \tag{6}$$

As shown in Fig. 6.10, $dH_c / dT \leqslant 0$, so (6) shows that the entropy in the normal state is larger than in the superconducting state (i.e., there is more order in the superconducting state). Thus, the latent heat of transition from the superconducting phase to the normal phase, as seen in Eq. 6.09(7), is $L_{sn} = T(S_n - S_s) \geqslant 0$. When the transition takes place at $T = T_c$, $H_c = 0$ and the latent heat is zero since the entropy vanishes there, by (6). According to the definitions of types of phase transformation given in Section 6.09, the superconducting–normal phase transformation is second order at $T = T_c$. The third law of thermodynamics states that as $T \to 0$ the entropy of a system approaches a limit S_0 that is independent of all its parameters.[8] Therefore, $S_n - S_s \to 0$ as $T \to 0$. Thus the latent heat of transformation is zero at $T = 0$, so the transition is second order there also. Note that at temperatures between zero and T_c the latent heat is not zero and the transition is first order. The vanishing of the difference of entropies at $T = 0$ also shows, from (6), that dH_c/dT is zero, so the slope of the phase boundary is identically zero there.

From (6) and the relation $c = T(dS/dT)$, one can readily show that there is a discontinuity in the specific heat $T = T_c$, where $H_c(T) = 0$ and there is a second-order transition. This is the discontinuity that we introduced in Fig. 1.06 as one of the early pieces of evidence concerning the superconducting state; its value per unit volume is

$$c_s(T_c) - c_n(T_c) = \mu_0 T_c (dH_c/dT)^2 \big|_{T_c} \tag{7}$$

Problems

6.10a. Show that for any temperature below T_c the difference of specific heats per unit volume between the superconducting and normal phases is given by

$$c_s(T) - c_n(T) = \mu_0 T \left[H_c(d^2 H_c/dT^2) + (dH_c/dT)^2 \right]$$

6.10b. An early model of the superconducting phase assumed the existence of interpenetrating normal and superconducting fluids. The specific heat of the normal fluid was taken to be the usual $c_n = \gamma T$ as given in Eq. 1.06(7). That of the superconducting fluid was taken to be $c_s = 3\gamma T^3/T_c^2$. Show that these forms are consistent with the result in Prob. 6.10a and Eq. 6.10(1).

6.10c. If we had left out the magnetic energy $\mu_0 H^2/2$ [see Eq. 6.07(6)] associated with the field in vacuum when we formed the Gibbs function, we would have had the form Eq. 6.08(f5). Show that the difference of entropy $S_n - S_s$ and the specific-heat difference are unaffected by this choice for G.

6.10d. We know from Chapter 2 that the energy difference between the superconducting and normal states (condensation energy) is, at $T = 0$,

$$W_s - W_n \cong -\tfrac{1}{2} N(0) \Delta^2(0)$$

where $N(0)$ is the density of single-particle states at the Fermi energy and $\Delta(0)$ is the gap parameter at $T = 0$. Show that the difference of Gibbs free energies for the superconducting and normal states (thermodynamic condensation energy) is $(G_s - G_n)_{T,H=0} = -\mu_0 H_c^2(0)/2$. By comparing the two condensation energies, obtain an expression for the critical magnetic field at $T = 0$ in terms of the critical temperature.

---

[8] F. Reif, *op cit.*, pp. 145–148.

Chapter 7

Spatially Dependent Behavior in Superconductors: The Ginzburg–Landau Equations and Departures from the Meissner State

7.01. Introduction

In Chapter 2, the BCS ground-state wave function was identified with a macroscopic electron-pair wave function $\psi(\vec{r}) = |\psi(\vec{r})| \exp i\theta(\vec{r})$, which was used extensively in Chapters 3–5. It was assumed throughout that $|\psi(\vec{r})|$ is spatially invariant and independent of the magnetic field. These assumptions are only justified in situations where the magnetic field is small compared to the local thermodynamic critical field and where no inhomogeneities are present. In many circumstances of physical or technological interest, however, these restrictions are not appropriate and $|\psi(\vec{r})|$ is not independent of magnetic field and position. In this chapter, the theoretical foundations for the treatment of spatially dependent behavior in superconductors will be presented. Much of the remainder of the book will be devoted to a variety of applications of this theory.

The phenomenological theory, published by Ginzburg and Landau[1] in 1950, represents a remarkable achievement of physical intuition. It has been corroborated by experiment and was confirmed and extended in subsequent microscopic theory by Gor'kov[2] during 1959–1960, based on the BCS theory. Ginzburg and Landau postulated the existence of an order parameter which could be used as a measure of the condensation in a superconductor. Unlike the spatial order of the atoms in a crystal, or the spin alignment in a ferromagnet, it is necessary to regard the order parameter in a superconductor as a complex quantity. If we write the order parameter as

$$\psi(\vec{r}) = |\psi(\vec{r})| \exp i\theta(\vec{r}) \tag{1}$$

---

[1] See the collection of papers by I. D. ter Harr, *Men of Physics: L. D. Landau.* Oxford: Pergamon Press, 1965, p. 138.
[2] A review of the Gor'kov theory is given by N. R. Werthamer in *Superconductivity*, R. D. Parks (Ed.). New York: Marcel Dekker, 1969, Chapter 6.

where $\theta(\vec{r})$ is the position-dependent phase, it is seen to have the same form as the macroscopic wave function.

As was seen in Section 3.03, the long-range order present in a superconductor allows $\theta(\vec{r})$ to be a meaningful quantity. Though absolute values of phase cannot be measured, weak connections between superconductors, as in the Josephson junction, provide means for measuring phase *differences* between superconducting regions.[3] It is clear from Eq. 3.03(7) that transport currents in weak fields are related to the gradient of $\theta(\vec{r})$; only the phase is affected by the presence of the magnetic field in that approximation.

In a uniform system without a magnetic field, the order parameter near T_c is proportional to the energy gap for excitations 2Δ [Eq. 2.08(4)]. Accordingly the normalized order parameter is frequently referred to as the *gap parameter* or *pair potential* $\Delta(\vec{r})$; this point will be discussed more fully in Section 7.06.[4]

In the earlier chapters we considered only the Meissner state, in which the magnetic flux is totally excluded from all but the surface penetration region. The Ginzburg–Landau solutions of coupled nonlinear differential equations, in which $|\psi|$ varies spatially and is a function of $\vec{A}$, show that the Meissner state is more complicated than the simple picture suggests, especially for bodies that have dimensions as small as the penetration depth. More significantly, gross departures from the Meissner state are shown to occur, even for large specimens, for a wide range of superconducting materials. This is because of transitions to states of lower free energy, with inhomogeneous distribution of the superconducting phase, induced by magnetic fields above certain critical values. It is the way in which $|\psi|$ changes in response to applied magnetic fields that provides the greatest practical interest in the application of the Ginzburg–Landau theory. In contrast to the London theory in which the magnetization of the whole body is studied, the Ginzburg–Landau approach concentrates attention on the fine detail of the internal structure of the superconducting state.

The Ginzburg–Landau equations, and the microscopic theory by Gor′kov which justifies them, also make possible the analysis of systems of materials in which the physical properties are spatially variable. In particular, the abrupt discontinuity at the interface of contiguous normal-metal

---

[3] An interesting discussion of the order parameter by P. W. Anderson may be found in E. R. Caianiello (Ed.), *Lectures on the Many-Body Problem*, Vol. 2. New York: Academic Press, 1964, p. 132.

[4] There is, however, a phenomenon known as "gapless" superconductivity in the presence of a magnetic field where this identification is not valid. In this case there is a nonvanishing order parameter but no gap in the excitation spectrum because the edges of the gap are smeared out. See M. Tinkham, *Introduction to Superconductivity*. New York: McGraw-Hill, 1975, p. 263.

and superconducting materials reduces the order in the superconductor and introduces some into the normal metal. These phenomena are called the *proximity effects* and are presented in Section 7.09. Josephson junctions that utilize the leakage of superconducting order into a conductor are studied in Section 7.10.

7.02.   Ginzburg–Landau Free-Energy Functional

The Ginzburg–Landau (GL) theory is based on the hypothesis that the degree of order at each point in a superconductor can be described by a continuous function, the order parameter introduced in the previous section. Ginzburg and Landau constructed an expression for the free energy of a superconducting body, and by a minimization procedure, obtained the differential equations describing the distribution of the magnetic induction and the order parameter in the equilibrium state. In the original theory, GL restricted their analysis to temperatures in the neighborhood of T_c. This allowed the expansion of the order-dependent part of the free-energy functional in a power series in the order parameter. Subsequent work has extended the theory to a wider range of temperature.

The analysis leading to the GL equations can be done either in terms of the Helmholtz free energy, as was done by Ginzburg and Landau, or in terms of the Gibbs free energy. We choose the latter since it is convenient to conceive of the minimization in terms of an experiment with a long thin sample parallel to the magnetic field (zero demagnetization coefficient). In that case there is a constant magnetic field inside, irrespective of the distribution of flux density attained as the system seeks the state of minimum free energy. We saw in Section 6.08 that the appropriate function for minimization in this situation is the Gibbs free energy.

From Eq. 6.08(9) we see that the Gibbs free energy can be obtained by a transformation of the Helmholtz free energy, which for constant pressure and volume can be written on a per-unit-volume basis as[5]

$$g = f - b(\vec{r})H \tag{1}$$

where it is assumed that the flux density is parallel to the field H. Here we use the symbol $b(\vec{r})$ to denote the local value of the magnitude of the magnetic flux density with variations on a scale of the penetration depth. We reserve $B(\vec{r})$ for the average magnitude of flux density over tens of penetration depths. The reason for the distinction is that there are fine-grained variations that are revealed by the GL theory, but there are also instances when only the larger-scale variations need be considered.

Let us first consider the construction of the Helmholtz free energy and

---

[5] We use the lower case letters for volume densities.

then make the transformation (1) to get the Gibbs free energy. Because of the presence of increased order in the superconducting state, there is a lowering of the Helmholtz free energy by an amount $\Delta f_s(|\psi|^2)$ at each point, corresponding to the local condensation energy, the precise dependence being left unspecified for the present. Ginzburg and Landau postulated an additional contribution to the free energy, associated with spatial variations of the order parameter and given by

$$(\hbar^2/2m^*)|\nabla\psi|^2$$

The magnetic flux density $\vec{b}(\vec{r}) = \nabla \times \vec{A}$ also affects the free energy, increasing it by $b^2/2\mu_0$ (Section 6.08). We must also require the free energy to be invariant to a change of the gauge chosen for $\vec{A}$. As discussed in Section 3.04, if one makes the substituion $\vec{A}' = \vec{A} + \nabla\chi(\vec{r})$, the magnetic flux density is unaffected, but the phase of the order parameter transforms according to the relation

$$\psi'(\vec{r}) = \psi(\vec{r})\exp\left[\frac{ie^*\chi(\vec{r})}{\hbar}\right]$$

where $\chi(\vec{r})$ is an arbitrary scalar function of position. This change would be reflected in the free energy through $\nabla\psi$, unless, to cancel the effect of the change of phase caused by the gauge transformation, we replace $(\hbar^2/2m^*)|\nabla\psi|^2$ by

$$(1/2m^*)|(i\hbar\nabla + e^*\vec{A})\psi|^2 \tag{2a}$$

To see what this means physically, we note that it can be rewritten as

$$\tfrac{1}{2}n_s^*m^*v_s^2 + (1/2m^*)(\hbar\nabla|\psi|)^2 \tag{2b}$$

by using Eq. 3.03(6). This shows that the added term (2a) contains the kinetic energy of the superfluid together with the effect of the stiffness of $|\psi|$ in opposing rapid spatial variations.

In the orignal GL equations the charge and mass were assumed to be those of the free electron. The microscopic theory of Gor'kov[6] showed that the correct value of charge e^* is the pair value $2e$, and this has been corroborated by flux-quantization experiments (Section 3.10). The mass m^* is generally taken to be twice that of unpaired electrons in the solid and the latter is nearly equal to the free-electron rest mass.

From the above arguments, we can write the Gibbs free-energy density for the superconductor using (1) as

$$g_s = g_{n0} + \Delta f(|\psi|^2) + \frac{1}{2m^*}|(i\hbar\nabla + e^*\vec{A})\psi|^2 + \frac{b^2}{2\mu_0} - bH \tag{3}$$

---

[6] See footnote 2.

where g_{n0} is the Gibbs free-energy density that would obtain for the same material in the normal state, at the same temperature, without a magnetic field, which is the same as the Helmholtz free-energy density under the same conditions.

In the GL theory, it is assumed that with T near T_c and with zero magnetic field and gradients of ψ, the order parameter goes smoothly to zero, as in Fig. 7.02, so the free energy can be expanded in a power series in $|\psi|^2$ and only the first two terms need to be used. Equation (3) becomes

$$\Delta g(|\psi|^2) = g_s - g_n = \Delta f(|\psi|^2) = \alpha(T)|\psi|^2 + \tfrac{1}{2}\beta(T)|\psi|^4 \qquad (4)$$

Since the last term dominates for sufficiently large $|\psi|^2$, the coefficient $\beta(T)$ must not be negative or there would be no limit to the decrease of the free energy with increasing $|\psi|^2$ where the expansion is clearly invalid. To find a minimum of Δg with $\beta(T) > 0$ and nonzero $|\psi|^2$, $\alpha(T)$ must be negative. We find the equilibrium value $|\psi_0|^2$ by finding the conditions for a minimum of Δg:

$$\left.\frac{\partial(\Delta g)}{\partial|\psi|^2}\right|_{\text{equilib}} = \alpha(T) + \beta(T)|\psi_0|^2 = 0 \qquad (5)$$

Thus

$$|\psi_0|^2 = -\alpha(T)/\beta(T) \qquad (6)$$

At the minimum, Δg must equal the condensation energy per unit volume, which can be expressed in terms of the critical magnetic field by $-\mu_0 H_c^2(T)/2$ (Prob. 6.10d). Substituting (6) in (4),

$$\Delta g_0 = g_{s0} - g_{n0} = \tfrac{1}{2}\mu_0 H_c^2(T) = -\tfrac{1}{2}\alpha^2(T)/\beta(T) \qquad (7)$$

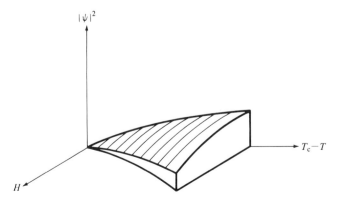

Figure 7.02. Dependence of the order parameter near T_c, shown schematically.

Thus α and β can be found from (6) and (7) to be

$$\alpha(T) = -\mu_0 H_c^2(T)/|\psi_0(T)|^2 \tag{8}$$

and

$$\beta(T) = \mu_0 H_c^2(T)/|\psi_0(T)|^4 \tag{9}$$

That $\beta(T) \cong$ constant can readily be seen from the two-fluid model, for $T \cong T_c$. Using (8) and (9), the general free-energy-density functional (2) can be written as

$$g_s = g_{n0} - \frac{1}{2}\,\mu_0 H_c^2(T)\left[\frac{2|\psi|^2}{|\psi_0|^2} - \frac{|\psi|^4}{|\psi_0|^4}\right]$$

$$+ \frac{1}{2m^*}\,|(i\hbar\,\nabla + e^*\vec{A})\psi|^2 + \frac{b^2(\vec{r})}{2\mu_0} - b(\vec{r})H \tag{10}$$

It should be noted that, although a special situation was used to evaluate $\alpha(T)$ and β, the resulting expression (10) is valid in any situation where the contribution to the free energy from the presence of order can be represented by the first two terms of a power series. There are numerous situations with nonvanishing magnetic fields and gradients of ψ in which the order parameter goes smoothly to zero at the transition, that is, so-called *second-order phase transitions*.

Problems

7.02a. Verify that expressions (2a) and (2b) are equivalent.

7.02b. Show that the free-energy functional (3), assuming (4), is gauge invariant.

7.02c. Discuss the significance of the signs and magnitudes of the coefficients α and β given by (8) and (9). Show that the temperature dependences near T_c of the $|\psi|^2$ and $|\psi|^4$ terms in the free-energy expansion are the same and sketch the $\Delta g[|\psi/\psi_0|, (T_c - T)]$ surface near the origin. Using Taylor's theorem, explain why the GL series expansion is valid near the transition temperature.

7.03. Ginzburg–Landau Differential Equations

The free energy given by Eq. 7.02(3) is a function of the distribution of the order parameter ψ and the magnetic vector potential $\vec{A}$. We can obtain the Ginzburg–Landau differential equations relating these quantities in equilibrium by minimizing the total free energy [the integral of Eq. 7.02(3)].[7]

---

[7] See, for example, D. Saint-James, G. Sarma, and E. J. Thomas, *Type II Superconductivity*. Oxford: Pergamon Press, 1969, p. 24.

Minimization with respect to $\vec{A}$ leads to the quantum-mechanical expression for current where all electrons are in the same state, with the order parameter playing the role of a wave function:

$$-\vec{J}_s = \frac{\nabla^2 \vec{A}}{\mu_0} = \frac{ie^* \hbar}{2m^*}(\psi^* \nabla \psi - \psi \nabla \psi^*) + \frac{e^{*2}}{m^*}|\psi|^2 \vec{A} \qquad (1)$$

Minimization with respect to ψ^* gives

$$\alpha(T)\psi + \beta|\psi|^2 \psi + (1/2m^*)(i\hbar \nabla + e^* \vec{A})^2 \psi = 0 \qquad (2)$$

The boundary condition on the magnetic vector potential is

$$(\nabla \times \vec{A})_t = \mu_0 \vec{H}_{0t} \qquad (3)$$

where $\vec{H}_{0t}$ is the component of magnetic field tangential to the surface. Making the order parameter zero at the boundary may at first sight seem to be an appropriate boundary condition. However, this would imply that superconductivity would vanish in very thin specimens, in contradiction to experimental results. Instead, the normal component of the conduction current is required to vanish at a superconductor–insulator boundary, giving (see Section 3.03):

$$\hat{n} \cdot (i\hbar \nabla + e^* \vec{A})\psi = 0 \qquad (4)$$

where $\hat{n}$ is the surface normal. The situation of a normal metal contiguous with the superconductor surface is treated separately in Section 7.10.

If the superconducting body is simply connected and there is no transport current flowing, the phase angle $\theta(\vec{r})$ in the above relations can be reduced to zero by an appropriate choice of gauge to make ψ real. In one-dimensional systems, the GL equations become

$$\frac{d^2 \vec{A}}{dx^2} = \frac{e^{*2}}{m^*} \mu_0 \psi^2 \vec{A} \qquad (5)$$

$$\frac{\hbar^2}{2m^*}\frac{d^2 \psi}{dx^2} = \left(\alpha(T) + \beta\psi^2 + \frac{e^{*2}}{2m^*}A^2\right)\psi \qquad (6)$$

Substituting in (6) from Eqs. 7.02(8) and 7.02(9), we have

$$\left(\frac{\hbar^2 \psi_0^2}{2m^* \mu_0 H_c^2}\right)\frac{d^2}{dx^2}\left(\frac{\psi}{\psi_0}\right) = \left(\frac{e^{*2}\psi_0^2 A^2}{2m^* \mu_0 H_c^2} - 1\right)\frac{\psi}{\psi_0} + \left(\frac{\psi}{\psi_0}\right)^3 \qquad (7)$$

The boundary condition on $\vec{A}$ is as in (3). That for ψ is, from (4),

$$d\psi/dx = 0 \qquad (8)$$

if the surrounding material is an insulator.

In the formulation of the GL equations, we have assumed that the only value of vector potential of importance is that at the point to which the GL differential equations are being applied. This is a so-called local approximation which is also made in the London equations.

Now let us examine how to interpret ψ_0. Ginzburg and Landau considered it to measure the equilibrium value of the density of superconducting electrons. The pairing theory suggests that $|\psi_0|^2$ is the density of electron pairs. For the purposes of practical calculations, we may usefully extend its meaning to be an *effective density of pairs*. Notice that in the absence of gradients of ψ, the situation that exists in weak magnetic fields for a uniform material, (1) becomes identical in form with the London relation, Eq. 3.05(1). The weak-field solutions of the distribution of magnetic flux therefore are the same as in Chapter 3. This suggests that the penetration depths in Section 3.12, given for situations where scattering and nonlocal effects are important, apply for the present analysis. If we assume that the exponential solution in Section 3.06 applies, as it does in the situations with local electrodynamics (categories b and c in Section 3.12), we can use a generalization of the relation 3.06(4),

$$\lambda^2(T) = m^*/e^{*2}\mu_0(n_s^*)_{\text{eff}} \tag{9}$$

to define the effective density of pairs $(n_s^*)_{\text{eff}} = |\psi_0|^2$. This is known to give accurate results for local electrodynamics; we shall also assume it to be useful as an approximation in the nonlocal cases. Thus we shall take $|\psi_0|^2$ to be given by

$$|\psi_0(T)|^2 = m^*/\mu_0 e^{*2}\lambda^2(T) \tag{10}$$

where $\lambda(T)$ is the appropriate penetration depth in Section 3.12.

Problems

7.03a. Verify that (1) and (2) reduce to (5) and (6) for the one-dimensional simply connected superconductor.

7.03b. Show that the boundary condition (8) is consistent with (4).

7.04. Examples of Solutions of the Ginzburg–Landau Equations; The Ginzburg–Landau Parameters

The Ginzburg–Landau equations are coupled nonlinear differential equations. Solutions generally must be obtained numerically, but some special cases can be treated in closed form. Let us consider first two one-dimensional, simply connected configurations to which we can apply the simpler form of the GL equations, Eqs. 7.03(5) and 7.03(6). In both of these problems, the applied field is parallel to the plane surface of the superconducting body, which is of infinite extent in this dimension. In this geometry, therefore, the problems of demagnetization are avoided and the effects of the magnetic field can be treated more easily.

Superconducting Half-Space

Consider the superconducting half-space shown in Fig. 7.04a. Let us assume, for simplicity, that the applied magnetic field H is sufficiently small, compared with the thermodynamic critical field $H_c(T)$, to cause only a minor weakening of the order parameter. Equation 7.03(5) can then be solved by assuming that $\psi(\vec{r}) = \psi_0$ as a first approximation. If the expression obtained for $\vec{A}$ is substituted in Eq. 7.03(6), the resulting *linear* second-order differential equation can be solved in the normal way. It is left to Prob. 7.04a for the reader to show that the solution for ψ that satisfies the boundary conditions 7.03(3) and (9) is given by

$$\frac{\psi(x, H)}{\psi_0} = 1 - \frac{\kappa}{2\sqrt{2}\,(2 - \kappa^2)} \left(\frac{H}{H_c(T)} \right)^2$$

$$\times \left[\exp\left(\frac{-\sqrt{2}\,x}{\xi_{GL}} \right) - \frac{\kappa}{\sqrt{2}} \exp\left(\frac{-2x}{\lambda(T)} \right) \right] \qquad (1)$$

where ψ_0 is the unperturbed value of the order parameter. The solution for

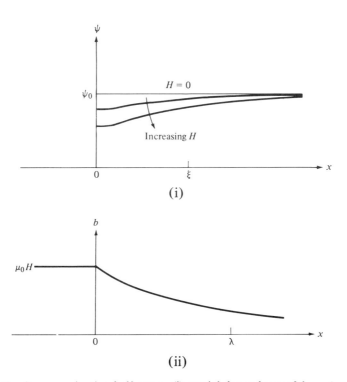

(i)

(ii)

Figure 7.04a. Superconducting half-space. (i) spatial dependence of the order parameter (shown exaggerated); (ii) spatial dependence of the magnetic flux density.

the magnetic flux density inside the specimen is given by

$$b(x) = \mu_0 H \exp\left[-x/\lambda(T)\right] \tag{2}$$

The penetration depth $\lambda(T)$ appearing in (1) and (2) is the appropriate weak-field value discussed in connection with Eqs. 7.03(9) and 7.03(10). The other characteristic length ξ_{GL} is the smallest distance over which the order parameter can make large fractional changes, as illustrated in Fig. 7.04a(i). It is called the *temperature-dependent coherence length* or *Ginzburg–Landau coherence length* and is given by

$$\xi_{GL}(T) = \frac{\hbar}{|2m^*\alpha(T)|^{1/2}} = \frac{\hbar|\psi_0(T)|}{(2m^*\mu_0)^{1/2}H_c(T)} \tag{3}$$

This coherence length has a completely different significance from those of the (temperature-independent) Pippard coherence lengths, the intrinsic value $\xi_0 = 0.18\hbar v_F/k_B T_c$, and the mean-free-path-dependent value $\xi(l)$ given by Eq. 3.11(1). Some confusion is caused by the terminology, but it is strongly entrenched in the literature. Also appearing in (1) is the ratio of $\lambda(T)$ and ξ_{GL}, designated κ and called the *Ginzburg–Landau parameter*:

$$\kappa = \frac{\sqrt{2}\,\mu_0 e^* \lambda^2(T) H_c(T)}{\hbar} = \frac{\lambda(T)}{\xi_{GL}(T)} \tag{4}$$

The relations (1) and (2) are plotted schematically in Fig. 7.04a where it is seen that as H is increased, the small depression of ψ at the boundary also grows.

The asymptotic form of (1) for $\kappa \ll 1$ gives the relative depression of ψ at the surface as

$$\frac{\psi_0 - \psi(0)}{\psi_0} \approx \frac{\kappa}{4\sqrt{2}}\left[\frac{H}{H_c(T)}\right]^2 \tag{5}$$

From this expression, it can be seen that superconductors having very small values of κ behave according to the rigid London model. Most of the soft superconducting elements in pure bulk form, such as indium, tin, and aluminum, have κ values less than 0.3, so that $\psi_0 - \psi(0)$ is only a small fraction of ψ_0, even when $H \approx H_c(T)$. Thus, the initial assumption of constant ψ used to solve the GL equations is valid only for these materials, known as type I superconductors. A more detailed calculation shows that λ itself exhibits a weak dependence on magnetic field, even for materials with small κ values, and that the magnetic flux penetration does not follow exactly an exponential decay.

It should be kept in mind that for (1) to be valid, the power-series expansion of the order-induced Δg, Eq. 7.02(4), must apply; this requires T to be near T_c.

Thin Superconducting Film

For a sufficiently thin film in a parallel magnetic field [Fig. 7.04b(i)], it is reasonable to assume ψ to be independent of position but dependent on magnetic field, as shown in Fig. 7.04b(ii). It can be shown[8] that this occurs exactly where $\kappa = 0$. Using the invariance of ψ in Eq. 7.03(5), we obtain

$$A_y(x) = \frac{\mu_0 H \lambda}{\omega} \left[\frac{\sinh(\omega x/\lambda)}{\cosh(\omega d/2\lambda)} \right], \qquad -\frac{d}{2} \leqslant x \leqslant \frac{d}{2} \qquad (6)$$

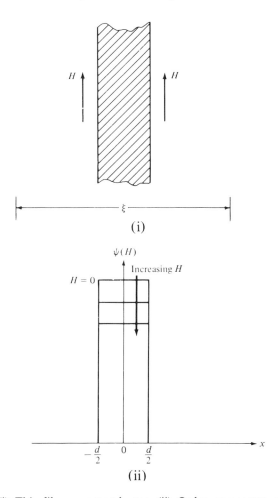

(i)

(ii)

Figure 7.04b. (i) Thin-film superconductor. (ii) Order parameter, assumed to be independent of position but dependent on magnetic field.

---

[8] See footnote 1.

where $\omega = \psi(H)/\psi_0$, and λ is given by Eq. 7.03(9) but with $(n_s^*)_{\text{eff}}$ dependent on film thickness through the mean free path, as is discussed in Section 8.07. If $d \leqslant \lambda$, then A^2 can be approximated by its average over the film in Eq. 7.03(6). It can then be shown that, for small H,

$$\frac{\psi(H)}{\psi_0} = 1 - \frac{1}{8}\left(\frac{H}{H_c}\right)^2 \frac{\sinh(d/\lambda) - (d/\lambda)}{(d/\lambda)\cosh^2(d/\lambda)} \tag{7}$$

where H_c is the bulk critical field. The critical field $H_\parallel$ for the film is given by the relation[9]

$$H_\parallel^2 = \frac{H_c^2 \omega_c^2 (2 - \omega_c^2)}{1 - (2\lambda/\omega_c d)\tanh(\omega_c d/2\lambda)} \tag{8}$$

Here ω_c is the value of ω at the critical field, that is, the field for which the Gibbs free energy of the film in the superconducting state equals that for the normal state.

Figure 7.04c[10] shows some representative forms of the variation of ω^2 as a function of $(H/H_\parallel)^2$. It is seen that for films thinner than $d = \sqrt{5}\,\lambda$, the order parameter goes smoothly to zero, but for thicker films there is a nonzero value of the order parameter at $H_\parallel$. The corresponding phase transitions are second- and first-order, respectively. It should be noted that

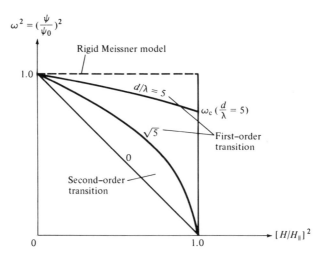

Figure 7.04c. Order parameter as a function of applied magnetic field for various film thicknesses.

[9] See footnote 1.

[10] D. H. Douglass, Jr., "Transition behavior of thin film in parallel magnetic fields," *IBM J. Res. Dev.*, Vol. 6, pp. 44–48, January 1962.

this result only applies near T_c, for the magnetic field H parallel to the plane of the film. For this arrangement there are no demagnetizing effects and the externally applied field is uniform both inside and outside the superconducting film.

There is, of course, appreciable penetration of the magnetic flux into the film in this case because d is assumed to be comparable to or smaller than λ. Since λ is temperature dependent, even relatively large samples will undergo a second-order transition at temperatures sufficiently close to the transition temperature T_c. Figure 7.04d gives the critical value ω_c of the parameter ω at the transition to the normal state as a function of d/λ. It can be seen that the classical rigid "Meissner" superconductor is exemplified by a thick specimen $(d \gg \lambda)$.

For $d < \sqrt{5}\ \lambda$ it can be shown that

$$H_{\parallel} = \sqrt{24}\ (\lambda/d)H_c \tag{9}$$

and for films with $d/\lambda \to 0$,

$$\frac{\psi(H)}{\psi_0} = \left[1 - \left(\frac{H}{H_{\parallel}} \right)^2 \right]^{1/2} = \left(1 - \frac{H^2 d^2}{24 H_c^2 \lambda^2} \right)^{1/2} \tag{10}$$

Comparing the results with those for the bulk superconductor, it is notable that, for very thin films, (9) shows a considerable increase in the critical field $H_{\parallel}$ over the bulk value H_c for the same materials.

It is of interest to note that in the case of a thin film where the magnetic field is H on one side only and zero on the other side (e.g., a cylindrical film carrying a transport current) the transition at the critical magnetic field $H_{\parallel}$ is always of first order. In that case, $H_{\parallel}$ is always less than H_c and is inversely proportional to d, the film thickness, for $d \ll \lambda$.

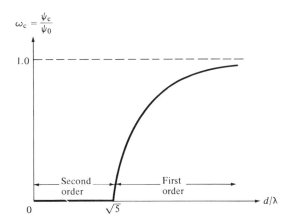

Figure 7.04d. Critical value of the order parameter at the transition between superconducting and normal states as a function of film thickness.

Problems

7.04a. Derive Equations (1) and (2) by solving Eqs. 7.03(5) and 7.03(7), and using the boundary condition $d\psi/dx = 0$.

7.04b. Using (8) show that for $d < \sqrt{5}\,\lambda$ the critical field is given by $H_\parallel = \sqrt{24}\,(\lambda/d)H_c$.

7.05.   Gor′kov's Microscopic Justification for the Ginzburg–Landau Theory

The Gor′kov formulation[11] of the BCS theory near the zero-field transition temperature T_c has provided a microscopic foundation for the GL equations and includes the effect of a finite mean free path l. The justification of the phenomenological approach of Ginzburg and Landau by the use of the microscopic theory has also helped to improve the understanding of the GL equations and to define more closely the limits of their validity. The Gor′kov approach has also played a key role in the extension of the application of the GL equations outside the neighborhood of T_c, but that work is beyond the scope of this text.

Gor′kov introduced a *pair potential* $\Delta(\vec{r})$ which satisfies relations of precisely the Ginzburg–Landau forms, Eqs. 7.03(5) and (6), near T_c. The parameter $\Delta(\vec{r})$, which may be regarded as a spatially varying form of the BCS gap parameter Δ, is proportional to $\psi(\vec{r})$ and, near T_c, is given by

$$\Delta(\vec{r}) = \left[3.07 k_B T_c/(n\mathrm{X})^{1/2}\right]\psi(\vec{r}) \tag{1}$$

where n is the density of conduction electrons and X is the function shown in Fig. 7.05.[12] Thus the pair potential $\Delta(\vec{r})$ is a continuous function of position and magnetic field. The energy gap itself, therefore, is also not rigid with respect to the magnetic field and will be reduced to zero at the critical magnetic field, either continuously at a second-order transition or discontinuously at a first-order transition.[13]

The Gor′kov theory shows that the GL equations are in the correct form for the case of a finite mean free path for conduction electrons, but the effect of impurities has to be taken into account in the characteristic parameters. From a practical point of view, most important superconducting materials have the mean free path of normal electrons reduced by impurities to be comparable to or smaller than the Pippard coherence

---

[11] See Footnote 2.
[12] Footnote 2, p. 338.
[13] For a refinement of this picture, see footnote 4.

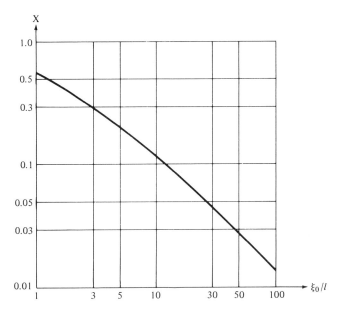

Figure 7.05. The function X used in the Gor'kov theory to account for finite mean free path. The argument is modfied here for convenience.

length ξ_0. Materials are classified according to the ratio l/ξ_0:

$$l/\xi_0 \gg 1, \qquad \textit{clean} \text{ or } \textit{pure} \text{ materials}$$
$$l/\xi_0 \ll 1, \qquad \textit{dirty} \text{ or } \textit{impure} \text{ materials} \tag{2}$$

For most superconductors, an impurity content of only a few percent reduces the mean free path to the *dirty* limit.

Gor'kov's formulation of the GL equations permits the evaluation of terms that play the roles of $\alpha(T)$ and β in both the pure and dirty limits, denoted, respectively, by the subscripts p and d. In the pure limit,

$$\alpha_p = -1.83(\hbar^2/2m^*)\xi_0^{-2}(1 - t) \tag{3}$$

where $t = T/T_c$ and

$$\beta_p = \left[0.35/N(0)\right]\left(\hbar^2/2m^*\xi_0^2 k_B T_c\right)^2 \tag{4}$$

where $N(0)$ is the normal density of states at the Fermi level. In the dirty limit,

$$\alpha_d = -1.36(\hbar^2/2m^*\xi_0 l)(1 - t) \tag{5}$$

and

$$\beta_d = \left[0.2/N(0)\right]\left(\hbar^2/2m^*\xi_0 l k_B T_c\right)^2 \tag{6}$$

Using (3), the temperature-dependent coherence length [Eq. 7.04(3)] becomes, for the pure limit,

$$\xi_{GLp}(T) = 0.74\xi_0/(1 - t)^{1/2} \tag{7}$$

and using (5), one finds for the dirty limit,

$$\xi_{GLd}(T) = 0.85(\xi_0 l)^{1/2}/(1 - t)^{1/2} \tag{8}$$

The penetration depth [Eq. 7.03(9)] can be expressed in terms of the GL α and β by using Eq. 7.02(6), with the result

$$\lambda(T) = \left(m^*\beta(T)/e^{*2}|\alpha(T)|\right)^{1/2} \tag{9}$$

Using (3) and (4), this becomes for the pure limit

$$\lambda_p(T) = \lambda_L(0)/\sqrt{2}\,(1 - t)^{1/2} = \lambda_L(T) \tag{10}$$

and with (5) and (6), the penetration depth in the dirty limit is

$$\lambda_d(T) = \left[0.615\lambda_L(0)/(1 - t)^{1/2}\right](\xi_0/l)^{1/2} \tag{11}$$

The temperature dependence of $\lambda(T)$ in both (10) and (11) is the same as that obtained from applying the two-fluid model to the London penetration depth near T_c.

It is of interest to note from the above expressions that, in both the pure and dirty limits, the GL parameter $\kappa = \lambda(T)/\xi_{GL}(T)$ is independent of temperature for T near T_c. For arbitrary values of the mean free path, Gor'kov has given

$$\kappa = 0.96\lambda_L(0)/\xi_0 X \tag{12}$$

where X is the function in Fig. 7.05. The parameter κ becomes

$$\kappa_p = 0.96\lambda_L(0)/\xi_0 \tag{13}$$

and

$$\kappa_d = 0.725\lambda_L(0)/l \tag{14}$$

in the pure and dirty limits, respectively. The function X approaches the limit $1.33l/\xi_0$ as l becomes much smaller than ξ_0.

Equation (12) has been approximated by Goodman[14] as

$$\kappa = \kappa_p + 7.5 \times 10^5 \rho\gamma^{1/2}$$

where ρ is the normal-state resistivity and γ is the electronic-specific-heat constant at the temperature of interest. In the dirty limit, the mean-free-path-dependent part dominates and thus κ is essentially controlled by the presence of impurities and lattice defects.

---

[14] B. B. Goodman, "The magnetic behavior of superconductors of negative surface energy," *IBM J. Res. Dev.*, Vol. 6, pp. 63–67, January 1962.

7.06. Surface Energy at the Boundary Between Normal and Superconducting Phases in a Homogeneous Medium

Magnetic flux can penetrate a bulk superconductor nonuniformly, provided that there is an inhomogeneous distribution of normal and superconducting regions. In these cases the magnetic induction $b(\vec{r})$ is virtually excluded from the superconducting phase but can pass through the normal regions. At the boundaries between normal and superconducting regions there is a decay of $b(\vec{r})$ in a distance on the order of the penetration depth λ in the superconducting region. The order parameter ψ vanishes in the regions of normal phase and rises nearly to its equilibrium value ψ_0 within about a GL coherence length of the boundary.

We consider here only superconducting bodies of constant cross section in the direction parallel to the applied magnetic field. This leads to the simplification that the magnetizing field H inside the superconductor is everywhere equal to the applied field, regardless of the magnetization (or equivalently, the induction) in the superconductor. Since H is the fixed quantity here, the appropriate functional to consider is the Gibbs free energy. In particular, it is of interest to calculate the incremental Gibbs free energy involved in the formation of a boundary between normal and superconducting regions. From the discussion of the previous sections, it is clear that the state with the lowest Gibbs free energy is that which exists in equilibrium with a given magnetic field H. Therefore, if a decrease of Gibbs free energy is produced by the existence of a boundary, the formation of boundaries is energetically favorable, and vice versa. In this section we analyze the idealized situation shown in Fig. 7.06a to determine the conditions under which boundary formation is favored. This leads to a criterion of fundamental importance in determining which of two distinct types of magnetic behavior a superconducting material will exhibit.

Consider Fig. 7.06a, where a magnetic field H equal to H_c, the thermodynamic critical field value, is applied. Let us consider the values of the

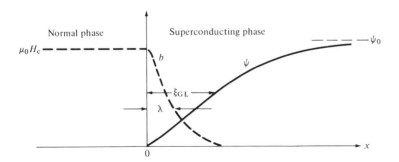

Figure 7.06a. Variation of magnetic flux density and order parameter at a plane interphase boundary in an infinite superconducting medium.

Gibbs free-energy density at $x = \pm \infty$. Since

$$g = f - bH \tag{1}$$

and (see Section 6.08)

$$f_{nH} = f_{n0} + \tfrac{1}{2} \mu_0 H^2 = f_{n0} + \tfrac{1}{2} \mu_0 H_c^2 \tag{2}$$

where f_{nH} is the Helmholtz free-energy density for the normal phase in the presence of magnetic field, we have, as $x \to -\infty$, $\psi = 0$ and

$$g(-\infty) = g_n = f_{nH} - bH = f_{n0} + \tfrac{1}{2}\mu_0 H_c^2 - \mu_0 H_c^2$$

$$= f_{n0} - \tfrac{1}{2}\mu_0 H_c^2 \tag{3}$$

As $x \to \infty$, $b \to 0$ so

$$g(\infty) = g_s = g_{s0} = f_{n0} - \tfrac{1}{2}\mu_0 H_c^2 \tag{4}$$

where the subscript s refers to the superconducting phase. The last term in (4) is the condensation energy. In the vicinity of the boundary, b and ψ vary smoothly. We have already seen that abrupt variations of the order parameter increase the free energy through the term in $(\nabla|\psi|)^2$. As a result, we expect ψ to increase smoothly from zero to the bulk value ψ_0 in a distance on the order of a coherence length ξ_{GL}. Likewise, b is expected to decrease from the external value in the normal region to zero inside the superconducting region within about a penetration depth λ. The relative sizes of ξ_{GL} and λ determine the physics of boundary surface formation in the following way. The penetration of the magnetic induction into the superconductor lowers the free energy by roughly $\tfrac{1}{2}\mu_0 H_c^2 \lambda$, whereas the decay of the order parameter raises the free energy by an amount equal to the loss of condensation energy, approximately $\tfrac{1}{2}\mu_0 H_c^2 \xi_{GL}$. From this semiquantitative argument, it can be seen that the presence of an interphase boundary raises the free energy by $\tfrac{1}{2}\mu_0 H_c^2(\xi_{GL} - \lambda)$ per unit area. If $\xi_{GL} > \lambda$, it is energetically unfavorable for the boundary to exist, whereas if the converse is true, solutions in which the superconductor contains many normal regions may be expected.

   This result can be deduced in a more precise manner by using the Ginzburg–Landau equations. The interphase Gibbs free energy per unit area of boundary is defined as

$$\sigma_{ns} = \int_{-\infty}^{\infty} dx \left[g_s(b) - g_n \right] \tag{5}$$

Using (3) this becomes

$$\sigma_{ns} = \int_{-\infty}^{\infty} dx \left[g_s(b) - f_{n0} + \tfrac{1}{2}\mu_0 H_c^2 \right] \tag{6}$$

Substituting for $g_s(b)$ in (6) using Eqs. 7.02(3) and 7.02(4), we obtain in one-dimensional form

$$\sigma_{ns} = \int_{-\infty}^{\infty} dx \left[\alpha\psi^2 + \frac{\beta}{2}\psi^4 + \frac{1}{2m^*} \left| \left(i\hbar\frac{\partial}{\partial x} + e^*\vec{A} \right)\psi \right|^2 \right.$$

$$\left. + \frac{[b(x) - \mu_0 H_c]^2}{2\mu_0} \right] \qquad (7)$$

where α and β are the GL coefficients given by Eqs. 7.02(8) and 7.02(9). This expression for σ_{ns} implicitly contains the magnetization energy of the superconducting region in which the flux has penetrated. By multiplying the GL Eq. 7.03(6) by ψ and integrating by parts, it can be shown that

$$\int_{-\infty}^{\infty} dx \left[\alpha\psi^2 + \beta\psi^4 + \frac{1}{2m^*} \left| \left(i\hbar\frac{\partial}{\partial x} + e^*\vec{A} \right)\psi \right|^2 \right] = 0 \qquad (8)$$

Substituting (8) in (7) we obtain

$$\sigma_{ns} = \int_{-\infty}^{\infty} dx \left[-\frac{\beta}{2}\psi^4 + \frac{[b(x) - \mu_0 H_c]^2}{2\mu_0} \right] \qquad (9)$$

From the form of the integrand in (9) we can see that there is no contribution to the integral from the region of normal phase where $\psi = 0$ and $b = \mu_0 H_c$. Using Eq. 7.02(9), we can recast (9) in the form

$$\sigma_{ns} = \frac{1}{2}\mu_0 H_c^2 \int_0^{\infty} dx \left[\left(1 - \frac{\psi^4}{\psi_0^4} \right) + \frac{(b^2/2\mu_0) - bH_c}{\mu_0 H_c^2/2} \right] \qquad (10)$$

We can readily see that the integrand vanishes deep inside the region of superconducting phase where $\psi = \psi_0$ and $b = 0$. Thus the only contribution to the Gibbs free energy is close to the boundary inside the superconducting region, as suggested by Fig. 7.06b.

We can write (10) as

$$\sigma_{ns} = \frac{1}{2}\mu_0 H_c^2 \delta \qquad (11)$$

where δ is the integral in (10) having the dimension of length; it cannot be evaluated in closed form except for certain selected values of the GL parameter κ (see Probs. 7.06b–d).

For materials with $\kappa < 1/\sqrt{2}$ (type I), the existence of an interphase boundary leads to a raising of the Gibbs free energy over that of a uniformly superconducting sample. Therefore, it is energetically unfavorable for boundaries to exist in a sample with zero demagnetization factor (long, thin sample with parallel magnetic field). We shall see in Section 7.08 that, for samples of other shapes, the energy involved in the distortion of the applied field makes a subdivision into superconducting and normal

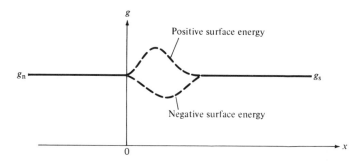

Figure 7.06b. Gibbs free-energy density in the neighborhood of a plane interphase boundary. The broken lines show two possible types of result for real superconductors.

phases energetically favorable. However, this behavior is fundamentally different in character from that discussed below for materials with $\kappa > 1/\sqrt{2}$.

Similar reasoning leads one to conclude that a material with $\kappa > 1/\sqrt{2}$ undergoes a transition at a relatively low value of applied field to a state in which phase boundaries have a negative surface energy. For these materials (type II superconductors), the formation of a structure involving a multitude of interphase boundaries is favored above a certain critical field, as will be discussed in Chapter 8.

The classification of superconducting materials into these two classes, by applying the Ginzburg–Landau theory, represents one of the most significant landmarks in the history of the subject, although, strangely, it was several years before its practical importance was recognized.

Problems

7.06a. The GL equations are often treated in normalized form. Starting from the Eqs. 7.03(5) and 7.03(7), obtain the normalized equations

$$\frac{d^2\vec{A}'}{dx'^2} = u^2\vec{A}'$$

$$\frac{1}{\kappa^2}\frac{d^2u}{dx'^2} = -u + u^3 + \frac{|\vec{A}'|^2u}{2}$$

where $\vec{A}'$ and x' are the appropriately normalized vector potential and distance coordinate, respectively. Use the appropriate relations for α, β, ξ_{GL}, and λ. Normalize the integral (10) by the same means.

7.06b. Evaluate the integral δ in (11) in the limit of $\kappa \ll 1$ by assuming essentially zero penetration of the magnetic flux in the second equation in Prob. 7.06a, which can then be integrated. Show that $\delta = 1.89\xi_{GL}$ for this case.

7.06c. Evaluate δ in the limit of $\kappa \gg 1$ by a suitable approximation in the second equation in Prob. 7.06a and show that $\delta = -1.1\lambda$.

7.06d. Evaluate δ for $\kappa = 1/\sqrt{2}$, showing that the surface energy is zero for this value of κ.

7.07. Intrinsic Magnetic Behavior of Superconductors

In the preceding section, the criterion for the interphase surface energy to be positive or negative was obtained for a single plane boundary of infinite extent in terms of the Ginzburg–Landau parameter κ. The surface contributions to the free energy originate within a layer of thickness approximately equal to the larger of λ or ξ_{GL}. We considered a single interface but solutions of the GL equations can be found in which there are innumerable interphase boundaries. These may be divided into two categories. In one, the contribution of the interphase boundary region to the total free energy is fractionally small. In the other, the boundary regions occupy a significant fraction of the total volume, so their contribution to the free energy is appreciable.

Those bulk materials with $\kappa < 1/\sqrt{2}$ (type I) would not be expected to contain a mixture of n and s phases since the lowest energy state has a minimum of interphase boundaries. Type I samples of zero demagnetization factor allow no flux penetration into the sample other than for a distance of a penetration depth at the exterior surface. At the critical field H_c, the transition to the normal state occurs abruptly and the equivalent magnetization vanishes as the order parameter goes to zero throughout the sample. This transition is shown in Fig. 7.07a. It is assumed here that the sample dimensions are much larger than the penetration depth, so the free energy associated with the penetration at the surface is negligible. For

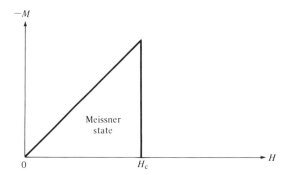

Figure 7.07a. Magnetization for a bulk type I sample of zero demagnetization factor in a parallel field. The phase transition at H_c is first order.

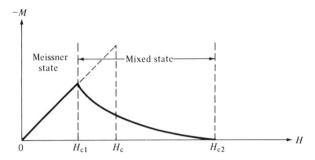

Figure 7.07b. Magnetization for a bulk type II sample of zero demagnetization factor in a parallel magnetic field. The transitions at H_{c1} and H_{c2} are second order.

small samples, such as thin films in magnetic fields parallel to their surface, the magnetic field can penetrate throughout the sample. This causes an appreciable reduction of the free energy and leads to a higher critical field. Thin films will be discussed more extensively in Section 8.07.

The second group, in which interphase surface energy plays a decisive role, includes both type II superconductors ($\kappa > 1/\sqrt{2}$) and thin films in fields perpendicular to their surfaces. The latter will be discussed in Section 8.07. The existence of an inhomogeneous, or *mixed*, state above a certain critical field H_{c1} in type II materials is purely a result of the intrinsic magnetic properties; that is, the interphase energy is negative for

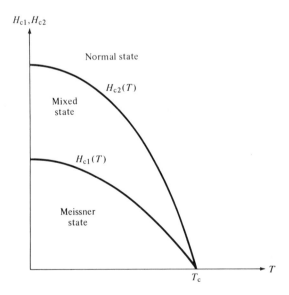

Figure 7.07c. Phase boundaries for a type II superconductor.

materials with $\kappa > 1/\sqrt{2}$ and therefore the formation of interphase boundaries is energetically favored. The transition to the mixed state at H_{c1} is shown in the magnetization curve, Fig. 7.07b. The magnetization is reduced when the transistion to the mixed state occurs. With increased magnetic field the order parameter is reduced further. At H_{c2}, the order parameter reaches zero and the magnetization vanishes. Figure 7.07c shows the phase boundaries in the $H_c - T$ plane between the various states for a type II superconductor with zero demagnetization factor.

Problem

7.07. Compare the Pippard and Ginzburg–Landau coherence lengths ξ and ξ_{GL}, respectively, in the pure and dirty limits to show that if $\xi_{GL} \ll \lambda$, then $\xi \ll \lambda$. Thus, strongly type II materials have local electrodynamics (Section 3.11). Use the Gor'kov formulas for ξ_{GL}.

7.08. Geometrical Effects: The Intermediate State

The most remarkable result of geometrical influence on superconductor properties is the *intermediate state* induced in samples where demagnetization effects are present. The magnetization of a bulk type I specimen is illustrated in Fig. 7.08a, where it is seen that the peak value is reached when the applied field H_0 equals $H_c(1 - \mathcal{D})$ far from the surface of a body with a demagnetization coefficient $\mathcal{D}$. This result applies strictly only to bodies of ellipsoidal geometry inside which the magnetization is uniform in magnitude and direction, but the concept can be used generally, for example, to explain the behavior at geometrical irregularities on the otherwise smooth surface of a superconductor. In particular, it is useful in

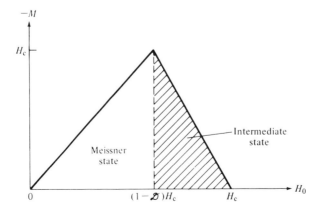

Figure 7.08a. Magnetization for a body with demagnetization coefficient $\mathcal{D}$.

explaining the irreversible magnetic properties and alternating-current losses in superconducting surface layers.

Taking a spherical specimen as an example, we have seen in Section 6.06 that the distortion of the magnetic field caused by the expulsion of flux from the interior of the superconductor results in the interior value of H, and therefore also the exterior equatorial value, rising to $H_0/(1 - \mathcal{D})$. Since $\mathcal{D} = \frac{1}{3}$ for a sphere, we see that $H = \frac{3}{2} H_0$ at the equator. Referring to Fig. 7.08a, the equatorial field reaches the critical value when $H_0 = \frac{2}{3} H_c$. Although the surface region at the equator would be expected to undergo a transition to the normal state at this value of applied field, it can be seen that the resultant penetration of flux would tend to restore the equatorial field to slightly below the critical value. That is, the demagnetization coefficient $\mathcal{D}$ becomes a decreasing function of H. However, it is known that any intrusion of normal regions into the superconducting sample must conform to certain rules. For example, for the two phases to exist in equilibrium, the magnetic field at the interphase boundary must be tangential and equal to H_c, the thermodynamic critical field. The positive free-energy contribution of the interphase surface will determine the equilibrium configuration of normal and superconducting regions, favoring a relatively coarse structure (Fig. 7.08b).

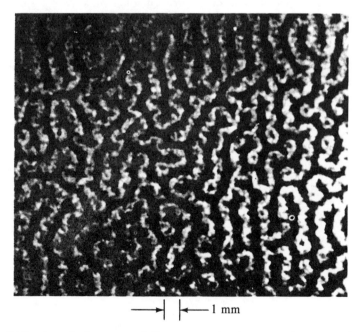

$\longrightarrow\!|\quad|\!\longleftarrow\!1$ mm

Figure 7.08b. A typical pattern of flux penetration in a type I superconductor in the intermediate state. (From T. E. Faber, "The intermediate state in superconducting plates," *Proc. Roy. Soc. (London)* Vol. A248, plate 25 after p. 464, 9 December 1958.)

A precise analytical description of this phenomenon has so far proved elusive. Experimental results have given convincing evidence of the complexity of the intermediate state, which has been revealed as a heavily convoluted interpenetrating structure of normal and superconducting phases. For low-κ, type I superconductors, a structure with a periodicity of millimeters is observed commonly. For pure, annealed samples, the growth of the normal phase within the superconductor takes the form of laminae emanating from the equatorial region and orientated parallel to the internal field. Clearly, the magnetic field must be at least equal to H_c in the normal regions and less than H_c throughout the superconducting regions. The laminar model in fact leads to inconsistent results at the boundaries of the sample unless branching of the laminae is allowed as the normal regions reach the surface.[15] The main theoretical difficulty arises from the first-order nature of the transition, away from T_c, which places the problem beyond the reach of the Ginzburg–Landau theory.

Although the intermediate state in macroscopic bodies is, by itself, of no particular technological importance, the related intermediate state in superconducting films (Section 8.07) and the irreversible penetration of magnetic flux into irregular-surface intermediate-state regions are topics of considerable practical importance.

7.09. Proximity Effects: Contiguous Normal and Superconductive Materials

If a superconductor and a normal metal are in intimate contact, as they are when one has been deposited on the other without allowing any oxide or contamination to accumulate on the first, there is a leakage of pairs from the superconductor s into the normal metal n and a leakage of quasiparticles from n into s. The result is a reduction of the pair density in the superconductor and the appearance in the normal metal of a pair density; these can extend several hundred nanometers in each medium.

The transition temperature of the superconductor is reduced by the presence of the contiguous normal metal. A typical experimental result[16] is shown in Fig. 7.09, where the critical temperature of the composite structure T_{cns}, normalized to that of the superconductor T_c, is shown as a function of the thickness of the normal metal d_n, for various thicknesses d_s of the superconductor. Notice that if the superconductor is much thicker

---

[15] A more complete discussion is given by C. G. Kuper, *Theory of Superconductivity*. New York: Oxford University Press, 1968, pp. 78–86. Many examples of experimental results are given by J. D. Livingston and W. DeSorbo, "The intermediate state in type I superconductors," in *Superconductivity* (R. D. Parks Ed.). New York: Marcel Dekker, 1969, Chapter 21.

[16] N. R. Werthamer, "Theory of the superconducting transition temperature and energy gap function of superposed metal films," *Phys. Rev.*, Vol. 132, pp. 2440–2445, 15 December, 1963.

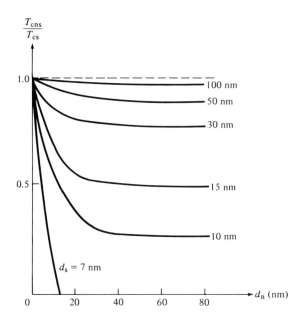

Figure 7.09. Typical experimental data on reduction of the critical temperature of an *ns* layered composite film as functions of the component film thicknesses. Here the materials are lead and copper. (From N. R. Werthamer, *Phys. Rev.*, Vol. 132, p. 2440, 15 December, 1963.)

than a certain value, which can be shown to be the coherence length, T_{cns} decreases with increasing d_n but reaches a limiting value. On the other hand, for thinner superconductive films (e.g., curve for $d_s = 7$ nm), T_{cns} decreases to zero with increasing d_n. The superconductivity is suppressed completely. The value of d_n beyond which no significant decrease of T_{cns} takes place is the coherence length ξ_n of the normal metal, which will be discussed further below. The decrease of T_{cns} is not a result of interdiffusion or alloying or it would not have these thickness dependences.

The *ns* composite structure has been analyzed extensively, both with the Ginzburg–Landau equations and with the corresponding microscopic Gor'kov equations. A major problem in the theories is the choice of boundary conditions. One approach[17] has compared theory and experiment by means of the temperature dependence of the critical magnetic field $H_{\parallel ns}$ (field aligned parallel to the film as in Section 7.04) to determine the correct boundary condition. Different choices of boundary conditions were tried and the best fit to the experimental data was found by assuming

---

[17] H. J. Fink, M. Sheikholeslam, A. Gilabert, J. P. Laheurte, J. P. Romagnan, J. C. Noiray, and E. Guyon, "Proximity effect and boundary conditions in superconducting–normal double layers," *Phys. Rev. B.*, Vol. 14, pp. 1052–1061, 1 August 1976.

continuity of the Gor'kov pair potential $\Delta(\vec{r})$. In the framework of the Gor'kov theory,[18] one can express the pair potential as the product of the BCS electron–electron interaction potential, $V(\vec{r})$ and the probability amplitude of the condensation of pairs $F_{co}(\vec{r})$:

$$\Delta(\vec{r}) = V(\vec{r})F_{co}(\vec{r}) \tag{1}$$

Since $V(\vec{r})$ is of very short range (approximately one atomic spacing), it should drop abruptly at the boundary to its near-zero value in the normal metal; thus the deduced continuity of $\Delta(\vec{r})$ appears to be inconsistent.[19] The more intuitively satisfying boundary condition is that F_{co} is continuous at the ns boundary (assuming, for convenience that the normal densities of Bloch states are equal in the two materials).[20] The resolution of this matter will have to await further analytical and experimental results.

Both theoretical approaches show a nearly exponential decay of the condensation amplitude in the n region. Thus, we take it in the form

$$F_{co}(x) = \Phi(x)e^{-k_n|x|} \tag{2}$$

where $\Phi(x)$ is a slowly varying function of x. The parameter k_n depends on whether the material is clean or dirty and on whether the interaction potential in the normal-metal regions, V_n, is positive, zero, or negative. Note that if V_n is positive, there is a nonvanishing transition temperature T_{cn} for the normal metal that appears in the equations. The solution (2) assumes that $d_n \gg k_n^{-1}$; its region of validity is $|x| \gg k_n^{-1}$. For clean n and s materials and $V_n = 0$,

$$k_n^{-1} = \hbar v_{Fn}/2\pi k_B T \tag{3}$$

where v_{Fn} is the Fermi velocity in the n material [Eq. 1.04(7)]. For n and s materials in the dirty limit with $V_n > 0$ and $T_{cns} > T > T_{cn}$,

$$k_n^{-1} = \xi_n\left[1 + 2/\ln(T/T_{cn})\right]^{1/2} \tag{4}$$

which defines the coherence length ξ_n for a normal metal. In (4),

$$\xi_n = (\hbar D/2\pi k_B T)^{1/2} = (\hbar v_{Fn} l_n/6\pi k_B T)^{1/2} \tag{5}$$

where D is the diffusion constant for the normal metal. Note that as $V_n \to 0$, $T_{cn} \to 0$ and $k_n^{-1} \to \xi_n$.

For $V_n < 0$ (Coulomb repulsion exceeds the electron–phonon–electron attraction), studies have indicated that $k_n^{-1} = \xi_n$, independent of the magnitude of the negative V_n. This applies to dirty materials; no information is available for the negative V_n case in clean materials.

---

[18] Footnote 7, p. 126.
[19] See footnote 17.
[20] G. Deutcher and P. G. deGennes, "Proximity effects," in *Superconductivity* (R. D. Parks, Ed.). New York: Marcel Dekker, 1969, pp. 1005–1034.

7.10. Normal-Metal- and Semiconductor-Coupled Sandwich-Type Josephson Junctions

It was pointed out in Section 5.02 that the Josephson effects depend on the existence of a weak connection between the wave functions on the two sides of the junction. It has been demonstrated that such a weak connection can be achieved by making a sandwich structure with either a normal metal or a semiconductor between the superconducting electrodes. In this section we adapt the theory of the proximity effects given in the preceding section to the analysis of these kinds of junction.

Normal-Metal-Coupled Junctions

The model for the analysis is shown in Fig. 7.10a. It is assumed that the normal-metal layer is thick enough that the simple exponential decay given in Eq. 7.09(2) applies near the center ($x = 0$) for the condensate leaked in from both sides. As pointed out in Section 7.09, the exponential is not a complete solution near the interfaces.

To simplify the analysis, we assume the two superconductors are identical. Thus, $F_{co}(a) = F_{co}(-a)$. The phases of the condensation amplitudes at a and $-a$ are designated θ_a and θ_{-a}, respectively. It is assumed that the magnitudes of the condensation amplitudes decay in from each side but their phases retain the values at a and $-a$. Adapting Eq. 7.09(2) to the two edges of the normal region, we write the condensation amplitude near the center of the normal region as the sum of the two amplitudes:

$$F_{co}(x) = A(T)\{\exp[-k_n(a-x) + i\theta_a] + \exp[-k_n(x+a) + i\theta_{-a}]\}$$

$$(1)$$

To calculate the junction current density, we make use of Eq. 7.03(1).

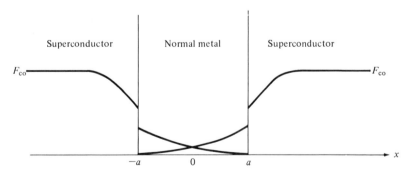

Figure 7.10a. Variation of the magnitudes of the complex condensation amplitudes originating on the two sides of an SNS junction. Each condensation amplitude is assumed independent of the other.

Where there is no applied magnetic field and the self-magnetic fields are negligible, the term involving the vector potential can be neglected. Thus,

$$J_s = -(ie^*\hbar/2m^*)(\psi^*\nabla\psi - \psi\nabla\psi^*) \tag{2}$$

Note that for a uniform medium, $\Delta(\vec{r}) = VF_{co}(\vec{r})$ by Eq. 7.09(1) and, therefore, $3.5k_BT_c = 2\Delta(0) = 2VF_{co}(0)$, where $F_{co}(0)$ is the zero-temperature condensation amplitude. With this, Eq. 7.05(1) reveals a simple proportionality between $F_{co}(\vec{r})$ and $\psi(\vec{r})$. Then we can write from (2), for one-dimensional variations,

$$J_s \propto F_{co}^* \frac{\partial F_{co}}{\partial x} - F_{co} \frac{\partial F_{co}^*}{\partial x} \tag{3}$$

Because of the uncertainties in the boundary conditions discussed in Section 7.09, we do not try to find the magnitude of J_s but rather obtain important dependences. Substituting (1) into (3),

$$J_s = k_n A(T)\exp(-2k_n a)\sin\phi = J_c(T)\sin\phi \tag{4}$$

where $\phi = \theta_a - \theta_{-a}$.

In one set of measurements, Josephson coupling was observed in SNS junctions employing thin-film lead electrodes and a copper–aluminum alloy thin film as the normal metal.[21] The normal layers had thicknesses in the range 200–700 nm. Very high ($> 10^4$ A cm^{-2}) current densities should be possible for thin (200-nm) barriers at low temperatures; however, measurements of the thin-film devices made so far were on junctions so large that their current densities had to be limited to about 200 A cm^{-2} to avoid self-field limiting (Section 4.06). Other measurements at low temperatures ($\lesssim 0.5$ K) have shown Josephson coupling through copper foils with deposited lead electrodes for foil thicknesses as large as 40 μm.[22] The temperature T below which supercurrents appeared in these junctions was related to the thickness $2a$ according to the empirical relation $T = 19/2a$, where T is in kelvins and $2a$ is in μm. Current densities as high as 10^4 A cm^{-2} were observed.

Semiconductor-Coupled Junctions

Semiconductor-coupled junctions have advantages over those using normal metal in having a higher resistance for a given junction size, which is important in applications. They can also be made with intermediate amounts of hysteresis in the $I-V$ characteristics (intermediate values of β_c;

---

[21] J. Clarke, "Supercurrents in Lead–Copper–Lead Sandwiches," *Proc. Roy. Soc. (London)*, Vol. A308, pp. 447–471, 28 January 1969.

[22] J. T. Shepherd, "Supercurrents through thick, clean S–N–S sandwiches," *Proc. Roy. Soc. (London)*, Vol. A326, pp. 421–430, 25 January, 1972.

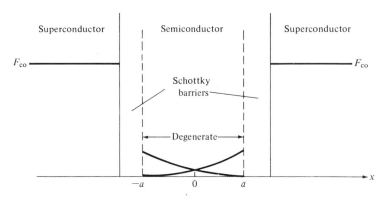

Figure 7.10b. Variation of the magnitudes of the condensation amplitudes originating on the two sides of an SSeS junction. Each condensation amplitude is assumed independent of the other.

see Section 5.03), which can be of importance in digital applications (Section 5.14).

The model that has been proposed[23] for the semiconductor-coupled Josephson junction is shown in Fig. 7.10b. Schottky barriers form at the interfaces between the semiconductor and the superconductors. The region between the Schottky barriers has a weak metallic behavior since the semiconductor is strongly degenerate. The condensation amplitude in the superconductors is assumed to be unaffected by the semiconductor because of the insulating Schottky barriers that isolate the conductive region in the semiconductor from the superconductors. The coupling of the pairs into the degenerate region of the semiconductor is understood to be by tunneling through the Schottky barriers. Therefore, there is a very substantial reduction of the condensation amplitude across the Schottky barriers. The pairs that tunnel into the degenerate region then diffuse toward the other side and there is a reduction of the magnitude of the condensation amplitude, as in the case of the normal-metal junction. The theory assumes that the two condensation amplitudes are independent; this is justified by the idea that each is too weak in the semiconductor to modify the other. Each of the condensation amplitudes has a phase that is independent of x; the difference of the phases leads to the Josephson relation, as in the case of the normal-metal-coupled junction. The coupling process just described does not apply if the combination of semiconductor doping and thickness are such that the two Schottky barriers merge sufficiently to preclude a metallic region; in that case, the coupling is by tunneling.

[23] J. Seto and T. Van Duzer, "Theory and measurements on lead–tellurium–lead supercurrent junctions," in *Low Temperature Physics – LT 13*, Vol. 3 (K. D. Timmerhouse, W. J. O'Sullivan, and E. F. Hammel Eds.). New York: Plenum Press, 1974.

The theoretical approach followed is the same as in the case of the SNS junction except that the magnitudes of the condensation amplitudes at $-a$ and a are determined differently. Here $F_{co}(x)$ is assumed constant at the value F_{co} up to the edge of the semiconductor and is reduced by the tunneling probability T_j to $F_{co}(a) = F_{co}(-a)$. Semiconductors have been treated as dirty materials, so the parameter k_n^{-1} [Eq. 7.09(4)] that characterizes the rate of decay in metallic regions can be conveniently rewritten for semiconductors in the form

$$k_{Se}^{-1} = \left(\hbar^3\mu/6\pi k_B Tem_{Se}^* \right)^{1/2}(3\pi^2 n)^{1/3}\left[1 + 2/\ln(T/T_{cSe})\right]^{1/2} \qquad (5)$$

where μ, m_{Se}^*, and n are the mobility, density-of-states carrier effective mass, and carrier density, respectively, all of which are assumed to be independent of position. The carriers, of charge e, may be electrons or holes. Here T_{cSe} is the transition temperature of the semiconductor, which we henceforth assume to be zero, so $k_{Se}^{-1} = \xi_{Se}$, the coherence length in the degenerate semiconductor. In the same way as for the SNS junction, the Josephson relation $J = J_c \sin \phi$ is found with

$$J_c \propto \frac{T_j^2}{\xi_{Se}} \exp(-2a/\xi_{Se}) \qquad (6)$$

Again, it is not possible in this simple theory to determine the magnitude of J_c, but (6) usefully shows the exponential dependence on the ratio of thickness to the coherence length ξ_{Se} and the dependence on tunneling probability.[24]

Various semiconductors have been used to form Josephson junctions.[25] These generally have been evaporated films of thicknesses up to several tens of nanometers. Crystalline silicon membranes formed by a special etching technique have also been used; current densities as high as 10^4 Acm^{-2} and $I_c R$ products higher than $(I_c R)_{tu}$ of Eq. 4.02(11) were demonstrated.[26]

---

[24] Semiconductor barriers of various doping levels in clean and dirty limits are treated in L. G. Aslamazov and M. V. Fistul', "Critical current of Josephson junctions with a semiconductor layer," *JETP Lett.*, Vol. 30, pp. 213–217, 20 August 1979.

[25] H. Kroger, "Josephson devices coupled by semiconductor links," *IEEE Trans. Electron Devices*, Vol. ED-27, pp. 2016–2026, October 1980.

[26] C. L. Huang and T. Van Duzer, "Schottky diodes and other devices on thin silicon membranes," *IEEE Trans. Electron Devices*, Vol. ED-23, pp. 579–583, June 1976.

Chapter 8

Type II Superconductivity: Theory and Technology

8.01. Introduction

The class of superconductive materials for which the Ginzburg–Landau parameter κ is greater than $1/\sqrt{2}$, known as type II, has become of great importance for high-power applications. This is because these materials retain zero resistivity for steady currents in the presence of magnetic fields considerably greater than their thermodynamic critical fields (which, for the most important materials, are larger than those of type I materials). This crucial practical advantage results from the partial magnetic flux penetration into the body of the superconductor for the range of magnetic-field strengths defining the mixed state. The currents that can be carried by type II superconductors in the mixed state are also larger than for type I because the flow is distributed in the bulk rather than just in the surface penetration layer.

The mixed state, introduced in Section 7.08 as an example of an inhomogeneous superconducting phase with negative interphase surface energy, is well suited to the use of the Ginzburg–Landau theory because of the occurrence of second-order transitions in the interior at the upper critical field H_{c2} and, under certain circumstances, on the surface at a higher field H_{c3}. In contrast to type I materials, in which only first-order transitions occur when any magnetic field is present, a variety of type II properties can be treated by the GL approach. (As we shall see in Section 8.07, thin films of type I materials are exceptions, having second-order transitions in some circumstances.)

The first part of this chapter presents an analysis of the way in which magnetic flux penetrates a type II superconductor. This leads to the determination of the lower critical field H_{c1} at which the flux first penetrates the bulk, and the upper critical field H_{c2}, where the order parameter becomes completely suppressed in the bulk and the transition to the normal state takes place. The concept of a surface sheath of nonvanishing order parameter which can exist, under some circumstances, to a still higher field H_{c3} is then introduced.

The special properties of thin films in magnetic fields either parallel or perpendicular to the film surface are analyzed. This subject has its major application in superconducting electronics and is a good illustration of the fact that the GL equations can play an important role even in relatively weak magnetic fields.

Flux penetration in the presence of a transport current is a subject of central importance to the design of superconducting magnets and power cables. Flux motion and the attendant dissipation are considered in detail and the use of material defects as pinning centers to prevent losses is shown to be an essential part of superconductor technology.

The final parts of the chapter deal with the behavior of type II super-conductors in the presence of the very large magnetic fields and currents encountered in superconducting magnets and cables.The basic concepts in the design of magnets and the mechanisms of ac losses in power cables and machines are also presented.

8.02. Mixed State in Type II Superconductors

In describing the intrinsic magnetic behavior of superconductors in Section 7.07, it was suggested that the consequence of negative interphase surface free energy, in materials where the Ginzburg–Landau parameter κ is greater than $1/\sqrt{2}$, would be a very high degree of subdividing into normal and superconducting regions to minimize the total free energy. However, the energy in the $|\nabla\psi|^2$ term limits the variations of the order parameter. Upon minimization of the free energy, it is seen that significant variations of the order parameter cannot exist on a scale smaller than the coherence length ξ_{GL}. In the theoretically defined mixed state, there are no regions that are completely in the normal state; rather, the order parameter is reduced in filamentary regions in the superconductor and reaches zero only exactly at the centers of these regions. The radial variation of the order parameter is shown in Fig. 8.02a. One quantum of magnetic flux, distributed as shown in Fig. 8.02a, passes through each cylindrical region. The order parameter rises from zero at the center to an approximately constant value at a radius equal to twice the coherence length. That value depends on the external magnetic field and varies from roughly the zero-field value at H_{c1}, where flux and regions of reduced ψ begin to appear in the superconductor, to zero at the upper critical field H_{c2}, where the transition to the normal state takes place.

A circulating current is associated with the magnetic field, and serves to screen it from the more strongly superconducting region outside. The current vectors are sketched in Fig. 8.02b and the current-density distribution is shown in Fig. 8.02a. The circulation of current in the region of depressed ψ has led to the use of the term *vortex*; this cylindrical distribu-

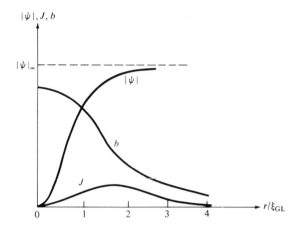

Figure 8.02a. Radial variation of the magnitudes of the order parameter ψ, the magnetic flux density $\vec{b}$, and current density $\vec{J}$ comprising a vortex.

tion of ψ, $\vec{J}$, and $\vec{b}$ is normally less than 1 μm in diameter and passes like a filament through the superconductor.

When the field is raised above H_{c1}, it becomes energetically more favorable to admit individual flux quanta in vortices than to maintain the Meissner state with total flux exclusion. Above H_{c1}, in an ideal material, there are many vortices present, ideally in a regular, two-dimensional array or lattice. The lattice spacing is determined by the applied magnetic field and the mutual repulsion between neighboring vortices. The large-scale average B of the magnetic induction b taken over many vortices approaches the externally applied value in the limit, as H approaches H_{c2}. This can be seen in the magnetization curve of Fig. 8.02c, where $B \approx \mu_0 H$ for $H \gg H_{c1}$. For magnetic fields just above H_{c1}, the superconducting sample retains appreciable magnetization and $B \ll \mu_0 H$.

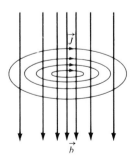

Figure 8.02b. Circulating currents and magnetic flux in a vortex.

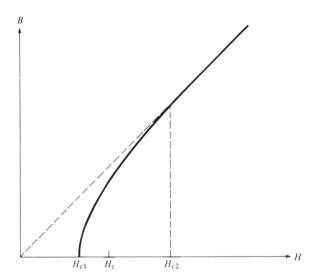

Figure 8.02c. Magnetization curve for a type II superconductor with $\kappa \cong 1.2$.

When a transport current of density $\vec{J}_T$ passes through a superconductor in the mixed state, there is a Lorentz force $\vec{J}_T \times \vec{b}$ acting on the vortices. At the same time, chemical or physical defects in the superconductor exert forces on the vortices to keep them trapped or "pinned" at the locations of the defects. If the Lorentz forces exceed the pinning forces, the vortices move and generate an electromotive force, leading to dissipation. This motion can be initiated by thermal activation and has been divided into various categories which will be discussed in Section 8.09. The heat produced by vortex motion places a practical limit on the application of type II superconductors in high-power systems.

An understanding of the structure and behavior of vortices provides the key to the macroscopic description of the mixed state; these will be examined in more detail in the following sections.

8.03. London Model of the Mixed State

An extreme type II superconductor ($\kappa \gg 1$) in the mixed state near the lower critical field, $H - H_{c1} \ll H_{c1}$, contains an array of vortices in which the regions of depressed order parameter ("cores") comprise a small fraction of the volume of the superconductor. The major part of the volume contains what is essentially the zero-field order parameter. In this case, the current and magnetic-field distribution in an individual vortex can be found, to a good approximation, from a simplified model. The vortices can then be assembled mathematically to describe the vortex lattice.[1]

An isolated vortex, under the above-stated conditions, can be usefully described by the solution of a simple modification of the London equation [cf. Eqs. 3.03(9) and 3.06(4)]:

$$\mu_0\lambda^2\nabla \times \vec{J}_s + \vec{b} = 0 \qquad (1)$$

The use of the London equation is appropriate here because with $\xi \ll \lambda$, the relation between $\vec{J}_s$ and $\vec{A}$ is a local one, as is assumed in the London theory (see Prob. 7.07). The penetration depth is the appropriate one for local electrodynamics for pure or impure materials, as discussed in Section 3.12.

A two-dimensional delta function weighted with a flux quantum Φ_0 is introduced on the right-hand side of (1) to provide a source for the London equation (this assumes, as can be shown,[2] that there is one quantum of flux in a vortex):

$$\mu_0\lambda^2\nabla \times \vec{J}_s + \vec{b} = \hat{z}\Phi_0\delta(r) \qquad (2)$$

where the magnetic field is along the z axis. Using $\nabla \times \vec{b} = \mu_0\vec{J}_s$, from Ampere's law, (2) becomes

$$\lambda^2\nabla \times \nabla \times \vec{b} + \vec{b} = \hat{z}\Phi_0\delta(r) \qquad (3)$$

Using a vector identity and noting that $\nabla \cdot \vec{b} = 0$, we have

$$\lambda^2\nabla^2\vec{b} - \vec{b} = -\hat{z}\Phi_0\delta(r) \qquad (4)$$

The solution for (4) in circular cylindrical coordinates can be found to be

$$\vec{b}(r) = \hat{z}(\Phi_0/2\pi\lambda^2)K_0(r/\lambda) \qquad (5)$$

where K_0 is the modified Bessel function of zero order.

In this model, the region of depressed order parameter is of zero radius rather than having a radius of order ξ_{GL}, so the details of the core of the vortex are obscured. For $r \gg \xi_{GL}$, this "London model" gives reasonably accurate results. For $r \gg \lambda$, the solution (5) approaches an exponential form. The modified Bessel function K_0 in (5) has a logarithmic form for $r \ll \lambda$.

The circulating supercurrent has only a circumferential component and its density is proportional to $\partial b/\partial r$:

$$\vec{J}_s(r) = \hat{\phi}(\Phi_0/2\pi\mu_0\lambda^3)K_1(r/\lambda) \qquad (6)$$

---

[1] The treatment given in Sections 8.03–8.06 follows A. L. Fetter and P. C. Hohenberg, "Theory of type II superconductors," in R. D. Parks (Ed.), *Superconductivity*. New York: Marcel Dekker, 1969.

[2] See footnote 1.

where K_1 is a modified Bessel function of first order and, like K_0, decays exponentially for $r \gg \lambda$. For radii such that $r/\lambda \ll 1$, the function $K_1(r/\lambda)$ approaches a $1/r$ variation.

The London model of a vortex assumes that $|\psi|$ is constant everywhere except at $r = 0$, where there is a singularity. The effect of the depression of $|\psi|$ in the core region ($r \lesssim \xi_{GL}$) is therefore not taken into account. The analyses that do include order-parameter depression use the Ginzburg–Landau equations, so they are only valid for $T \to T_c$. The London model of a vortex is more approximate and applies only where $\kappa \gg 1$ and $(H - H_{c1}) \ll H_{c1}$ but is valid for all T not too close to T_c. (Very near T_c, the cores become large and the assumption of uniform $|\psi|$ fails.)

A model of the mixed state can be constructed as the superposition of a large number of vortices of the form described. Close to H_{c1}, where the vortices are widely separated, the interaction between them is very weak. As the field is increased, the vortices are more densely packed and their interaction must be taken into account.

8.04. Behavior Near H_{c1}

At the lower critical field H_{c1}, the transition to the mixed state occurs with the entry of the first few vortices.[3] The separation of these vortices is much greater than λ for fields near H_{c1}, making it possible to calculate the energy of an isolated vortex by neglecting the small contribution from interaction with other vortices.

At H_{c1} the Meissner state with no vortices and the mixed state with a low density of noninteracting vortices are in equilibrium. At the common boundary between these two phases (or "states"), the Gibbs free energies must be equal, as discussed in Section 6.09. In a long, thin sample parallel to the magnetic field, the internal field is uniform and equal to the applied field. The local flux density b varies across the plane perpendicular to the field having maxima along the axes of the vortices, which can be assumed to be uniformly distributed. All quantities are independent of the coordinate along the field direction.

Now we shall consider the Gibbs free energy of the sample. Using the subscripts "M" and "mix" to denote the Meissner and mixed states, respectively, we require

$$G_M = G_{mix} \tag{1}$$

The Gibbs and Helmholtz free energies per unit length at H_{c1} are related

---

[3] The presence of surface barriers may delay vortex entry until a field somewhat above H_{c1} is reached, as discussed in Section 8.09.

by

$$G_M = F_M - H_{c1} \int_S b \, dS \qquad (2a)$$

$$G_{mix} = F_{mix} - H_{c1} \int_S b \, dS \qquad (2b)$$

The field H and flux density b can be treated as scalars since they are parallel. The flux density in the Meissner state is zero (neglecting the small penetration at the surface), so $G_M = F_M$. Then combining this with (1) and (2b), we have

$$F_M = F_{mix} - H_{c1} \int_S b \, dS \qquad (3)$$

The Helmholtz free energies of the two states differ only by virtue of the energy in the vortices which has a value per unit length of ϵ_1 for each vortex:

$$F_{mix} = F_M + n\epsilon_1 \qquad (4)$$

where n is the number of vortices in the sample. Noting also that the integral in (3) is the total flux and assuming that each vortex contains one flux quantum, the integral is $n\Phi_0$. Combining this result with (4), we have

$$H_{c1} = \epsilon_1 / \Phi_0 \qquad (5)$$

In order to find H_{c1}, we must evaluate ϵ_1. To do this, let us use (4) with $n = 1$. The mixed state in the sample then differs from the Meissner state by the presence of one isolated vortex. The Helmholtz free energy in the mixed state is raised by the loss of condensation energy in the core, the presence of circulating currents, and the penetration of magnetic flux. We treat only materials with $\kappa \gg 1$, so the core is very small and the reduction of condensation energy there is neglected. Beyond a few penetration lengths from the center of the vortex, both the circulating currents and the magnetic flux die away to negligible values and the free energy densities in the two states tend to become equal. We can obtain the difference of Helmholtz free-energy densities $f_{mix} - f_M$ as follows. We note from Eqs. 7.02(1) and 7.02(3) that

$$f_s = f_{n0} + \Delta f(|\psi|^2) + (1/2m^*)|(i\hbar \nabla + e^* \vec{A})\psi|^2 + b^2/2\mu_0 \qquad (6)$$

where we have used $g_{n0} = f_{n0}$, since b = 0 for that term. In the Meissner state only the first two terms on the right side of (6) are present, whereas in the mixed state all four terms are nonzero. The difference $f_{mix} - f_M$ arises only from the last two terms. To apply (4) with $n = 1$, we integrate this difference over the sample (assuming a unit length, for simplicity):

$$\epsilon_1 = \int_S \left(\frac{1}{2m^*} |(i\hbar \nabla + e^* A)\psi|^2 + \frac{b^2}{2\mu_0} \right) dS \qquad (7)$$

Since $|\psi|$ is constant in the London model that we are using here, the first term in (7) can be identified with the current density by Eq. 3.03(7) so (7) becomes

$$\epsilon_1 = \int_S \left(\frac{1}{2} \frac{m^*}{n_s^* e^{*2}} J_s^2 + \frac{b^2}{2\mu_0} \right) dS \tag{8}$$

By using $|\nabla \times b| = \mu_0 J_s$ and cutting off the integral at $r = \xi_{GL}$ to eliminate the artificial singularity at the origin in the London model, one can find

$$\epsilon_1 = (\Phi_0^2/4\pi\mu_0\lambda^2)\ln \kappa \quad \text{joules/meter} \tag{9}$$

In this approximation, the precise nature of the vortex core does not enter since it has been assumed that κ is large and, therefore, the contribution to free energy by the core is negligible. Combining (5) and (9), we find

$$H_{c1} = (\Phi_0/4\pi\mu_0\lambda^2)\ln \kappa \quad \kappa \gg 1 \tag{10}$$

Then recasting Eq. 7.04(4) in the form

$$H_c = \frac{\kappa}{2\sqrt{2}\,\pi\lambda^2\mu_0} \left(\frac{h}{e^*} \right) = \frac{\kappa\Phi_0}{2\sqrt{2}\,\pi\lambda^2\mu_0} \tag{11}$$

and substituting it in (10) gives H_{c1} in terms of the thermodynamic field H_c:

$$\boxed{H_{c1} = \left(H_c/\sqrt{2}\,\kappa \right)\ln \kappa} \tag{12}$$

The flux density at the center of an isolated vortex can be found through a series of transformations[4] to be

$$b(0) = 2\mu_0\epsilon_1/\Phi_0 = 2\mu_0 H_{c1} \tag{13}$$

8.05. The Vortex Lattice

The large slope of the $B-H$ curve at H_{c1} shown in Fig. 8.02c implies that the entry of the first vortex is accompanied by a rapid influx of many others as the magnetic field is raised marginally above H_{c1}. Close to H_{c1} the average density of vortices n is small compared to that at the upper critical field, $\mu_0 H/\Phi_0$, and will only approach this limit when the magnetic flux penetrates the sample completely. In fact, it can be shown[5] that in the mixed state, where $H_{c1} < H < H_{c2}$, the vortices are always (in the ideal

---

[4] Footnote 1, p. 860.
[5] A. A. Abrikosov, "On the magnetic properties of superconductors of the second group," *Sov. Phys., JETP*, Vol. 5, pp. 1174–1182, 15 December 1957.

case of a pure crystalline material) located at the lattice sites of a regular array. This result can be obtained by calculating the free-energy contribution arising from the repulsive interaction between neighboring vortices and minimizing the energy as a function of lattice configuration. It could have been shown in Abrikosov's theoretical work that the triangular array has a slightly lower free energy than has a square lattice.[6] The existence of a triangular lattice has been shown theoretically[7] and confirmed in some elegant experiments[8] (see Fig. 8.05). The difference in free energy for triangular and square arrays is sufficiently small to lead to anomalies in practice, because of defects and other factors, and the triangular lattice is observed only in specially prepared specimens.

The broad features of the analysis for determination of the equilibrium lattice structure can be explained with the aid of the London model introduced in Section 8.03. For n vortices per unit area located on sites $\vec{r}_j$, the London equation can be modified to the form

$$\mu_0 \lambda^2 \nabla \times \vec{J}_s + \vec{b} = \hat{z} \Phi_0 \sum_j \delta(\vec{r} - \vec{r}_j) \tag{1}$$

To get the solution for (1), we use that obtained previously for $b(\vec{r})$ in a single isolated vortex and superimpose the results for all vortices:

$$\vec{b}(\vec{r}) = \hat{z} \frac{\Phi_0}{2\pi\lambda^2} \sum_j K_0\left(\frac{|\vec{r} - \vec{r}_j|}{\lambda}\right) \tag{2}$$

where it is assumed there is negligible effect on λ caused by the interaction of vortices.

The total free energy per unit volume resulting from n vortices per unit area can be calculated following the same approach that led to Eq. 8.04(9), but using the magnetic flux density given by (2). The result is

$$F = n\epsilon_1 + \frac{n\Phi_0^2}{4\pi\mu_0\lambda^2} \sum_j K_0\left(\frac{|\vec{r} - \vec{r}_j|}{\lambda}\right) \tag{3}$$

where j is summed over all vortices but the one at the origin. The first term is simply the sum for the n vortices of the self-energy contributions. The second term gives the increase in free energy resulting from the repulsive interaction between vortices.

The equilibrium lattice structure can be found by minimizing the Gibbs function $G = F - BH$ with respect to B, the average flux-density vector

---

[6] Abrikosov mistook a saddle point for a minimum and this led him to the conclusion that a square lattice has the least free energy.

[7] W. H. Kleiner, L. M. Roth, and S. H. Autler, "Bulk solution of Ginzburg–Landau equations for type II superconductors: Upper critical field region," *Phys. Rev.*, Vol. A 133, pp. 1226–1227, 2 March 1964.

[8] H. Träuble and U. Essman, "Flux-line arrangement in superconductors as revealed by direct observation," *J. Appl. Phys.*, Vol. 39, pp. 4052–4059, August 1968.

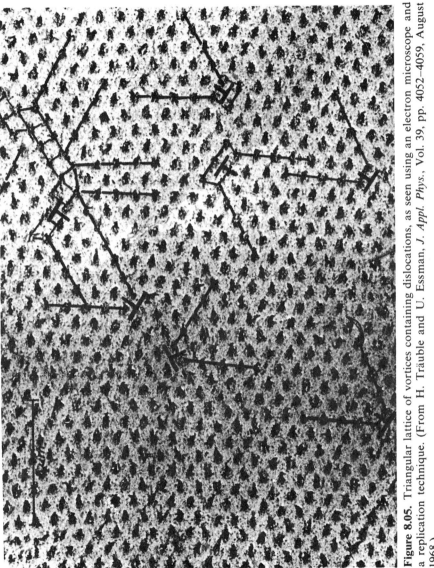

Figure 8.05. Triangular lattice of vortices containing dislocations, as seen using an electron microscope and a replication technique. (From H. Träuble and U. Essman, *J. Appl. Phys.*, Vol. 39, pp. 4052–4059, August 1968.)

taken over all n vortices using (3) for F. From $\partial G/\partial B = 0$ one obtains a constitutive relation between B and the applied magnetic field H. It is useful to introduce some approximations, of which the simplest is the restriction to fields marginally above H_{c1}. This allows consideration of only nearest neighbors since the intervortex interactions are then not of long range compared to λ.

Assuming that, in a regular array of vortices, each nearest neighbor is a distance d away, the repulsive interaction term from (3) can be written

$$\frac{n\Phi_0^2 z}{4\pi\lambda^2} K_0\left(\frac{d}{\lambda}\right) = \frac{Bz\Phi_0}{4\pi\lambda^2}\left(\frac{n\lambda}{2d}\right)^{1/2} e^{-d/\lambda} \tag{4}$$

where z is the number of nearest neighbors and the asymptotic form of $K_0(d/\lambda)$ for $d \gg \lambda$ is used. Choosing a minimum value of z (4 for a square array, 6 for a triangular array) does not yield the equilibrium configuration because d, the nearest-neighbor distance, depends on z and B and dominates through the exponential term. Hence, we can show that, at least near H_{c1}, the triangular lattice gives the lowest free energy.

It can also be shown[9] that

$$B \propto \left[\ln\left(3\Phi_0/4\pi\mu_0\lambda^2(H - H_{c1})\right)\right]^2 \tag{5}$$

giving infinite initial slope to the $B-H$ curve at H_{c1}, as seen in Fig. 8.02c.

Further calculations are needed to determine the lattice structure at higher fields where next-nearest neighbors, and so on, must be included in the interaction term and some overlapping of vortices occurs. The results show that a triangular lattice yields the minimum free energy in all cases. Near H_{c2} the superconductor is virtually filled with vortex cores, closely packed in a regular triangular array; the Ginzburg–Landau equations are employed to study this limiting case in the next section.

8.06. Behavior Near H_{c2} and Surface Superconductivity

At low fields the vortex cores occupy a negligible fraction of the total volume. At the higher fields, the entire superconductor becomes a mosaic of weakly superconducting core regions through which magnetic flux penetrates almost uniformly. At some upper critical field H_{c2}, the order parameter is quenched and the bulk of the sample makes a second-order transition to the normal state (although superconductivity may persist in a shallow surface region up to a yet higher critical field H_{c3}). The continuous depression of the order parameter ψ to vanishingly small values as H approaches H_{c2} presents a situation in which the Ginzburg–Landau theory can be readily applied.

---

[9] M. Tinkham, *Introduction to Superconductivity*. New York: McGraw-Hill, 1975, p. 151.

Determination of H_{c2}

Abrikosov[10] solved the GL equations for H near H_{c2} under the assumption that $|\psi|$ is everywhere small compared to its value with zero magnetic field $|\psi_0|$ and that the sample makes a second-order phase transition to the normal state at H_{c2}. The GL equations can then be linearized with respect to $\psi(r)$ and take the form

$$(1/2m^*)(i\hbar\,\nabla + e^*\vec{A})^2\psi + \alpha\psi = 0 \qquad (1)$$

$$\vec{A} = \vec{a}_y\mu_0 Hx \qquad (2)$$

where α is the GL parameter introduced in Section 7.02 and the vector potential $\vec{A}$ is that for a uniform magnetic field applied in the z direction. It is assumed that the magnetic-field perturbations produced on the scale of the vortex-screening-current distribution are negligible in the comparison to the applied field. Expanding (1) and substituting for $\vec{A}$ from (2) we obtain

$$\frac{\hbar^2}{2m^*}\nabla^2\psi - \frac{i\hbar e^*\mu_0 Hx}{m^*}\frac{\partial\psi}{\partial y} - \frac{e^{*2}\mu_0^2 H^2 x^2}{2m^*}\psi - \alpha\psi = 0 \qquad (3)$$

which may be written in the form

$$\frac{\partial^2\psi}{\partial x^2} + \left[\left(\frac{1}{\xi_{GL}^2}\right) - \left(\frac{2\pi\mu_0 Hx}{\Phi_0} + i\frac{\partial}{\partial y}\right)^2\right]\psi = 0 \qquad (4)$$

A solution of the partial differential equation (4) is assumed to be of the form

$$\psi(x, y) = u(x)\exp(ik_y y) \qquad (5)$$

Substituting (5) in (4), it can be seen that $u(x)$ satisfies a one-dimensional harmonic-oscillator type of equation

$$\frac{d^2u}{dx^2} + \left[\frac{1}{\xi_{GL}^2} - \left(\frac{2\pi\mu_0 Hx}{\Phi_0} - k_y\right)^2\right]u = 0 \qquad (6)$$

The eigenvalues H_n are determined by the relation

$$2\pi\mu_0 H_n/\Phi_0 = 1/(2n + 1)\xi_{GL}^2 \qquad (7)$$

where n is an integer. The eigenvalue corresponding to $n = 0$ gives the largest value of H for which a solution $\psi \neq 0$ exists. The linear approximation made in (1) becomes increasingly valid as H approaches its maximum value, which is taken to be the upper critical field H_{c2}.

$$H(n = 0) = H_{c2} = \Phi_0/2\pi\mu_0\xi_{GL}^2$$

---

[10] See footnote 5.

or

$$H_{c2} = \sqrt{2}\,\kappa H_c \qquad\qquad (8)$$

since

$$H_c = \frac{\Phi_0}{2\sqrt{2}\,\pi\mu_0\lambda\xi_{GL}} \qquad \text{and} \qquad \kappa = \frac{\lambda}{\xi}$$

The eigenfunction for $n = 0$ has the form

$$\psi(x, y) = \psi_0 \exp\left[\frac{-(x - x_0)^2}{2\xi_{GL}^2}\right] \exp\left[i\,\frac{2\pi\mu_0 H_{c2} x_0}{\Phi_0}\right] y \qquad (9)$$

where

$$x_0 = k_y \Phi_0 / 2\pi\mu_0 H_{c2}$$

It has been shown that H_{c2}, given by (8), is the largest field for which the order parameter may exist in the *bulk* of a type II superconductor. The parameter x_0 is a continuous variable, so the solution (9) may be located at

Figure 8.06. Spatial distribution of $|\psi|^2$ near H_{c2} for the equilibrium vortex array. The contours are labeled with the square of the reduced order parameter. (From W. H. Kleiner, L. M. Roth, and S. H. Autler, *Phys. Rev.*, Vol. A 133, p. 1227, 2 March 1964.)

any interior point of the sample without affecting the free energy. It follows from the linearity of (4) that any linear combination of these vortex-type solutions may be assembled as a general solution with the values of x_0 arranged as the points of a lattice. Abrikosov[11] constructed such a solution, periodic in both x and y, taking into account the nonlinear terms in the GL equations omitted from the calculation given here. He showed that by this approach it is possible to obtain the lattice configuration with minimum free energy. Subsequent work[12] has given the equilibrium distribution of $|\psi|$ (see Fig. 8.06) and shown that the triangular lattice is the minimum-free-energy configuration near H_{c2}.

Surface Sheath

The above analysis that led to an upper critical field H_{c2} has not taken boundaries into consideration and thus strictly applies to an infinite medium. Here we present the results of similar analyses when the boundary condition Eq. 7.03(4) is satisfied for a superconductor–insulator interface. Different results are obtained depending on whether the applied field is parallel or perpendicular to the boundary. If the field is perpendicular to the boundary, the solution (9) satisfies the boundary conditions and the highest field for a nonvanishing ψ is still H_{c2} given by (8). On the other hand, if the field is parallel to the boundary, a nonvanishing solution is found with an even higher maximum field.[13] The solution vanishes in the bulk of the sample but is nonzero in a sheath at the surface roughly of thickness ξ_{GL}. The field at which the sheath is suppressed is

$$\boxed{H_{c3} = 1.7 H_{c2}} \qquad (10)$$

The presence of this sheath has been verified experimentally. It does not exist, however, if the surface of the superconductor is in contact with a normal metal rather than an insulator, because of the different boundary condition on the normal derivative of ψ.

8.07. Flux Penetration in Thin Films: Critical Fields

The simple division of bulk superconductors into type I and type II for the Ginzburg–Landau κ less or greater than $1/\sqrt{2}$, respectively, does not apply to specimens that have at least one dimension comparable to λ or ξ_{GL}. Very thin films can have second-order transitions to the normal state even

---

[11] See footnote 5.
[12] See footnote 7.
[13] D. Saint-James and P. G. de Gennes, "Onset of superconductivity in decreasing fields," *Phys. Lett.*, Vol. 7, pp. 306–308, 15 December 1963.

if they are strongly type I, and the mixed state can exist in type I films with perpendicular magnetic fields. Also, the parameters λ and κ depend on both film thickness and temperature. For films, then, the magnetic field behavior depends on the orientation of the film relative to the field, the thickness of the film, and the intrinsic properties of the film material.

For analysis of the magnetic behavior of films, the dependences of the penetration depth and κ on film thickness d are required.[14] If the film is thin enough or the intrinsic mean free path short enough, local electrodynamics applies and one has the adaptation of Eq. 3.12(5):

$$\lambda(T,d) = \lambda_L(T)\left[\xi_0/l(d)\right]^{1/2} \tag{1}$$

The thickness-dependent mean free path $l(d)$ has the value

$$1/l(d) = (1/l_0) + (\tfrac{3}{8}d) \tag{2}$$

In (2), l_0 is the intrinsic mean free path for a bulk sample of the same material with the same impurity and defect content, and diffuse scattering is assumed at the film surfaces. In the nonlocal case, a better approximation for the penetration depth is given by

$$\lambda(T,d) = \lambda_{nl}(T)\left[1 + \lambda_L^2(T)\xi_0/\lambda_{nl}^2(T)l(d)\right]^{1/2} \tag{3}$$

where $\lambda_{nl}(T)$ is the bulk weak-field penetration depth for nonlocal materials, Eq. 3.12(2). The penetration depths in (1) and (3) are reasonable approximations for either the perpendicular or parallel orientation of $\vec{H}$ relative to the film. The Ginzburg–Landau κ can be expressed by the relation given in Eq. 7.04(4) but with temperature and film-thickness dependences as

$$\kappa(T,d) = 2\sqrt{2\pi}\ \lambda^2(T,d)\,\mu_0 H_c(T)/\Phi_0 \tag{4}$$

In keeping with the variability inherent in thin-film properties and the difficulties of precise thickness control, we neglect here the differences between Maki's κ_1 and κ_2, which should ideally appear in the equations and graphs of this section.[15] Figure 8.07a shows how $\kappa(T,d)$ varies for two important soft superconductors, lead and tin.[16] Reasonably accurate interpolation for the bulk value $\kappa(T,\infty)$ for other temperatures can be done with the two-fluid model in which

$$\kappa(T,\infty) = C/(1 + t^2) \tag{5}$$

where C is a constant.

---

[14] G. D. Cody and R. E. Miller, "Magnetic transitions of superconducting thin films and foils: I. Lead," *Phys. Rev.*, Vol. 173, pp. 481–493, 10 September 1968.

[15] Footnote 1, p. 864 ff.

[16] R. E. Miller and G. D. Cody, "Magnetic transitions of superconducting thin films and foils: II. Tin," *Phys. Rev.*, Vol. 173, pp. 494–503, 10 September 1968.

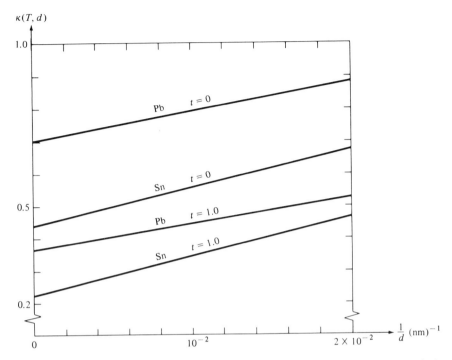

$\kappa(T, d)$

Figure 8.07a. Thickness and temperature dependence of κ for pure lead and tin films. (Data from Cody and Miller, footnotes 14 and 16.)

Field Parallel to Film

The Ginzburg–Landau solution for a film thinner than the coherence length, and therefore with uniform order parameter, was found for a parallel magnetic field in Eq. 7.04(9) to be

$$H_\parallel(T, d) = \sqrt{24}\ [\lambda(T, d)/d] H_c(T) \tag{6}$$

The magnetic field is assumed to be of equal strength on both sides of the film. We saw in Section 7.04 that for $\kappa \to 0$ a second-order transition occurs at $H_\parallel$ if $d < \sqrt{5}\ \lambda$, whereas the transition is first-order for thicker films. The maximum thickness for which a second-order transition occurs remains equal to $\sqrt{5}\ \lambda$ for $\kappa < 0.4$ but then increases slightly for $0.4 < \kappa < 1/\sqrt{2}$. Equation (6) has been extensively verified assuming the two-fluid model for the temperature dependences of λ and H_c [see Eqs. 3.13(2) and 6.10(1)]. With this assumption,

$$H_\parallel(T, d) = \sqrt{24}\ [\lambda(0, d)/d] H_c(0) [(1 - t^2)/(1 + t^2)]^{1/2} \tag{7}$$

where $\lambda(0, d)$ is given by (3) with $T = 0$, and $t = T/T_c$. Since the above expressions for $H_\parallel$ are based on a solution of the GL equations, their validity at temperatures away from T_c may be questionable but, in fact, good results are found even at very low temperatures.

The appropriate expression for $H_\parallel$ for thicker films depends on the value of $\kappa(T, d)$. If κ is large enough that the surface-sheath critical field H_{c3} exceeds the thermodynamic field H_c, the highest field for which superconductivity can persist is given by Eq. 8.06(10):

$$H_\parallel(T, d) = 1.7\sqrt{2}\ \kappa(T, d)H_c(T) \qquad (8)$$

where $\kappa(T, d)$ is given by (4). On the other hand, if κ is less than the above-mentioned value, the transition at the upper critical field is a first-order bulk transition. For films much thicker than the penetration depth,[17]

$$H_\parallel(T, d) = H_c(T)(1 + \lambda/d) \qquad (9)$$

Examples of these different types of dependence of $H_\parallel$ are seen in Fig. 8.07b where $H_\parallel$ is plotted as a function of film thickness for lead at 4.2 K and tin at 2.9 K. The lead data are not normalized and those for tin are normalized to the $H_c(T, d)$ (as in the works cited in footnotes 14 and 16). For each film the transition temperature is slightly different depending on the film thickness and structure; $H_c(T, d)$ was calculated using the correspondence principle, $H_c(0, d)/T_c(d) = $ constant for tin and had values of about 1.8×10^4 A/m $\pm$ 10%. From Fig. 8.07b it may be seen that for lead the theoretical curve given by (6) well describes the thin-film results. At larger thicknesses $H_\parallel$ becomes the nearly constant value expected from (8). [Notice from Fig. 8.07a that there is very little change in $\kappa(T, d)$ for $d > 200$ nm.] Tin has smaller $\kappa(T, d)$ and although it follows (6) for very thin films, the thick films fit reasonably well to (9), as seen in Fig. 8.07b. It should be noted that (8) and (9) do not apply exactly at the boundary for behavior described by (6). There is a transition region not well described by any of (6), (8), or (9).

These dependences and others for different materials can be categorized in terms of the chart in Fig. 8.07c, which maps the behavior for different combinations of $\kappa(T, d)$ and $d/\lambda(T, d)$.[18] For sufficiently thin films, the order parameter is independent of position in the film and goes gradually to zero as the upper field $H_\parallel$ is approached; thus a second-order transition is made there. For films thicker than $1.8\lambda(T, d)$, ψ can vary enough for a row a vortices to exist; this dividing line is shown broken in Fig. 8.07c. For combinations of $\kappa(T, d)$ and d to the right of the broken line, the behavior

[17] V. L. Ginzburg and L. D. Landau, see I. D. ter Harr, *Men of Physics: L. D. Landau*. Oxford: Pergamon, 1965.

[18] E. Guyon, F. Meunier, and R. S. Thompson, "Thickness dependence of κ_2 and related problems for superconducting alloy films in strong fields," *Phys. Rev.*, Vol. 156, pp. 452–469, 10 April 1967.

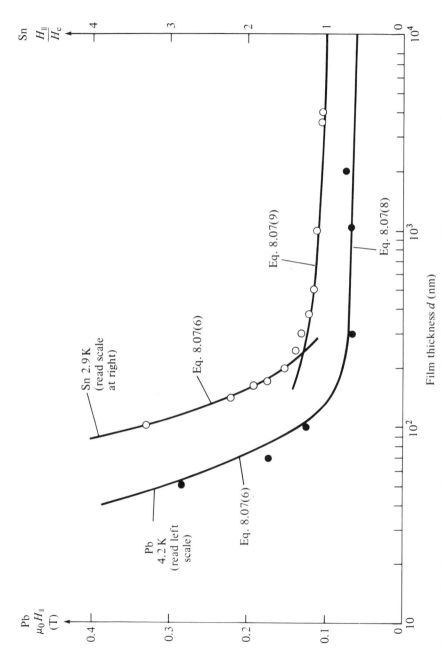

Figure 8.07b. Upper critical field for pure lead and tin films in magnetic fields parallel to the film surface. (Data from Cody and Miller, footnotes 14 and 16.)

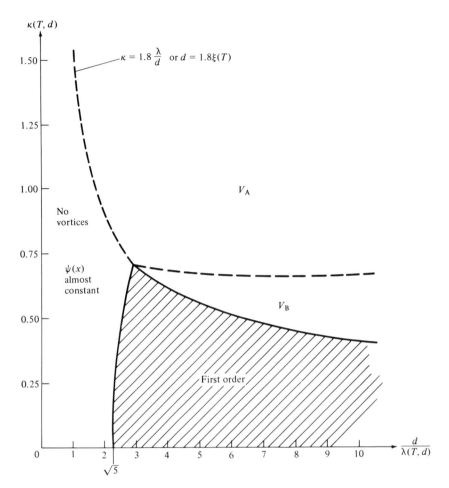

Figure 8.07c. Regimes of different behaviors for films of normalized thickness $d/\lambda(T, d)$ and Ginzburg–Landau parameter $\kappa(T, d)$. Vortices form in regimes V_A and V_B. All transitions to the normal state resulting from raising the magnetic field are second-order except where indicated.

of the film as it approaches the upper field $H_\parallel$ is like a type II superconductor in which surface sheaths of order parameter are the last remnants of a superconducting state, and these remain until H_{c3} given by (8). At lower fields in the region to the right of the broken line, the film contains vortices as in a bulk type II material.

On the other hand, for very small $\kappa(T, d)$ the very-thin-film behavior stops at $d = \sqrt{5}\,\lambda(T, d)$. As d is further increased, the magnetic flux in the center of the film becomes progressively weaker. The transition at $H_\parallel$ is first-order and is given by (9). When the penetration depth becomes

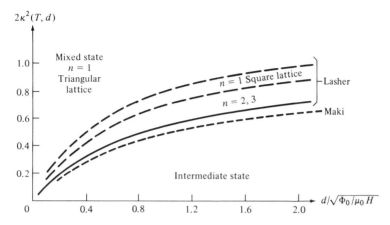

Figure 8.07d. Domains in which different kinds of flux penetration occur in thin films oriented perpendicular to the applied magnetic field.

negligible compared with the film thickness, $H_\parallel \cong H_c$. The entire region of first-order behavior requires analysis outside the scope of this text and is shown by the cross-hatching in Fig. 8.07c. In the region marked V_B the surface sheath and even a row of vortices can exist at fields above H_c and these vanish in a second-order manner at $H_\parallel$. The larger the value of d, the weaker the vortex structure.

Field Perpendicular to Film

We have previously seen that for bulk materials the vortex (mixed) state exists only if the GL parameter κ is greater than $1/\sqrt{2}$; that is, the material is type II. In films with perpendicular magnetic fields, the mixed state can be found even for type I materials if the film is sufficiently thin.[19] This results from the reduced effectiveness of the shielding of the circulating currents so that the range of penetration of magnetic field becomes larger as the film is made thinner. Theoretical studies[20,21] of this situation with fields near the upper critical field, using the Ginzburg–Landau equations, support the existence of the mixed state and give the required conditions. An experimental "decoration" technique like that used to get a visualiza-

---

[19] M. Tinkham, "Effect of fluxoid quantization on transitions of superconducting films," *Phys. Rev.*, Vol. 129, pp. 2413–2422, 15 March 1963.

[20] K. Maki, "Fluxoid structure in superconducting films," *Ann. Phys.*, Vol. 34, pp. 363–372, 6 October 1965.

[21] G. Lasher, "Mixed state of type I superconducting films in a perpendicular magnetic field," *Phys. Rev.*, Vol. 154, pp. 345–348, 10 February 1967.

tion of the vortex array in bulk type II material (Fig. 8.05) has been used for thin films as a way to determine which state exists.[22] The intermediate state having the form in Fig. 7.08b is seen in type I films that are not too thin. The single-quantum vortex mixed state is found for sufficiently thin samples of type I or type II materials. The regular array found in bulk crystalline materials has not been seen in any of the thin-film samples. This is probably a result of the polycrystalline state of the films since crystal boundaries can form pinning sites with energies that could exceed those associated with vortex interaction in an array.

For very thin films, Tinkham's calculation and other more rigorous theoretical treatments show that the magnetic field $H_\perp$ at which the order parameter vanishes completely is given by the same form of expression as that for H_{c2} in bulk materials,

$$H_\perp(T,d) = \sqrt{2}\,\kappa(T,d)H_c(T) \tag{10}$$

except that in this case the GL parameter depends on the film thickness and an approximate temperature dependence is assumed; thus $\kappa(T,d)$ is given by (4). The transition at $H_\perp$ given by (10) is second order.

Films that are sufficiently thick behave like bulk slabs, so if $\kappa(T,d)$ is not too large, the behavior will be that of the intermediate state of type I materials which exhibits the large domains shown in Fig. 7.08b and has a first-order transition to the normal state at the critical field. The dependence of $H_\perp$ on the temperature and thickness in this case is given by[23]

$$H_\perp(d,T) = H_c(T)\left\{1 - \left[C\,\delta(T)/d\right]^{1/2}\right\} \tag{11}$$

where $\delta(T)$ is the interphase surface-energy parameter in Eq. 7.06(11). There is about a factor of 2 uncertainty in the constant C with values being in the range 1–2. For lead at 4.2 K, an experimetal value of $C\delta$ was 63 nm.[24]

Theoretical studies have yielded the boundary between the mixed- and intermediate-state behaviors,[25,26] which is shown in Fig. 8.07d on a graph of $2\kappa^2(T,d)$ vs $d/(\Phi_0/\mu_0 H_\perp)^{1/2}$. Lasher's calculation also showed that there are some regions on the graph in which the mixed state has a triangular lattice, as in bulk type II materials, and in other regions the mixed state can have a square lattice. There are even some places where more than one flux quantum per lattice point is possible theoretically. It was pointed out above that the existence of the single-flux-quantum state

[22] G. J. Dolan, "Critical thicknesses for the transition from intermediate to mixed state behavior in superconducting thin films of Pb, Sn, and In," *J. Low Temp. Phys.*, Vol. 15, pp. 133–160, April 1974.
[23] See footnote 14.
[24] See footnote 14.
[25] See footnote 20.
[26] See footnote 21.

has been verified experimentally but that no lattice pattern could be found. The experiments that used the decoration method to determine the conditions for the mixed- and intermediate-state patterns have largely verified the boundary in Fig. 8.07d.

The difference between the thickness dependences given by (10) and (11) upon crossing the boundary in Fig. 8.07d is vividly demonstrated in the data in Fig. 8.07e for lead at 4.2 K. From Fig. 8.07a and (5) it can be seen that for $d \lesssim 10^3$ nm, where the transition between the two types of dependences apparently takes place, $\kappa(T, d) \approx 0.5$. The parameter $2\kappa^2(T, d)$ is also ≈ 0.5, and one would expect from Fig. 8.07d that intermediate-state patterns would be observed in the films with $d \gtrsim 0.8$ $(\Phi_0/\mu_0 H_\perp)^{1/2}$. Using $\mu_0 H_\perp \cong 0.04T$ from Fig. 8.07e, we find $d = 180$ nm. This is not far from the value found by Dolan.[27] Apparently, the intersection of the two curves in Fig. 8.07e is not the place where intermediate-state behavior is first found; the region near the transition is not well defined theoretically.

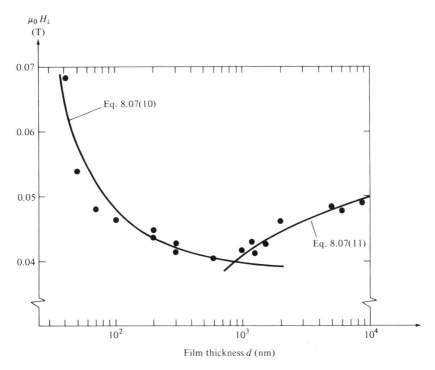

Figure 8.07e. Upper critical field for pure lead films in magnetic fields perpendicular to the film surface at $T = 4.2$ K. (Data from Cody and Miller, footnote 14.)

---

[27] See footnote 22, Fig. 4.

Field at Arbitrary Angle to Film

For very thin films $(d < \sqrt{5} \, \lambda(T,d))$ with the field direction at an angle θ with the plane of the film, the critical field $H_c(\theta)$ is given by

$$\left| \frac{H_c(\theta) \sin \theta}{H_\perp} \right| + \left| \frac{H_c(\theta) \cos \theta}{H_\parallel} \right|^2 = 1 \qquad (12)$$

This relation can be derived on the basis of the linearized GL equation[28] and has been confirmed experimentally.

Problems

8.07a. Consider pure lead films in a parallel magnetic field and operated at 4.2 K as in the data in Fig. 8.07b. Assume that the nonlocal and London penetration depths have the same temperature dependences, Eq. 3.13(2), and that $T_c = 7.2$ K for all the films. Determine and sketch the locus in the $\kappa(T,d)$-vs-$d/\lambda(T,d)$ plane of Fig. 8.07c for various thicknesses of the lead films. Discuss the data of Fig. 8.07b as it relates to the above-determined locus.

8.07b. Suppose a series of tin films of 200-nm thickness are made with different impurity contents and tested at 2.9 K. Assume that the nonlocal and London penetration depths have the same temperature dependence, Eq. 3.13(2), and that $T_c = 3.8$ K for all the films. Find the locus of points in Fig. 8.07c as the impurity content is increased, taking values of l_0 as follows: ∞, 2000, 1000, 500, 300, 150, and 50 nm.

8.07c. Pure tin films at 2.9 K are found to have a broad minimum of $H_\perp(T,d)$ of about 1.1×10^3 A/m in the range of 150–500 nm. Estimate the thickness above which intermediate-state behavior is to be expected.

8.07d. Suppose a lead film containing an alloying element is made 600-nm thick. The alloying reduces the mean free path sufficiently that local electrodynamics can be assumed. Use the nonlocal form for λ and assume all λs vary with temperature according to the two-fluid model. Find the shortest inherent mean free path l_0 for which intermediate-state behavior is to be expected at 4.2 K with perpendicular magnetic field.

8.07e. Plot the critical field for a 200-nm-thick Pb film operated at 4.2 K using the values of $H_\parallel$ and $H_\perp$ from the theoretically fitted curves in Figs. 8.07b, e.

---

[28] Footnote 9, pp. 133–135.

8.08. Vortex Motion and Flux-Flow Resistance

When a transport current passes through a superconductor threaded by vortices, a Lorentz force acts to move the vortices. Their movement leads to the development of a longitudinal potential gradient in the superconductor or, equivalently, the onset of resistance. However, the vortices may be pinned by defects in the material with sufficient force to prevent continuous motion below a certain critical current density. Resistanceless operation of type II materials above H_{c1} therefore is achievable only in specially prepared so-called *hard* superconductors in which the pinning force is sufficiently large to prevent flux motion.

When a magnetic field greater than the lower critical field H_{c1} is applied to a superconducting body, the material is penetrated by vortices, as shown in Fig. 8.05. Transport currents applied by an external source pass through the body of the material, in contrast to the surface currents characteristic of the Meissner state. The transport current interacts with the magnetic flux in the vortices as described by the Lorentz relation $\vec{J} \times \vec{b}$. The transport current is constrained to flow longitudinally, and because of the intimate relation between the magnetic flux density in the vortex and the associated screening currents, the entire vortex is displaced laterally. We can calculate the magnitude of the force on an isolated vortex for large κ as follows. The y-directed force per unit volume between the z-directed magnetic flux and x-directed transport current for a stationary vortex is given by

$$f_y = -n_s^* e^* v_x b_z \tag{1}$$

where v_x is the average drift velocity associated with the transport current. (This uniform current is superimposed on the circulating vortex currents.) Using the usual relation between current density and charge velocity $J_T = n_s^* e v_x$ and the London model of Eq. 8.03(5) for the magnetic field, (1) becomes

$$f_y = -J_T(\Phi_0/2\pi\lambda^2)K_0(r/\lambda) \tag{2}$$

The magnitude of the force per unit length of a vortex is obtained by integrating (2) over the cross-sectional area extending to a radius of several penetration depths, assuming the vortex to be isolated:

$$f_L = J_T\Phi_0 \tag{3}$$

If the applied magnetic field is not perpendicular to the transport current but at an angle θ to it, (3) is generalized to

$$f_L = J_T\Phi_0 \sin\theta \tag{4}$$

since only the component of $\vec{b}$ perpendicular to $\vec{J}_T$ contributes to the Lorentz force.[29]

In an ideal, perfectly annealed, pure superconductor, unimpeded vortex motion would occur for any value of transport current and the mixed state could not for any practical purpose be considered to be superconducting. However, in practice, inhomogeneities in both the interior and on the surface of a sample produce barriers to vortex motion and cause the vortices to be pinned locally at defect sites. Superconducting materials contain a great many such defects which act in concert to prevent the motion of the vortex array. Vortices that are not pinned are constrained, to some extent, by the intervortex interactions to stay with those that are. As the transport current is raised, the Lorentz force is more easily able to overcome the potential barriers at the pinning sites. At the "depinning" current, the total Lorentz force on the array of vortices exceeds the total pinning force and the vortex lattice moves with a steady drift velocity. Thermally activated flux motion also occurs as vortices are shaken free from their pinning sites. Both types of motion result in dissipation and heat generation. It is to be expected that there are random deviations from uniform motion caused by encounters with pinning sites, but we shall consider only the time-average motion here.

In moving through the superconductor, the vortices experience a velocity-dependent force. Its proportionality to velocity has led to its designation as a viscous force:

$$\vec{f}_v = -\eta\vec{v} \tag{5}$$

where η is the viscosity coefficient and $\vec{v}$ is the vortex velocity. There have been some theoretical efforts to evaluate η in terms of material parameters. Bardeen and Stephen[30] used a model in which it is assumed that the superconductor is strongly type II (a vortex "core" is defined with radius equal to the coherence length ξ_{GL}, which is much smaller than the penetration depth), so the flux density can be taken to be uniform in the vicinity of the core. The order parameter is assumed for simplicity to vanish entirely in the core; thus, the current there is entirely normal. Outside, there are both quasiparticle and superconducting components of current. As the vortex moves along the superconductor, the pairs at the front of the core are split and electrons at the rear edge of the core must rejoin into pairs. The relaxation back to pairs is assumed to occur in time equal to the collision time in the normal metal and, for the model to be valid, this must be small compared with the time required for the vortex

---

[29] The circulating supercurrent does not contribute to the force on the vortex, which is assumed to be in equilibrium in the absence of the transport current.

[30] J. Bardeen and M. J. Stephen, "Theory of the motion of vortices in superconductors," *Phys. Rev.*, Vol. 140, pp. A1197–A1207, 15 November 1965.

to move the distance of the core radius. The movement of the flux induces an electromotive force in the core (as well as in the surrounding region) which drives current through the normal region. Bardeen and Stephen demonstrate that this current is just equal to the transport current when the vortices are moving. When the vortex is pinned (or is part of a pinned lattice), there is no emf induced and no current flows in the core; the transport current flows around the core without energy loss.

Typical experimental results[31] on voltages developed in type II samples thinner than the penetration depth carrying a transport current are shown in Fig. 8.08a. It is seen that no measurable time-average voltage is developed until the current exceeds a certain value and, for slightly higher currents, the voltage variation becomes linear. The maximum zero-voltage current depends on the density of defects in the samples; the broken line is the expected result for a defect-free sample.

The shapes of these curves can be explained by the following phenomenological model. The viscous force (5) is equated to the difference between the Lorentz force (3) and a pinning force that averages the effect of the vortices' encounters with the potential wells at the defect pinning sites. Thus

$$\eta v = f_{\mathrm{L}} - f_{\mathrm{p}} \qquad (6)$$

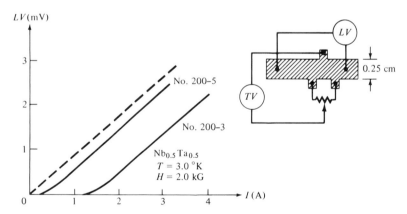

Figure 8.08a. $V-I$ characteristics of two flat-sheet Nb–Ta samples containing different amount of defects in a magnetic field $H_{c1} < H < H_{c2}$. The broken line shows the behavior expected for a defect-free sample. (From Y. B. Kim, C. F. Hempstead, and A. R. Strnad, *Phys. Rev.*, Vol. 139 A, p. 1165, 16 August 1965.)

[31] Y. B. Kim and M. J. Stephen, "Flux flow and irreversible effects," in R. D. Parks (Ed.) *Superconductivity*. New York: Marcel Dekker, 1969. Y. B. Kim, C. F. Hempstead, and A. R. Strnad, "Flux-flow resistance in type-II superconductors," *Phys. Rev.*, Vol. 139, pp. A1163–A1172, 16 August 1965.

The quantities in (6) can be written as scalars because they have the same or opposite directions. A reasonable, empirically useful picture of flux-flow resistance can be based on the assumption that an electric field is produced by the flux motion in a manner analogous to Faraday's law of induction:

$$E = nv\Phi_0 = vB \tag{7}$$

where n is the number of vortices per unit area and B is the average flux density. Taking the derivative of (6) with respect to f_L and substituting in (3), one obtains

$$\frac{dv}{dJ_T} = \frac{\Phi_0}{\eta} \tag{8}$$

Combining this result with the derivative of (7) with respect to v, it is seen that the differential *flow resistivity* $\rho_f \overset{\Delta}{=} dE/dJ_T$ is

$$\rho_f = \Phi_0 B/\eta \tag{9}$$

From (6), (7), and (9) we see, as in Fig. 8.08a, that no voltage should be developed until f_L exceeds f_p and that the $V-I$ relation should subsequently be linear and increase proportionally with the average flux density. The slopes of the curves are independent of the defect concentration in the samples and measure the viscosity η.[32]

If the differential flux-flow resistivity, normalized to the normal-state resistance at the same temperature, is plotted as a function of magnetic field H, curves such as Fig. 8.08b result. These measurements were made

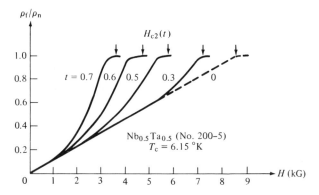

Figure 8.08b. Differential flow resistivity as a function of H and $t = T/T_c$. The arrows show the values of H_{c2} measured resistively. The broken line shows the behavior extrapolated to $t = 0$. (From Y. B. Kim, C. F. Hempstead, and A. R. Strnad, *Phys. Rev.*, Vol. 139A, p. 1166, 16 August 1965.)

---

[32] Experimental results for flux-flow conditions depend strongly on the sample geometry and the heat-transfer efficiency. Those shown in Fig. 8.08a are for a moderately well-cooled specimen.

on thin-sheet samples in which the flux density was nearly proportional to the applied field even down to fairly small fields. The linear dependence on H is seen to be increasingly valid as the temperature $t = T/T_c$ is decreased. At low temperatures, $t \ll 1$, one finds the approximate, general relationship

$$\rho_f/\rho_n = H/H_{c2}(0) \qquad (10)$$

An important consequence of this result stems from the relatively high normal resistivity of type II superconductors, typically three orders of magnitude greater than that of copper at the same temperature. It is clear that no appreciable transport current can be tolerated in the flux-flow state except for brief transients. In practice, the superconductor must be surrounded by a normal metal of good thermal conductivity to be able to withstand intermittent operation under flux-flow conditions. Not only is efficient heat transfer from the superconductor to the helium bath required, but also a temporary current-sharing path is necessary to divert a major part of the transport current from the superconductor until resistanceless operation is restored (see Section 8.12).

8.09. Thermally Activated Flux Motion: Flux Creep and Flux Jumps

In the flux-flow condition the Lorentz force is very much larger than the pinning force. The V–I curves of thin-film specimens with good heat transfer show well-defined regions of constant-resistance behavior, as shown in Fig. 8.08a. As the current is progressively reduced, the "excess" driving force falls and at the knee of the curve a dynamic equilibrium exists between the Lorentz force and the pinning force. The precise form of the V–I curve in the neighborhood of this value of current is, strictly, indeterminate. Although the resistive state is most sensibly defined in terms of the current at which a measurable voltage is detected between the ends of the sample, clearly the sensitivity of the experimental measurement is the key factor in the determination of the precise value of the critical current.

In high-field applications of type II materials, ideally one would wish to operate as close as possible to the critical current at which the Lorentz force and the pinning force are, in a statistical sense, balanced, to achieve optimum utilization of the current-carrying capacity of the superconductor. Since flux motion is necessarily attended by heat generation and because the pinning force itself is temperature dependent, thermally activated flux motion plays a crucial role in the stability of this balance (e.g., as in the critical-state model described in Section 8.10).

Thermally activated flux motion can be simply described by referring to a familiar physical picture. Flux pinning is closely analogous to the trapping of a mobile charged particle in a potential well and is therefore similarly affected by thermal fluctuations. A vortex pinned at a particular site will need to surmount a potential-energy barrier before being able to move under the influence of the local Lorentz force. Thermal energy, even at cryogenic temperatures, is sufficient to free pinned vortices at a constant average rate. Once released, the vortices are propelled by the driving force $\vec{J} \times \vec{B}$ generating noise voltages and heat until becoming trapped again at another pinning center. In fact, the vortices move in groups known as flux bundles, each containing many vortices (perhaps as many as 100) because of the magnetic interaction between them (Section 8.05).

The flux motion can be divided into two closely related types[33]:

a. *flux creep*, which tends to stabilize the flux distribution in the super-conductor by relieving the magnetic pressure in a controlled manner and

b. *flux jumps*, which may lead to sufficient heat generation to cause a catastrophic instability.

Flux creep, under steady-state conditions well below the critical current, proceeds at an orderly pace which becomes progressively slower with time as the flux-density gradients are gradually reduced by vortex displacement. In practice, flux creep can be detected easily only immediately after a transient change in externally applied magnetic field or current has been made, because it decays logarithmically with time. Equally, flux creep never disappears completely, but the motion reverts to a randomly directed form as the $\vec{J} \times \vec{B}$ driving force decays. Here, the current density $\vec{J}$ may be the result of externally applied transport currents or macroscopic screening currents induced in the bulk of a hard type II material. In both cases a gradient of flux density is supported by the available pinning force and is related to the current density through Ampere's law:

$$\nabla \times \vec{B} = \mu_0 \vec{J} \tag{1}$$

As the current density is increased under external control towards the critical level, flux creep increases. The amount of heat generated by flux creep is usually sufficiently small not to be of practical importance, but because of the very small specific heat and thermal conductivity of superconductors, the heat produces relatively large local changes in temperature. Since the average pinning force decreases exponentially as the temperature rises, a positive-feedback mechanism is readily identified. On a time scale of about a millisecond, the creep rate can build up to a level

---

[33] P. W. Anderson and Y. B. Kim, "Hard superconductivity: Theory of the motion of Abrikosov flux lines," *Rev. Mod. Phys.*, Vol. 36, pp. 39–43, January 1964. (M. R. Beasley, R. Labusch, and W. W. Webb, "Flux creep in type II superconductors," *Phys. Rev.*, Vol. 181, pp. 682–700, 10 May 1969.)

where an avalanche of flux bundles known as a *flux jump* is released. The overall temperature rise produced may even be sufficient to drive the superconductor normal locally unless some form of thermal stabilization is provided.

Flux jumps are a common feature of mixed-state behavior for near-critical levels of current where the creep rate is enhanced and the super-conductor is most sensitive to temperature fluctuations. A simple calculation shows that the amount of heat generated by a flux jump is proportional to the total flux released. If we assume that a small fluctuation in temperature δT, resulting from a perturbation of the flux distribution, leads directly to a further increment in temperature ΔT because of the additional flux motion excited, a stable condition would be ensured if $\Delta T < \delta T$. This inequality is governed by three factors only, if we ignore the possibility of heat flow away from the vicinity of the flux jump: the specific heat of the superconductor c, the temperature coefficient of the critical current $\partial J_c / \partial T$, and the thickness d of the superconductor, which is taken to be an infinite plate.

For stability against flux jumps, it can be shown that[34]

$$d^2 < \frac{8c}{\mu_0 J_c |\partial J_c / \partial T|} \tag{2}$$

Typical values of d satisfying (2) for hard type II materials are around 0.1 mm. Plates or layers of wires thinner than the critical value are free from the flux-jump type of instability but necessarily have a relatively modest current-carrying capacity unless some provision for heat removal is made. The small value of c for superconductors and the difficulty of transferring excess heat to the helium bath point to the possible use of composite conductors for improved stabilization. The addition of a normal metal (e.g., copper) matrix in which superconducting wires or foils are embedded enables rapid heat removal from "hot spots" and also minimizes the temperature rise because of the extra heat capacity (see Section 8.11).

Reviewing the discussion of flux motion in this and the previous section, from the point of view of possible applications of type II materials in the mixed state, it is clear that zero-resistance operation with steady currents is possible only in strongly pinned (i.e., hard) superconductors. Weakly pinned materials cannot be used for high-field applications because flux-flow conditions would be encountered at relatively small critical currents, with unacceptably large dissipation of heat.

The subject of flux pinning in superconductors has been extensively investigated since the first practical application of type II materials to high-field magnets. Metallurgically, the procedures used in manufacturing hard superconductors follow closely those familiar in the production of

---

[34] J. E. C. Williams, *Superconductivity and Its Applications*. London: Pion Press, 1970, p. 94.

high-yield-strength materials; i.e., it is the introduction of defects of the correct type and density that determines the pinning strength of the material. Many different types of defect have been used as pinning agents, including impurities and precipitates, dislocations induced by cold working or by the method of preparation, and neutron irradiation. It has been shown that the physical mechanism behind the pinning phenomenon depends directly on the local change of superconducting properties at the defect site.[35] Various models for different types of pinning center have been proposed which are in broad agreement with the experimental evidence obtained from mixed-state measurements. The scale of the distribution of pinning centers required for effective pinning is roughly the same as that of the vortex structure itself, e.g., on the order of 10 nm.

As in the case of mechanically strong alloys, hard superconductors showing the highest pinning strengths are frequently very brittle or are difficult to manufacture. Consequently, it is very expensive to produce conductors in a suitable form for practical applications, e.g., substantial lengths of very fine continuous and flexible wires capable of being wound into a small-bore solenoid. The production of ductile alloys such as Nb–Ti allowed the commercial development of superconducting magnets to advance, but it is the A15 intermetallic compounds based on niobium that offer the greatest potential for the future.

The niobium compounds are especially brittle, but because of their superior performance for fields above 10 T and high critical temperature (> 18 K) these problems have been largely overcome. Nb_3Sn has become the most important superconductor commercially produced (usually by diffusing tin into niobium tape, or by chemical vapor deposition of Nb_3Sn onto stainless-steel tape). A copper backing is provided for stabilization of the type used for filamentary conductors (Section 8.12). Tape conductors are also the preferred form for V_3Ga which does not, however, suffer from the brittleness characteristic of Nb_3Sn. Multifilamentary composites are being developed for both V_3Ga and Nb_3Sn, with matrix materials other than copper, such as Cu–Ni and other alloys and intermetallic compounds.

8.10. The Critical-State Model for Hard Superconductors

If it were possible to reduce flux pinning to arbitrarily low levels, reversible magnetization curves would be obtained for bulk type II materials, even for field excursions over the complete range $-H_{c2} < H < H_{c2}$. These materials, which would need to be perfectly pure and annealed, would be incapable of carrying a transport current in the mixed state without resistance (Section 8.08) and would be of little practical interest. It is

---

[35] D. Dew-Hughes, "The metallurgical enhancement of type II superconductors," *Rep. Prog. Phys.*, Vol. 34, pp. 821–873, September 1971.

useful, however, to begin by considering a material with no pinning centers and then to examine the mixed-state behavior as the pinning strength is increased. Irreversible magnetic behavior is usually discussed in terms of the hysteresis losses observed under cyclic magnetization conditions; in type II superconductors it is equally important to determine the effect of irreversibility on the maximum direct current that can be carried without loss in the presence of a high ambient magnetic field, as in a solenoid, for example.

The critical-state model, first proposed by Bean,[36,37] provides a phenomenological description of the way in which the critical current density is limited by the Lorentz force. We can illustrate this approach by applying it to the case shown in Fig. 8.10a. The locally averaged flux density and screening current density are given for a type II superconducting plate immersed in a magnetic field H applied parallel to the plate surfaces. As H is increased above H_{c1}, flux enters the interior; in the absence of pinning, there is no bulk screening current because the flux density is uniform throughout the plate. In the London penetration regions at the plate surfaces, the Meissner screening currents persist until H approaches H_{c2} and the diamagnetism of the plate disappears. If a moderate amount of pinning is present, the flux-density profile in the interior of the plate depends upon the pinning strength, and macroscopic screening currents are induced in the bulk in addition to the Meissner currents at the surface. In the Bean model, for simplicity, the flux-density profile is taken to follow a constant gradient which gives a uniform screening current density J_{scr}, where

$$\mu_0 J_{scr} = \frac{dB}{dx} \qquad (1)$$

Increasing the available pinning force per unit volume α permits larger flux-density gradients and, therefore, larger screening current densities. For a stable configuration of flux in the plate, the Lorentz force at any point must not exceed the available local value of pinning strength α, so we may write

$$|\vec{J}_{scr} \times \vec{B}| \leq \alpha_c(B) \qquad (2)$$

where α_c is a function of local average flux density and temperature. Its value will also depend on the density and the type of pinning center present.

Since (2), which defines the critical state, must be satisfied everywhere in the plate, in principle it should be possible to determine from (1) and (2)

---

[36] C. P. Bean, "Magnetization of hard superconductors," *Phys. Rev. Lett.*, Vol. 8, pp. 250–253, 15 March 1962.

[37] Y. B. Kim, C. F. Hempstead, and A. R. Strnad, "Magnetization and critical supercurrents," *Phys. Rev.*, Vol. 129, pp. 528–535, 15 January 1963.

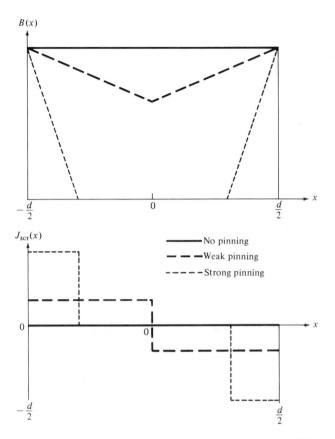

Figure 8.10a. Flux density and screening-current density for different pinning strengths according to the Bean critical-state model for a type II plate immersed in a parallel magnetic field, $H_{c1} < H < H_{c2}$.

the distribution of flux and current. For an increasing magnetizing field, for example, flux entering the plate at the surface will tend to upset the balance between the pinning force and the Lorentz force. Transient movements of flux will take place to adjust gradients or screening current densities, allowing the flux profile to relax towards equilibrium. The left-hand side of (2) can be equated to the "magnetic pressure" in a region containing a very large number of vortices. The excess magnetomechanical stress resulting from an external input driving additional flux into the plate can only be relieved by a process of internal adjustment of the flux-density profile by flux creep.

In the steady state, flux creep diminishes to insignificant levels and the gradients and current density are limited everywhere to the maximum values that the local pinning strength can support. The total amount of flux contained in a unit cross-sectional area of the plate Φ_T and the total current carried per unit length I_T are both determined by the available pinning strength. Through a succession of critical states, created under isothermal conditions by an extremely slow monotonic increase of the applied magnetic field, the flux and current ultimately reach their maximum stable values. Beyond this point it is no longer possible to balance the critical-state relation (2) by flux creep alone and intolerably vigorous flux motion will ensue. A similar picture would be obtained if the straight-line flux-density profiles were to be generalized to allow other forms of flux-density and current-density solutions. Although the critical-state model is simple in approach, its use has been vindicated by extensive experimental studies of hard superconductors.

The screening current $\vec{J}_{scr}$ is, in practice, accompanied by a transport current $\vec{J}_T$ as in the case of a superconducting solenoid. Figure 8.10b shows

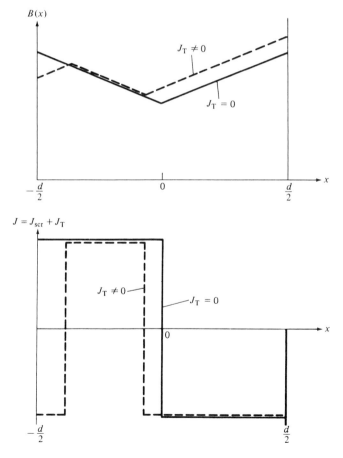

Figure 8.10b. Magnetic flux density and critical-current-density profiles for a magnetized sample with and without transport current.

that, for the case where the ambient field is parallel to the conductor surface, $\vec{J}_{scr}$ has odd symmetry about the midplane of the plate, whereas $\vec{J}_T$ flows in one direction only. If $\vec{J}_T$ is gradually increased from zero in a plate already biased into a critical state by the ambient magnetic field, the flux and current profiles will be adjusted by flux movement to attain a new critical state as shown. The maximum externally supplied current that can be supported stably by the superconductor, known as the *saturation current*, will be that for which the current density just becomes unidirectional everywhere. It can be seen that, apart from the complete reversal of the current in one half of the plate, no substantial changes have taken place in the magnitude of $\vec{J} \times \vec{B}$, even though the plate now carries a large transport current. Thus, provided the reversal is brought about in a smooth, controlled fashion, a plate able to support a screening-current density $\vec{J}_{scr}$ will carry a transport-current density $\vec{J}_T$ of the same magnitude under stable conditions. The discussion of thermally activated flux motion in the previous section points to the importance of the way in which the reversal of current flow is brought about, i.e., the relative rates at which the ambient field and the transport current are increased.[38]

The assumption of constant-gradient flux-density profiles, employed to simplify the description of the critical-state model, does not take into account the influence of the flux density on the pinning force. Models for various types of pinning center have been proposed,[39] yielding different functions $\alpha(B)$ for the pinning force. The experimental evidence is consistent with $\alpha(B)$ reaching a flat maximum value between H_{c1} and H_{c2}, so that α can be taken to be roughly constant over a wide range of intermediate fields.

In this section, no reference has been made to the Abrikosov vortex lattice. It was noted in Section 8.05 that the free-energy difference between various regular lattice configurations is relatively small; in practice, the material structure will have a greater influence on the vortex pattern. Moreover, we have been concerned here with a nonequilibrium situation far removed from that in which the Abrikosov result was obtained (i.e., the minimization of the free energy in the absence of transport currents and pinning forces).

If the screening or transport currents are cycled, the critical-state model predicts that substantial flux trapping occurs. This is shown in Fig. 8.10c, where the applied field has been first reduced to zero and then reversed, for a plate carrying no transport current. The hysteresis curve resulting from cycling the magnetization of the plate is illustrated in Fig. 8.10d. The

[38] P. S. Swartz and C. P. Bean, "A model for magnetic instabilities in hard superconductors: The adiabatic critical state," *J. Appl. Phys.*, Vol. 39, pp. 4991–4998, October 1968.

[39] D. Dew-Hughes, "Practical superconducting materials," in S. Foner and B. B. Schwartz, (Eds.) *Superconducting Machines and Devices*. New York: Plenum Press, 1973.

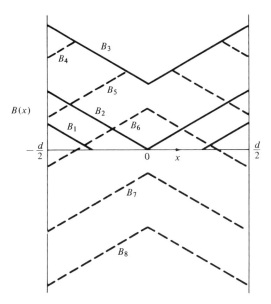

Figure 8.10c. Flux shielding and trapping according to the critical-state model. (——— field increasing; – – – field decreasing and reversing.)

area contained in a complete $B-H$ loop increases with the pinning strength; therefore ac operation of hard superconductors would be accompanied by unacceptably large losses. Similarly, transient or switched behavior in these materials depends strongly on the previous history of the sample magnetization.

The relation between the available pinning force and the ability to carry transport currents in a large ambient magnetic field is thus seen to produce

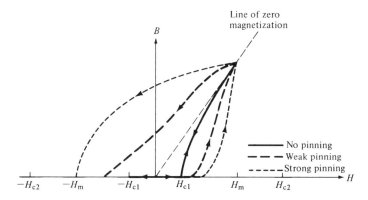

Figure 8.10d. Hysteresis curves for a hard type II material from the critical-state model for different values of pinning strength as in Fig. 8.10a.

conflicting requirements. High-field solenoids need strong-pinning super-conductors, but their thermal stability and their use with time-varying currents are inevitably threatened.

Problems

8.10a. Referring to Fig. 8.10c, calculate the magnetization of the plate as a function of applied magnetic field, following the sequence $B_1, B_2, \ldots, B_8$.

8.10b. Deduce from the arguments presented in this section the form of the J_c vs H curves for zero-pinning, weak-pinning, and strong-pinning materials.

8.10c. Under what conditions is the Bean model (J_c independent of average flux density) likely to be a useful representation of the critical state? Refer to plots of the critical current density and pinning force.

8.10d. Show that if the pinning force per unit length F_p is taken to be inversely proportional to B, the Kim–Anderson model results, in which $J_c(B + B_0)$ = const, and the flux profiles are parabolic instead of straight lines as in the Bean model.

8.11. The Surface Barrier to Flux Entry

Irreversible effects are a notable feature of the behavior at the surfaces of type II superconductors. The presence of a potential-energy barrier at the surface causes the entry of flux into the bulk to be delayed to field strengths above H_{c1}; the exit of flux is similarly delayed until the external field has fallen below H_{c1}. The nature of the surface barrier can be understood with the aid of a simple physical picture using the method of images[40] for the case where the external applied magnetic field is parallel to the surface. In Fig. 8.11a(i) the surface of a superconductor, near which a single vortex is assumed to be present, has been replaced by a mathematical plane in a continuous superconducting medium containing the image vortex as shown. The image is of opposite polarity to the real vortex to ensure that the screening current has no component normal to the surface and therefore satisfies the boundary condition of the physical problem. The attractive force between the vortex at a distance x from the surface and its image an equal distance beyond the surface opposes further penetration of the vortex into the superconductor giving a contribution to

---

[40] C. P. Bean and J. D. Livingston, "Surface barrier in type II superconductors," *Phys. Rev. Lett.*, Vol. 12, pp. 14–16, 6 January 1964.

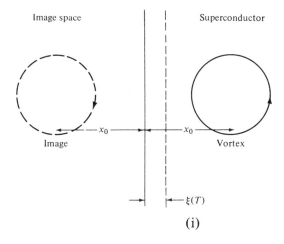

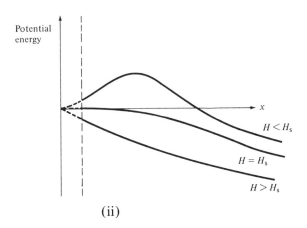

Figure 8.11a. Surface barrier to vortex entry: (i) vortex inside superconductor and its image outside; (ii) potential energy showing a maximum, and hence a barrier for $H < H_s$.

potential energy of the form [Eq. 8.05(3)]

$$V_A(x) = \frac{\Phi_0^2 K_0(2x/\lambda(T))}{4\pi\mu_0\lambda^2(T)} \tag{1}$$

for $x \gg \xi_{GL}(T)$. The details of the vortex core are ignored here since this result was derived for the GL parameter $\kappa \gg 1$.

The London penetration region, on the order of $\lambda(T)$ in extent, will contain the Meissner screening current, which tends to push the vortex deeper into the bulk, giving a repulsive potential energy term

$$V_R(x) = -\Phi_0 H \exp\left\{-\left[x/\lambda(T)\right]\right\} \qquad (2)$$

where H is the external applied field.

Combining (1) and (2), the potential-energy function will have a maximum value near the surface for external magnetic fields below a certain threshold value H_s, as shown in Fig. 8.11a(ii). Taking H_s as the field for which the potential barrier disappears, an estimate can be obtained from (1) and (2) by using suitable approximations. It can be shown[41] that, for large values of κ, H_s is roughly equal to the thermodynamic critical field H_c, where

$$H_c = \sqrt{2}\ \Phi_0/4\pi\mu_0\lambda(T)\xi_{GL}(T) \qquad (3)$$

An analysis[42] using the Ginzburg–Landau theory, taking into account the change in the order parameter above H_{c1}, shows that H_s is appreciably larger than H_c for small values of κ, as sketched in Fig. 8.11b.

Usually H_s is written in the form

$$H_s = H_{c1} + \Delta H \qquad (4)$$

where ΔH is always positive for increasing applied fields. The theoretical values for ΔH are rarely attained in practice; surface roughness produces local field enhancement in convex regions (as in the discussion of the intermediate state in Section 7.08). Premature flux entry occurs because the barrier is effectively lowered at these points. In a decreasing field, however, the barrier preventing the flux leaving the superconductor is raised where field enhancement is present and flux trapping occurs for fields well below H_{c1}.

Under ac excitation, surface trapping of this type produces the major contribution to hysteresis losses at power frequencies in thin-film superconductors.[43] Experimental results are very strongly dependent on the quality and type of surface treatment applied during processing. Similar difficulties confront accurate determinations of H_{c1}.

Problem

8.11. Using the asymptotic forms of equations (1) and (2) for $\xi_{GL}(T) \ll x \ll \lambda(T)$, plot the potential-energy curve $V_A + V_R$ and show that for $H \approx H_c$ the potential barrier disappears.

---

[41] P. E. de Gennes, "Vortex nucleation in type II superconductors," *Solid State Commun.*, Vol. 3, pp. 127–130, June 1965.

[42] J. Matricon and D. Saint-James, "Superheating fields in superconductors," *Phys. Lett.*, Vol. 24A, pp. 241–242, 27 February 1967.

[43] R. M. Easson and P. Hlawiczka, "Surface structure and ac losses in superconducting niobium," *J. Phys. D.* Vol. 1, pp. 1477–1485, November 1968.

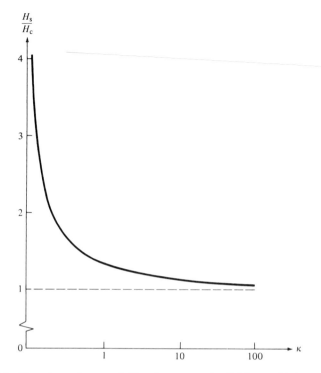

Figure 8.11b. The dependence of H_s, the magnetic field at which vortex entry occurs, on the Ginzburg–Landau parameter κ.

8.12. Stabilization of Superconducting Cables by the Use of Composite Conductors

The initial efforts to realize the full potential of high-field type II super-conductors in solenoids were thwarted by the severe degradation of the performance of complete coils when compared with the current-carrying capacity of the same material as measured in a "short sample" test. It became clear that flux jumps were the principal cause of the transition to the normal state; the probability of failure because of flux jumps, although insignificant in short samples, increased to virtual certainty in the long conductors required for multiturn solenoid coils.

The discussion in Section 8.09 of the magnetothermal instability did not allow for heat transfer to the helium bath or to some intermediate heat sink. If adequate means for removing the generated heat can be provided, it is possible to operate a superconducting cable under stable conditions for thicknesses greater than the limiting value obtained for adiabatically stabilized conductors satisfying the stability criterion Eq. 8.09(2). In prac-tice, however, the maximum thickness of superconducting cables is usually limited to about 1 mm because the poor thermal conductivity of superconductors leads to large temperature gradients. Nevertheless, enormous advances in superconductor technology have been made through the use of composite conductors in which superconducting cores or filaments are embedded in a host matrix of normal metal.

There are two types of composite conductor in common use for steady currents: cryostatically stabilized and dynamically stabilized. Under time-varying excitation, multifilament composite cables require an additional feature to ensure stability: the twisting or transposing of the filaments within the normal-metal matrix.

Cryostatic Stabilization

In the approach known as *cryostatic stabilization*, a composite cable is designed to carry the transport current entirely in the superconductor in the zero-resistance state during subcritical operation. The onset of flux jumps, or perhaps a transient increase in transport current above the critical value, is accommodated by allowing a transition to the flux-flow state or even to the normal state. The current is then shared between the superconducting core and a normal-metal (usually copper) sheath. The stability criterion requires that the steady-state generation of heat in both superconductor and normal metal is at least equalled by a sufficient rate of transfer to the liquid-helium bath to maintain the superconductor temperature below the critical value. In the extreme case where the superconductor is driven normal and all of the transport current flows in the copper sheath, the heat-transfer rate must allow the composite conductor to cool sufficiently to restore the superconducting core to its design temperature.

The heat-transfer coefficient for a superconducting wire immersed in a liquid-helium bath depends on the heat-flux density, so the use of a linear relation of the type

$$W = \gamma p (T - T_0) \qquad (1)$$

where W is the power dissipation per unit length, p is the wire perimeter, and γ is the heat-transfer coefficient, must be used with caution. Nevertheless, a reasonably satisfactory picture of the effect of heat transfer on the transition from flux-flow behavior to the normal-resistance state can be obtained from (1). As the transport current in an unclad filamentary superconducting wire is increased, a steady voltage is first measured when it reaches the critical value I_c (Section 8.10). The heat dissipation just above I_c will be governed by the flux-flow resistance (Section 8.08) through a relation of the type

$$W = I_c E \qquad (W/m) \qquad (2)$$

where E is the voltage drop per unit length in the flux-flow state. Combining (1) and (2) and assuming that the critical current varies as

$$I_c(T) = I_c(T_0)[(T_c - T)/(T_c - T_0)] \qquad (3)$$

where T_c is the critical temperature of the superconductor, the locus in the current–voltage plane can be obtained for various values of the heat-transfer coefficient γ. Typical solutions corresponding to well-cooled, moderately cooled, and poorly cooled wires are shown in Figure 8.12a. It can be seen that the ideal flux-flow solution of the type described in Section 8.08 is only possible for wires in which the heat-transfer coefficient is sufficiently large to ensure stable operation at a constant temperature, for $I > I_c$. For smaller values of γ, a thermal instability causes a rapid transition to the normal state to occur along loci such as (b) and (c), with the temperature reaching T_c at the intersections A and B.

If the wire is coated with a high-conductivity normal metal such as copper, with a resistivity perhaps two orders of magnitude smaller than the flux-flow value for the superconductor, the heat dissipation above I_c will be greatly reduced because a significant proportion of the current will flow in the copper sheath for $I > I_c$. The high thermal conductivity of copper ensures that good heat transfer is maintained between the superconductor and the helium bath and that a locus of the type (a) is followed. Although in practice the variation of γ with heat flux gives a nonlinear heat-transfer relation and leads to a more complicated behavior about this locus,[44] for simplicity the stability criterion can be assumed to be of the form found from (1) and (2):

$$I_c^2 \rho_n / A_n < \gamma p (T_c - T_0) \qquad (4)$$

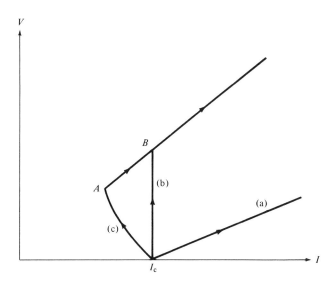

Figure 8.12a. Voltage–current loci for (a) well-cooled, (b) moderately cooled, and (c) poorly cooled wires.

[44] J. E. C. Williams, *Superconductivity and Its Applications.* London: Pion Press, 1970, p. 108.

where ρ_n is the resistivity and A_n the cross-sectional area of the copper cladding. Strictly, ρ_n should be calculated from magnetoresistance data to give a realistic estimate of I_c.

Cryostatically stabilized conductors were the first successful solution to solenoid failure and typically use Nb–Ti alloy cores about 0.25 mm in diameter drawn inside a copper matrix, with a cross-sectional area ratio of about 1:10 (Nb–Ti:Cu). Single-core composites are commonly used up to about 50 A; multicore composites have been designed from currents in excess of 2000 A. Good thermal contact between superconductor and cladding is essential in cryostatically stabilized composites since efficient heat transfer is the basis of the method. It is a particularly robust form of stabilization, able to withstand large transient disturbances without failure and is therefore especially suitable for large-scale applications. The principal disadvantage is the restricted overall current density obtainable because of the high proportion of normal-metal cladding used, but this is offset by the degree of mechanical stability provided. The enormous forces generated in large magnets are a potential source of instability because microscopic movements can lead to significant local temperature changes.[45] The performance of cryostatically stabilized conductors depends strongly on the design of the cooling channels carrying the liquid-helium refrigerant.

Dynamic Stabilization

The stabilization methods discussed above and in Section 8.09 are based on the steady-state magnetothermal behavior of superconductors carrying transport currents in the critical state. If the diffusion rates of magnetic flux and heat are compared, it becomes clear that by a suitable choice of composite conductor it should be possible to achieve stability on a dynamic basis. This approach, based on the transient behavior of the superconductor, gives a more compact and more efficient form of composite conductor than cryostatic stabilization.

The gross movement of flux, initiated by a flux jump, across a composite conductor containing a number of superconducting filaments is dependent upon the flux-flow resistivity of the superconductor and the resistivity of the normal matrix material, as well as their cross-sectional dimensions. The low resistivity of copper, the most common matrix choice, gives a relatively slow diffusion of magnetic flux[46] through the composite and therefore moderates the rate of production of heat by flux motion. On the other hand, the removal of this heat is governed by the efficiency of thermal

---

[45] M. N. Wilson, "Stabilization of superconductors for use in magnets," *IEEE Trans. Magn.*, Vol. MAG-13, pp. 440–446, January 1977.

[46] The diffusion constant for magnetic flux in a highly conducting medium can be shown to be proportional to the resistivity, whereas that for heat flux is proportional to the thermal conductivity.

conduction within both the superconductor and the normal metal, as well as by heat transfer to the liquid-helium bath. In fact, the heat flow in the superconductor is the limiting factor (the thermal conductivity of copper is several orders of magnitude greater than that of either Nb–Ti or Nb_3Sn, the most commonly used type II materials), since relatively rapid heat transfer to the liquid-helium bath from the superconducting filaments can be obtained via the copper.

By adjustment of the relative dimensions of the paths within the superconducting filaments and the copper matrix, across which both magnetic flux and heat are transported, it is possible to ensure that a multifilament composite is dynamically stable not only for quasi-steady-state currents and fields, but also for low-frequency time-varying conditions. The maximum cross-sectional area of each filament can be shown to be proportional to the thermal conductivity of the superconductor and inversely proportional to the resistivity of the normal-metal matrix.

In practice, the filaments are required to be of smaller cross-sectional area than those designed for adiabatic stability, i.e., less than 50 μm in diameter, and as in the case of adiabatically stabilized multifilament conductors, a much lower ratio of copper to superconductor can be employed than for cryostatically stabilized composites, typically about 2:1. As a result, the overall current density of dynamically stabilized composites is considerably greater than for cryostatically stabilized types.

The distinction drawn here between adiabatic and dynamic (isothermal) stability is somewhat artificial in the case of multifilamentary conductors, since a copper matrix is likely to be used in either case. The essential difference is that adiabatically stabilized superconducting wires can be used without a normal-metal cladding as single-strand conductors, but their current-carrying capacity is limited to about 10 A per wire.

Under dc conditions, the stability of a multifilament composite cable is assured if the individual filaments satisfy the dynamic-stability criterion. The presence of the normal-metal matrix does, however, introduce mutual coupling between the superconducting filaments under ac conditions so that they no longer act independently in response to flux jumps. Unless some means for decoupling is introduced, the dynamic-stability condition would be violated because the effective cross-sectional area of the superconductor would considerably exceed that of a single filament. The simplest method of decoupling requires the filament to be transposed by twisting within the normal-metal matrix. Provided that the pitch of the twist is sufficiently small, for a given rate of change of solenoid current or ambient magnetic field, the composite conductor will remain stable.[47,48]

[47] Y. Iwasa and D. B. Montgomery, "High-field superconducting magnets," in V. L. Newhouse (Ed.), *Applied Superconductivity*, Vol. 2. New York: Academic Press, 1975.
[48] M. N. Wilson, C. R. Walters, J. D. Lewin, P. F. Smith, and A. H. Spurway, "Experimental and theoretical studies of filamentary superconducting composites," *J. Phys. D.*, Vol. 3, pp. 1517–1585, November 1970.

The critical pitch l_c is proportional to the square root of the resistivity of the normal-metal matrix and inversely proportional to the square root of the rate of change of magnetic field. For a rate of change of field of 10^4 $A\,m^{-1}s^{-1}$, a typical value for l_c is about 15 cm.

Composite Conductors

Since some degree of compatibility exists between the adiabatic and dynamic schemes for stabilization, the two approaches may be combined in a single design that will be primarily influenced by the choice of superconductor through its upper critical field.

In addition to the electrical and thermal properties of the materials used in the composite conductor, the mechanical properties of the superconductor are of considerable importance in the construction of multiturn solenoid coils. Only a few type II materials have been used in commercially produced cables—the alloy Nb–Ti and the intermetallic compounds

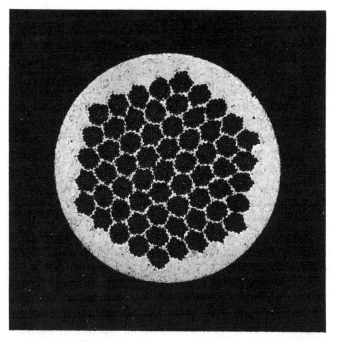

Figure 8.12b. Nb_3Sn–bronze composite conductor with 4453 filaments and 0.025-cm diameter. Overall view of cross section. (©1979 IEEE. Reprinted, with permission, from D. L. Martin, M. R. Daniel, J. M. Cutro, and R. E. Schwall, "Reaction treatment, critical current, transition temperature and bend properties of a niobium–bronze process multifilamentary superconductor," *IEEE Transactions on Magnetics*, Vol. MAG-15, pp. 185, January 1979.)

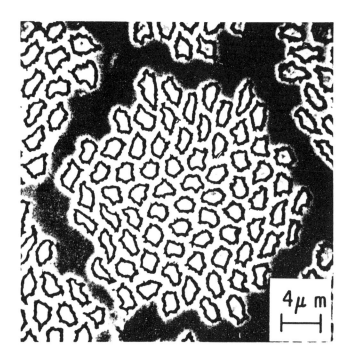

Figure 8.12c. Scanning electron micrograph of cross section of a 73-filament group showing Nb_3Sn-reacted zones as dark rings around the niobium filaments. (From D. L. Martin, A. Petrovich, and M. S. Walker, "Formation of Nb_3Sn and superconducting properties of a multifilamentary niobium–bronze composite," in *New Developments and Applications in Composites*, D. Kuhlmann-Wilsdorf and W. C. Harrigan, Jr. (Eds.) ©1979 AIME, New York, NY.)

Nb_3Sn and V_3Ga. Each has advantages for particular applications, but Nb–Ti is used only for intermediate fields up to 9 T, whereas Nb_3Sn can be used up to 15 T and V_3Ga up to 20 T.

The Nb–Ti-based composites have been widely used in solenoids in both single-wire and multifilament form, and are easily wound into compact coils a few centimeters in bore diameter. The cryostatically stabilized composites described earlier consist of a modest number of relatively thick Nb–Ti cores about 0.25 mm in diameter, each carrying 20 A. Adiabatically stabilized composites, on the other hand, consist of hundreds or even thousands of superconducting filaments. (See Figs. 8.12b and 8.12c.)

8.13. ac Losses at Power Frequencies

At power frequencies, quasiparticle losses calculated from the two-fluid model are negligible in comparison with the hysteresis losses resulting from the irreversible magnetization of practical superconductors. Moreover, the hysteresis losses are strongly dependent on the maximum amplitude of alternating fields and currents relative to the critical values; therefore, the design of ac power systems employing superconductors is influenced greatly by these considerations. The two most important factors determining the ac losses in superconductors are the surface condition and the bulk pinning force. In composite cables, losses are generally too great to allow operation at frequencies higher than a few hertz because of the additional eddy-current losses in the matrix.

In view of the discussion of hysteresis in Section 8.10, the restriction of ac operation to the Meissner state would appear to allow the losses to be kept to a minimum. The transport current would be confined to the London penetration region at the surface where essentially reversible behavior can be obtained. Either type I operating below H_c or type II operating below H_{c1} (taking account of demagnetization factors) could be used. There are, however, two difficulties to be overcome: type I materials afford only a small working margin between T_c and the helium bath temperature 4.2 K, and type II materials mostly have low values of H_{c1}.

Both of these factors are of great importance to ac applications of superconductors because they limit the power-handling capability of superconducting transmission lines and the tolerance of fault conditions, as well as pose refrigeration problems. Lead is the only type I material considered so far ($T_c = 7$ K, $H_c = 4 \times 10^4$ A/m at 4.2 K) and would probably have been exploited more widely if pure niobium had not been available. As has been noted elsewhere, niobium is an anomalous superconductor with the smallest possible κ of type II materials ($T_c = 9$ K, $H_c = 1.2 \times 10^5$ A/m at 4.2 K) and also the largest value of H_{c1}. It offers, therefore, a considerable improvement in performance over lead in the Meissner state, and has, in addition, more satisfactory mechanical and chemical properties. Figure 8.13a shows the measured losses at 50 Hz in a niobium strip at 4.2 K as a function of peak surface magnetic field H_{max} produced by its own transport current. The notable feature is the dependence of the losses on the peak value of the self-magnetic field, which shows something between a H_{max}^3 and H_{max}^4 relationship. Above H_{c1} the losses rise much more steeply as bulk penetration of flux begins to contribute to hysteresis, although it should be noted at this point that the term "bulk" implies simply that vortices are entering the superconductor, although it may, in fact, be a thin film only a few penetration depths in thickness. The losses below H_{c1} are believed to result mainly from surface roughness on a microscopic scale and from physical impurities and imperfections. As in the cases of the intermediate state (Section 7.08) and the surface barrier (Section 8.11), small surface irregularities produce perturbations in the applied field since the local demagnetization factor is changed by surface roughness. If simple geometrical forms of surface roughness are taken into account, it is possible to model the hysteresis losses in reasonable agreement with

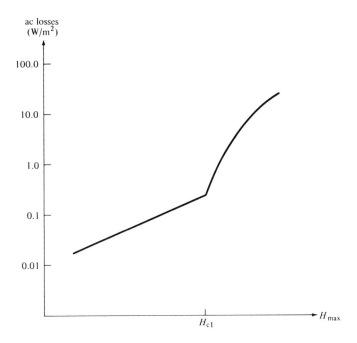

Figure 8.13a. Measured losses at 50 Hz and 4.2 K in niobium strip vs peak surface value of tangential magnetic field.

experimental results; an expression of the type

$$W = Cs\left(H_{max}^{n}/H_{c1}^{2}\right) \qquad (W/m^2) \qquad (1)$$

is obtained.[49] Here C is a constant incorporating the influence of surface contamination (adsorbed gases), s is a measure of the degree of surface roughness, and n lies between 3 and 4. The temperature dependence of the losses follows that expected from the parabolic variation of H_{c1}; it is obviously desirable to operate as far below T_c as possible, consistent with containing refrigeration costs within acceptable limits.

Looking to materials with larger values of T_c, such as Nb_3Sn (18 K), it is possible either to take advantage of the reduced losses obtainable at 4.2 K or to operate at a higher helium-bath temperature with consequent savings on refrigeration (each watt of heat dissipated at 4.2 K requires about 400 W of refrigeration power to maintain equilibrium). The principal disadvantage with the high-T_c materials is their low value of H_{c1}, which makes it essential to abandon the Meissner state with purely surface currents and to

---

[49] P. H. Melville, "Theory of ac loss in type II superconductors in the Meissner state," *J. Phys. C*, Vol. 4, pp. 2833–2848, 9 December 1971.

tolerate losses arising from bulk pinning. Although pinning is usually synonymous with magnetic hysteresis and, therefore, potentially high ac losses, it must be kept in mind that one important function of pinning is the raising of critical-current levels, and that the losses can be controlled through the pinning strength.[50]

Experimentally, it has been found that the onset of appreciable ac loss occurs for fields well above H_{c1}. This is attributed to the presence of the surface barrier (Section 8.11) which effectively raises H_{c1} to a value $H_{c1} + \Delta H$, in the neighborhood of H_c for the material.[51] The use of thin layers is also found to limit the losses in strong-pinning materials such as Nb_3Sn to roughly the level measured in pure niobium at the same current density, as shown in Figure 8.13b.

The contribution of the bulk losses can, in fact, be reduced below that of surface losses by suitable choice of film thickness and pinning strength, so

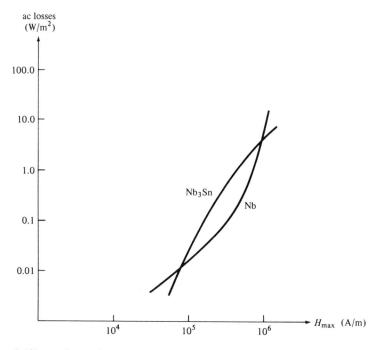

Figure 8.13b. ac losses in Nb_3Sn and niobium at 50 Hz and 4.2 K vs H_{max}, the peak surface magnetic field.

---

[50] Generally it is observed that strong pinning reduces ac losses if $H_{max} < H_p$, but increases losses if $H_{max} > H_p$, where H_p is the field at which the magnetization reaches a maximum.

[51] See footnote 43.

that, as with Meissner-state operation, it is the condition of the surface that is paramount.

The preceding discussion is of direct relevance to the design of superconducting ac power-transmission lines, which are usually constructed in the form of a thin layer (or a number of layers) of superconductor deposited on a normal-metal substrate. Great care is taken to ensure that the self-magnetic field is precisely parallel to the superconductor surface; therefore, accurately symmetrical coaxial geometry is favored. If the normal component of magnetic field is not zero, the ac losses rise appreciably above the levels obtained with only parallel fields. Applications other than the power-transmission line, such as superconducting motors and generators, in general are not able to conform to this condition; hence, the problem of ac loss, e.g., in superconducting armatures, is much more serious and requires the use of screening.

Appendix A

Elements of Electron Tunneling

Here we derive an expression for the tunneling current through a rectangular barrier, with a single electron in a plane-wave state incident on the barrier, and find the corresponding tunneling matrix element. The choice of a rectangular barrier is a simplification; barriers generally have more complicated shapes. Even though the rectangular barrier does not fit real conditions, the results are important because they reveal some important approximate facts about the effect of the barrier. Methods for treating more complicated shapes are treated in texts on tunneling.[1,2]

Consider the one-dimensional potential distribution shown in Fig. A1 with an electron incident on the barrier (region b) from region 1 with an energy less than the potential energy of the barrier. For convenience we take the zero of potential energy to be that in region 1. Let us first find the general solutions of Schrödinger's equation

$$- \frac{\hbar^2}{2m} \frac{d^2\Psi}{dx^2} + V\Psi = U\Psi \tag{1}$$

in regions 1 and b. These will have the form

$$\Psi(x) = ae^{ikx} + be^{-ikx} \tag{2}$$

where $k^2 = 2m(U - V)/\hbar^2$. In region 1, $U > V_1$, so we have propagating-type states. In region b we assume that $U < V_b$, and we can let $k = i\alpha$, so $\alpha^2 = 2m(V_b - U)/\hbar^2$. Then for region b, (2) becomes

$$\Psi_b(x) = a_b e^{-\alpha x} + b_b e^{\alpha x} \tag{3}$$

By matching the wave functions and their derivatives across the boundary (x_1) between regions 1 and b, we obtain a set of two equations linear in

---

[1] E. Burstein and S. Lundqvist, *Tunneling Phenomena in Solids*. New York: Plenum Press. 1969. The treatment in this appendix largely follows that in Chapter 1 of this reference.

[2] C. B. Duke, *Tunneling in Solids*, Solid-State Physics Series, Suppl. No. 10. New York: Academic Press, 1969.

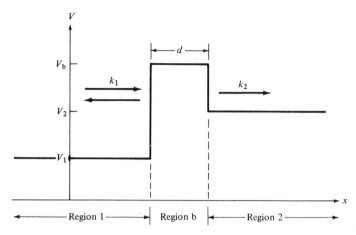

Figure A1. Potential variation assumed for tunneling calculations. The potential energy in region 1 is the lowest, so this represents a barrier between two regions with a bias $V_2 - V_1$ applied to the left side relative to the right side.

the wave amplitudes a_1, b_1, a_b, and b_b. These can be arranged in the form

$$\begin{bmatrix} a_1 \\ b_1 \end{bmatrix} = [R_1] \begin{bmatrix} a_b \\ b_b \end{bmatrix} \tag{4}$$

where

$$[R_1] = \frac{1}{2k_1}$$

$$\times \begin{bmatrix} (k_1 + i\alpha)\exp[-i(k_1 - i\alpha)x_1] & (k_1 - i\alpha)\exp[-i(k_1 + i\alpha)x_1] \\ (k_1 - i\alpha)\exp[i(k_1 + i\alpha)x_1] & (k_1 + i\alpha)\exp[i(k_1 - i\alpha)x_1] \end{bmatrix} \tag{5}$$

In the same way we can find a relation between the amplitudes in regions b and 2:

$$\begin{bmatrix} a_b \\ b_b \end{bmatrix} = [R_2] \begin{bmatrix} a_2 \\ b_2 \end{bmatrix} \tag{6}$$

Substituting (6) in (4), we obtain

$$\begin{bmatrix} a_1 \\ b_1 \end{bmatrix} = [R_1][R_2] \begin{bmatrix} a_2 \\ b_2 \end{bmatrix} \tag{7}$$

We are concerned with an electron incident on the barrier from the left and with the resulting electron wave traveling to the right in region 2. There is no leftward-traveling wave in region 2, since that region is assumed to extend to infinity; thus, $b_2 = 0$. The relation between a_1 and a_2

is therefore

$$a_1 = [R_1 R_2]_{11} a_2 \tag{8}$$

If the details are worked out and the barrier is strong so $e^{-ad} \ll 1$, where d is the barrier thickness, (8) is found to have the form

$$a_2 = \frac{4 k_1 \alpha \varphi e^{-ad}}{\left(k_1^2 + \alpha^2\right)^{1/2} \left(k_2^2 + \alpha^2\right)^{1/2}} a_1 \tag{9}$$

where φ is a phase factor whose magnitude is unity.

The momentum of a free electron is $\hbar k$ and the electron density is $|a|^2$ for a single traveling electron, so the incident and transmitted current densities are

$$J_1 = -\hbar k_1 e |a_1|^2 / m \qquad \text{and} \qquad J_2 = -\hbar k_2 e |a_2|^2 / m$$

respectively. Using (9) we can find the ratio of the transmitted to incident current densities to be

$$\frac{J_2}{J_1} = \frac{16 k_1 k_2 \alpha^2}{\left(k_1^2 + \alpha^2\right)\left(k_2^2 + \alpha^2\right)} e^{-2ad} \tag{10}$$

The exponential factor has a value typically in the range 10^{-5}–10^{-10}; its value cannot be calculated very accurately in real problems, so the prefactor cannot be determined from experiment. Note the symmetry in (10) which shows that the same relation holds for tunneling through the barrier in either direction. Note also the important result that the tunneling current has an exponential dependence on the product of the thickness and the square root of the energy difference $V_b - U$.

Let us evaluate the tunneling matrix element for the rectangular barrier by comparing Eq. 2.13(1) with (10). Noting that $J_1 = -\hbar k_1 e |a_1|^2 / m$, we can write the latter as

$$J_2 = -\left[\frac{16 k_1 k_2 \alpha^2 e^{-2ad}}{\left(k_1^2 + \alpha^2\right)\left(k_2^2 + \alpha^2\right)} \right] \frac{\hbar k_1 e}{m} |a_1|^2 \tag{11}$$

We can relate $N_2(\mathcal{E})$ to k_2 in Eq. 2.13(1) by using

$$N_2(\mathcal{E}) \, d\mathcal{E} = N_2(k) \, dk \tag{12}$$

finding the relation between the differential energy $d\mathcal{E}$ and the differential wave number dk, and evaluating $N_2(k)$. We are interested in the one-dimensional density of states because all tunneling electrons have their momenta normal to the plane of the junction, and so can only tunnel into the set of states with that direction of momentum. If L_2 is the length of the metal in region 2 normal to the barrier surface, $N_2(k) = L_2/2\pi$. Furthermore, the normalization condition on the amplitude of the state k_2 is that $|a_2|^2 = 1/L_2$. Therefore, $N_2(k) = 1/2\pi |a_2|^2$. Also, since we are using the free-electron model for the metals, $\mathcal{E} = \hbar^2 k^2 / 2m$, so $d\mathcal{E} = \hbar^2 k \, dk / m$. Combining these relations with (12), we obtain

$$2\pi |a_2|^2 \hbar^2 k_2 N_2(\mathcal{E}) / m = 1 \tag{13}$$

Multiplying (11) by (13) and rearranging, we obtain the form Eq. (2.13(1)), where

$$|T_{12}|^2 = \frac{\hbar^4 \alpha^2}{m^2} \cdot \frac{16 k_1^2 k_2^2 |a_1|^2 |a_2|^2 e^{-2\alpha d}}{(k_1^2 + \alpha^2)(k_2^2 + \alpha^2)} \tag{14}$$

The form of $|T_{12}|^2$ is independent of whether the metals are in the normal or superconducting state. It should be kept in mind, however, that it represents the tunneling of single electrons.

We have chosen to treat the simplest of barriers for this analysis. Real barriers have more complex forms, as seen in Section 2.13; approximate methods exist for calculating the tunneling matrix elements in those cases.

Problems

A1. Verify (5).

A2. Equation (10) can be used to evaluate the fraction of the current incident on a barrier that tunnels through, assuming that the states in region 2 are unoccupied. Assume a negligible bias in the junction and a rectangular barrier of height 1.0 eV above the Fermi level and width of 2.5 nm. Take the incident electrons of interest to have an energy of 0.1 eV above the Fermi energy ($\mathcal{E}_F = 7.3$ eV). Find $J_2(k_2) / J_1(k_1)$.

Appendix B

Determination of Materials Parameters $N(0), v_F, \xi_0$, and $\lambda_L(0)$ from Experimental Data

The free-electron model, which forms the basis of the theoretical treatments of normal and superconducting metals, fails to account for the complex shapes of real Fermi surfaces. Those values of London penetration depth and intrinsic coherence length calculated on the basis of a spherical Fermi surface, with each atom contributing to the Fermi gas those electrons in its outer shell, do not agree well with experimental values. We outline here the procedure used to get better values for most of those few cases that have been done.

Calculations of the intrinsic coherence length and the London penetration depth will be seen to require knowledge of the average Fermi velocity and area of the Fermi surface. The intrinsic coherence length was given by Eq. 3.11(2) as

$$\xi_0 = 0.18\hbar v_F / k_B T_c \qquad (1)$$

From the theory of the anomalous skin effect,[1] it can be seen that the coefficient Λ appearing in Eq. 3.03(15), which is the same as that in Eq. 1.10(5) (assuming $e^* = -2e$, $m^* = 2m$, and $n_s^* = 2n$), is given by

$$\lambda = \frac{12\pi^3\hbar}{e^2} \left[\int v_F(\vec{k}) \, dS_F \right]^{-1} = \frac{12\pi^3\hbar}{e^2 v_F S_F} \qquad (2)$$

where the final form contains the mean Fermi velocity v_F and the area of the Fermi surface S_F. The London penetration depth is found from Λ by Eq. 3.06(4) using (2):

$$\lambda_L(0) = (\Lambda/\mu_0)^{1/2} = \left(12\pi^3\hbar / \mu_0 e^2 v_F S_F \right)^{1/2} \qquad (3)$$

To proceed, we need S_F and v_F. The Fermi surface area S_F can be found from measurements of the anomalous skin effect. And v_F can then be determined from S_F and the density of states at the Fermi surface $N(0)$,

---

[1] A. B. Pippard, *Dynamics of Conduction Electrons*. New York: Gordon and Breach, 1965, p. 62.

the latter being proportional to the measurable electronic heat coefficient γ. Faber and Pippard have given a relation for the area of the Fermi surface in terms of the anomalous surface conductance (in the long-mean-free-path limit) Σ_∞, which is measured at frequency ω[2,3]:

$$S_F = 4 \times 10^{-14} 3^{3/2} \pi^4 \hbar e^{-2} (\omega^2 \Sigma_\infty^3) \tag{4}$$

The density of states at the Fermi surface $N(0)$ can be related to the mean inverse Fermi velocity taken over the surface by[4]

$$N(0) = \frac{1}{4\pi^3 \hbar} \int \frac{dS_F}{v_F} = \frac{S_F}{4\pi^3 \hbar} \overline{\left(\frac{1}{v_F}\right)} \tag{5}$$

The density of states can also be expressed in terms of the electronic specific heat constant by using Eq. 1.06(7):

$$N(0) = 3\gamma / \pi^2 k_B^2 \tag{6}$$

Neglecting the difference between the mean of the reciprocal of the velocity and the reciprocal of the mean, (5) and (6) can be rearranged to give

$$v_F = k_B^2 S_F / 12\pi \hbar \gamma \tag{7}$$

Then inserting the Fermi surface area (4), one obtains the following expression for the mean Fermi velocity:

$$v_F = \sqrt{3} \times 10^{-14} \pi^3 k_B^2 e^{-2} (\omega^2 \Sigma_\infty^3 / \gamma) \tag{8}$$

Then using (4) and (8) in (1) and (3), the values of intrinsic coherence length and penetration depth are found. The values of ξ_0 and $\lambda_L(0)$ given on the inside back cover were found in the above-described manner[5,6] except in the case of niobium.[7] In some cases, two sets of numbers are given; the ones without parentheses are the usual values found in the literature and those in parentheses are recalculations based on more recently published values of the electronic specific heat constant.

---

[2] T. E. Faber and A. B. Pippard, "The penetration depth and high-frequency resistance of superconducting aluminum," *Proc. Roy. Soc.*, Vol. A231, pp. 336–353, 6 September 1955.

[3] We have changed their units so that the Fermi surface area is given in $\vec{k}$ space rather than $\vec{p}$ space and all quantities are in MKS units.

[4] Footnote 1, p. 35.

[5] R. G. Chambers, "The anomalous skin effect," *Proc. Roy. Soc.*, Vol. A215, pp. 481–497, 22 December 1952.

[6] P. N. Dheer, "The surface impedance of normal and superconducting indium at 3000 Mc/s," *Proc. Roy. Soc.*, Vol. A260, pp. 333–349, 7 March 1961.

[7] B. W. Maxfield and W. L. McLean, "Superconducting penetration depth of niobium," *Phys. Rev.*, Vol. 139, pp. A1515–A1522, 30 August 1965.

Index

COMPOUNDS AND ALLOYS[†]

MATERIAL	T_c (K)	$\mu_0 H_{c2}$ (T)*
Nb_3Ge	23.2	36
$Nb_3(Al_{75}Ge_{25})$	21	40
Nb_3Sn	18.4	22
V_3Ga	15	23
Nb–Ti	9.5	13

[†]G. Bogner, "Large scale applications of superconductivity," in *Superconductor Applications: SQUIDs and Machines*, B. B. Schwartz and S. Foner (Eds.). New York: Plenum, 1977.
*$I = 0$, $T = 4.2$ K.

PHYSICAL CONSTANTS

Speed of light in vacuum	$c = 2.9979 \times 10^8$ m/s
Permittivity of free space	$\varepsilon_0 = 8.8542 \times 10^{-12}$ F/m
Permeability of free space	$\mu_0 = 4\pi \times 10^{-7}$ H/m
Planck's constant	$h = 6.6262 \times 10^{-34}$ J-s
Reduced Planck's constant	$\hbar = h/2\pi = 1.0546 \times 10^{-34}$ J-s
Electron charge magnitude	$e = 1.6022 \times 10^{-19}$ C
Electron rest mass	$m = 9.1096 \times 10^{-31}$ kg
Electron volt	$eV = 1.6022 \times 10^{-19}$ J
Boltzmann's constant	$k_B = 1.3806 \times 10^{-23}$ J/K
Avogadro's number	$N_A = 6.0222 \times 10^{23}$ mole^{-1}
Magnetic flux quantum	$\Phi_0 = 2.0679 \times 10^{-15}$ Wb
Josephson frequency-voltage ratio	$f/V = 4.8360 \times 10^{-14}$ Hz/V
Boiling point of liquid hydrogen (1 atm.)	20.39 K
Boiling point of liquid He^4 (1 atm.)	4.216 K
Boiling point of liquid He^3 (1 atm.)	3.20 K
Superfluid transition temperature of He^4 (1 atm.)	2.178 K